Data Structures and Algorithms using Python

Efficiently using data structures to collect, organize, and retrieve information is one of the core abilities modern computer engineers are expected to have. Python currently is one of the most popular programming languages, and as such, it has become vital for students to understand this concept in this language.

This student-friendly textbook provides a complete view of data structures and algorithms using the Python programming language, striking a balance between theory and practical application. All major algorithms have been discussed and analysed in detail, and the corresponding codes in Python have been provided. Diagrams and examples have been extensively used for better understanding. Running time complexities are also discussed for each algorithm, allowing the student to better understand how to select the appropriate one.

The book has been written with both undergraduate and graduate students in mind. Each chapter ends with a large number of problems, including multiple choice questions, to help consolidate the knowledge gained. This will also be helpful with competitive examinations for engineering in India such as GATE and NET. As such, the book will be a vital resource for students as well as professionals who are looking for a handbook on data structures in Python.

Subrata Saha is Head of the Department of Computer Applications at Techno India Hooghly, West Bengal. He has more than 20 years of teaching experience in various subjects in computer science and engineering, including data structures and algorithms, programming in C, C++, Java, and Python, basic computation, operating systems, and so on. He has previously published *Basic Computations and Programming with C* with Cambridge University Press in 2016.

Data Structures and Algorithms using Python

Subrata Saha

CAMBRIDGE
UNIVERSITY PRESS

CAMBRIDGE
UNIVERSITY PRESS

University Printing House, Cambridge CB2 8BS, United Kingdom

One Liberty Plaza, 20th Floor, New York, NY 10006, USA

477 Williamstown Road, Port Melbourne, vic 3207, Australia

314 to 321, 3rd Floor, Plot No.3, Splendor Forum, Jasola District Centre, New Delhi 110025, India

103 Penang Road, #05–06/07, Visioncrest Commercial, Singapore 238467

Cambridge University Press is part of the University of Cambridge.

It furthers the University's mission by disseminating knowledge in the pursuit of education, learning and research at the highest international levels of excellence.

www.cambridge.org
Information on this title: www.cambridge.org/9781009276979

First published 2023

Printed in India by Nutech Print Services, New Delhi 110020

A catalogue record for this publication is available from the British Library

ISBN 978-1-009-27697-9 Paperback

To my beloved wife,
Mrs Sriparna Saha, and my princess, Miss Shreya
Saha, whose constant support motivated me to
write this book

Contents

Preface

In computer science and engineering, data structure and algorithm are two very important parts. Data structure is the logical representation of data, so that insertion, deletion, and retrieval can be done efficiently, and an algorithm is the step-by-step procedure to solve any problem. By studying different data structures, we are able to know their merits and demerits, which enriches our knowledge and our ability to apply the appropriate data structures at proper places when we try to write new applications. Studying different standard algorithms provides us much knowledge about solving new problems. Both data structures and algorithms are interrelated and are complementary to each other. By studying both data structures and algorithms, we may acquire a solid foundation of writing good code. This comprehensive knowledge helps to understand new frameworks as well.

With the studying of data structures and algorithms, it is very important to implement them using proper languages. Several books have been written on this topic using the C language. But today Python has become very popular because of its features such as being easy, open source, object oriented, portable, multi-threaded, extensive libraries, embeddable, etc. Hence, in this book data structures and algorithms are implemented using Python.

About the Book

This book is written to serve the purposes of a textbook for undergraduate courses of computer science and information technology and for undergraduate and postgraduate courses of computer application where data structure is one of the subjects in the syllabus. In this book different data structures and algorithms are discussed in a lucid manner so that students can understand the concept easily. All the relevant data structures and their operations are discussed with diagrams and examples for better understanding. After discussing relevant algorithms in detail, the algorithmic representation and the corresponding code in Python are given. Various programming examples along with new problems for practice and a set of MCQ questions at the end of each chapter increase the self-learning process of the students.

The salient features of this book are:

- This book is written in very simple English for better understanding the complex concepts.

- In order to make the presentation visually interactive for students, neat labelled diagrams are provided wherever necessary. For each topic, explanations are clear and concise, avoiding verbosity as much as possible.

- Each topic is discussed in detail with proper examples.

- Algorithms are presented with algorithmic representation as well as with the corresponding code in Python.

- Complexity analysis is discussed for almost all problems discussed in this book and in very lucid manner for better understanding.

- A large number of solved programming examples.

- MCQ questions and their solutions.

Acknowledgments

I thank my beloved students for their constant motivation which made me write this book. My students are extremely fond of and fascinated by my 'teaching from the ground up' style and their demand inspired me to write this book. My heartiest thanks to them.

I would like to thank my student Sayandip Naskar for drawing the figures of stack and queue.

My heartiest thanks to my family members and friends for their constant support, encouragement, and unconditional love, which helped to conclude the book.

Finally, I would like to thank all the reviewers of this book for their critical comments and suggestions. I convey my sincere gratitude to Mr Agnibesh Das and the entire editing team at Cambridge University Press, India, for their great work.

Data Structure Preliminaries

Our basic aim is to write a good program. A program must give correct results. But a correct program may not be a good program. It should possess some characteristics such as readability, well documented, easy to debug and modify, etc. But the most important feature is that it should efficiently. Efficient means that the program should take minimum time and minimum space to execute. To achieve this, we need to store and retrieve data in memory following some logical models. These are called data structures.

1.1   Concept of Data Type

Before discussing data structures let us recapitulate what data are and what data type is. Data are raw facts. Through a program we convert data into our required information. For example, marks scored by a student in some examination are data. But total marks, average marks, grade, whether the student has passed or failed – these are information. The nature of all data is not the same. Some of them are whole numbers, some are real numbers that contain some fractional value, some are of character type, etc. These types of data are known as data type. Data type indicates the nature of the data stored in a particular variable. Different programming languages support different data types. Some are common, some are different. Integer, character, float, double, etc., are examples of data types. We can group data types into two categories. One is primitive or basic data type and the other is user defined data type.

1.1.1   Primitive data type

The data types which are predefined and in-built are known as primitive or basic data type. In Python, the primitive data types are number, string, and Boolean. Number data types are of three types in Python. These are integers, floating-point numbers and complex numbers. Strings are collections of characters. There are several types of strings in Python.

These are escape sequences, raw strings, and triple quoted strings. Boolean data type represents only two values: `True` and `False`. There is another basic data type, named `None`, which represents the absence of any value.

1.1.2 User defined data type

The data types which are defined by user, i.e. programmer here, according to the needs of the application, are known as user defined data type. Generally this data type consists of one or more primitive data types. In C, examples of user defined data types are structure, union, and enumerated list. In Python, user defined data type is class.

1.1.3 Abstract data type

Here the term 'abstract' means hiding the internal details. Hence, abstract data type (ADT) represents the type of an object whose internal structure for storing data and the operations on that data is hidden. It just provides an interface by which its behavior is understandable but does not have the implementation details. For example, `Stack` is an abstract data type which follows the LIFO operations of data. It has two basic operations – `Push` for inserting data into a stack and `Pop` for retrieving data from a stack. But as an ADT it is not known whether it is implemented through linked list, list, or array. ADT does not even disclose in which programming language it is implemented.

1.2   What Is Data Structure?

Data structure is the logical representation of data so that insertion, deletion, and retrieval can be done efficiently. Here efficiently means we need to consider two constraints. One is time complexity and the other is space complexity. These are two comparative measures. Time complexity denotes how fast an algorithm executes a specific task in comparison to another algorithm. Space complexity is a comparative measure among algorithms which depicts which algorithm takes less space in comparison to others for a specific job. Hence, data structure helps us to store, delete, and retrieve data with less time and space.

1.3   Definition and Brief Description of Various Data Structures

Based on the ordering of elements, data structures are classified into two categories: **linear data structures** and **non-linear data structures.** The data structures whose elements form a sequence are known as linear data structures. In linear data structures every element has a distinct predecessor element and a successor element. Examples are array, linked list, stack, queue, etc. On the other hand, data structures whose elements do not form a sequence are known as non-linear data structures. In non-linear data structures we cannot specify exactly which is the predecessor or successor element of an element. There may be multiple options for specifying the predecessor or successor element of each element. Examples of non-linear data structures are tree, graph, etc.

Based on the nature of the elements in a particular data structure, data structures are further classified into two groups. They are homogeneous and heterogeneous data structures. The data structure whose elements are similar in nature, i.e. belong to a specific data type, is known as homogeneous data structure. An example of this type of data structure is an array. But if the elements of a data structure are not similar type, i.e. if their data types are different, it is known as heterogeneous data structure. A list in Python is an example of heterogeneous data structure.

Based on allocation style, data structures are of two types. These are static and non-static data structures. If the number of elements in a data structure is fixed and is defined before compilation, it is known as static data structure. Example is an array. But if the number of elements in a data structure is not fixed, and we may insert or delete elements as and when required during program execution, it is known as dynamic data structure. Linked list is an example of dynamic data structure.

In the following section we will discuss various data structures in brief.

1.3.1 Array

An array is a linear, homogeneous, and static data structure. We can define an array as a collection of homogeneous (i.e., same data type) data elements described by a single name and placed in contiguous memory locations. Each individual element of an array is referenced by a subscripted variable, formed by affixing to the array name a subscript or index enclosed in brackets.

Thus by declaring an array we can store a set of values, say 60 of a particular type, e.g. *int*, in a single variable without declaring 60 different variables of different names. All these values will be stored under a unique identifier (array name).

To access an array element we need to mention the array name followed by the array index enclosed within [ ]. The general format to access an array element is:

```
Array_name [ index ]
```

Hence, if we declare an array, arr, of size 5, then to access the first element of the above array we have to write arr[0] as in Python, array index always starts from 0. Similarly, to access the next elements we have to write arr[1], arr[2], and so on.

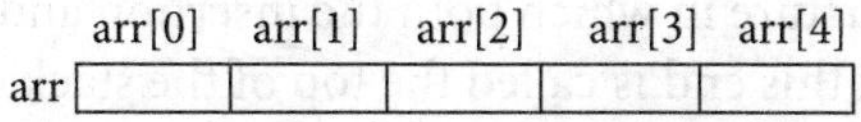

Figure 1.1   Representation of an array in memory

The advantage of array data structure is that it is very simple, easy to implement, and both sequential and random access are possible in an array. But the disadvantage is that its size is fixed. So, there is a chance of wastage of memory as well as lack of memory during execution. Another disadvantage is in insertion and deletion operations, as we need to shift the elements.

1.3.2 Linked list

A linked list is a linear and dynamic data structure. It is a linear collection of data items which are known as nodes. Each node contains two parts: one is the data part that stores one or more data values, and the other is the reference part which keeps the reference of the next node. The first node, along with data values, keeps the reference of the second node; the second node keeps the reference of the third node; and so on. And the last node contains None to indicate the end of the list. In this way each node is linked with the others to form a list. Thus this type of list is popularly known as linked list.

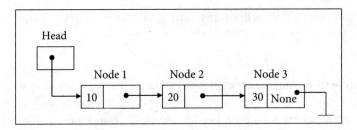

Figure 1.2   Representation of a singly linked list in memory

A linked list is a dynamic data structure. Hence the size of the linked list may increase or decrease at run time efficiently. We can create or delete node as and when required. As a result, there is no chance of wastage of memory due to prior allocation. Similarly, there is no chance of shortage of memory either. Unlike an array, we need not allocate a large contiguous memory chunk. Every time when the allocation is required, we will allocate only a single node. Moreover, it provides flexibility in rearranging the items efficiently. It is possible to insert and/or delete a node at any point in the linked list very efficiently with a few and constant number of operations. Here we need not shift items. What we have to do is just update some links.

1.3.3 Stack

A stack is a linear data structure in which both the insertion and deletion operations occur only at one end. Generally this end is called the top of the stack. The insertion operation is commonly known as PUSH and the deletion operation is known as POP. As both operations occur at one end, when the elements are pushed into a stack, the elements are stored one after another and when the elements need to be popped, only the top-most element can be removed first and then the next element gets the scope of being popped. Hence, stack follows the Last-In-First-Out (LIFO) order. Another operation related to stack is PEEK by which the top element of the stack is retrieved without removing it.

When we want to push an element into a stack, it is necessary to check whether the stack is full or not. If the stack is full it is not possible to insert more items, and this situation is known as **Stack Overflow**. Similarly, when we want to pop or peek any element, we have to check whether the stack is empty or not. This empty situation is known as **Stack Underflow**.

A stack may be implemented statically as well as dynamically in memory. For static representation we may use an array to implement a stack, and for dynamic representation a linked list is used. In Python, we may also use the in-built **list** data structure for dynamic representation as the list grows and shrinks dynamically.

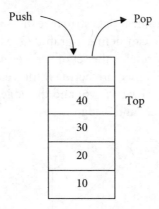

Figure 1.3   Representation of stack

1.3.4 Queue

A queue is a linear data structure in which insertion and deletion operations take place at two different ends. The insertion operation is commonly known as ENQUE and the deletion operation is known as DEQUE. These two operations take place at two different ends. The end at which elements are inserted is known as the **rear** end, and the other end through which elements are deleted from the queue is known as the **front** end. The elements are inserted through the **rear** end and removed through the **front** end following the First-In-First-Out (FIFO) order, i.e. elements will leave a queue maintaining the same order in the order in which they entered the queue. Like stack, a peek operation also may be applied with queue – by which the front element of the queue is retrieved without removing it.

To enqueue an element into a queue, it is necessary to check whether the queue is full or not. If the queue is full, it is not possible to insert more items, and this situation is known as **Queue Overflow**. Similarly, when we want to dequeue or peek any element we have to check whether the queue is empty or not. This empty situation is known as **Queue Underflow**.

Similar to a stack, a queue may be implemented statically as well as dynamically in memory. For static representation we may use an array to implement a queue and for dynamic representation a linked list or Python's in-built **list** data structure may be used.

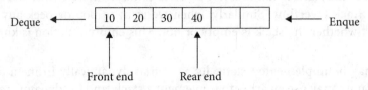

Figure 1.4   Representation of queue

1.3.5 Graph

A graph is a very important non-linear data structure in computer science. A graph consists of some vertices and edges. We can define a graph, G, as an ordered set of vertices and edges, i.e. G = {v, e}, where v represents the set of vertices, which are also called nodes, and e represents the edges, i.e. the connectors between the vertices. Figure 1.5 shows a graph where the vertex set v = {v1, v2, v3, v4, v5, v6} and the edge set e = {e1, e2, e3, e4, e5, e6, e7, e8, e9}, i.e. the graph has 6 vertices and 9 edges.

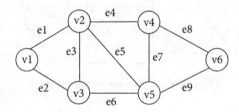

Figure 1.5   A graph

In memory a graph is represented using an array as well as a linked list. However, to represent a graph in memory a 2D array is required. There are two ways in which a graph can be represented. These are:

- Using Adjacency matrix
- Using Incidence matrix

To represent a graph using a linked list there are also two ways. These are:

- Using Adjacency list
- Using Adjacency multi-list

As a graph is a non-linear data structure, for standardization we need to traverse the graph following some specific algorithms. Traversal of graph means examining or reading data from each and every vertex and edge of the graph. There are two standard algorithms to traverse a graph. These are:

- BFS (Breadth First Search)
- DFS (Depth First Search)

In Breadth First Search (BFS) algorithm, starting from a source vertex all the adjacent vertices are traversed first. Then the adjacent vertices of these traversed vertices are traversed one by one. This process continues until all the vertices are traversed. Another graph traversal algorithm is Depth First Search (DFS) algorithm. In this algorithm starting from the source vertex, instead of traversing all the adjacent vertices, we need to move deeper and deeper until we reach a dead end. Then by backtracking we return to the most recently visited vertex and from that position again we start to move to a deeper level through unvisited vertices. This process continues until we reach the goal node or traverse the entire graph.

1.3.6 Tree

A tree is a non-linear data structure which is used to represent hierarchical relationship among data items. Basically a tree is an acyclic and connected graph. It consists of some **nodes** and these nodes are connected by **edges**. The topmost node or starting node is known as **root**. Zero or more nodes can be connected with this root node through edges. The structure of a tree is recursive by its nature. Each node connected with the root node may be further considered as a root node with which some other nodes can be connected and form a sub-tree. Thus, a **tree**, T, can be defined as a finite non-empty set of elements among which one is the root and others are partitioned into trees, known as sub-trees of T. Figure 1.6 shows a sample tree structure.

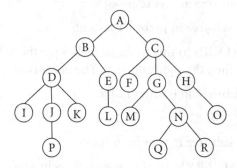

Figure 1.6 A tree

If the degree of a tree is 2, it is called a binary tree. Hence, each node in a binary tree can have a maximum of two children. It is either empty or consists of a root node and zero or one or two binary trees as children of the root. These are known as left sub-tree and right sub-tree. The starting node of each sub-tree is considered as their root node and can have further left sub-tree and right sub-tree, if any. Figure 1.7 shows a binary tree.

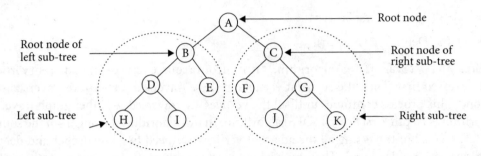

Figure 1.7 A binary tree

Here, A is the root node and the nodes B, D, E, H, and I form the left sub-tree and the nodes C, F, G, J, and K form the right sub-tree. Again B is the root node of this left sub-tree whose left sub-tree consists of D, H, and I nodes and the right sub-tree consists of a single node, E, and so on. If any node does not have a left sub-tree and/or a right sub-tree, that means it consists of empty sub-trees.

As a binary tree is also a non-linear data structure, we need to traverse the tree in a systematic manner. Based on the way nodes of a tree are traversed, the traversal technique of a binary tree can be classified mainly into three categories. These are:

1. **Preorder traversal (VLR):** In this traversal technique the root is visited before its child. The order is as follows:

   i.   Visit the root

   ii. Visit the left sub-tree in preorder fashion

   iii. Visit the right sub-tree in preorder fashion

2. **Inorder traversal (LVR):** In this traversal technique the left sub-tree is visited first, then the root, and then the right sub-tree. The order is as follows:

   i.   Visit the left sub-tree in inorder fashion

   ii. Visit the root

   iii. Visit the right sub-tree in inorder fashion

3. **Postorder traversal (LRV):** In this traversal technique the root is visited after traversing its both children. The order is as follows:

   i.   Visit the left sub-tree in postorder fashion

   ii. Visit the right sub-tree in postorder fashion

   iii. Visit the root

Apart from the above three traversal techniques, there is another traversal technique, named **level order traversal**. In this technique nodes are visited level by level, starting from the root and in each level from left to right.

The advantage of the tree structure is that it provides faster insertion, deletion, and search operations.

1.3.7 Heap

A heap is a very important tree-based data structure. It is widely used in computer science. We can define a heap as a binary tree which has two properties. These are: shape property and order property. By the shape property, a heap must be a complete binary tree. By the order property, there are two types of heaps. One is max heap and the other is min heap. By default a heap means it is a max heap. In a max heap, the root should be larger than or equal to its children. There is no order in between the children. This is true for its sub-trees also. In a min heap the order is reversed. Here the root is smaller than or equal to any of its children. Thus the root of a max heap always provides the largest element of a list whereas the root of a min heap always provides the smallest element. Figure 1.8 shows a max heap and a min heap.

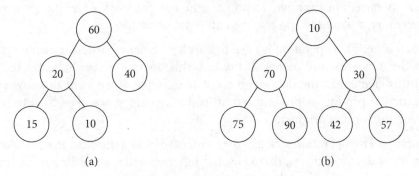

(a)   (b)

Figure 1.8   (a) Max heap and (b) Min heap

As a heap is a complete binary tree, it can be implemented using an array or list. One of the important applications of the heap data structure is to implement priority queue. Another application is in heap sort, which is a relatively very fast sorting algorithm.

1.4   Data Structures versus Data Types

We have already discussed that data type represents the type of the data stored in a variable, whereas data structure represents the logical representation of data in order to store and retrieve data efficiently. We have also noticed that using data structures we are able to create ADT which represents some user defined data type. On the other hand, primitive data structures are the basic data type in any programming language. Hence, these are very close in meaning. If we consider the data types in Python, i.e. integer(int), string(str), list, dictionary(dict), etc., we find that all the data types are represented as class, which is nothing but a data structure.

1.5   Operations on Data Structures

In general the operations that can be performed on different data structures can be summarized as the following:

- **Insertion:** By this operation new elements are added in the data structure. When new elements are added, they follow the properties of the corresponding data structure. For example, when a new product needs to be added in the inventory, all the information regarding the new product will be inserted in the appropriate data structure.

- **Deletion:** This operation removes or deletes one or more elements from the data structure. For example, when a product needs to be removed from the inventory, all the information regarding the product will be deleted from the appropriate data structure.

- **Traversing:** This operation indicates accessing all the elements in a data structure exactly once. For example, to prepare the current stock of all the elements in the inventory, we need to traverse the entire data structure.

- **Searching:** This operation is used to check whether a particular element is present in the data structure or not. If present, this operation also indicates the position of this element in the data structure. For example, if we want to know whether a particular product is present or not in the inventory, we need to search the data structure for that product.

- **Sorting:** This operation arranges the elements of a data structure in a particular order. In some data structures, there is some inherent order according to the properties of that data structure; otherwise we may sort the elements in either ascending or descending order. For example, we may sort the products of an inventory in the descending order of their stock.

- **Merging:** This operation is generally done between two or more sorted lists. After the operation, the lists are combined into one list maintaining the initial order of the lists. For example, if we have two lists sorted in ascending order, after merging they becomes a single list where all the elements would be present in ascending order.

Data Structure Preliminaries At a Glance

✓ Data type represents the type of the data stored in a variable.

✓ The data types which are predefined and in-built are known as primitive or basic data type.

✓ The data types which are defined by the user according to the needs of the applications are known as user defined data type.

✓ Abstract data type (ADT) represents the type of an object whose internal structure for storing data and the operations on that data are hidden. It just provides an interface by which its behavior is understandable but does not have the implementation details.

✓ Data structure is the logical representation of data so that insertion, deletion, and retrieval can be done efficiently. Efficiently means in relatively less time and using less space.

✓ Based on the ordering of data, data structures are broadly categorized into linear and non-linear data structures.

✓ Examples of linear data structures are array, linked list, stack, queue, etc., whereas graph and tree are examples of non-linear data structures.

Multiple Choice Questions

1. Which of the following is not a data type in Python?
   a) int
   b) char
   c) float
   d) bool

2. Which of the following is a valid string literal in Python?
   a) 'Data Structure'
   b) "Data Structure"
   c) '''Data Structure'''
   d) All of these

3. Which of the following is an ADT?
   a) Stack
   b) Queue
   c) Both (a) and (b)
   d) None of these

4. Which of the following is a linear data structure?
    a) Array
    b) List
    c) Queue
    d) All of these

5. Which of the following is a non-linear data structure?
    a) Heap
    b) Graph
    c) Tree
    d) All of these

6. Which of the following is not a linear data structure?
    a) Heap
    b) Stack
    c) Queue
    d) None of these

7. Which of the following is not a non-linear data structure?
    a) Heap
    b) Linked List
    c) B Tree
    d) None of these

8. Array is a data structure of which type?
    a) Linear
    b) Homogeneous
    c) Static
    d) All of these

9. Linked list is a data structure of which type?
    i.   Linear
    ii. Homogeneous
    iii. Static
    iv. Dynamic
    a) i and ii only
    b) i, ii and iv
    c) ii and iii only
    d) All of these

10. Which of the following is not a operation of stack?

    a) Push

    b) Pop

    c) Peek

    d) Retrieve

11. Which of the given data structures supports all the following operations?

    i.   Insert an element at the beginning

    ii.   Insert an element at the end

    iii. Insert an element at any intermediate position

    iv.   Delete an element from any intermediate position

    a) Stack

    b) Queue

    c) Linked List

    d) Graph

12. Stack follows which of the following?

    a) FIFO

    b) LIFO

    c) FILO

    d) LILO

13. Queue follows which of the following?

    a) FIFO

    b) LIFO

    c) FILO

    d) LILO

14. Which of the following is/are the common operation/s on data structures?

    a) Searching

    b) Sorting

    c) Merging

    d) All of these

15. A graph can be represented in memory using which of the following?

    a) Adjacency Matrix

    b) Incidence Matrix

    c) Adjacency multi-list

    d) All of these

16. Which of the following is not a tree traversal technique?

    a)   Preorder

    b)   Inorder

    c)   Level order

    d)   None of these

Review Exercises

1.   What do you mean by data type? Give an example.

2.   What are the different data types? Explain with an example.

3.   What is primitive data type?

4.   What do you mean by user defined data type?

5.   What is data structure?

6.   Discuss about different type of data structures.

7.   What is the difference between an array and a linked list?

8.   What are the advantages and disadvantages of array over linked list?

9.   Compare stack and queue. Explain their operations with an example.

10.   What is the use of heap data structure?

Introduction to Algorithm

Algorithm is a very common word in computer science, especially in case of any procedural programming languages. In this chapter we will know about algorithms, different types of algorithms, different approaches to designing an algorithm, analysis of algorithms, etc. We will also be able to learn how an algorithm can be written using different control structures.

2.1 What Is an Algorithm?

We can define an algorithm as a step-by-step procedure to solve a problem. This is much like a recipe for cooking an item. To cook a new item, we follow the instructions one by one as given in its recipe. Similarly, to write a program we need to follow the algorithm. Once we are able to generate the algorithm of a problem, then writing its code is not a huge task at all. But before writing an algorithm we have to keep in mind that any algorithm must have the following characteristics:

- **Input:** Inputs are the values that are supplied externally. Inputs are those without which we cannot proceed with the problems. Every algorithm must have zero or any number of inputs.

- **Output:** Output is the outcome of an algorithm. Every algorithm produces at least one output.

- **Definiteness:** All the instructions in the algorithm must be clear and should not be ambiguous.

- **Finiteness:** Whatever may be the inputs for all possible values, every algorithm must terminate after executing a finite number of steps.

- **Effectiveness:** All the instructions in the algorithm should be very basic so that every instruction of the algorithm can be converted to programming instruction easily. Effectiveness indicates that every instruction is a step towards the solution.

- **Feasible:** Every instruction must be a feasible instruction.

2.2 Importance of an Algorithm

When we try to write a program, first we need to identify all the tasks. Some tasks are easily identifiable while some tasks maybe hidden within the problem definition. For that a detailed analysis of the problem is required. After proper analysis we are able to find what the expected output is. What are the inputs required using which we can get the output? Using the inputs how we reach the solution? To accomplish this 'how', after identifying all the tasks we need to arrange them in a proper sequence. This is called an algorithm and in common words 'Program Logic'. A small and well-known program may be written arbitrarily, but for a large program or programs about which we are not much familiar, we must prepare an algorithm first.

Though algorithm provides us with the step-by-step procedures towards a solution, the importance of algorithms is not restricted only to providing a solution. The study of an algorithm helps us to find the best possible solution of a given problem. Comparative study of algorithms helps us develop efficient algorithms in terms of time and space. Studying different types of algorithms we are able to learn different program-solving approaches which helps us to develop new algorithms.

2.3 Different Approaches to Designing an Algorithm

When we solve a large problem it is better to divide it into some smaller modules. Breaking up a large program into a few smaller modules is known as modular programming. There are several advantages of modular programming. First of all, it increases readability and decreases line of code (LOC). It also increases reusability, and helps in testing, debugging, and maintenance. Developing of algorithms using modular programming may follow two different approaches. These are top-down approach and bottom-up approach.

In the top-down approach, first the overall algorithm is decomposed into smaller modules. Then each module is fragmented into further sub-modules. These sub-modules may further be divided into sub-sub-modules, and so on. Hence, in this approach from an abstract model of the problem, in every iteration we move toward more concrete modules. Generally procedural programming follows this approach.

The bottom-up approach is the reverse form of the top-down approach. In bottom-up approach, we first design all the elementary modules. Then a driver module is created to solve some specific tasks, which invokes some elementary modules and provides a primary level of abstraction. In this way several driver modules are created. Then some of these driver modules are grouped together to form a higher level module. This process of combining modules into higher level modules continues until the complete algorithm is developed. Generally object oriented programming follows this approach.

2.4 Algorithm Design Tools: Flowchart and Pseudocode

Now we will learn how an algorithm can be written. We have already discussed the characteristics of any algorithms. Keeping in mind all these characteristics we have to write the instructions of any algorithm step by step. Not only that; the algorithm we write should be efficient, which means it should use minimum resources like processor's time and memory space. To write an algorithm, first we need to identify the inputs, if any. Suppose we have to print all two digit prime numbers. In this case, we do not have any input because no extra information is required; we know what the two digit numbers are and what the criteria are for any number becoming a prime number. But if our problem is to find the area of a rectangle, we have to take two inputs – length and breadth of the rectangle. Unless these two values are provided externally, we are not able to calculate the area. Consider the following example.

Example 2.1: Write an algorithm to find the area and perimeter of a rectangle.

Solution:

1. Input "Enter length:" to `length`

2. Input "Enter breadth:" to `breadth`

3. Set `area = length * breadth`

4. Set `peri = 2*(length+breadth)`

5. Print "Area =", `area`

6. Print "Perimeter =", `peri`

7. Stop

It is a very simple algorithm; only sequential statements are used here. As we move to harder problems, we need to use control structures. The notation and use of different control structures are shown in the next section. Now we will discuss about two tools of designing algorithms. These are flowchart and pseudo code.

2.4.1   Flowchart

A flowchart is a pictorial or diagrammatic representation of an algorithm. It is a type of diagram that represents an algorithm or process, showing the steps as boxes of various kinds, and their order by connecting them with arrows. This diagrammatic representation illustrates a solution to a given problem. The purpose of a flowchart is to provide people with a common language or reference point when dealing with a project or process.

Flowcharts are broadly classified into two categories:

1. Program flowchart

2. System flowchart

Program flowcharts are symbolic or graphical representation of computer programs in terms of flowchart symbols. They contain the steps for solving a problem unit for a specific result.

System flowcharts, on the other hand, contain solutions of many problem units together that are closely related to each other and interact with each other to achieve a goal.

In this book we will concentrate on program flowcharts as this book is mainly on data structures and different programming algorithms. A program flowchart is an extremely useful tool in program development activity in the following respects:

1. Any error, omission, or commission can be more easily detected from a program flowchart than it can be from a program.

2. A program flowchart can be followed easily and quickly.

3. It can be referred to if program modifications are needed in future.

To draw a flowchart we have to be familiar with the standard symbols of flowcharts. Table 2.1 shows the list of symbols used in program flowcharts along with their brief descriptions.

Table 2.1   Flowchart symbols

SYMBOL	NAME	USAGE
	Terminal	Used to show the beginning and end of a set of computer-related process.
	Input/Output	Used to show any input/output operation.
	Process	Used to show any processing including all types of calculations performed by a computer system.
	Comment	Used to write any explanatory statement required to clarify something. It is used for documentation purposes only.
	Flow line.	Used to connect the symbols. The direction of the arrow indicates the direction of flow.
	Document Input/Output	Used when input comes from a document and output goes to a document.
	Decision	Used to show any point in the process where a decision must be made to determine further action.
	On-page connector	Used to connect parts of a flowchart continued on the same page.
	Off-page connector	Used to connect parts of a flowchart continued on separate pages.

The following rules should be adhered to while drawing program flowcharts:

- Only the standard symbols should be used in program flowcharts.

- Program logic should depict the flow from top to bottom and from left to right.

- Each symbol used in a program flowchart should contain only one entry point and one exit point, with the exception of the decision symbol.

- The operations shown within a symbol of a program flowchart should be expressed independent of any particular programming language.

- All decision branches should be well labeled.

Here is an example of a flowchart.

Example 2.2: Draw a flowchart to find the area and perimeter of a rectangle.

Solution:

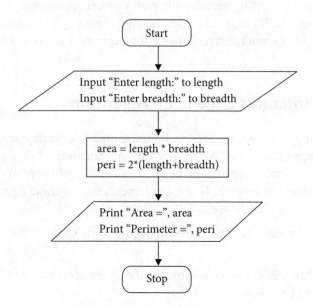

Figure 2.1 Example of a flowchart

2.4.2 Pseudocode

Another tool to represent an algorithm is pseudocode. 'Pseudo' means false and 'code' represents instructions written in any programming language. Hence, pseudocode means false coding. This implies that it looks like a programming code but actually it is not that. There is no compiler or interpreter to execute this. Pseudocodes are written in any natural language, mostly English. Instead of writing in a solid text or using some symbols, it follows the control structures of programming languages. Pseudocode follows all the basic programming control structures like sequence, selection, and iteration. As it follows the control structures of programming languages, it should be written for computer professionals; at least they should know a programming language. It is very helpful for project leaders of any software development team to explain the algorithm to his/her team members.

A pseudocode has several advantages over a flowchart. It is easy to convert a pseudocode into the code of any programming language. If any modification needs to be done on the algorithm, the changes that need to be carried out due to this will require less effort in a pseudocode than in a flowchart. If any programming language is known, it is much easier to write a pseudocode than drawing a flowchart. In case of a complex problem, instead of directly writing a code, it is better to write a pseudocode of that problem first, because writing a pseudocode is much easier than to write the actual code. Instead of concentrating on the hazards of syntax, programmers can concentrate more on the algorithm of the problem. However there are some disadvantages also. As there are no standard rules for writing a pseudocode, the style of writing pseudocode varies from programmer to programmer and hence may create some difficulties in understanding. Another drawback of this tool is that writing a pseudocode is much more difficult for beginners in comparison to drawing a flowchart.

2.5 Control Structures Used in an Algorithm

In any programming construct we need to follow some basic control structures. These are sequence, selection, and iteration. When we write an algorithm, using some basic structure to represent these control structures makes the task easy and more understandable than writing only statements in English. In the implementation of these control structures, we follow some conventions. These are as follows:

1.   We have used indentation to represent a block. One may use Begin–End to indicate a block.

2.   Elements of an array are accessed by specifying the array name followed by an index within square brackets.

3.   Variables used in the algorithm are local to the function/procedure.

4.   Parameters passed in the function/procedure follow call by value mechanism.

5.   Compound data are organized as an object, and every object is composed of attributes and methods. These members are accessed using the dot (.) operator.

Now we will discuss the implementation of control structures in an algorithm.

Sequence: The sequence control structure represents sequential execution of statements. Example 2.1 is an example of a sequence control structure in an algorithm.

Selection: The selection or decision control structure is used when we need to take a decision within the algorithm. The decision should be taken based on some condition. Sometimes it may so happen that only for the condition being true, we need to do something; but if the condition is false, we have nothing to do. This is called simple If construct. The general form of an If construct in an algorithm may be shown as

```
If condition, Then
      Statement or Statements
```

When a set of statement or statements are executed based on if a condition is true, otherwise another set of statement or statements are executed, we need to follow the If–Else control structure. The general form of an If–Else construct in an algorithm may be shown as

```
If condition, Then
      Statement or Statements
Else
      Statement or Statements
```

Both the If and If–Else constructs may also be nested. The `Statement or Statements` may further contain an If or If–Else construct. Here is an example to show the selection control structure in an algorithm.

Example 2.3: In a shop, a discount of 10% on purchase amount is given only if purchase amount exceeds ₹5000; otherwise 5% discount is given. Write an algorithm to find net payable amount.

[Net Payable Amount = Purchase Amount – Discount]

Solution:

1. Input "Enter Purchase Amount:" to P_amount
2. If P_amount > 5000, Then
   a. Set Discount = P_amount * 10 /100
3. Else
   a. Set Discount = P_amount * 5 /100
4. Set NetPay = P_amount – Discount
5. Print "Net Payable Amount =", NetPay
6. Stop

Iteration: When a set of statements need to be executed again and again, the iteration or repetition control structure is used. Several control structures are used in an algorithm for iteration or repetition. These are While, Do–While, For, Repeat–Until, etc.

The While statement is an entry control type loop statement. The general form of a While control structure is as follows:

```
While Condition, Do
      Statement or Statements
```

The `Statement or Statements` under a While statement will be executed repeatedly till the condition associated with the While is true. When the condition becomes false, the control comes out of the loop. Consider the following example.

Example 2.4: Write an algorithm to find the factorial of a number.

Solution:

1. Input "Enter any number:" to Num

2. Set `Fact = 1`

3. Set `I = 1`

4. While `I <= Num`, do

   a. Set `Fact = Fact * I`

   b. Set `I = I + 1`

5. Print "Factorial value =", `Fact`

6. Stop

The Do–While statement is an exit control type loop statement. The general form of a Do–While control structure is as follows:

```
Do
      Statement or Statements
While Condition
```

The `Statement or Statements` under a Do–While statement will be executed repeatedly till the condition associated with the While is true. When the condition becomes false, the control comes out of the loop. Consider the following example:

Example 2.5: Write an algorithm to display the first n natural numbers.

Solution:

1. Input "Enter the value of n:" to N

2. Set `I = 1`

3. Do

   a. Print `I`

   b. Set `I = I + 1`

4. While I <= N

5. Stop

The For construct is another entry control loop. It is a definite loop statement. When starting value, final value, and proper increment or decrement value are known, the For construct can be used. The general form of a For control structure is as follows:

```
For indexvariable = Startvalue To Finalvalue [Step
                                     StepValue],Do
        Statement or Statements
```

The indexvariable iterates from Startvalue to Finalvalue and in each iteration it is incremented by StepValue. StepValue is optional and its default value is 1. Negative StepValue indicates that the value of indexvariable will be decremented. Consider the following example:

Example 2.6: Write an algorithm to find the sum of the first n natural numbers.

Solution:

1. Input "Enter the value of n:" to N

2. Set Sum = 0

3. For I = 1 to N, Do

    a. Set Sum = Sum + I

4. Print "Sum =", Sum

5. Stop

Another iterative construct is Repeat–Until. This is like the While construct but the condition is given in reverse form. This loop continues its execution as long as the condition remains false. When the condition becomes true, this loop construct terminates its execution. The general form of a Repeat–Until control structure is as follows:

```
Repeat Until condition, Do
     Statement or Statements
```

Consider the following example:

Example 2.7: Write an algorithm to display the first n odd natural numbers.

Solution:

1. Input "Enter the value of n:" to N

2. Set I = 1

3. Set `C = 1`

4. Repeat until `C > N`, do
   a. Print `I`
   b. Set `I = I + 2`
   c. Set `C = C + 1`

5. Stop

2.6   Time and space complexity

The main task to analyze an algorithm is to determine how much resource is required to execute the algorithm. Here recourse means execution time of the CPU and the amount of memory consumed. Based on these criteria, the efficiency of an algorithm is measured and also compared with other algorithms of the same purpose. The first criterion is known as the time complexity and the second criterion the space complexity. Both these criteria depend on the input size of the problem. Hence we can define the time complexity as the total time required to execute the problem as a function of the input size. Similarly, the space complexity is the total space required in the computer memory to execute the problem as a function of the input size. Nowadays, the cost of memories has come down considerably. Hence, the execution speed of an algorithm becomes more crucial than the memory requirement, and in this book we shall mainly discuss the time complexity of different algorithms and data structures. Before discussing how we can calculate the time complexity, let us discuss some related terms.

2.7   Best Case, Worst Case, Average Case Time Complexity

When we analyze an algorithm, the calculation of its exact running time is not possible. There may be several constraints. Generally running time depends on the input size of the problem. With the increase of input size, running time also increases. Hence time complexity is measured in terms of a function whose argument is the input size of the problem. But this is not the only constraint. The order of the inputs also affects the running time calculation. Therefore, instead of an exact calculation, a boundary is calculated. Here we will discuss some terms that represent different types of complexity calculation.

Best Case Time Complexity: By this term we denote the performance of an algorithm when the situation is the most favorable. An example is if we are doing a search operation and the element is found at the first check.. The best case time complexity denotes the least time required to execute that algorithm.

Worst Case Time Complexity: This denotes the performance of an algorithm when the situation is the most adverse. As an example, if we are doing a search operation and the element is not found at all or found at the last comparison. The worst case time complexity denotes the maximum time required to execute that algorithm. The importance of it is that it makes us sure that in any condition the execution time does not cross this value.

Average Case Time Complexity: This denotes the estimation of execution time on an average. The importance of this case is that it shows the expected behavior of an algorithm when input size is randomly chosen, i.e., it represents the overall performance.

Amortized Time Complexity: In some problem, it may be found that some operations are expensive while many others are cheap. In that situation amortized complexity is used. This represents the time complexity for the algorithms in which the worst situation (and for that expensive operation) occurs very rarely, and it considers the steps that are performed frequently. The importance of amortized time complexity is that it guarantees at least average case complexity in all case, even in the worst case.

2.8   Time–Space Trade-off

Though the cost of memories has reduced, still the calculation of space complexity does not lose its importance. Hence to choose the best one among several algorithms to solve a particular problem, we have to consider time complexity as well as space complexity. If we get an algorithm that takes minimal time as well as minimal memory, it is well and good. But in practice this is hardly achieved. One algorithm may take less memory but it may require more time to execute in comparison with others. On the other hand, another algorithm may execute in lesser time but allocate more memory space. To gain on one we may have to sacrifice the other. There is always a trade-off between time and space. There is no specific rule that one we shall opt for; we have to take the decision based on the situation, constraints, and a comparative study. When time is the main constraint, we may sacrifice space. On the other hand, if space is the main constraint, we may need to sacrifice speed. Sometimes it may so happen that we choose an algorithm that neither shows the best running time complexity nor the best space complexity, but the overall performance is very good. So, considering all these things, we need to decide which algorithm has to be chosen.

2.9   Frequency Count and Its Importance

Frequency count or step count is the simplest method for finding the complexity of an algorithm. In this method, the frequency or occurrence of execution of each statement or step is calculated. Adding all these values we get a polynomial which represents the total number of executable statements or steps. Ignoring coefficient and lower terms, the term containing the highest power is considered the order of time complexity.

To illustrate the concept, let us consider the algorithm to find the factorial of a number:

Algorithm	Frequency of each statement
Factorial (n)	1
Set fact = 1	1
Set i = 1	1
While i <= n, do	n+1
fact = fact * i	n
i = i + 1	n
Return (fact)	1
Total number of executable statements	3n+5

Hence, the time complexity of the above problem is O(n).

Let us consider another example where a nested loop is used. The problem is to sort an array using the bubble sort. In the following, function *Arr* is an array and *n* is its size.

Algorithm	Frequency of each statement
BubbleSort (Arr, n)	1
For i = 1 to n-1, do	1+n+(n-1) = 2n
For j = 1 to n-1, do	(1+n+(n-1))*(n-1) = 2n²-2n
If Arr[j+1] > Arr[j], Then	(n-1)*(n-1)= n²-2n+1
Set temp = Arr[j+1]	n²-2n+1
Set Arr[j+1] = Arr[j]	n²-2n+1
Set Arr[j] = temp	n²-2n+1
Return (Arr)	1
Total number of executable statements	6n²-8n+6

In the above example each For statement contains a single initialization, n times checking and n-1 times increment. Hence, the total number of executable statements in the For statement is $1+n+(n-1) = 2n$. The body of the i loop will execute n-1 times. So, all the statements under the i loop should execute n-1 times. Again the number of executable statements in the For statement is $2n$, which should be executed $n-\underline{1}$ times. Thus the total number of executable statements for this statement is $2n*(n-1) = 2n^2-2n$. Similarly all the statements under the j loop should execute $(n-1)*(n-1)$ times in the worst case, i.e., n^2-2n+1 times. Hence, the total number of executable statements is $6n^2-8n+6$. Ignoring the coefficient, the term with the highest power in the polynomial is n^2. Hence, the time complexity of the bubble sort algorithm is $O(n^2)$.

Calculating the frequency count is not so easy for all problems, especially when the loop index does not increase or decrease linearly. We need to make an extra effort for calculating in those situations. However, the frequency count or step count method provides us with an idea about the order of execution easily.

2.10 Analyzing Algorithms

The main intention behind analyzing an algorithm is to find the efficiency of that algorithm. We have already discussed that efficiency indicates how much time and space is required to execute an algorithm. To formulate the efficiency of an algorithm we need to find the order of growth of the running time of the algorithm. Based on these we may also compare with other algorithms. We generally find that the 'order of growth' is effective for a large input size. Asymptotic efficiency of an algorithm indicates that the 'order of growth' is effective for a large enough input size. Now we discuss some asymptotic notation.

2.10.1 Big O Notation

The most popular asymptotic notation is the Big O notation. It is also known as 'Big-Oh'. We have already discussed that complexity is expressed as a function of input size, i.e., $f(n)$, where n is the number of elements. Whether the function is simple or complicated, the performance of the function is greatly dependent on n. $f(n)$ increases with the increase of n but we will now find the rate of growth.

If $f(n)$ and $g(n)$ are functions for all positive integers n, then $f(n) = O(g(n))$, read as 'f of n is Big oh of g of n' or '$f(n)$ is of the order of $g(n)$', if and only if there exists positive constants c and n_0 such that $f(n) \leq c\,g(n)$, $\forall\, n \geq n_0$, which means for all sufficiently large input values $(n > n_0)$, $f(n)$ will grow no more than a constant factor than $g(n)$. Therefore, g provides an upper bound for $f(n)$. In other words,

$O(g(n)) = \{f(n) :$ there exist positive constants c and n_0 such that $0 \leq f(n) \leq c\,g(n)$, $\forall\, n \geq n_0\}$

Figure 2.2 shows for all values of n to the right of n_0, the value of the function $f(n)$ is on or below $g(n)$.

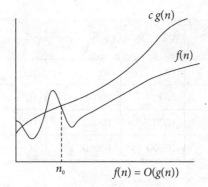

$$c\,g(n)$$
$$f(n)$$
$$n_0$$
$$f(n) = O(g(n))$$

Figure 2.2   Big O notation

The Big O notation provides an upper bound on a function within a constant factor. That is, the function $f(n)$ never performs worse than the specified value. Obviously it may perform better than that. As it provides the worst case complexity, this is widely used to analyze an algorithm.

Some examples of $g(n)$ and the corresponding $f(n)$ are shown in Table 2.2.

Table 2.2 Examples of $g(n)$ and the corresponding $f(n)$

$g(n)$	$f(n) = O(g(n))$
12	$O(1)$ i.e., Constant
$3n + 5$	$O(n)$
$5n^2 + 6n + 2$	$O(n^2)$
$n^3 - 4n^2 + 13n + 9$	$O(n^3)$
$2\log_2 n + 16$	$O(\log_2 n)$

According to the Big O notation, there are several types of algorithms. These are as follows.

- Constant time algorithm whose running time complexity is $O(1)$
- Logarithmic time algorithm whose running time complexity is $O(\log n)$
- Linear time algorithm whose running time complexity is $O(n)$
- Polynomial time algorithm whose running time complexity is $O(n^k)$ for $k > 1$
- Exponential time algorithm whose running time complexity is $O(k^n)$ for $k > 1$

To compare the above algorithms let us prepare a comparative study on the growth of these algorithms from which we can predict the number of operations in each case. Consider Table 2.3.

Table 2.3   Rate of growth for different types of algorithms

$f(n)$ / n	$O(\log_2 n)$	$O(n)$	$O(n \log_2 n)$	$O(n^2)$	$O(n^3)$	$O(2^n)$
10	$3.32 \approx 4$	10	40	10^2	10^3	1024
100	$6.64 \approx 7$	100	700	10^4	10^6	1.26×10^{30}
1000	$9.96 \approx 10$	1000	10000	10^6	10^9	1.07×10^{301}
10000	$13.28 \approx 14$	10000	140000	10^8	10^{12}	1.99×10^{3010}

From the Table 2.3 it is observed that the rate of growth is the slowest for the logarithmic function $\log_2 n$ and the fastest for the exponential function 2^n. The rate of growth depends on k for the polynomial function n^k.

However, the Big O notation suffers from some drawbacks. These are as follows:

- The Big O notation ignores the coefficient of the terms as well as the terms with lower powers of n. For example, if T(n) of an algorithm is $n^3 + 15$ and that of another algorithm is $10000n^2 + 8$, then according to the Big O notation, the time complexity of the first algorithm is $O(n^3)$, which is slower than the other, whose complexity is $O(n^2)$. But in reality this is not true for n < 10000. Similarly, if T(n) of an algorithm is $3n^2 + 6n + 5$ and that of another algorithm is $12n^2 + 108n + 60000$, then according to the big O notation, the time complexity of both algorithms is the same and it is $O(n^2)$. But practically there is a great difference between these considerations.

- It does not consider the programming effort.

- Sometimes it is very difficult to analyze mathematically.

2.10.2 Ω (Omega) Notation

As an inverse to the Big O notation, there is another notation, named Ω, which provides a lower bound on a function. It indicates that the function $f(n)$ never performs better than the specified value. However, it may perform worse than that. Hence, it provides the best case complexity of an algorithm.

If $f(n)$ and $g(n)$ are functions for all positive integers n, then $f(n) = \Omega(g(n))$, read as 'f of n is Omega of g of n', if and only if there exists positive constants c and n_0 such that $c\,g(n) \leq f(n)$, $\forall n \geq n_0$, which means for all sufficiently large input values $(n > n_0)$, $f(n)$ will grow no less than a constant factor than $g(n)$. Therefore, g provides a lower bound for $f(n)$. In other words,

$$\Omega(g(n)) = \{f(n): \text{there exist positive constants } c \text{ and } n_0 \text{ such that } 0 \leq c\,g(n) \leq f(n), \ \forall n \geq n_0\}$$

The Omega (Ω) notation provides a lower bound on a function within a constant factor. Figure 2.3 shows for all values of n to the right of n_0, the value of the function $f(n)$ is on or above $g(n)$.

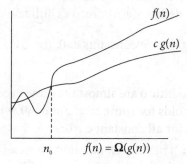

$f(n) = \Omega(g(n))$

Figure 2.3 Ω (Omega) notation

2.10.3 Θ (Theta) Notation

Another important notation, Θ, provides both upper and lower bounds on a function. If $f(n)$ and $g(n)$ are functions for all positive integers n, then $f(n) = \Theta(g(n))$, read as 'f of n is Theta of g of n', if and only if there exist positive constants c_1, c_2, and n_0 such that $c_1 g(n) \leq f(n) \leq c_2 g(n)$, $\forall\, n \geq n_0$, which means for all sufficiently large input values ($n > n_0$), $f(n)$ will grow no less than a constant factor than $g(n)$ and no more than another constant factor than $g(n)$. Therefore, g provides an asymptotic tight bound for $f(n)$. In other words,

$$\Theta(g(n)) = \{ f(n) : \text{there exist positive constants } c_1, c_2 \text{ and } n_0 \text{ such that } 0 \leq c_1 g(n) \leq f(n) \leq c_2 g(n), \forall n \geq n_0 \}$$

The Theta (Θ) notation provides an asymptotic tight bound for $f(n)$. Figure 2.4 shows an intuitive diagram of functions $f(n)$ and $g(n)$ where $f(n) = \Theta(g(n))$. For all values of n to the right of n_0, the value of the function $f(n)$ is on or above $c_1 g(n)$ and on or below $c_2 g(n)$.

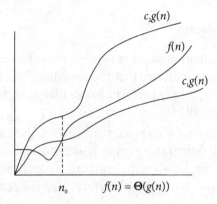

Figure 2.4   Θ (Theta) notation

2.10.4 Other Useful Notations

Now we will discuss another two notations. These are little Oh (o) and little Omega (ω).

Little Oh (o) Notation: This notation is used to represent an upper bound that is not asymptotically tight. We may define $o(g(n))$, read as 'little oh of g of n', as the set

$$o(g(n)) = \{ f(n) : \text{for any positive constants } c > 0, \text{ there exist a constant } n_0 > 0, \text{ such that } 0 \leq f(n) < cg(n), \forall n \geq n_0 \}.$$

Definitions of the Big O and little o are almost the same except that in the Big O notation the bound $0 \leq f(n) \leq c\, g(n)$ holds for **some** constant $c > 0$, whereas in little o notation the bound $0 \leq f(n) < cg(n)$ holds for **all** constant $c > 0$.

Little Omega (ω) Notation: The Big O notation represents an upper bound that is asymptotically tight and the little o represents an upper bound that is not asymptotically tight. Similarly Ω notation represents a lower bound that is asymptotically tight and little omega, i.e., ω, represents a lower bound that is **not** asymptotically tight.

We may define $\omega(g(n))$, read as 'little omega of g of n', as the set

$\omega(g(n)) = \{f(n) :$ there exist a constant $n_0 > 0$, for any positive constants $c > 0$, such that $0 \le cg(n) < f(n), \forall n \ge n_0\}$.

We may notice that the definitions of the big Omega (Ω) and little omega (ω) are almost the same except that in the big Omega notation the bound $0 \le cg(n) \le f(n)$ holds for **some** constant $c > 0$, whereas in the little omega notation the bound $0 \le cg(n) < f(n)$ holds for **all** constant $c > 0$.

2.11 Divide and Conquer Strategy

Divide and conquer is a design paradigm of algorithms. This paradigm breaks a problem into smaller sub-problems of similar type recursively until these sub-problems are simple enough to be solved directly. These solutions of the sub-problems are then combined to find the solution of the whole problem. There are several efficient algorithms which follow the divide and conquer strategy. Merge sort, quick sort in sorting algorithms, Karatsuba algorithm for multiplying large numbers, top-down parser in syntactic analysis, and computation of discrete Fourier transform are some common examples where the divide and conquer design paradigm is used. This type of algorithms follows three basic steps:

1. **Divide:** A problem is divided into a number of sub-problems of same type.
2. **Conquer:** Solutions to the sub-problems have to be found by recursively calling them.
3. **Combine:** By combining the solutions to the sub-problems, get the solution of the whole problem.

To understand the concept of divide and conquer algorithm let us discuss merge sort as an example. In merge sort:

1. **Divide:** First original sequence is divided into two sub-sequences.
2. **Conquer:** Then merge sort algorithm is applied recursively on each of the sub-sequences. Hence, each sub-sequence is further divided into two sub-sub-sequences. This procedure continues until the size of each sub-sequence becomes 1.
3. **Combine:** Finally two sorted sub-sequences are merged to get a sorted sequence.

Consider the example in Figure 2.5.

Actually the key operation is done at the 'combine' step. At the last level of recursion each sub-sequence contains a single element. Hence they are sorted. Now on every two sub-sequences merging operation is applied and we get a sorted sequence of two elements. These sub-sequences now move into the upper level and the same merging operations are applied on them. In this way gradually the entire sequence becomes sorted.

As recursion is used, it is relatively difficult to find the running time complexity of any algorithm that follows divide and conquer strategy. This is generally done using recurrence relation. In Chapter 6, we will discuss how we find the complexity of an algorithm where recursion is used.

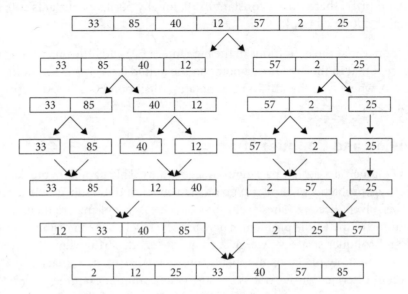

Figure 2.5   Merge sort operation

The main advantage of the divide and conquer paradigm is that we can simplify a large problem easily by breaking it into smaller unit. Another advantage is that as every time it is broken into two sub-sequences, the algorithm helps to achieve running time complexity in terms of $O(\log_2 n)$. For example, running time complexity of merge sort is $O(n \log_2 n)$.

2.12 Dynamic Programming

Dynamic programming is a sophisticated technique that optimizes recursion algorithms. It is mainly effective for the type of problems that have overlapping sub-problems. Like divide and conquer algorithms, this also combines the solutions of sub-problems to find the solution of the original problem. We may find that recursion repeatedly solves some common sub-sub-problems, i.e., for specific arguments the function is called several times. This wastes time as well as memory space. Dynamic programming helps us by solving this problem. Instead of calling a recursive function several times for the same argument(s), it computes the results of sub-sub-problems only once, stores in a table and uses that values in the rest calls. Hence, it reduces our efforts by avoiding execution of the same procedure again and again.

Suppose we want to find the n-th Fibonacci number using recursion. We know that the first two Fibonacci numbers are 0 and 1 and the rest are generated by adding its previous two terms. Hence, recursively we may define the function as

```
def FibNum(n):
    if n == 1:
        return 0
    elif n == 2:
        return 1
    else:
        return FibNum(n - 1) + FibNum(n - 2)
```

Now, if we want to find the 5th term, the recursion tree of the function call will look like as shown in Figure 2.6.

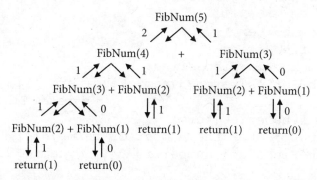

Figure 2.6 Recursive calls for n-th Fibonacci numbers

From the diagram we can find that to calculate **FibNum(5)** it recursively calls **FibNum(4)** and **FibNum(3)**. **FibNum(4)** further recursively calls **FibNum(3)** and **FibNum(2)**. **FibNum(3)** again recursively calls **FibNum(2)** and **FibNum(1)**. In the right sub tree of **FibNum(5)**, **FibNum(3)** again recursively calls **FibNum(2)** and **FibNum(1)**. All the **FibNum(2)** and **FibNum(1)** calls return 1 and 0 respectively.

But if we implement the above problem using dynamic programming, we need not call recursively again **FibNum(3)** at the right sub-tree of **FibNum(5)**, because this value is already calculated in the previous call. Hence, the recursion tree of the function call becomes as shown in Figure 2.7.

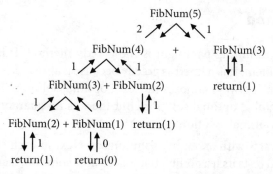

Figure 2.7 Recursive calls for n-th Fibonacci numbers using dynamic programming

From the diagram it is clear that we need not call **FibNum(3)** recursively at the right sub-tree of **FibNum(5)**. Similarly, if we call **FibNum(6)**, we will able to skip the recursive call of **FibNum(5)** at the right sub-tree. In this way, for larger terms we will get a great reduction of time and space. The following program illustrates the above concept:

Program 2.1 Program to find the n-th Fibonacci number using dynamic programming concept

```
#PRGD 2_1: Program to find n-th Fibonacci number using
#dynamic programming concept.
fiboSeries = {1:0,2:1}
def dynamicFibo(term):
    global fiboSeries
    if term not in fiboSeries:
        fiboSeries[term]=dynamicFibo(term-1)+
                                    dynamicFibo(term-2)
    return fiboSeries[term]
n = int(input("Enter the number of terms: "))
print(n,"th Fibonacci number is : ", dynamicFibo(n))
```

Output:

```
Enter the number of terms: 10
10 th Fibonacci number is :   34
```

It is very much cleare that dynamic programming is effective only for problems that have overlapping sub-problems. If we compare it with the divide and conquer algorithm, both use recursion but not at the same area. For example, merge sort is implemented using recursion. But there is no overlapping sub-problem in merge sort. Hence, dynamic programming cannot be applied here, wWhereas the divide and conquer strategy is perfectly applicable for merge sort.

2.13 Greedy Method

Another important programming paradigm is the greedy method. It is used to find the optimal solution of a problem. It is named as greedy because it always selects the best option available at that moment. It always chooses the local optimal solution in anticipation that this choice leads to the global optimal solution. But there is no guarantee that the greedy method always finds an optimal solution.

A greedy algorithm starts with an empty solution set. Next in each step, it chooses the best possible solution and tests its feasibility. If it is a feasible solution, it adds to the solution set; otherwise it is rejected forever. This process continues until a solution is reached.

Now we will illustrate the greedy method with an example. Suppose we have to find the change of ₹23 with minimum number of coins and the available coins are of ₹10, ₹5, ₹2, and ₹1. There is no limit to the number of each type of coins. To find the solution, we start with an empty set. Now, in each iteration we will choose the highest-valued coin to minimize the number of coins. So, we add a coin of ₹10 twice to the solution set and the sum of the set becomes 20. Now we cannot choose a coin of ₹10 or ₹5 as it is not feasible. So, we choose a coin of ₹2 and the set becomes {10, 10, 2}. Similarly, the next feasible coin to choose is a coin of ₹1. Hence, the final solution set is {10, 10, 2, 1}, which is also the optimal solution of the problem. But if the available coins are of ₹10, ₹6, and ₹1, the greedy method finds the solution as {10, 10, 1, 1, 1}, which is not an optimal solution. The optimal solution is {10, 6, 6, 1}.

To make sense of whether a problem can be solved using the greedy method we need to find two properties within the problem. These are the greedy choice property and the optimal sub-structure. The greedy choice property tells that an overall optimal solution is achieved by selecting the local best solution without considering the previous results coming from sub-problems. The optimal sub-structure indicates that the optimal solution of the whole problem contains the optimal solution of the sub-problems.

Both dynamic programming and the greedy method have optimal sub-structure properties. But they differ in the greedy choice property. In dynamic programming, choice taken at each step depends on the solutions of the sub-problems. But the greedy choice does not consider the solutions of the sub-problems. The greedy method is a top-down approach whereas dynamic programming is a bottom-up approach.

Though the greedy method may not find the best solution in all cases yet it shows very good performance for many algorithms like the Knapsack problem, job scheduling problem, finding minimum spanning tree using Prim's and Kruskal's algorithms, finding shortest path using Dijkstra's algorithm, Huffman coding, etc.

Introduction to Algorithm At a glance

- ✓ An algorithm is a step-by-step procedure to solve any problem.
- ✓ Algorithm helps us to solve complicated problems easily.
- ✓ The study of algorithms helps us to find the best possible solution of a given problem.
- ✓ Comparative study of algorithms helps us to develop efficient algorithms in terms of time and space.
- ✓ By studying different types of algorithms we are able to learn different program solving approaches which helps us to develop new algorithms.
- ✓ Two common algorithm design tools are flowchart and pseudocode.

✓ A flowchart is a pictorial or diagrammatical representation of an algorithm.

✓ Flowcharts are broadly classified into two categories: program flowchart and system flowchart.

✓ A pseudocode represents an algorithm in a form that looks like a programming code but actually it is not so.

✓ Best case time complexity denotes the minimum time required to execute an algorithm.

✓ Worst case time complexity denotes the maximum time required to execute an algorithm.

✓ Average case time complexity represents the overall performance.

✓ Big O notation provides an upper bound on a function within a constant factor, i.e., the algorithm never performs worse than the specified value.

✓ Ω notation provides a lower bound on a function. It indicates that the function $f(n)$ never performs better than the specified value.

✓ Θ notation provides both upper and lower bounds on a function.

✓ Divide and conquer breaks a problem into smaller sub-problems of similar type recursively until these sub-problems are simple enough to be solved directly and then these solutions to the sub-problems are combined to find the solution of the whole problem.

✓ If a problem has overlapping sub-problems, dynamic programming sophisticatedly optimizes the recursion algorithms by avoiding executing the same procedure again and again.

✓ Greedy method always selects the best option available at that moment. It always chooses the local optimal solution in anticipation that this choice leads to the global optimal solution.

Multiple Choice Questions

1. Which of the following is not a property of any algorithm?
   a) Definiteness
   b) Finiteness
   c) Fineness
   d) Effectiveness

2. Pictorial representation of an algorithm is known as
    a) Picture Chart
    b) Flowchart
    .c) Diagram chart
    d) None of these

3. By which of the following an algorithm can be better expressed when the audience does not have any programming knowledge?
    a) Flowchart
    b) Pseudocode
    c) Both a) and b)
    d) None of these

4. By which of the following an algorithm can be better expressed when the audience has programming knowledge?
    a) Flowchart
    b) Pseudocode
    c) Both a) and b)
    d) None of these

5. Which of the following is not a control structure of any algorithm?
    a) Sequence
    b) Selection
    c) Insertion
    d) Iteration

6. Which of the following denotes the minimum time requirement to execute that algorithm?
    a) Best case time complexity
    b) Worst case time complexity
    c) Average case time complexity
    d) Minimum case time complexity

7. Which of the following denotes the maximum time requirement to execute that algorithm?
    a) Best case time complexity
    b) Worst case time complexity
    c) Average case time complexity
    d) Minimum case time complexity

8. Which notation provides an upper bound on a function?
    a) Big O notation
    b) Ω notation

    c)   Θ notation

    d)   ω notation

9.   Which notation provides a lower bound on a function?

    a)   Big O notation

    b)   Ω notation

    c)   Θ notation

    d)   ω notation

10.   Which notation provides both upper and lower bound on a function?

    a)   Big O notation

    b)   Ω notation

    c)   Θ notation

    d)   ω notation

11.   Which notation provides an upper bound that is not asymptotically tight on a function?

    a)   Big O notation

    b)   Ω notation

    c)   Little Oh (o) notation

    d)   ω notation

12.   Which notation provides a lower bound that is not asymptotically tight on a function?

    a)   Big O notation

    b)   Ω notation

    c)   Little Oh (o) notation

    d)   ω notation

13.   Which of the following algorithms follows the divide and conquer design paradigm?

    a)   Prim's Algorithm

    b)   Quick Sort

    c)   Huffman Encoding

    d)   Radix Sort

14.   Which of the following algorithms follows the the greedy method?

    a)   Prim's Algorithm

    b)   Kruskal's Algorithm

    c)   Huffman Encoding

    d)   All of these

15.   Which of the following is true if we think about dynamic programming?

    a)   Effective for the problems that have overlapping sub problems

    b)   Combines the solutions of sub-problems to find the solution of original problem

c) Optimizes the recursion algorithms

d) All of these

Review Exercises

1. What do you mean by an algorithm? What is its importance?

2. What are the different criteria we need to keep in mind to write a good algorithm?

3. Explain the different approaches to designing an algorithm.

4. What do you mean by modular programming?

5. Differentiate between top-down approach and bottom-up approach.

6. What is a flowchart? What is its importance?

7. Explain the rules that need to be followed while drawing program flowcharts.

8. Draw a flowchart to find the smallest between 3 inputted numbers.

9. What is a pseudocode? What is its importance?

10. Explain the basic control structures of any programming languages/algorithms.

11. What do you mean by time complexity? What is space complexity? What is their importance?

12. Explain with example: best case, worst case and average case time complexity.

13. How is frequency count used to find the complexity of an algorithm? Explain with an example.

14. What are the different notations used to express time complexity?

15. Explain the big Oh (O), Ω, and Θ notations.

16. Explain with example the divide and conquer design paradigm of any algorithm.

17. What is dynamic programming? Explain with an example.

18. What is the greedy method? Mention the algorithms that follow the greedy method.

19. Compare and contrast dynamic programming and the greedy method.

Array

We start to write programs using a limited number of variables, but in real life, plenty of elements are required to be dealt with. For example, first we learn to write a program to find out the maximum between two variables. Then gradually we move to writing the same program for three, four or five variables. But if our task is to find the highest marks in a class of 60 students or more, then it will become a tedious job for us. This will mean 60 variables are to be declared to store marks of 60 students, so 60 *input* statements have to be used to input the marks of each student, and finally 60 *if* statements to find the maximum of these marks, and so on. Not only that, if another class contains less or more than 60 students, we cannot not use this program for that class. We have to rewrite the program according to that new class. Thus, this approach of processing a large set of data is too cumbersome and surely not flexible enough. Almost all modern high level programming languages provide a more convenient way of processing such collections. The solution is **array** or **subscripted variables**.

3.1 Definition

An array is a collection of homogeneous (i.e., same data type) data elements described by a single name and placed in contiguous memory locations. Each individual element of an array is referenced by a subscripted variable, formed by affixing to the array name with a subscript or index enclosed in brackets.

Thus, by declaring an array we can store a set of values, say 60 of a particular type, say, *int*, in a single variable without declaring 60 different variables of different names. All these values will be stored under a unique identifier (array name).

3.2 Creating an Array

In Python, we can create an array by importing the 'array' module. After importing we can declare an array as:

```
array(type_code, value_list)
```

Here,

value_list: specifies the list of elements which will be the content of the array.

type_code: specifies the data type of the elements which is going to be stored in the array. Table 3.1 shows commonly used type codes for declaring array.

Example:

```
import array as arr

myIntArray = arr.array('i', [10, 20, 30])
myFloatArray = arr.array('f', [10.2, 5.8, 23.71])
```

Table 3.1   Commonly used Type Codes for declaring array

Code	C Type	Python Type	Min bytes
b	signed char	int	1
B	unsigned char	int	1
u	Py_UNICODE	Unicode	2
h	signed short	int	2
H	unsigned short	int	2
i	signed int	int	2
I	unsigned int	int	2
l	signed long	int	4
L	unsigned long	int	4
q	signed long long	int	8
Q	unsigned long long	int	8
f	float	float	4
d	double	float	8

An array can also be created using the package NumPy. NumPy is a package in Python for scientific computing. It helps us to work with N-dimensional array. NumPy's array class is called ndarray. In NumPy we can declare an array as:

```
array(value_list, [dtype=type])
```

Example:

```
import numpy as npy

myIntArray = npy.array([10, 20, 30])    #Array of Integers
myFloatArray = npy.array( [10.2, 5.8, 23.71])
                                      #Array of Floats
myComplexArray = npy.array( [5, 10, 15], dtype=complex)
                          #Array of Complex numbers
myInt32Array = npy.array([1, 3, 5, 7], dtype=npy.int32)
                          #Array of 32 bit Integers
```

We can create an array of zeros and ones using the zeros() and ones() methods. zeros() method returns an array of given shape and data type containing all zeros. The general format of zeros() method is:

```
numpy.zeros(Shape[, dtype=type] [, order])
```

where **Shape** indicates the number of elements in case of a single dimensional array, **dtype** indicates the data type of the array and **order** is not required in case of single dimensional arrays. The default value of **dtype** is float.

Ones() is very similar to zeros() method. Instead of zeros it returns an array whose all values are set to 1. The general format of ones() method is:

```
numpy.ones(Shape[, dtype=type] [, order])
```

where **Shape** indicates the number of elements in case of a single dimensional array, **dtype** indicates the data type of the array, and **order** is not required in case of single dimensional arrays. The default value of **dtype** is float. Consider the following example:

```
import numpy as npy

myZerosArray1 = npy.zeros(5)
print(myZerosArray1)

myZerosArray2 = npy.zeros(5, dtype=int)
```

```
print(myZerosArray2)

myOnesArray1 = npy.ones(4)
print(myOnesArray1)

myOnesArray2 = npy.ones(4, dtype=npy.int32)
print(myOnesArray2)
```

Output:

```
[0. 0. 0. 0. 0.]
[0 0 0 0 0]
[1. 1. 1. 1.]
[1 1 1 1]
```

Another way to create an array is using `arange()` method. `arange()` method returns a single dimension ndarray containing evenly spaced values for a given range. The general format of `arange()` is:

$$\textbf{numpy.arange([Start,] End [, Step] [, dtype=type])}$$

where **Start** is the starting value of the range, **End** indicates the end value of the range but excluding **End** value, i.e., up to **End-1**, **Step** indicates the gap between values, and **dtype** indicates the data type of the array. The default value of **Step** is 1.

```
import numpy as npy

myArray1 = npy.arange(10)
print(myArray1)

myArray2 = npy.arange(1,24,2)
print(myArray2)

myArray3 = npy.arange(1,2,.2)
print(myArray3)
```

Output:

```
[0 1 2 3 4 5 6 7 8 9]
[ 1  3  5  7  9 11 13 15 17 19 21 23]
[1.  1.2 1.4 1.6 1.8]
```

3.3 Accessing Elements of an Array

Once an array is declared, we can access individual elements in the array. These elements are accessed with the help of array index which is nothing but the position of the element in that array. Array index always starts from 0. Hence, the first position of an array is 0, second is 1, and so on. To access an array element we need to mention the array name followed by the array index enclosed within [ ]. The general format to access an array element is:

```
Array_name[ index ]
```

If we declare an array, arr, of size 5, then to access the first element of the array we have to write arr[0] as in Python array index always starts from 0. Similarly, to access the next elements we have to write arr[1], arr[2], and so on.

	arr[0]	arr[1]	arr[2]	arr[3]	arr[4]
arr					

These elements can be accessed individually just like a normal variable. We can read as well as modify its value. For example, to assign the value 72 in the second cell of **arr**, we can write the statement as:

```
arr[1] = 72
```

Similarly, to assign the value of the second element of **arr** to a variable called **num**, we can write:

```
num = arr[1]
```

Thus, the expression arr[1] acts just like a variable of type *int*. Not only assignment, it can also be used in input statement, output statement, or in any arithmetic expression – everywhere its use is similar to a numeric variable.

Notice that the second element of **arr** is specified as **arr**[1], since the first one is **arr**[0]. Therefore, the third element will be **arr**[2], fourth element will be **arr**[3], and the last element will be **arr**[4]. Thus, if we write **arr**[5], it would be the sixth element of the array **arr** and therefore exceeding the size of the array, which is an error.

We can use a variable as a subscript or array index to access the array elements. At runtime this variable may contain several values and thus different array elements are accessed accordingly. This facility of using variables as subscripts makes array so useful.

The following code snippet shows how easily we can take 60 inputs in an array using a variable as subscript:

```
import array as arr

myArray=arr.array('i',[0]*60)
for i in range(60):
    myArray[i]=int(input("Enter Any Number: "))
```

Similarly, we can display the content of an array of size 60 as :

```
for i in range(60):
    print(myArray[i])
```

Some other valid operations with arrays:

```
arr[0] = a
arr[a] = 75
b = arr [a+2]
arr[2] = arr[0] + arr[1]
arr[arr[a]] = arr[2] + 5  etc.
```

Now we will write a complete program that will demonstrate the operations of the array.

Program 3.1 Write a program to find the highest marks in a class of n students.

```
# PRGD3_1: Program to find the highest marks in a class of
#n students.

import array as arr

n=int(input("Enter number of Students: "))
marks=arr.array('i',[0]*n)
for i in range(n):
    marks[i]=int(input("Enter Marks of Student%d:"%(i+1)))
max=marks[0]
for i in range(1,n):
    if marks[i]>max:
        max=marks[i]
print("The highest marks is :", max)
```

In the above program, first we take the number of students as input. Based on that inputted number we declare an integer array named marks with the statement

```
marks=arr.array('i',[0]*n)
```

Next we take the input to the array. To find the highest marks we store the first element into the **max** variable and compare it with the rest elements of the array. If the array element is larger than **max**, it will be stored within the **max** variable. So, **max** variable contains the highest marks.

From the above program we can see now with a single statement we are able to store marks of **n** number of students. A **for** loop and an **input** statement are able to take input of the marks of **n** students and similarly a **for** loop and an **if** statement are able to find the maximum of these marks. This is the advantage of using an array.

Not only a single array, but we can also use as many arrays as required in a program. Here is another example where we use two arrays in a program.

Program 3.2 Write a program that will store the positive numbers first, then zeros if any, and the negative numbers at the end in a different array from a group of numbers.

```
# PRGD3_2: Program that will store the positive numbers
# first, then zeros if any, and the negative numbers at
# the end in a different array from a group of numbers.

import array as arr
n=int(input("Enter number of Elements: "))
elements=arr.array('i',[0]*n)
arranged=arr.array('i',[0]*n)
for i in range(n):            #  Input to array
    elements[i]=int(input("Enter Element%d: "%(i+1)))
j=0
for i in range(n):            # Copy of positive elements
    if elements[i]>0:
        arranged[j]=elements[i]
        j+=1

for i in range(n):            # Copy of zeros
    if elements[i]==0:
        arranged[j]=elements[i]
        j+=1
for i in range(n):            # Copy of negative elements
    if elements[i]<0:
        arranged[j]=elements[i]
        j+=1

print("The Newly Arranged Elements are : ")
for i in range(n):            # Printing of array elements
    print(arranged[i], end=' ')
```

Apart from this general convention of accessing element, Python also provides the flexibility to access array elements from the end. When we access an array from the left or the beginning, the array index is started from 0. But if we start accessing elements from the end, array index starts from -1. Python uses negative index numbers to access elements in the backward direction.

	-5	-4	-3	-2	-1
arr	10	1234	563	27	98
	0	1	2	3	4

Figure 3.1 Positive and negative index to access array elements

Consider Figure 3.1. Here, arr[-1] returns 98, arr[-2] returns 27, and so on. Hence, Python gives us the opportunity to access array elements in the forward as well as in the backward direction.

3.4 Operations on an Array

Python is enriched by its operator and its vast library functions. We can add elements into an array, remove elements from an array, modify the content of an array, extract a portion of an array (slicing), search an element from an array and concatenate multiple arrays. We can also create a new array by repeating the elements of an existing array.

3.4.1 Adding Elements to an Array

We can add one or more elements into an array using append(), extend(), and insert(). Using append() we can add a single element at the end of an array whereas extend() helps us to add multiple elements at the end of an array. On the other hand, insert() helps us to insert an element at the beginning, end, or at any index position in an array. The following program explains the operations of these functions:

Program 3.3: Write a program to show the use of append(), insert(), and extend().

```
#PRGD3_3: Program to show the use of append(), insert()
#and extend()
import array as arr

elements=arr.array('i',[10,20,30])
print ("Before insertion : ", end =" ")
print(elements)
```

```
elements.append(40)                       #Inserts 40 at end
print ("After appending 40 : ", end =" ")
print(elements)

elements.extend([50, 60, 70])             #Inserts 50, 60 and
                                          #70 at end
print ("After extending the array with 50, 60 and 70 : ")
print(elements)

elements.insert(0,5)                      #Inserts 5 at index
                                          #position 0
print ("After inserting 5 at 0th position : ")
print(elements)

elements.insert(2,15)                     #Inserts 15 at index
                                          #position 2
print ("After inserting 15 at position 2 : ")
print(elements)
```

Output:

Before insertion : array('i', [10, 20, 30])
After appending 40 : array('i', [10, 20, 30, 40])
After extending the array with 50, 60 and 70 :
array('i', [10, 20, 30, 40, 50, 60, 70])
After inserting 5 at 0th position :
array('i', [5, 10, 20, 30, 40, 50, 60, 70])
After inserting 15 at position 2 :
array('i', [5, 10, 15, 20, 30, 40, 50, 60, 70])

3.4.2   Removing Elements from an Array

Elements can be removed from an array using the del statement or remove() and pop(). Using the del statement we can remove an element of a specific index position. If we want to delete the entire array, we need to mention the array name only with del. remove() deletes the first occurrence of an element in an array. But if the element does not exist in the array, it raises an error. pop() removes an element from a specified index position. If we do not mention the index position, pop() removes the last element. In both cases, after removing the element it also returns the element. The following program explains the operations of these functions:

Program 3.4: Write a program to show the use of del, remove(), and pop().

```
#PRGD3_4: Program to show the use of del, remove() and
# pop()
import array as arr

elements=arr.array('i',[10,20,30,40,10])
print ("Before deletion : ", end =" ")
print(elements)

del elements[2]        #Deleting element of index position 2
print ("After deleting element of index position 2 : ")
print(elements)

elements.remove(10)   #Deleting first occurrence of 10
print ("After deleting the first occurrence of 10 : ")
print(elements)

num=elements.pop()     #Last element is deleted and returned
print("Popped element is : ",num)
print ("After popping without argument : ")
print(elements)

num=elements.pop(0)   #First element is deleted and returned
print("Popped element is : ",num)
print ("After popping element of index position 0 : ")
print(elements)

del elements               # Delete entire array
```

Output:

Before deletion : array('i', [10, 20, 30, 40, 10])
After deleting element of index position 2 :
array('i', [10, 20, 40, 10])
After deleting the first occurrence of 10 :
array('i', [20, 40, 10])
Popped element is : 10
After popping without argument :
array('i', [20, 40])
Popped element is : 20
After popping element of index position 0 :
array('i', [40])

3.4.3   Slicing of an Array

By using the slicing operation we can extract one or more elements from an array. This operation can be done using (:) operator within the subscript operator ([ ]). The general format of a slicing operation on an array is:

```
Array_name[ Start : End : Step]
```

where **Start** is the starting index position from which the extraction operation starts. The extraction operation continues up to the **End – 1** index position, and **Step** represents the incremented or decremented value needed to calculate the next index position to extract elements. If **Start** is omitted, the beginning of the array is considered, i.e., the default value of **Start** is 0. If **End** is omitted, the end of the array is considered and the default **Step** value is 1. If we use negative **Step** value, elements will be extracted in the reverse direction. Thus, for negative **Step** value, the default value of **Start** is -1 and that of **End** indicates the beginning of the array. The following example illustrates these concepts:

Program 3.5 Write a program to show the slicing operation on an array.

```
#PRGD3_5: Program to show the slicing operation on an
#array

import array as arr

elements=arr.array('i',[10,20,30,40,50])
print ("Before slicing operation : ", end =" ")
print(elements)

slice1 = elements[1:4]
#Extracts elements from index position 1 to 3
print ("New extracted array is : ", end =" ")
print(slice1)

slice2 = elements[:4]
#Extracts elements from index position 0 to 3
print ("New extracted array is : ", end =" ")
print(slice2)

slice3 = elements[1:]
#Extracts elements from index position 1 to end
print ("New extracted array is : ", end =" ")
print(slice3)
```

```
slice4 = elements[1:4:2]
```
#Extracts elements from index position 1 and 3
```
print ("New extracted array is : ", end =" ")
print(slice4)
```

```
slice4 = elements[::2]
```
#Extracts elements from index position 0, 2 and 4
```
print ("New extracted array is : ", end =" ")
print(slice4)
```

```
slice5 = elements[4:1:-1]
```
#Extracts elements from index position 4 to 2
```
print ("New extracted array is : ", end =" ")
print(slice5)
```

```
slice6 = elements[-1:-4:-1]
```
#Extracts elements from index position -1 to -3
```
print ("New extracted array is : ", end =" ")
print(slice6)
```

```
slice7 = elements[-1:1:-1]
```
#Extracts elements from index position -1 to 2
```
print ("New extracted array is : ", end =" ")
print(slice7)
```

```
slice8 = elements[-3::-1]
```
#Extracts elements from index position -3 to beginning of the array
```
print ("New extracted array is : ", end =" ")
print(slice8)
```

```
slice9 = elements[:-4:-1]
```
#Extracts elements from end to index position -3
```
print ("New extracted array is : ", end =" ")
print(slice9)
```

```
slice10 = elements[::-1]
```
#Extracts all elements but in reverse direction
```
print ("New extracted array is : ", end =" ")
print(slice10)
```

Output:

```
Before slicing operation : array('i', [10, 20, 30, 40, 50])
New extracted array is : array('i', [20, 30, 40])
New extracted array is : array('i', [10, 20, 30, 40])
New extracted array is : array('i', [20, 30, 40, 50])
New extracted array is : array('i', [20, 40])
New extracted array is : array('i', [10, 30, 50])
New extracted array is : array('i', [50, 40, 30])
New extracted array is : array('i', [50, 40, 30])
New extracted array is : array('i', [50, 40, 30])
New extracted array is : array('i', [30, 20, 10])
New extracted array is : array('i', [50, 40, 30])
New extracted array is : array('i', [50, 40, 30, 20, 10])
```

3.4.4 Searching Element in an Array

To search an element within an array index () is used. This function returns the index position of the first occurrence of element passed as an argument with this function. But if the element is not found in the array, it raises an error.

The membership operators **in** and **not in** can also be applied on an array for searching an element. The operator in returns **True** if the element is found in the array; otherwise it returns **False**. The operator not in works as its reverse. If the element is found in the array, it returns **False**; otherwise it returns **True**. Hence, using the membership operator, whether an element is present in an array or not can be confirmed. After confirmation we can determine its position using the index () method. There is another function, count (), which counts the occurrence of a element, passed as argument with this method, in an array.

The following program explains the searching operation in an array:

Program 3.6 Write a program to show the search operation in an array.

```
#PRGD3_6: Program to show the search operation in an array

import array as arr

elements=arr.array('i',[10,20,30,40,10])
print ("The Array : ", end =" ")
print(elements)

num = int(input("Enter any number: "))
if num in elements:
```

```
    posn = elements.index(num)      #Returns first
                                    #occurrence of 10
    print("The index of 1st occurrence of %d is : "%(num),
                                            end ="")
    print(posn)
    print("And total occurrence of %d is : %d"
                            %(num,elements.count(num)))
else:
    print("Number not found")
```

Sample Output:

The Array : array('i', [10, 20, 30, 40, 10])
Enter any number: 10
The index of 1st occurrence of 10 is : 0
And total occurrence of 10 is : 2

The Array : array('i', [10, 20, 30, 40, 10])
Enter any number: 22
Number not found

3.4.5 Updating Elements in an Array

Arrays are mutable in Python. We can easily update the array elements by just assigning value at the required index position. With the help of the slicing operation certain portions of an array can be modified. Consider the following example:

Program 3.7 Write a program to show the updating operation in an array.

```
#PRGD3_7: Program to show the updating operation in an
#array
import array as arr

elements=arr.array('i',[10,20,30,40,10])
print ("Before updation : ", end =" ")
print(elements)
elements[2]=55              #Updating element of index
                                        #position 2
print ("After updating element of index position 2 : ")
print(elements)

arr2=arr.array('i',[22,33,44])
```

```
elements[1:4]=arr2        #Updating elements of index
                                   #position 1 to 3
print ("After updating elements from index position 1 to
                                            3: ")
print(elements)
```

Output:

Before updation : array('i', [10, 20, 30, 40, 10])
After updating element of index position 2 :
array('i', [10, 20, 55, 40, 10])
After updating elements from index position 1 to 3:
array('i', [10, 22, 33, 44, 10])

3.4.6 Concatenation of Arrays

We can also concatenate two or more arrays. By this operation two or more arrays can be joined together. Concatenation is done using the + operator. Consider the following example:

Program 3.8 Write a program to show the concatenation operation of arrays.

```
#PRGD3_8: Program to show the concatenation operation of
#arrays

import array as arr

arr1=arr.array('i',[10,20,30,40])
arr2=arr.array('i',[5,10,15,20,25])
arr3=arr.array('i',[22,33,44])
print ("1st Array : ", end =" ")
print(arr1)
print ("2nd Array : ", end =" ")
print(arr2)
print ("3rd Array : ", end =" ")
print(arr3)

myArr = arr1+arr2+arr3        #Concatenation of 3 arrays
print ("Concatenated Array : ")
print(myArr)
```

Output:

1st Array : array('i', [10, 20, 30, 40])
2nd Array : array('i', [5, 10, 15, 20, 25])
3rd Array : array('i', [22, 33, 44])
Concatenated Array :
array('i', [10, 20, 30, 40, 5, 10, 15, 20, 25, 22, 33, 44])

3.4.7 Multiplication or Repetition on Array

A unique feature of Python is the repetition of elements of an object and this is done using the * operator. This is applicable for arrays also. We can repeat the entire array or a single element multiple times. Consider the following example:

Program 3.9 Write a program to show the repetition operation on an array.

```
#PRGD3_9: Program to show the repetition operation on
#array

import array as arr

arr1=arr.array('i',[10,20,30,40])
arr2=arr.array('i',[1])

print ("1st Array : ", end =" ")
print(arr1)
print ("After repeting twice: ", end =" ")
print(arr1*2)          #Repeating the entire array twice

print ("2nd Array : ", end =" ")
print(arr2)
arr3=arr2*5            #Repeating the entire array 5 times
print ("After repeting 5 times : ", end =" ")
print(arr3)

myArr=arr.array('i',[0]*6)     #Creating an array of 6
                                              #zeros
print ("Array of 6 zeros: ", end =" ")
print(myArr)
```

Output:

1st Array : array('i', [10, 20, 30, 40])
After repeting twice: array('i', [10, 20, 30, 40, 10, 20, 30, 40])

2nd Array : array('i', [1])
After repeting 5 times : array('i', [1, 1, 1, 1, 1])
Array of 6 zeros: array('i', [0, 0, 0, 0, 0, 0])

3.5   Representation of Polynomials

There are huge applications of arrays in computer programming. Here we are showing an example. A polynomial can be easily represented using an array. The general form of a polynomial of degree n is:

$$f(x) = a_n x^n + a_{n-1} x^{n-1} + a_{n-2} x^{n-2} + \ldots\ldots + a_1 x + a_0$$

where a_n , a_{n-1} , ... , a_1 , a_0 are the coefficients and n, n-1, n-2,.... are exponents or powers of the term x of the polynomial. As each term of a polynomial consists of coefficient and exponent or power, to represent a polynomial we may consider the array indices as the power and the value of a particular index position as the coefficient of that term. Hence, if a polynomial is $f(x) = 3x^6 + 5x^3 + 9x + 2$, it will be represented as follows:

2	9	0	5	0	0	3
0	1	2	3	4	5	6

 This representation is very easy. Consider the following program which illustrates how a polynomial can be created, displayed, and added with another polynomial:

Program 3.10 Write a program to add two polynomials.

```
#PRGD3_10: Program to add two Polynomials

import array as arr

def create_poly(poly): # Function to create a Polynomial
    while True:
        cof=int(input("Enter Coefficient : "))
        pr=int(input("Enter Power : "))
        poly[pr]=cof
        ch=input("Continue?(y/n): ")
        if ch.upper()=='N':
            break

def display(poly): # Function to display the Polynomial
    size=len(poly)
```

```
    for i in range(size-1,-1,-1):
        if poly[i]!=0:
            print(str(poly[i])+"x^"+str(i),end="+")
    print("\b ")

def add_poly(pol1, pol2): # Function to Add two Polynomials
    l=len(pol1)
    pol3=arr.array('i',[0]*l)
    for i in range(l):
        pol3[i]=pol1[i]+pol2[i]
    return pol3

p1=int(input("Enter the highest power of 1st Polynomial:
                                                      "))
p2=int(input("Enter the highest power of 2nd Polynomial:
                                                      "))
p=max(p1,p2)
poly1=arr.array('i',[0]*(p+1))
poly2=arr.array('i',[0]*(p+1))
print("Enter values for 1st Polynomials:-")
create_poly(poly1)
print("Enter values for 2nd Polynomials:-")
create_poly(poly2)

poly3=add_poly(poly1, poly2)
print("\n1st Polynomial : ",end="")
display(poly1)
print("2nd Polynomial : ",end="")
display(poly2)
print("Resultant Polynomial : ",end="")
display(poly3)
```

Though the representation of polynomials using arrays is very easy to implement, yet the main drawback of this representation is that if most of the terms of a polynomial are missing, there is a huge wastage of memory as most of the cells contain zero. Suppose we have a polynomial $f(x) = 3x^{36} + 7$; it will be represented as follows:

7	0	0	0	0	0	0	0	0	0	0	0	0	...	0	0	0	0	0	0	3
0	1	2	3	4	5	6	7	8	9	10	11	12	...	30	31	32	33	34	35	36

This problem can be overcome if we implement it using a linked list. We will discuss about linked list and its advantage and implementation in Chapter 7.

3.6   Two Dimensional Array

So far, we have discussed arrays with only one dimension. It is also possible to declare two or more dimensions for arrays. In a one dimensional array we can store a list of values but in a two dimensional array we can store values in tabular format.

A two dimensional array consists of a few rows and columns. The conceptual view of a two dimensional array named arr2d, whose number of rows is 3 and number of columns in each row is 5, is shown in the following figure:

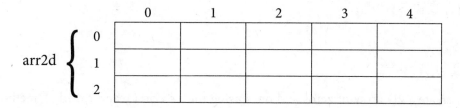

Figure 3.2   Conceptual view of a two dimensional array

3.7   Creation of a Two Dimensional Array

Like single dimensional arrays, a two dimensional as well as any multidimensional array can be created in Python. This can be achieved easily using the Numpy package. NumPy has powerful features for operations on matrices and for multidimensional arrays. Hence, here we are using the NumPy package for two dimensional as well as multidimensional arrays.

Basically in Python a two dimensional array is considered as an array of arrays. In NumPy there are several ways by which we can create two dimensional arrays. First, we are creating a 2D array providing some value list. Consider the following example:

```
import numpy as npy

myInt2DArray = npy.array([[10, 20, 30], [40, 50, 60]])
print(myInt2DArray)          #2D Array of Integers
myFloat2DArray = npy.array( [[10.2, 5.8, 23.71],[4.5, 6,
                                                 9.3]])
print(myFloat2DArray)        #2D Array of Floats
myComplex2DArray = npy.array([[5,10,15],[20,25,30]],
                                            dtype=complex)
print(myComplex2DArray)      #2D Array of Complex numbers
my2DInt32Array = npy.array([[1,3,5,7],[2,4,6,8]],
                                            dtype=npy.int32)
print(my2DInt32Array)        #2D Array of 32 bit Integers
```

Output:

```
[[10 20 30]
 [40 50 60]]

[[10.2 5.8 23.71]
 [4.5  6.  9.3 ]]

[[ 5.+0.j 10.+0.j 15.+0.j]
 [20.+0.j 25.+0.j 30.+0.j]]

[[1 3 5 7]
 [2 4 6 8]]
```

We can create a 2D array of zeros and ones using the `zeros()` and `ones()` methods also. In both methods we need to specify the length of the dimensions, i.e., the number of rows and columns, as argument. The general format of the `zeros()` method is:

`Numpy.zeros(Shape[, dtype=type][, order])`

where **Shape** indicates the dimensions of the array, i.e. the number of rows and columns of the array, **dtype** indicates the data type of the array, and **order** represents whether it follows row major or column major representation of data in memory.

The general format of `ones()` method is:

`Numpy.ones(Shape[, dtype=type][, order])`

where **Shape** indicates the dimensions of the array, i.e. the number of rows and columns of the array, **dtype** indicates the data type of the array, and **order** represents whether it follows row major or column major representation of data in memory. Consider the following example:

```
import numpy as npy

my2DZerosArray = npy.zeros((2,3))
print(my2DZerosArray)

my2DOnesArray = npy.ones((4,3), dtype=npy.int32)
print(my2DOnesArray)

myMixArray = npy.ones((3,2), dtype=[('x','int'),('y',
                                              'float')])
print(myMixArray)
```

Output:

```
[[0. 0. 0.]
 [0. 0. 0.]]


[[1 1 1]
 [1 1 1]
 [1 1 1]
 [1 1 1]]


[[(1, 1.) (1, 1.)]
 [(1, 1.) (1, 1.)]
 [(1, 1.) (1, 1.)]]
```

Another way to create a 2D array is using the arange() and reshape() methods. The arange() method returns a single dimension ndarray containing evenly spaced values for a given range. The general format of arange() is:

numpy.arange([Start,] End [, Step] [, dtype=type])

where **Start** is the starting value of the range, **End** indicates the end value of the range but excluding **End** value, i.e., up to **End-1**, **step** indicates the gap between values, and **dtype** indicates the data type of the array.

On the other hand, the reshape() method changes the shape of the array without changing the data of the array. The number of rows and columns are needed to be sent as argument with this method. But we have to be careful that the product of rows and columns must be the same as the total elements in the array.

Hence, by using arange() and reshape() methods together we can easily create a 2D array.

```
import numpy as npy

my2DArray = npy.arange(1,24,2).reshape(3,4)
print(my2DArray)

[[ 1  3  5  7]
 [ 9 11 13 15]
 [17 19 21 23]]
```

3.8   Accessing Elements of a Two Dimensional Array

To access an element of a 2D array we have to specify the row number and column number of the element. The general format is:

```
Array_name[row] [column]
```

In Python, row number and column number both start from zero, as described in Figure 3.3. So, to access the second element vertically and the fourth horizontally from the array named arr2d the expression would be:

arr2d[1][3]

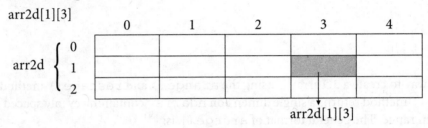

Figure 3.3 Accessing elements in a two dimensional array

Other operations are the same as in a one dimensional array. Some valid operations with two dimensional arrays are:

```
arr2d[0] [0] = a;   /* a is an integer variable   */
arr2d[i] [j] = 75; /* i and j are integer variables
a = arr2d[i+2] [j];
```

We can access the rows and columns of a 2D array like single elements. To access the rows we need to specify only the row index along with the array name. Hence, arr2d[0] represents the first row, arr2d[1] represents the second row, and arr2d[2] represents the third row. And yes obviously! We can specify negative index also to access from the end. To access the columns we have to specify a (:) followed by a (,) followed by the column index within the subscript operator. The following example illustrates these:

```
import numpy as npy
myInt2DArray = npy.array([[10, 20, 30], [40, 50, 60], [70, 80,
                                                             90]])
print("Entire array:")
print(myInt2DArray)
print("First row:")
print(myInt2DArray[0])
print("Second row:")
print(myInt2DArray[1])
```

```
print("Third row:")
print(myInt2DArray[2])
print("First & Second row:")
print(myInt2DArray[0:2])
print("Second & third row:")
print(myInt2DArray[1:])
print("Second & third row in reverse order:")
print(myInt2DArray[:0:-1])
print("First column:")
print(myInt2DArray[:,0])
print("Second column:")
print(myInt2DArray[:,1])
print("Third column:")
print(myInt2DArray[:,2])
```

3.9   Representation of a Two Dimensional Array in Memory

Though we have shown the two dimensional array in tabular form, which consists of rows and columns, yet actually in memory it is a linear sequence of bytes. Our view is fully conceptual. Now in this conceptual view there are two ways by which elements are stored in a two dimensional array. These are:

- Row Major Representation
- Column Major Representation

3.9.1 Row Major Representation

In this representation, elements are stored row-wise. If a 2D array has m rows and n columns, the first n elements of the first row will be stored in the first n memory locations, then n elements of the second row will be stored in the next n memory locations, then n elements of the third row will be stored in the next n memory locations, and so on. Thus, elements are stored row by row. This is followed in most of the programming languages like C, C++, Java, and so on. This concept has been shown in Figure 3.4.

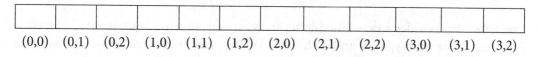

(0,0)   (0,1)   (0,2)   (1,0)   (1,1)   (1,2)   (2,0)   (2,1)   (2,2)   (3,0)   (3,1)   (3,2)

Figure 3.4   Row major representation of a 4×3 two dimensional array

Like single dimensional arrays, two dimensional arrays also store only the base address, i.e., the starting address of the array. Based on the base address, the addresses of other positions are calculated. Suppose we have a 2D array, **arr**, of size *m×n* and the lower index of row is **r_ind** and that of column is **c_ind**. Therefore, the address of the element at the i-th row and j-th column position can be calculated as:

Address of arr[i][j] = Base Address of arr +
$$[\{ n * (i-r\_ind) \} + (j-c\_ind)] * \text{Size of the data type}$$

As in C, C++ or Java, both the value of r_ind and c_ind is 0, above formula is converted to,

Address of arr[i][j] = Base Address of arr + $[(n * i) + j] * \text{Size of the data type}$

3.9.2 Column Major Representation

In this representation, elements are stored column-wise. If a 2D array has *m* rows and *n* columns, the first *m* elements of the first column will be stored in the first *m* memory locations, then *m* elements of the second column will be stored in the next *m* memory locations, then *m* elements of the third column will be stored in the next *m* memory locations, and so on. Thus elements are stored column by column. This is followed in the FORTRAN programming language. This concept has been shown in Figure 3.5.

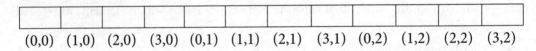

(0,0) (1,0) (2,0) (3,0) (0,1) (1,1) (2,1) (3,1) (0,2) (1,2) (2,2) (3,2)

Figure 3.5   Column major representation of a 4×3 two dimensional array

Suppose we have a 2D array, **arr**, of size *m×n* and the lower index of row is **r_ind** and that of column is **c_ind**. Therefore, following the column major representation, the address of the element at the i-th row and j-th column position can be calculated as:

Address of arr[i][j] = Base Address of arr +
$$[\{ m * (j-c\_ind) \} + (i-r\_ind)] * \text{Size of the data type}$$

As in C, C++ or Java, both the value of r_ind and c_ind is 0, above formula is converted to,

Address of arr[i][j] = Base Address of arr + $[(m * j) + i] * \text{Size of the data type}$

Example 3.1: Consider a two dimensional array, myArr, of size 10×12. Its base address is 2060, size of the data type is 2 and both the lower index of row and column is 0. Compute the address of the element

i.   myArr[5][6], if the elements are stored in row major order.

ii. myArr[11][8], if the elements are stored in column major order.

Solution:

i.   According to row major representation,

Address of arr[i][j] = Base Address of arr + [(n * i) + j] * Size of the data type; when both the lower index of row and column is 0.

$$\begin{aligned}\text{Address of myArr}[5][6] &= 2060 + [\,(12 * 5) + 6\,] * 2 \\ &= 2060 + [\,60 + 6\,] * 2 \\ &= 2060 + 66 * 2 \\ &= 2060 + 132 \\ &= 2192\end{aligned}$$

ii. According to column major representation,

Address of arr[i][j] = Base Address of arr + [(m * j) + i] * Size of the data type; when both the lower index of row and column is 0.

$$\begin{aligned}\text{Address of myArr}[11][8] &= 2060 + [\,(10 * 8) + 11\,] * 2 \\ &= 2060 + [\,80 + 11\,] * 2 \\ &= 2060 + 91 * 2 \\ &= 2060 + 182 \\ &= 2242\end{aligned}$$

3.10 Operations on Two Dimensional Arrays

Two dimensional arrays can be considered as matrices and NumPy supports various operations on matrices. In this section a few common operations on matrices have been shown.

3.10.1 Matrix Addition

A simple + operator is used to add two or more matrices. Corresponding elements of the matrices are added to form a new matrix. But remember, dimensions of all matrices should be the same. Consider the following example:

```
import numpy as npy

my2DArray1 = npy.array([[100, 200, 300], [400, 500, 600]])
my2DArray2 = npy.array([[10, 20, 30], [40, 50, 60]])
my2DArray3 = npy.array([[1, 2, 3], [4, 5, 6]])
newArray = my2DArray1 + my2DArray2 + my2DArray3
print(newArray)
```

Output:

```
[[111 222 333]
 [444 555 666]]
```

3.10.2 Matrix Multiplication

Matrix multiplication is done using the dot ( ) method. The * operator is used to multiply the corresponding elements of two matrices but not the matrix multiplication. Consider the following example:

```
import numpy as npy

my2DArray1 = npy.array([[10, 20, 30], [40, 50, 60]])
my2DArray2 = npy.array([[1, 2], [3, 4], [5, 6]])
newArray = npy.dot(my2DArray1, my2DArray2)
print("Resultant Matrix: ")
print(newArray)
```

Output:

Resultant Matrix:
[[220 280]
 [490 640]]

3.10.3 Transpose of a Matrix

To transpose a matrix the transpose() method is used. Consider the following example:

```
import numpy as npy

my2DArray = npy.array([[10, 20, 30], [40, 50, 60]])
newArray=npy.transpose(my2DArray)
print("New Transposed Matrix: ")
print(newArray)
```

Output:

New Transposed Matrix:
[[10 40]
 [20 50]
 [30 60]]

3.10.4 Slicing of a Matrix

Slicing operation can also be done on a matrix. To extract *m* number of rows and *n* number of columns from a matrix, we need to write [:*m*, :*n*] along with the array name. If we omit *m*, it will consider all rows. Similarly, if we omit :*n*, it will consider all columns. If omitting

(:) only *n* is mentioned, it considers the *n*-th column only. To specify the range we need to mention the start and end before and after (:) correspondingly.

```
import numpy as npy

my2DArray = npy.array([[10, 20, 30], [40, 50, 60], [70,
80, 90], [5, 10, 15]])
print("my2DArray =")
print(my2DArray)
print("my2DArray[:2,:2] =" )
print(my2DArray[:2,:2])
print("my2DArray[:,:2] =")
print(my2DArray[:,:2])
print("my2DArray[:2,] =")
print(my2DArray[:2,])
print("my2DArray[:,2] =")
print(my2DArray[:,2])
print("my2DArray[:2,2] =")
print(my2DArray[:2,2])
print("my2DArray[1:3,1:3] =")
print(my2DArray[1:3,1:3])
```

Output:

```
my2DArray =
[[10 20 30]
 [40 50 60]
 [70 80 90]
 [ 5 10 15]]

my2DArray[:2,:2] =
[[10 20]
 [40 50]]

my2DArray[:,:2] =
[[10 20]
 [40 50]
 [70 80]
 [ 5 10]]

my2DArray[:2,] =
```

```
[[10 20 30]
 [40 50 60]]

my2DArray[:,2] =
[30 60 90 15]

my2DArray[:2,2] =
[30 60]

my2DArray[1:3,1:3] =
[[50 60]
 [80 90]]
```

3.11 Sparse Matrix

A sparse matrix is a special type of matrix. When a large number of elements in a matrix are zero, the matrix is known as sparse matrix. On the other hand, if most of the elements in a matrix are non-zero, it is known as dense matrix. If a matrix element is zero, it represents the absence of the requisite data for that cell. Hence, in case of a sparse matrix, though we are allocating a large memory space, yet only a few portions are utilized, resulting in a huge wastage of memory. To solve this problem we may store a sparse matrix using a different data structure. We may consider an array whose number of columns is 3. The first column represents row index, second column represents column index and third column represents non-zero elements of the sparse matrix. As each row represents a single non-zero element, the number of rows in this new data structure will be the same as the number of non-zero elements in the sparse matrix. In addition to these rows, an extra row called header row is also needed, which is the first row of this structure and represents the overall information of the original sparse matrix. The first column of this header row stores the number of rows in the original matrix, second column stores the number of columns in the original matrix and third column stores the total number of non-zero elements in the original matrix. Hence, instead of allocating memory for the entire matrix, we need to allocate an array whose number of columns is 3 and number of rows is just one more than the number of non-zero elements in the original matrix. The following example illustrates this representation:

Example 3.2: Convert the following sparse matrix into a proper sparse matrix form.

	0	1	2	3	4	5	6	7	8	9
0	0	0	0	6	0	0	0	0	0	0
1	0	0	0	0	0	0	15	0	0	0
2	0	23	0	0	0	0	0	0	7	0
3	0	0	0	0	0	0	0	0	0	0

4	0	0	0	0	0	21	0	0	0	0
5	0	0	4	0	0	0	0	0	11	0

Solution:

In the original matrix, number of rows is 10, number of columns is 6 and total number of elements is 7. Hence, number of rows in the new sparse matrix will be 7+1=8 and the resultant array will be as follows:

10	6	7
0	3	6
1	6	15
2	1	23
2	8	7
4	5	21
5	2	4
5	8	11

The main disadvantage of this representation is in predicting the number of non-zero elements in the original array. To solve this problem we may use a similar data structure named list which is dynamic in nature and therefore need not predict in advance. Another advantage of the list structure is that we may store the elements of any data type in the third column.

Program 3.11 Write a program to convert a matrix to a sparse matrix.

```
# PRGD3_11: Program to convert a matrix to sparse matrix
import numpy as npy

def OriginalToSparse(matrix):
    row = len(matrix)
    col = len(matrix[0])
    c = 0
    sparseMatrix =npy.array([[row, col, 0]])
    temp = npy.array([0, 0, 0])

    for i in range(row):
        for j in range(col):
            if matrix[i][j] != 0 :
                temp[0] = i
                temp[1] = j
                temp[2] = matrix[i][j]
```

```
                sparseMatrix =
                    npy.append(sparseMatrix,[temp],axis=0)
                c+=1
    sparseMatrix[0][2] = c
    return sparseMatrix

myMatrix = npy.array([[0, 0, 0, 6, 0, 0, 0],
                      [0, 2, 0, 0, 0, 0, 0],
                      [0, 0, 0, 0, 0, 0, 0],
                      [0, 0, 5, 0, 0, 7, 0],
                      [4, 0, 0, 0, 0, 0, 0]])

print("\nOriginal Matrix: ")
print(myMatrix)            # displaying the Original matrix

sparseMatrix = OriginalToSparse(myMatrix)

print("\nSparse Matrix: ")
print(sparseMatrix)        # displaying the Sparse matrix
```

Output:

```
Original Matrix:
[[0 0 0 6 0 0 0]
 [0 2 0 0 0 0 0]
 [0 0 0 0 0 0 0]
 [0 0 5 0 0 7 0]
 [4 0 0 0 0 0 0]]

Sparse Matrix:
[[5 7 5]
 [0 3 6]
 [1 1 2]
 [3 2 5]
 [3 5 7]
 [4 0 4]]
```

Program 3.12 Write a program to convert a sparse matrix into a general matrix.

```
# PRGD3_12: Program to convert a sparse matrix into a
#general matrix
```

```python
import numpy as npy

def SparseToOriginal(sparseMatrix):
    row = sparseMatrix[0][0]
    col = sparseMatrix[0][1]
    c = 0
    myMatrix = npy.zeros((row, col))

    for i in range(1, row+1):
        r = sparseMatrix[i][0]
        c = sparseMatrix[i][1]
        element = sparseMatrix[i][2]
        myMatrix[r][c] = element
    return myMatrix

sparseMatrix = npy.array([[5, 7, 5],
                          [0, 3, 6],
                          [1, 1, 2],
                          [3, 2, 5],
                          [3, 5, 7],
                          [4, 0, 4]])

print("\nSparse Matrix: ")
print(sparseMatrix)          # displaying the Sparse matrix

originalMatrix = SparseToOriginal(sparseMatrix)

print("\nOriginal Matrix: ")
print(originalMatrix)     # displaying the Original matrix
```

Output:

Sparse Matrix:
[[5 7 5]
 [0 3 6]
 [1 1 2]
 [3 2 5]
 [3 5 7]
 [4 0 4]]

Original Matrix:
[[0. 0. 0. 6. 0. 0. 0.]

[0. 2. 0. 0. 0. 0. 0.]
[0. 0. 0. 0. 0. 0. 0.]
[0. 0. 5. 0. 0. 7. 0.]
[4. 0. 0. 0. 0. 0. 0.]]

Program 3.13 Write a program to add two sparse matrices.

```
# PRGD3_13: Addition of two Sparse Matrices

import numpy as npy

def addSparse(Matrix1, Matrix2):
    row1 = Matrix1[0][0]
    col1 = Matrix1[0][1]
    row2 = Matrix2[0][0]
    col2 = Matrix2[0][1]
    i = j = 1
    c=0
    sparseMatrix =npy.array([[row1, col1, 0]])
    temp = npy.array([0, 0, 0])
    while i <= row1 and j <= row2:
        if Matrix1[i][0] < Matrix2[j][0]:
            sparseMatrix =
            npy.append(sparseMatrix,[Matrix1[i]],axis=0)
            i+=1
        elif Matrix1[i][0] > Matrix2[j][0]:
            sparseMatrix =
            npy.append(sparseMatrix,[Matrix2[j]],axis=0)
            j+=1
        elif Matrix1[i][1] < Matrix2[j][1]:
            sparseMatrix =
            npy.append(sparseMatrix,[Matrix1[i]],axis=0)
            i+=1
        elif Matrix1[i][1] > Matrix2[j][1]:
            sparseMatrix =
            npy.append(sparseMatrix,[Matrix2[j]],axis=0)
            j+=1
        else:
            temp[0]= Matrix1[i][0]
            temp[1]= Matrix1[i][1]
            temp[2]= Matrix1[i][2]+Matrix2[j][2]
            sparseMatrix =
```

```
                    npy.append(sparseMatrix, [temp],axis=0)
            i+=1
            j+=1
        c+=1

    sparseMatrix[0][2] = c
    return sparseMatrix

sparseMatrix1 = npy.array([[5, 7, 5],
                           [0, 2, 6],
                           [1, 1, 2],
                           [3, 2, 5],
                           [3, 5, 7],
                           [4, 0, 4]])

sparseMatrix2 = npy.array([[5, 7, 5],
                           [0, 3, 6],
                           [1, 1, 2],
                           [3, 2, 5],
                           [3, 5, 7],
                           [4, 0, 4]])

print("\n1st Sparse Matrix: ")
print(sparseMatrix1)
print("\n2nd Sparse Matrix: ")
print(sparseMatrix2)

finalMatrix = addSparse(sparseMatrix1, sparseMatrix2)
print("\nResultant Matrix: ")
print(finalMatrix)
```

Output:

```
1st Sparse Matrix:
[[5 7 5]
 [0 2 6]
 [1 1 2]
 [3 2 5]
 [3 5 7]
 [4 0 4]]


2nd Sparse Matrix:
```

[[5 7 5]

[0 3 6]

[1 1 2]

[3 2 5]

[3 5 7]

[4 0 4]]

Resultant Matrix:

[[5 7 6]

 [0 2 6]

 [0 3 6]

 [1 1 4]

 [3 2 10]

 [3 5 14]

 [4 0 8]]

3.12 Programming Examples

Here are a few programming examples that will help us understand the various operations that can be performed on an array.

Program 3.14 Write a program to store n numbers in an array and find their average.

```
#PRGD3_14Program to store n numbers in an array and find
#their average
import array as arr

n=int(input("Enter number of Elements: "))
elements=arr.array('i')
sum=0
for i in range(n):
    elements.append(int(input("Enter any number: ")))
    sum+=elements[i]
avg = sum/n
print("Average = ",avg)
```

Output:

Enter number of Elements: 4

Enter any number: 12

Enter any number: 33

Enter any number: 56
Enter any number: 72
Average = 43.25

Program 3.15 Write a program to input five numbers through the keyboard. Compute and display the sum of even numbers and the product of odd numbers.

```
#PRGD3_15 : Program to input numbers through the keyboard.
#Compute & display sum of even numbers and product of odd
#numbers.

import array as arr

n=int(input("Enter number of Elements: "))
myArray=arr.array('i')
for i in range(n):
    myArray.append(int(input("Enter any number: ")))

sum=0
prod=1
for i in range(n):
    if myArray[i]%2==0:

        sum+=myArray[i]
    else:
        prod*=myArray[i]

print("Sum of Even Numbers : ",sum)
print("Product of Odd Numbers : ",prod)
```

Output:

Enter number of Elements: 5
Enter any number: 2
Enter any number: 4
Enter any number: 7
Enter any number: 3
Enter any number: 6
Sum of Even Numbers : 12
Product of Odd Numbers : 21

Program 3.16 Write a program to calculate variance of N numbers.

```
#PRGD3_16: Program to calculate variance of n numbers

import array as arr

n=int(input("Enter number of Elements: "))
elements=arr.array('i')
sum=0
for i in range(n):
    elements.append(int(input("Enter number %d: "%(i+1))))
    sum+=elements[i]
mean = sum/n
sqrDev = 0
for i in range(n):
    deviation = elements[i]-mean
    sqrDev += deviation*deviation
variance = sqrDev/n
print("Variance = ",variance)
```

Output:

Enter number of Elements: 6
Enter number 1: 23
Enter number 2: 78
Enter number 3: 57
Enter number 4: 7
Enter number 5: 43
Enter number 6: 39
41.166666666666664
Variance = 518.8055555555555

Program 3.17 The following figure is known as Pascal's triangle.

```
1
1  1
1  2  1
1  3  3  1
1  4  6  4  1
1  5 10 10  5  1
.....

.....
```

Write a program to display Pascal's triangle up to a specified number of rows.

```
#PRGD3_17: Program to display the Pascal's Triangle

import numpy as npy

n=int(input("Enter number of lines: "))
pascal = npy.zeros((n, n))
for i in range(n):
    for j in range(i+1):
        if j==0 or i==j:
            pascal[i][j] = 1    # To set 1 in 1st column
                                # and diagonal
        else:
            pascal[i][j] = pascal[i-1][j]+pascal[i-1][j-1]
        print("%2d"%(pascal[i][j]), end=' ')
    print()
```

Program 3.18 In an organization monthly sales figures of employees are available. Write a program to find the total sales of each employee and total sales of each month. Also find the total sales of the organization.

```
# PRGD3_11: Program to find employeewise & Monthwise total
#Sales

import numpy as npy

row = int(input("Enter number of Employees: "))
col = int(input("Enter number of Months: "))
sales = npy.zeros((row, col))
for i in range(row):
    for j in range(col):
        sales[i][j] = int(input("Enter Sales Value of
                        Employee%d of Month%d: "%(i+1, j+1)))
print('\n\t\t', end = '\t')
for i in range(1,col+1):
    print('Month%d'%(i), end='\t\t')
print('Total')
for i in range(row):
    tot=0
    print("Employee",i+1, end='\t')
    for j in range(col):
```

```
            print("%5d"%(sales[i][j]), end='\t\t')
            tot+=sales[i][j]
        print("%5d"%(tot))

grandTotal=0
print('Total', end ='\t\t')
for j in range(col):
    tot=0
    for i in range(row):
        tot+=sales[i][j]
    print("%5d"%(tot), end='\t\t')
    grandTotal+=tot

print("%5d"%(grandTotal))
```

Output:

Enter number of Employees: 4
Enter number of Months: 3

Enter Sales Value of Employee1 of Month1: 25
Enter Sales Value of Employee1 of Month2: 365
Enter Sales Value of Employee1 of Month3: 121
Enter Sales Value of Employee2 of Month1: 23
Enter Sales Value of Employee2 of Month2: 2356
Enter Sales Value of Employee2 of Month3: 420
Enter Sales Value of Employee3 of Month1: 225
Enter Sales Value of Employee3 of Month2: 65
Enter Sales Value of Employee3 of Month3: 320
Enter Sales Value of Employee4 of Month1: 110
Enter Sales Value of Employee4 of Month2: 80
Enter Sales Value of Employee4 of Month3: 275

	Month1	Month2	Month3	Total
Employee 1	25	365	121	511
Employee 2	23	2356	420	2799
Employee 3	225	65	320	610
Employee 4	110	80	275	465
Total	383	2866	1136	4385

Array at a Glance

✓ An array is a collection of homogeneous data elements.

✓ Array elements are always stored in contiguous memory locations.

✓ Array index always starts with 0.

✓ The subscript or array index may be any valid integer constant, integer variable or integer expression.

✓ Python uses negative index numbers to access elements in backward direction. Negative index starts from -1.

✓ Operations on an array are: addition, deletion, searching, updating, slicing, concatenation, and repetition or multiplication.

✓ Multidimensional arrays are better accessed through the numPy package.

✓ In memory there are two types of representation of two dimensional arrays: row major representation and column major representation.

✓ Common operations on matrix are addition, multiplication, transpose, and slicing.

✓ When a large number of elements in a matrix are zero, the matrix is known as sparse matrix.

✓ If most of the elements in a matrix are non-zero, it is known as dense matrix.

Multiple Choice Questions

1. What is an array?
   a) Collection of homogeneous data elements.
   b) Collection of heterogeneous data elements.
   c) Collection of homogeneous or heterogeneous data elements that depend on compiler.
   d) None of these.

2. Which of the following is true with respect to array?
   a) Array elements are always stored in contiguous memory locations.
   b) Array elements are always stored in scattered way in the memory.
   c) There is no fixed rule about allocation of an array. Depending on the availability of memory, operating system allocates memory for an array.
   d) None of these.

3. In Python language the array index always starts with
   a) 0
   b) 1
   c) -1
   d) 0 or -1, depending on which direction the array will be accessed.

4. Which of the following is not true?
   a) The array index may be a floating value.
   b) The array index may be an integer.
   c) The array index may be any expression which yields an integer.
   d) The array index may be a constant.

5. Array cannot be used to store
   a) Price of cars.
   b) Roll no., name, address, and age of a student.
   c) Weekly expenditures of an organization.
   d) Marks of an examination.

6. What is the proper syntax to declare an integer array using array module after executing the statement: import array as arr
   a) `myArray=arr.array('i',[10,20,30])`
   b) `myArray=arr.array('i',(10,20,30))`
   c) `myArray=arr.array('i',{10,20,30})`
   d) All of the above

7. NumPy's array class is called
   a) `narray`
   b) `ndarray`
   c) `nd_array`
   d) `darray`

8. Which of the following method in NumPy can be used to create an array?
   a) `zeros()`
   b) `ones()`
   c) `arange()`
   d) All of these

9. Multiple elements can be added in an existing array using
   a) `insert()`
   b) `append()`

c) `extend ()`

d) Multiple elements cannot be added

10. `pop()` is used

    a)   to remove the last element only.

    b)   to return the last element only.

    c)   to remove as well as return the last element.

    d)   to remove and return the last element as well as any other element from an array.

11. Which of the following statements is correct to declare an array containing 5 zeros, considering the statement: import array

    a)   `zeroArra=array.array('i',[0]*5)`

    b)   `zeroArra=array.array('i',[0*5])`

    c)   `zeroArra=array.array([0,0,0,0,0])`

    d)   All are correct

12. For matrix multiplication which of the following is used in `NumPy`?

    a)   `multiply()`

    b)   `*` operator

    c)   `dot ()`

    d)   All of the above

13. A sparse matrix is a matrix

    a)   whose all elements are zero.

    b)   which is a unit matrix.

    c)   whose most of the elements are zero.

    d)   whose few elements are zero.

14. A is an array of size m * n, stored in the row major order. If the address of the first element in the array is M, the address of the element A(i, j) (A(0, 0) is the first element of the array and each element occupies one location in memory) is

    a)   M+(i-j)*m+j-1

    b)   M+(i -1)*m+i-1

    c)   M+i*m+j

    d)   M+(i-1)*n+j-1

Review Exercises

1.   What is an array? What is its need?

2.   What are subscripts?

3.   What are the different functions available in Python to add elements to an array?

4. Differentiate between `insert()`, `append()`, and `extend()`?

5. What are the different ways by which we can remove elements from an array in Python?

6. Differentiate between `remove()`, `pop()`, and `del` statements?

7. What will be the output of the following code?

```
import array as arr

elements=arr.array('i',[5,10,15,20,25,30,35,40,45,50])

print(elements[2:8])
print(elements[0:10])
print(elements[:8])
print(elements[8:])
print(elements[0:])
print(elements[-8:-2])
print(elements[-8:-2:-1])
print(elements[-2:-8]:-1)
print(elements[-2:-8:-2])
print(elements[::-2])
print(elements[::2])
```

8. What will be the output of the following code?

```
import numpy as npy

myArray1 = npy.arange(5)
print(myArray1)
myArray2 = npy.arange(5,50,5)
print(myArray2)
myArray3 = npy.arange(.5,5.5,.5)
print(myArray3)
```

9. What will be the output of the following code?

```
import array as arr

myArray=arr.array('f',[5,10,15,20])
myArray.append(2.5)
print(myArray)
myArray.append(25)
print(myArray)
```

```
myArray.insert(0,.5)
print(myArray)
myArray.insert(10,.5)
print(myArray)
myArray.extend([5,.5,5.5])
print(myArray)
```

10. What will be the output of the following code?

```
import array as arr

elements=arr.array('i',[1,2,2,3,4,2,1,3])
del elements[2]
print(elements)
elements.remove(1)
print(elements)
num=elements.pop()
print("Popped element is : ",num)
print(elements)
print("Popped element is : ", elements.pop(0))
print(elements)
```

11. What will be the output of the following code?

```
import array as arr
elements=arr.array('f',[1,1.5,2,2.5,3])
arr1=arr.array('f',[1.2])
elements[1:4]=arr1
print(elements)
arr2=arr.array('f',[1.4,1.6,1.8])
elements[1:4]=arr1
print(elements)
```

12. What will be the output of the following code?

```
import array as arr

odd =arr.array('i',[1,3,5,7])
even=arr.array('i',[2,4,6])
numbers=odd+even
print(numbers)
print(odd*3)
print(2*even)
```

Problems for Programming

1. Write a program to find the smallest element among N inputted numbers.

2. Write a program to rearrange an array in reverse order without using a second array.

3. Write a program to calculate standard deviation of N numbers.

4. Write a program to count odd numbers in a set of integers.

5. Write a program to find the largest odd number in a set of integers.

6. Write a program to count the total number of prime numbers in a set of integers.

7. Write a program to find the second highest element among N inputted numbers.

8. Write a program to find the largest difference in a set of numbers.

9. Write a program to find binary equivalent of a decimal number.

10. Write a program to delete an element from the k-th position of an array.

11. Write a program to sort an array in descending order.

12. Write a program to insert an element at its proper position in a previously sorted array.

13. Write a program to find the union of two sets of numbers.

14. Write a program to merge two sorted arrays.

15. Write a program to find the frequency of each element in an array.

16. Write a program to find the determinant of a matrix.

17. Write a program to find the sum of diagonal elements of a square matrix.

18. Maximum temperatures of each day for 20 cities are recorded for the month of January. Write a program to find the following:

    a) The highest temperature of each city in January.

    b) The day in which the highest temperature is recorded for the city.

    c) Average maximum temperature of each city.

Python Data Structures

In the previous chapter we have studied about arrays. An array is a widely used data structure in almost every high level programming languages. In this chapter we will discuss some very useful data structures of Python. These are lists, tuples, sets, and dictionaries. All these data structures are of type compound data structures since they consist of some basic or primitive data structure/data type.

4.1   Lists

List is a very important and useful data structure in Python. It has almost all the functionalities of an array but with more flexibility. Basically a list is a collection of heterogeneous elements. List items are ordered, which means elements of a list are stored in a specific index position. List items are mutable, which indicates that it is possible to change or edit the elements of a list, and duplicate items are allowed in a list. Another important feature of a list is that it is dynamic. It can grow or shrink during program execution according to our requirement.

4.1.1   Creating a List

A list is a collection of elements that are separated by commas (,) inside a pair of square brackets. Hence we can create a list by putting comma separated elements within square brackets. The general format to defining a list is:

```
List_variable = [ value1, value2, …. ]
```

Hence we may create a list of integers as:

```
myIntList = [10, 12, 25, 37, 49 ]
```

A list of string can be created as:

```
nameList = ["Amit", "Sudip", "Dibyendu", "Sourav"]
```

A list with heterogeneous data can be created as:

```
myList = [ 25, "Sudip Chowdhury", 87.2]
```

An empty list can be created as:

```
myList = [ ]
```

An empty list can also be created using a constructor as:

```
myList = list( )
```

4.1.2 Accessing List Elements

List elements are accessed just like array elements, i.e., the elements of a list are accessed using a list index. Like arrays, in case of lists also the index value starts from 0. Hence, the first position of a list is 0, second is 1, and so on. To access a list element we need to mention the list name followed by the list index enclosed within [ ]. The general format to access a list element is:

List_name[index]

Suppose we have a list, myList = [10, 12, 25, 37, 49], then to access the first element of the list we have to write myList [0]. Similarly, to access the next elements we have to write myList [1], myList [2], and so on.

	myList[0]	myList[1]	myList[2]	myList[3]	myList[4]
myList	10	12	25	37	49

These elements can be accessed individually just like a normal variable. We can read as well as modify its value. For example, to assign the value 53 in the second cell of **myList**, we can write the statement as:

```
myList [1] = 53
```

Similarly, to assign the value of the second element of **myList** to a variable called **num**, we can write:

```
num = myList [1]
```

Thus, the expression myList [1] acts just like a variable of some basic type. Not only assignment, it can also be used in input statement, output statement, in any arithmetic expression – everywhere its use is similar to a basic type variable.

Notice that the second element of **myList** is specified as **myList**[1], since the first one is **myList**[0]. Therefore, the third element will be **myList**[2], the fourth element will be **myList**[3], and the last element will be **myList**[4]. Thus, if we write **myList**[5], it will be the sixth element of the list **myList** and therefore exceeding the size of the list, which produces an error, "List index out of range".

We can use a variable as a subscript or list index to access the list elements. At runtime this variable may contain several values and thus different list elements are accessed accordingly. This facility of using variables as subscripts makes lists equally useful as arrays.

Some other valid operations with lists are:

```
myList[0] = a          # where a is any variable
myList[a] = 75         # where a is an integer
b = myList[a+2]        # where a is an integer
myList[2] = myList[0] + myList [1]
myList[myList[a]] = myList[2] + 5  etc..
```

Apart from this general convention of accessing elements, Python also provides the flexibility to access list elements from the end. When we access a list from the left or the beginning, the list index starts from 0. But if we start accessing elements from the end, the list index starts from -1. Python uses negative index numbers to access elements in backward direction.

	-5	-4	-3	-2	-1
myList	10	1234	563	27	98
	0	1	2	3	4

Figure 4.1   Positive and negative index to access list elements

Consider Figure 4.1. Here, myList[-1] returns 98, myList[-2] returns 27, and so on. Hence, Python gives us the opportunity to access array elements in forward direction as well as backward direction.

Example 4.1: What will be the output for the following code segment?

```
myList=[10, -3, 231, 2712, 57]
print("myList[0]   = ",myList[0])
print("myList[1]   = ",myList[1])
```

```
print ("myList [4]  =  ",myList [4])
print ("myList [-1] =  ",myList [-1])
print ("myList [-4] =  ",myList [-4])
```

Output:

```
myList[0] = 10
myList[1] = -3
myList[4] = 57
myList[-1] = 57
myList[-4] = -3
```

4.1.3 Operations on a List

Whatever operations we have done on an array can also be done on a list. We can add elements into a list, remove elements from a list, modify the contents of a list, extract a portion of a list (slicing), search an element from a list, and concatenate multiple lists. We can also create a new list by repeating the elements of an existing list.

4.1.3.1 Adding Elements to a List

Just like an array in Python, we are able to add one or more elements into a list using `append()`, `extend()`, and `insert()` methods. Using `append()` we can add a single element at the end of a list, whereas `extend()` helps us to add multiple elements at the end of a list. On the other hand, `insert()` helps us to insert an element at the beginning, end, or at any index position in a list. The following program explains the operations of these functions:

Example 4.2: Write a program to show the use of `append()`, `insert()` and `extend()`

```
elements=[10,20,30]
print ("Before insertion : ", end =" ")
print (elements)

elements.append(40)                      #Inserts 40 at end
print ("After appending 40 : ", end =" ")
print (elements)

elements.extend([50, 60, 70])   #Inserts 50, 60 and 70 at
                                                 #end
print ("After extending the array with 50, 60 and 70 : ")
print (elements)
```

```
elements.insert(0,5)        #Inserts 5 at index position 0
print("After inserting 5 at 0th position : ")
print(elements)

elements.insert(2,15)       #Inserts 15 at index position 2
print("After inserting 15 at position 2 : ")
print(elements)

elements.insert(-2,15)      #Inserts 15 at index position -2
print("After inserting 15 at position -2 : ")
print(elements)
```

Output:

Before insertion : [10, 20, 30]
After appending 40 : [10, 20, 30, 40]
After extending the array with 50, 60 and 70 :
[10, 20, 30, 40, 50, 60, 70]
After inserting 5 at 0th position :
[5, 10, 20, 30, 40, 50, 60, 70]
After inserting 15 at position 2 :
[5, 10, 15, 20, 30, 40, 50, 60, 70]
After inserting 15 at position -2 :
[5, 10, 15, 20, 30, 40, 50, 15, 60, 70]

4.1.3.2 Removing Elements from a List

Elements can be removed from a list using the del statement or remove(), pop(), and clear(). Using the del statement we can remove an element of a specific index position. If we want to delete the entire list, we need to mention the list name only with the del statement. remove() deletes the first occurrence of an element in a list. But if the element does not exist in the list, it raises an error. pop() removes an element from a specified index position. If we do not mention the index position, pop() removes the last element. In both cases, after removing the element it also returns the element. To remove all elements from a list, the clear() method is used. We can also remove a portion of a list by assigning an empty list to a slice of elements. The following program explains the operations of these functions:

Example 4.3: Write a program to show the use of del, remove(), pop() and clear().

```
elements=[10,20,30,40,10,50,60,70]
print("Before deletion : ", end =" ")
print(elements)
```

```python
del elements[2]        #Deleting element of index position 2
print("After deleting element of index position 2 : ")
print(elements)

elements.remove(10)        #Deleting first occurrence of 10
print("After deleting the first occurrence of 10 : ")
print(elements)

num=elements.pop()    #Last element is deleted and returned
print("Popped element is : ",num)
print("After popping without argument : ")
print(elements)

num=elements.pop(0) #First element is deleted and returned
print("Popped element is : ",num)
print("After popping element of index position 0 : ", end
                                                    =" ")
print(elements)

elements[1:3]=[]        #Deleting element of index
                                 #position 1 and 2
print("After removing element of index position 1 and 2 :
                                                        ")
print(elements)

elements.clear()        #Deleting all existing element
print("After removing all existing elements : ", end =" ")
print(elements)

del elements                # Delete entire array
```

Output:

Before deletion : [10, 20, 30, 40, 10, 50, 60, 70]
After deleting element of index position 2 :
[10, 20, 40, 10, 50, 60, 70]
After deleting the first occurrence of 10 :
[20, 40, 10, 50, 60, 70]
Popped element is : 70
After popping without argument :

[20, 40, 10, 50, 60]
Popped element is : 20
After popping element of index position 0 : [40, 10, 50, 60]
After removing element of index position 1 and 2 :
[40, 60]
After removing all existing elements : []

4.1.3.3 *Slicing of a List*

By using slicing operation we can extract one or more elements from a list. This operation
can be done using the (:) operator within the subscript operator ([ ]). The general format
of the slicing operation on a list is:

```
List_name[ Start : End : Step]
```

where, **Start** is the starting index position from which the extraction operation starts. The
extraction operation continues up to the **End** − **1** index position and **Step** represents the
incremented or decremented value needed to calculate the next index position to extract
elements. If **Start** is omitted, the beginning of the list is considered, i.e., the default value
of **Start** is 0. If **End** is omitted, the end of the list is considered and the default **Step**
value is 1. If we use negative **Step** value, elements will be extracted in reverse direction.
Thus, for negative **Step** value, the default value of **Start** is -1 and that of **End** indicates
the beginning of the list. The following example illustrates these concepts:

Example 4.4: Write a program to show the slicing operation on a list.

```
elements=[10,20,30,40,50]
print ("Before slicing operation : ", end =" ")
print(elements)

slice1 = elements[1:4]
#Extracts elements from index position 1 to 3
print ("New extracted List is : ", end =" ")
print(slice1)

slice2 = elements[:4]
#Extracts elements from index position 0 to 3
print ("New extracted List is : ", end =" ")
print(slice2)

slice3 = elements[1:]
#Extracts elements from index position 1 to end
```

```python
print ("New extracted List is : ", end =" ")
print(slice3)

slice4 = elements[1:4:2]
#Extracts elements from index position 1 and 3
print ("New extracted List is : ", end =" ")
print(slice4)

slice4 = elements[::2]
#Extracts elements from index position 0, 2 and 4
print ("New extracted List is : ", end =" ")
print(slice4)

slice5 = elements[4:1:-1]
#Extracts elements from index position 4 to 2
print ("New extracted List is : ", end =" ")
print(slice5)

slice6 = elements[-1:-4:-1]
#Extracts elements from index position -1 to -3
print ("New extracted List is : ", end =" ")
print(slice6)

slice7 = elements[-1:1:-1]
#Extracts elements from index position -1 to 2
print ("New extracted List is : ", end =" ")
print(slice7)

slice8 = elements[-3::-1]
#Extracts elements from index position -3 to beginning of
the List
print ("New extracted List is : ", end =" ")
print(slice8)

slice9 = elements[:-4:-1]
#Extracts elements from end to index position -3
print ("New extracted List is : ", end =" ")
print(slice9)

slice10 = elements[::-1]
#Extracts all elements but in reverse direction
print ("New extracted List is : ", end =" ")
```

```
print(slice10)
```

Output:

```
Before slicing operation : [10, 20, 30, 40, 50]
New extracted List is : [20, 30, 40]
New extracted List is : [10, 20, 30, 40]
New extracted List is : [20, 30, 40, 50]
New extracted List is : [20, 40]
New extracted List is : [10, 30, 50]
New extracted List is : [50, 40, 30]
New extracted List is : [50, 40, 30]
New extracted List is : [50, 40, 30]
New extracted List is : [30, 20, 10]
New extracted List is : [50, 40, 30]
New extracted List is : [50, 40, 30, 20, 10]
```

4.1.3.4 Searching Element in a List

To search an element within a list index() is used. This function returns the index position of the first occurrence of an element passed as an argument with this function. But if the element is not found in the list, it raises an error.

The membership operators **in** and **not in** can also be applied on a list for searching an element. The operator **in** returns **True** if the element is found in the list; otherwise it returns **False**. The operator **not in** works just as its reverse. If the element is found in the list, it returns **False**; otherwise **True**. Hence, using the membership operator it can be confirmed whether an element is present or not in a list. After confirmation we can determine its position using the index() method. There is another function, count(), which counts the occurrence of an element, passed as an argument with this method, in a list.

The following program explains the searching operation in a list:

Example 4.5: Write a program to show the search operation in a list.

```
elements=[10,20,30,40,10]
print ("The List : ", end =" ")
print(elements)

num = int(input("Enter any number: "))
if num in elements:
    posn = elements.index(num)        #Returns first
```

```
                                        #occurrence of num
    print("The index of 1st occurrence of %d is : "%(num),
                                           end ="")

    print(posn)
    print("And total occurrence of %d is : %d"
                            %(num,elements.count(num)))
else:
    print("Number not found")
```

Output:

The List : [10, 20, 30, 40, 10]
Enter any number: 10
The index of 1st occurrence of 10 is : 0
And total occurrence of 10 is : 2

The List : [10, 20, 30, 40, 10]
Enter any number: 25
Number not found

4.1.3.5 *Updating Elements in a List*

Lists are mutable in Python. We can easily update or modify the list elements just by assigning value at the required index position. With the help of the slicing operation certain portions of a list can be modified. Consider the following example:

Example 4.6: Write a program to show the updating operation in a list.

```
elements=[10,20,30,40,10]
print ("Before updation : ", end =" ")
print(elements)

elements[2]=55         #Updating element of index position 2
print("After updating element of index position 2 : ")
print(elements)

elements[1:4]=[22,33,44]    #Updating elements of index
                                   #position 1 to 3
print("After updating elements from index position 1 to
                                        3: ")
print(elements)
```

```
elements[1:3]=[55,66,77]    #Updating index position 1 & 2
                                     #by 3 elements
print("Updating index position 1 & 2 by 3 elements: ")
print(elements)
```

Output:

Before updation : [10, 20, 30, 40, 10]
After updating element of index position 2 :
[10, 20, 55, 40, 10]
After updating elements from index position 1 to 3:
[10, 22, 33, 44, 10]
Updating index position 1 & 2 by 3 elements:
[10, 55, 66, 77, 44, 10]

Note the last output. Here two existing elements are replaced by three new elements and thus the number of elements in the list increases.

4.1.3.6 Concatenation of Lists

We can also concatenate two or more lists. By this operation two or more lists can be joined together. Concatenation is done using the + operator. Consider the following example:

Example 4.7: Write a program to show the concatenation operation of lists.

```
myList1=[10,20,30,40]
myList2=[5,10,15,20,25]
myList3=[22,33,44]
print("1st List : ", end =" ")
print(myList1)
print("2nd List : ", end =" ")
print(myList2)
print("3rd List : ", end =" ")
print(myList3)

myNewList = myList1+myList2+myList3    #Concatenation of
                                             #3 lists
print ("Concatenated List : ")
print(myNewList)
```

Output:

1st List : [10, 20, 30, 40]
2nd List : [5, 10, 15, 20, 25]
3rd List : [22, 33, 44]
Concatenated List :
[10, 20, 30, 40, 5, 10, 15, 20, 25, 22, 33, 44]

4.1.3.7 Multiplication or Repetition of List

A unique feature of Python is the repetition of elements in an object and this is done using the * operator. This is applicable for lists as well. We can repeat the entire list or a single element multiple times. Consider the following example:

Example 4.8: Write a program to show the repetition operation on list.

```
list1=[10,20,30,40]
list2=[1]

print("1st List : ", end =" ")
print(list1)
print("After repeating twice: ", end =" ")
print(list1*2)            #Repeating the entire list twice

print("2nd List : ", end =" ")
print(list2)
list3=list2*5        #Repeating the entire array 5 times
print("After repeating 5 times : ", end =" ")
print(list3)

list4=[0]*6                #Creating an list of 6 zeros
print("List of 6 zeros: ", end =" ")
print(list4)
```

Output:

1st List : [10, 20, 30, 40]
After repeating twice: [10, 20, 30, 40, 10, 20, 30, 40]
2nd List : [1]
After repeating 5 times : [1, 1, 1, 1, 1]
List of 6 zeros: [0, 0, 0, 0, 0, 0]

4.1.4 Nested List

A list can also have another list as an item. This is called a nested list. To access a nested list, the list name along with the index value represents a single element in the list. But this single element is again a list. Hence, to access an element from that list we need to use a double index just like accessing a double array. The following example illustrates this:

Example 4.9: Write a program to show accessing of element from a nested list.

```
mylist = ["Techno", [8, 4, 6], [2.5,3.8]]

print("mylist = ",mylist)
print("mylist[0] = ",mylist[0])
print("mylist[1] = ",mylist[1])
print("mylist[2] = ",mylist[2])
print("mylist[0][2] = ",mylist[0][2])
print("mylist[1][2] = ",mylist[1][2])
print("mylist[2][1] = ",mylist[2][1])
```

Output:

```
mylist = ['Techno', [8, 4, 6], [2.5, 3.8]]
mylist[0] = Techno
mylist[1] = [8, 4, 6]
mylist[2] = [2.5, 3.8]
mylist[0][2] = c
mylist[1][2] = 6
mylist[2][1] = 3.8
```

4.1.5 List Functions

Python provides a set of functions that work on iterables, which include all sequence types (like list, string, tuples, etc.) and some non-sequence types (like dict, file objects, etc.). In this section we discuss some of these built-in functions. Here list is used as an argument of these functions. However, they are applicable on other iterables as well.

max( ): It returns the largest element of an iterable.

min( ): It returns the smallest element of an iterable.

sum( ): It returns the sum of all elements of an iterable.

sorted( ): It returns a new sorted list.

all( ): It returns True if for all the elements of an iterable, bool(element) returns True.

any( ): It returns True if for any of the element of an iterable, bool(element) returns True.

list( ): It constructs and returns a list from any iterable.

The following example illustrates the use of these functions:

Example 4.10: Write a program to show the use of list functions.

```
mylist = [34, 57, 69, 371, 4, 92]

print("mylist = ",mylist)
print("Max = ",max(mylist))
print("Min = ",min(mylist))
print("Sum = ",sum(mylist))
print("Sorted List : ",sorted(mylist))
print("all(mylist) : ",all(mylist))
print("any(mylist) : ",any(mylist))

newList = list("Python Program")
print("New List : ",newList)
```

Output:

```
mylist =  [34, 57, 69, 371, 4, 92]
Max =  371
Min =  4
Sum =  627
Sorted List :  [4, 34, 57, 69, 92, 371]
all(mylist) :  True
any(mylist) :  True
New List :['P','y','t','h','o','n',' ','P','r','o','g','r','a','m']
```

4.1.6 List Methods

We have already discussed some list methods. Here we are discussing some other methods.

copy( ): It returns the copy of the list for which the method is called. Though we can use '=' to copy the content of a list to another variable, '=' does not copy at all. It just assigns the reference of the last variable, which means any change to a variable also reflects in the other; for true copy we need to use the copy() method.

count( ): It returns the number of occurrences of an element passed as argument in a list.

reverse( ): This method reverses the order of the list elements.

sort( ): This method sorts the list elements in ascending order. To sort in descending order we need to pass the argument **reverse = True**.

The following example illustrates the use of these methods:

Example 4.11: Write a program to show the use of list methods.

```python
mylist = [2,3,4,2,1,2,3]

print("mylist = ",mylist)
newlist = mylist.copy()
reflist = mylist

print("Occurrence of 2 in list = ",mylist.count(2))
mylist.reverse()
print("Reverse list = ", mylist)
mylist.sort()
print("List sorted in ascending Order = ", mylist)
mylist.sort(reverse=True)
print("List sorted in descending Order = ", mylist)
print("Copied list = ", newlist)
print("reference list = ", reflist)
```

Output:

```
mylist = [2, 3, 4, 2, 1, 2, 3]
Occurrence of 2 in list = 3
Reverse list = [3, 2, 1, 2, 4, 3, 2]
List sorted in ascending Order = [1, 2, 2, 2, 3, 3, 4]
List sorted in descending Order = [4, 3, 3, 2, 2, 2, 1]
Copied list = [2, 3, 4, 2, 1, 2, 3]
reference list = [4, 3, 3, 2, 2, 2, 1]
```

4.1.7 Looping in a List

As a list is iterable, we can iterate through a list very easily using the for statement. Consider the following example:

Example 4.12: Write a program to show how to iterate through a list.

```python
my_list = [10,20,30,40]
for i in my_list:
    print(i, end=' ')
```

Output:

```
10 20 30 40
```

We can also iterate through a list using the list index as follows:

Example 4.13: Write a program to show how to iterate through a list using the loop index.

```
my_list = [10,20,30,40]
for i in range(len(my_list)):
    print(my_list[i], end=' ')
```

Output:

```
10 20 30 40
```

If we use the list index to iterate through a list, we may use the `while` loop also.

Example 4.14: Write a program to show how to iterate through a list using the `while` loop.

```
my_list = [10,20,30,40]
i=0
while i<len(my_list):
    print(my_list[i], end=' ')
    i+=1
```

Output:

```
10 20 30 40
```

4.1.8   List vs. Array

Though the operations of a list and an array are almost the same, still there are some differences between them. First of all, an array is a strictly homogeneous collection, whereas a list may contain heterogeneous elements. An array is a static data structure. We cannot change its size during program execution. But a list is dynamic. We may insert new elements or remove existing elements as and when required. Now the question is: which one is better? If its answer is not simple, then what to use and when? If our goal is to accumulate some elements only, then list is better as it is much more flexible than an array. But when we need to maintain strictly that elements should be homogeneous, array is the choice. In mathematics, matrix plays a very important role. Using NumPy we can do mathematical computations on arrays and matrices very easily. On the other hand, arrays of array module use less space and perform much faster. Hence, if our requirement is that we need not change the array size and it strictly stores homogeneous elements, use of arrays of array module is the better option. Otherwise it is better to use Numpy for mathematical computations on arrays and matrices and list for other uses.

4.2   Tuples

A tuple is another important in-built data structure in Python. A tuple is a comma separated collection of elements. Parentheses are used to define its elements. Actually any set of comma separated multiple values written without an identifying symbol like [ ], { }, ( ), etc., are treated as tuples by default. Like lists, tuples are also ordered and allow duplicate values, but elements of tuples are immutable. We cannot insert new elements, delete or modify existing elements in a tuple. Hence, it cannot be grown or shrunk dynamically.

4.2.1   Creating a Tuple

A tuple is a collection of elements that are separated by commas (,) inside parentheses. Hence we can create a tuple by putting comma separated elements within parentheses. The general format to defining a tuple is:

```
Tuple_variable  =  (value1, value2, …)
```

We may create a tuple of integers as:

```
myIntTuple = (10, 12, 25, 37, 49 )
```

A tuple of strings can be created as:

```
nameTuple = ("Gautam", "Arijit", "Rahul", "Sriparna")
```

A tuple with heterogeneous data can be created as:

```
myTuple = ( 25, "Sudip Chowdhury", 87.2)
```

We can also create a tuple without using parenthesis. This is called tuple **packing**.

```
myTuple = 25, "Sudip Chowdhury", 87.2
```

The above statement creates a tuple, myTuple. If we now print the tuple as

print (myTuple), it will show the output: (25, "Sudip Chowdhury", 87.2)

In contrast to packing there is another operation called **Unpacking**. By this feature, tuple elements are stored into different variables. For example, the statement

```
a, b, c = myTuple
```

stores the tuple elements into the variables a, b and c respectively. Thus, after the execution of this statement, a will contain 25, b will contain "Sudip Chowdhury" and c will contain 87.2.

We can also create an empty tuple. An empty tuple can be created as:

```
myTuple = ( )
```

An empty tuple can also be created using a constructor as:

```
myTuple = tuple( )
```

But to create a single element tuple we cannot write:

```
notTuple = (5)
```

This statement will execute well but the type of the variable notTuple is not a tuple. It is an integer. To declare a single element tuple we need to write:

```
myTuple = (5,)
```

4.2.2 Accessing Tuple Elements

Just as arrays and lists, tuple elements are also accessed using index values. Tuple index also starts from 0. Negative index is also allowed in accessing tuple elements. It always starts from -1. To access a tuple element we mention the tuple name followed by the tuple index enclosed within [ ]. Slicing operation is also applicable on tuples. The general format to access a tuple element is:

Tuple_name[index]

The following example illustrates how tuple elements are accessed and the slicing operation on a tuple:

Example 4.15: Write a program to show how to access tuple elements.

```
my_tuple = (10, 20, 30, 40, 50, 60, 70, 80)

print("my_tuple[2] =", my_tuple[2])
print("my_tuple[-3] =", my_tuple[-3])
print("my_tuple[2:5] =", my_tuple[2:5])
```

```
print("my_tuple[:5] =", my_tuple[:5])
print("my_tuple[5:] =", my_tuple[5:])
print("my_tuple[:-5] =", my_tuple[:-5])
print("my_tuple[-5:] =", my_tuple[-5:])
print("my_tuple[-2:-5:-1] =", my_tuple[-2:-5:-1])
```

Output:

```
my_tuple[2] = 30
my_tuple[-3] = 60
my_tuple[2:5] = (30, 40, 50)
my_tuple[:5] = (10, 20, 30, 40, 50)
my_tuple[5:] = (60, 70, 80)
my_tuple[:-5] = (10, 20, 30)
my_tuple[-5:] = (40, 50, 60, 70, 80)
my_tuple[-2:-5:-1] = (70, 60, 50)
```

4.2.3 Operations on Tuple

Tuples are immutable. Hence, we cannot use any type of insertion, deletion or modification operation. However, if any element of a tuple is mutable, then it can be modified. We can delete an entire tuple using the del statement. Like lists, tuples also support the concatenation and repetition operations. Membership operators (in and not in) also work on tuples. We can also compare two tuples. In case of comparison, corresponding members of two tuples are compared. If the corresponding members satisfy the condition, it proceeds for the next set of elements; otherwise it returns **False**. It returns **True** only if for all the corresponding set of members, the condition is satisfied. The following example illustrates these features:

Example 4.16: Write a program to show the operations on a tuple.

```
oddTuple = (1, 3, 5)
evenTuple = (2, 4, 6, 8)
numberTuple = oddTuple + evenTuple
print("oddTuple : ", oddTuple)
print("evenTuple : ", evenTuple)
print("Concatenated Tuple : ", numberTuple)
newTuple = oddTuple * 3
print("oddTuple repeated Thrice : ", newTuple)
print("Is 2 in oddTuple? : ", 2 in oddTuple)
print("Is 2 not in evenTuple? :", 2 not in evenTuple)
```

```
print("(1,2,3)==(1,2,3)? : ", (1,2,3)==(1,2,3))
print("(1,2,3)<(1,2,3,4)? : ", (1,2,3)<(1,2,3,4))
print("(1,20,30)>(10,2,3)? : ", (1,20,30)>(10,2,3))
print("(1,20,3)>=(1,2,30)? : ", (1,20,3)>=(1,2,30))
```

Output:

oddTuple : (1, 3, 5)
evenTuple : (2, 4, 6, 8)
Concatenated Tuple : (1, 3, 5, 2, 4, 6, 8)
oddTuple repeated Thrice : (1, 3, 5, 1, 3, 5, 1, 3, 5)
Is 2 in oddTuple? : False
Is 2 not in evenTuple? : False
(1,2,3)==(1,2,3)? : True
(1,2,3)<(1,2,3,4)? : True
(1,20,30)>(10,2,3)? : False
(1,20,3)>=(1,2,30)? : True

As tuples are also iterable, we can use basic Python functions that work on any iterable function. These functions have already been discussed with list. The following example shows their operation on tuples:

Example 4.17: Write a program to show the use of tuple functions.

```
myTuple = (34, 57, 69, 371, 4, 92)

print("myTuple = ",myTuple)
print("Max = ",max(myTuple))
print("Min = ",min(myTuple))
print("Sum = ",sum(myTuple))
print("Sorted List : ",sorted(myTuple))
print("all(myTuple) : ",all(myTuple))
print("any(myTuple) : ",any(myTuple))

newTuple1 = tuple("Python")
print("New Tuple 1 : ",newTuple1)
newTuple2 = tuple([5, 10, 15])
print("New Tuple 2 : ",newTuple2)
del myTuple          # Deletes entire tuple
```

Output:

```
myTuple = (34, 57, 69, 371, 4, 92)
Max = 371
Min = 4
Sum = 627
Sorted List : [4, 34, 57, 69, 92, 371]
all(myTuple) : True
any(myTuple) : True
New Tuple 1 : ('P', 'y', 't', 'h', 'o', 'n')
New Tuple 2 : (5, 10, 15)
```

4.2.4 Nested Tuples

Similar to a list, a tuple may contain another tuple or list as an element. This is called nested tuple. Accessing the nested tuple elements is just like accessing nested list elements. Consider the following example:

Example 4.18: Write a program to show the accessing of nested tuple elements.

```
my_tuple = ("Techno", (8, 4, 6), [2.5,3.8])

print("my_tuple =", my_tuple)
print("my_tuple[0] =", my_tuple[0])
print("my_tuple[1] =", my_tuple[1])
print("my_tuple[2] =", my_tuple[2])
print("my_tuple[1][2] =", my_tuple[1][2])
print("my_tuple[2][1] =", my_tuple[2][1])
```

Output:

```
my_tuple = ('Techno', (8, 4, 6), [2.5, 3.8])
my_tuple[0] = Techno
my_tuple[1] = (8, 4, 6)
my_tuple[2] = [2.5, 3.8]
my_tuple[1][2] = 6
my_tuple[2][1] = 3.8
```

4.2.5 Tuple Methods

Tuples have only two methods. These are count() and index(). The operations of these methods are similar to the corresponding method of list. The count() method counts the occurrence of a particular element supplied as an argument in a tuple and index() returns the index position of the first occurrence of an element supplied as argument in a tuple. Consider the following example:

Example 4.19: Write a program to show the use of tuple methods.

```
my_tuple=(2,4,5,2,6,2,7)

posn = my_tuple.index(2)     #Returns first occurrence of 2
c = my_tuple.count(2)         #Counts total occurrence of 2
print("my_tuple =", my_tuple)
print("The index of 1st occurrence of 2 is : ", posn)
print("And total occurrence of 2 is : " , c)

print("The index of 1st occurrence of 6 is : ", my_tuple.
                                              index(6))
print("And total occurrence of 6 is : " , my_tuple.
                                              count(6))
```

Output:

```
my_tuple = (2, 4, 5, 2, 6, 2, 7)
The index of 1st occurrence of 2 is : 0
And total occurrence of 2 is : 3
The index of 1st occurrence of 6 is : 4
And total occurrence of 6 is : 1
```

4.2.6 Looping in a Tuple

As a tuple is also iterable, we can iterate through a tuple just like a list very easily using the for statement. Consider the following example:

Example 4.20: Write a program to show how to iterate through a tuple.

```
my_tuple = (10,20,30,40)
for i in my_tuple:
    print(i, end=' ')
```

Output:

```
10 20 30 40
```

We can also iterate through a tuple using a tuple index and that can be performed using the for as well as while loop.

Example 4.21: Write a program to show how to iterate through a tuple using the loop index.

```
my_tuple = (10,20,30,40)
for i in range(len(my_tuple)):
    print(my_tuple[i], end=' ')
```

Output:

10 20 30 40

If we have a nested tuple, in each iteration the iterative variable contains a tuple.

Example 4.22: Write a program to show how to iterate through a nested tuple.

```
square_tuple = ((1,1), (2,4), (3,9))
for i in square_tuple:
    print(i, end=' ')
```

Output:

(1, 1) (2, 4) (3, 9)

But to access the individual member of nested tuples, we may write the code as:

Example 4.23: Write a program to show how to access individual members when iterate in a nested tuple.

```
square_tuple = ((1,1), (2,4), (3,9))
for i,j in square_tuple:
    print("Square of %d is %d" %(i,j))
```

Output:

Square of 1 is 1
Square of 2 is 4
Square of 3 is 9

4.3 Sets

Another important in-built data structure in Python is a set. A set is also a heterogeneous collection of elements but the elements of a set are not ordered. It means that we cannot access the set elements using some index values. Another property is that it does not allow duplicate values. However, set elements are mutable. We can insert new elements, delete or modify existing elements in a set. But any mutable element like a list cannot be an element of a set.

4.3.1   Creating a Set

A set is a collection of elements that are separated by commas (,) inside curly brackets { }. Hence we can create a set by putting comma separated elements within curly brackets. The general format to defining a set is:

```
Set_variable  = {value1, value2, …}
```

We may create a set of integers as:

```
myIntSet= {10, 12, 25, 37, 49}
```

A set of strings can be created as:

```
nameSet = {"Shreya", "Nandita", "Sudeshna", "Ushashi"}
```

A set with heterogeneous data can be created as:

```
mySet = {693, "Shreys Saha", 93.02}
```

Like lists and tuples, an empty set can also be created as:

```
mySet = {}
```

An empty set can also be created using set () as:

```
mySet = set ( )
```

A set can also be created from an existing list, tuple or string.

```
setFromList   = set([5, 10, 15])
setFromTuple  = set((5, 10, 15))
setFromString = set("AEIOU")
```

4.3.2   Operations on a Set

A set is a mutable and unordered data structure. Hence, we can add elements into a set but not in a specific position. We can remove elements from a set but elements of specific position cannot be removed. Searching is possible through the membership operator but it is not possible to find the index position of an item in a set. Slicing is also not possible as there is no specific index position of the elements. Set also does not support concatenation and repetition operations.

4.3.2.1 *Adding Elements to a Set*

To add an element into a set the add() method is used. We can add the elements of a set into other using the update() method. But remember, a set does not allow duplicate elements. Consider the following example:

Example 4.24: Write a program to add an element in a set.

```
mySet1= {10, 12, 25, 37, 49}
print("Initial Set :", mySet1)
mySet1.add(20)
print("After Adding 20:", mySet1)
mySet2= {15, 25, 35}
mySet1.update(mySet2)
print(("After updating by another set:", mySet1)
```

Output:

Initial Set : {49, 25, 10, 12, 37}
After Adding 20: {37, 10, 12, 49, 20, 25}
After updating by another set: {35, 37, 10, 12, 15, 49, 20, 25}

4.3.2.2 *Removing Elements from a Set*

To remove an element from a set we may use discard(), remove(), pop(), and clear(). Both discard() and remove() delete the specified element from a set. If the element does not exist in the set, remove() raises an error but discard() does not. The pop() method removes any arbitrary element and returns it. To remove all elements from a set, the clear() method is used. If we want to delete the entire set, we need to mention the set name with the del statement. The following program explains the operations of these functions:

Example 4.25: Write a program to remove elements from a set.

```
mySet= {10, 12, 25, 37, 49}
print ("Before deletion : ", end =" ")
print(mySet)

mySet.discard(10)                 #Deleting 10 using discard()
```

```
print ("After deleting 10 : ")
print(mySet)

mySet.remove(12)            #Deleting 12 using remove()
print ("After deleting 12 : ")
print(mySet)

num=mySet.pop() #An arbitrary element is deleted and returned
print("Popped element is : ",num)
print ("After popping : ")
print(mySet)

mySet.clear()               #Deleting all existing element
print ("After removing all existing elements : ", end =" ")
print(mySet)

del mySet              # Delete entire array
```

Output:

Before deletion : {49, 25, 10, 12, 37}
After deleting 10 :
{49, 25, 12, 37}
After deleting 12 :
{49, 25, 37}
Popped element is : 49
After popping :
{25, 37}
After removing all existing elements : set()

4.3.2.3 Searching an Element in a Set

Using the membership operator it is possible to check whether an element is present in a set or not.

Example 4.25: Application of membership operator in a set.

```
oddSet =  {1, 3, 5}
evenSet =  {2, 4, 6, 8}
print("oddSet : ", oddSet)
print("evenSet : ", evenSet)
print("Is 2 in oddSet? : ", 2 in oddSet)
print("Is 3 not in evenSet? : ", 3 not in evenSet)
```

Output:

oddSet : {1, 3, 5}
evenSet : {8, 2, 4, 6}
Is 2 in oddSet? : False
Is 3 not in evenSet? : True

4.3.3 Set Methods

Basic mathematical operations on a set are union, intersection, difference and symmetric difference. Python allows us do all these operations with its built-in data structure set. For these operations, methods as well as operators are available. Besides these methods there are also some other methods. Here we are discussing some of them.

union( ): This method finds the union of two sets. The '|' operator also does the same job.

intersection( ): This method finds the intersection of two sets. Using the '&' operator we can do the same operation.

intersection_update( ): This method updates the set for which this method is called by the intersection values of two sets.

difference( ): This method finds the difference between two sets. A new set contains the elements that are in first set (here for which this method is called) but not in the second set (which is passed as an argument). The operator '–' also does the same.

difference_update( ): This method updates the set for which this method is called by the difference between two sets.

symmetric_difference( ): This method finds the symmetric difference of two sets. A new set contains the elements that are either in the first set (here for which this method is called) or in the second set (which is passed as an argument) but not in both. The operator '^' also does the same.

isdisjoint( ): This method returns True if the two sets do not have any common element, i.e., their intersection produces a null set.

issubset( ): This method returns True if every element of the first set (i.e., for which this method is called) is also present in the second set (i.e., which is passed as an argument). The operator '<=' can also be used for this operation.

issuperset( ): This method returns True if every element of the second set (i.e., which is passed as an argument) is also present in the first set (i.e., for which this method is called). The operator '>=' can also be used for this operation.

copy( ): This method creates a new copy of a set.

Along with these methods sets are also used with Python's basic functions for iterables. These are `max()`, `min()`, `len()`, `sum()`, `all()`, `any()`, `sorted()`, etc. The following example illustrates the operations of set methods:

Example 4.26: Example to show operations of set methods.

```python
students = {'Jadu','Madhu','Parna','Pulak','Ram','Rabin','
Shreya','Shyam'}
physics =  {'Ram', 'Shyam', 'Jadu', 'Madhu'}
chemistry =  {'Rabin', 'Pulak', 'Shyam', 'Madhu'}
Mathematics = {'Shreya', 'Parna', 'Rabin'}

print("Passed in Physics : ", physics)
print("Passed in Chemistry : ", chemistry)
print("Passed in Mathematics : ", Mathematics)
unionSet1 = physics.union(chemistry)
print("Passed either in Physics or Chemistry or Both : ",
                                        unionSet1)
unionSet2 = physics | chemistry
print("Passed in physics | chemistry : ", unionSet2)
interSet1 = physics.intersection(chemistry)
print("Passed in both subjects : ", interSet1)
interSet2= physics & chemistry
print("Passed in physics & chemistry : ", interSet2)
physics.intersection_update(chemistry)
print("Set physics after using Intersection_update(): ",
                                        physics)

physics =  {'Ram', 'Shyam', 'Jadu', 'Madhu'}
diffSet1 = physics.difference(chemistry)
print("Passed only in Physics but not in Chemistry : ",
                                        diffSet1)

diffSet2 = physics - chemistry
print("physics - chemistry : ", diffSet2)
physics.difference_update(chemistry)
print("Set physics after using difference_update(): ",
                                        physics)

physics =  {'Ram', 'Shyam', 'Jadu', 'Madhu'}
symDiffSet1 = physics.symmetric_difference(chemistry)
print("Passed either in Physics or Chemistry but not
                            in both : ", symDiffSet1)
symDiffSet2 = physics ^ chemistry
print("physics ^ chemistry : ", symDiffSet2)

print("Is none of them passed in both Physics and
```

```
                Mathematics? :", physics.isdisjoint(Mathematics))
    print("Is none of them passed in both Physics and
                Chemistry? :", physics.isdisjoint(chemistry))
    print("Is Physics is a subset of students set? :",
                                physics.issubset(students))
    print("Is Students is a superset of Chemistry set? :",
                                physics.issubset(students))
```

Output:

Passed in Physics : {'Jadu', 'Shyam', 'Ram', 'Madhu'}

Passed in Chemistry : {'Rabin', 'Pulak', 'Shyam', 'Madhu'}

Passed in Mathematics : {'Parna', 'Shreya', 'Rabin'}

Passed either in Physics or Chemistry or Both : {'Shyam', 'Ram', 'Rabin', 'Pulak', 'Jadu', 'Madhu'}

Passed in physics | chemistry : {'Shyam', 'Ram', 'Rabin', 'Pulak', 'Jadu', 'Madhu'}

Passed in both subjects : {'Shyam', 'Madhu'}

Passed in physics & chemistry : {'Shyam', 'Madhu'}

Set physics after using Intersection_update(): {'Shyam', 'Madhu'}

Passed only in Physics but not in Chemistry : {'Jadu', 'Ram'}

physics - chemistry : {'Jadu', 'Ram'}

Set physics after using difference_update(): {'Ram', 'Jadu'}

Passed either in Physics or Chemistry but not in both : {'Ram', 'Rabin', 'Pulak', 'Jadu'}

physics ^ chemistry : {'Ram', 'Rabin', 'Pulak', 'Jadu'}

Is none of them passed in both Physics and Mathematics? : True

Is none of them passed in both Physics and Chemistry? : False

Is Physics is a subset of students set? : True

Is Students is a superset of Chemistry set? : True

Example 4.27: Example to show operations of set functions.

```
mySet = {34, 57, 69, 371, 4, 92}

print("mySet = ",mySet)
print("Max = ",max(mySet))
print("Min = ",min(mySet))
print("Sum = ",sum(mySet))
print("Sorted List : ",sorted(mySet))
print("all(mySet) : ",all(mySet))
print("any(mySet) : ",any(mySet))

copiedSet = mySet.copy()
print("Copied Set : ", copiedSet)
```

```
newSet1 = set("Python")
print("New Set created from string : ",newSet1)
newSet2 = set([5, 10, 15])
print("New Set created from list : ",newSet2)
del mySet          # Deletes entire Set
print("mySet = ",mySet)
```

Output:

mySet = {34, 4, 69, 371, 57, 92}

Max = 371

Min = 4

Sum = 627

Sorted List : [4, 34, 57, 69, 92, 371]

all(mySet) : True

any(mySet) : True

Copied Set : {34, 371, 4, 69, 57, 92}

New Set created from string : {'h', 'n', 'P', 'o', 'y', 't'}

New Set created from list : {10, 5, 15}

Traceback (most recent call last):

  File "D:/DSP Book/Python programs/set4.py", line 18, in <module>

   print("mySet = ",mySet)

NameError: name 'mySet' is not defined

4.3.4 Frozenset

A frozenset is a special set in Python whose elements are frozen, which means they become immutable. No further elements can be added or removed from that set. The built-in function `frozenset()` is used for this purpose. It takes any iterable as an argument and returns an immutable set.

Example 4.28: Example to show the creation of a frozenset.

```
mySet = {5, 10, 15, 20}
mySet.add(25)
print("mySet = ",mySet)
myFrozenSet=frozenset(mySet)
print("myFrozenSet = ",myFrozenSet)
myFrozenSet.add(25)
```

Output:

mySet = {25, 10, 20, 5, 15}

myFrozenSet = frozenset({25, 10, 20, 5, 15})

Traceback (most recent call last):

  File "D:/DSP Book/Python programs/frozenSet.py", line 6, in <module>

    myFrozenSet.add(25)

AttributeError: 'frozenset' object has no attribute 'add'

4.4   Dictionaries

Another very important and useful data structure in Python is a dictionary. It is also a collection but not just collection of values. It stores the data values as a pair of key and value. Each key is separated from its value by a colon ' : '. This key–value pair represents a single element and a comma separated set of these elements forms a dictionary. Basically dictionaries are not sequences; rather they are mappings. Mappings are collections of objects that store objects by key instead of by relative position. Hence, elements of a dictionary are not ordered, i.e., they do not have any specific index position. Keys in a dictionary are unique as well as immutable. However, elements in a dictionary are mutable. We can add new key–value pair, delete existing key–value pair or modify the value of a particular key.

4.4.1   Creating a Dictionary

We have already discussed that a dictionary stores data values as a pair of key and value. Each key is separated from its value by a colon ' : '. This key–value pair represents a single element and these elements are separated by commas inside curly brackets{ }. The general format to defining a dictionary is:

```
dictionary_name = { key 1 : value 1,
                    key 2 : value 2,
                    key 3 : value 3,
                    ….. }
```

Hence we may create a dictionary where keys are the roll numbers of students and names of the students are the corresponding values of the keys as:

```
studentList = {1:"Shreya", 2:"Sriparna", 3:"Subrata"}
```

A dictionary where attribute and values are the key–value pair may be defined as:

```
my_dict = {'Roll':3, 'Name':'Subrata'}
```

An empty dictionary can be created as:

```
mydict = { }
```

A dictionary can also be created using constructor as:

```
my_dict = dict([('Roll' , 3), ('Name', 'Subrata')])
```

4.4.2 Accessing Values in a Dictionary

Dictionaries are not ordered. Thus, elements of a dictionary cannot be accessed through index value. They are mappings. Hence, they are accessed by the key. The general format to access an element of a dictionary is:

Dictionary_name[Key]

The following example illustrates how an element of a dictionary is accessed:

Example 4.29: Write a program to show how to access dictionary elements.

```
my_dict = {'Roll' : 3, 'Name': 'Subrata'}
print('Roll : ', my_dict['Roll'])
print('Name : ', my_dict['Name'])
```

Output:

```
Roll : 3
Name : Subrata
```

4.4.3   Operations on a Dictionary

Keys in a dictionary are unique as well as immutable. Elements in a dictionary are mutable. We can add a new key–value pair, delete an existing key–value pair or modify the value of a particular key. But we cannot add duplicate keys; they are unique. Keys are immutable also; we cannot change them. Membership operators are also used with key values in a dictionary.

4.4.3.1 Adding and Modifying an Element in a Dictionary

To add an element we need not use any methods. This is true for modifying an element as well. And the fun is that the same statement may add or modify an element. What we simply need to do is specify a value against a key. If the key is not in the dictionary the key–value pair will be added to the dictionary; otherwise the key will be updated with the new value. The same operation can be done using the update( ) method. Consider the following example:

Example 4.30: Write a program to show how an element can be added or modified in a dictionary.

```
my_dict = {'Roll' : 1, 'Name': 'Subrata'}
print("Initial Dictionary : ", my_dict)
my_dict['Marks'] = 576        #New key, Marks added
print("After adding Marks : ",my_dict)
my_dict['Marks'] = 675        #The key, Marks modified with
                              #new value
print("After modifying Marks : ",my_dict)

print("Using Update() method :-")
my_dict = {'Roll' : 1, 'Name': 'Subrata'}
print("Initial Dictionary : ", my_dict)
new_dict={'Marks': 576}
my_dict.update(new_dict)                #New key, Marks added
print("After adding Marks : ", my_dict)
my_dict.update({'Marks': 675}) #The key, Marks modified
                              #with new value
print("After modifying Marks : ", my_dict)
```

Output:

Initial Dictionary : {'Roll': 1, 'Name': 'Subrata'}
After adding Marks : {'Roll': 1, 'Marks': 576, 'Name': 'Subrata'}
After modifying Marks : {'Roll': 1, 'Marks': 675, 'Name': 'Subrata'}
Using Update() method :-
Initial Dictionary : {'Roll': 1, 'Name': 'Subrata'}
After adding Marks : {'Roll': 1, 'Marks': 576, 'Name': 'Subrata'}
After modifying Marks : {'Roll': 1, 'Marks': 675, 'Name': 'Subrata'}

4.4.3.2 Removing an Element from a Dictionary

To remove a particular element from a dictionary or an entire dictionary we may use the del statement. To remove a particular element from a dictionary, with the del statement we need to specify the key that we want to delete as:

```
del dictionary_name[key]
```

If the key is present in the dictionary, it will be removed; otherwise it will raise `KeyError`. We may also use the `pop()` method to solve this problem. The `pop()` method removes the key, passed as an argument, from a dictionary and returns the corresponding value. If the key is not present in the dictionary, it will also raise `KeyError`. But we can solve this problem by supplying an additional argument with the `pop()` method:

```
dictionary_name.pop(key [, d])
```

where **d** is the default value that will be returned if the key is not present in the dictionary.

The `popitem()` method arbitrarily removes an item from a dictionary and returns a key–value pair as a tuple. However, it raises a `KeyError` if the dictionary is empty. The `clear()` method removes all the keys from a dictionary and makes it empty. To remove a dictionary from memory, only the dictionary name needs to be specified with the `del` statement. The following example illustrates the deletion operation on a dictionary:

Example 4.31: Write a program to show deletion operation on a dictionary.

```
my_dict = {'Roll' : 1, 'Name': 'Subrata', 'Marks': 675}
print("Initial Dictionary : ", my_dict)
del my_dict['Marks']
print("After deleting Marks : ", my_dict)
print("Again popping Marks, returned :",
                    my_dict.pop('Marks', 'Not found'))
print("Popping Name :", my_dict.pop('Name'))
my_dict.clear()
print("Clearing all elements from dictionary : ", my_dict)
del my_dict
```

Output:

Initial Dictionary : {'Marks': 675, 'Roll': 1, 'Name': 'Subrata'}
After deleting Marks : {'Roll': 1, 'Name': 'Subrata'}
Again popping Marks, returned : Not found
Popping Name : Subrata
Clearing all elements from dictionary : {}

4.4.3.3 Membership Test in a Dictionary

We may use the membership operators to check whether a particular key is present or not in a dictionary. The following example illustrates the use of membership operators:

Example 4.32: Write a program to show the use of membership operators on a dictionary.

```
my_dict = {'Roll' : 1, 'Name': 'Subrata'}
print("my_dict : ", my_dict)
print("'Roll' in my_dict : ", 'Roll' in my_dict)
print("'Marks' in my_dict : ", 'Marks' in my_dict)
print("'Roll' not in my_dict : ", 'Roll' not in my_dict)
print("'Marks' not in my_dict : ", 'Marks' not in my_dict)
```

Output:

my_dict : {'Name': 'Subrata', 'Roll': 1}

'Roll' in my_dict : True

'Marks' in my_dict : False

'Roll' not in my_dict : False

'Marks' not in my_dict : True

4.4.4 Looping in a Dictionary

The keys(), values() and items() methods return iterables containing keys, values and key–value pair respectively as tuples. Thus based on these iterables we may iterate through a dictionary. Consider the following example:

Example 4.33: Write a program to show how to iterate through a dictionary.

```
my_dict = {'Roll' : 1, 'Name': 'Subrata', 'Marks': 675}
print("my_dict : ", my_dict)
print("Keys are : ", end=' ')
for k in my_dict.keys():
    print(k, end=' ')
print("\nValues are : ", end=' ')
for v in my_dict.values():
    print(v, end=' ')
print("\nItems are : ")
for k,v in my_dict.items():
    print(k, v)
```

Output:

my_dict : {'Roll': 1, 'Name': 'Subrata', 'Marks': 675}

Keys are : Roll Name Marks

Values are : 1 Subrata 675

Items are :

Roll 1

Name Subrata

Marks 675

4.4.5 Nested Dictionaries

Like lists and tuples, a dictionary may also be nested. We may insert a dictionary as a value against a key. Consider the following example. Here names of the students are used as a key in the dictionary and against each key a dictionary is inserted which further represents the marks of three subjects as a pair of key–value. In this nested dictionary, subjects are the keys and corresponding marks are the values against each key.

Example 4.34: Write a program to show the use of a nested dictionary.

```
my_dict = { 'Ram':{'c':67,'Java':82,'Python':93},
            'Shyam':{'c':82,'Java':73,'Python':89},
            'Jadu':{'c':77,'Java':85,'Python':90}
          }
for k,v in my_dict.items():
    print("Name : ", k, "\tMarks : ", v)
```

Output:

```
Name : Ram        Marks : {'c': 67, 'Python': 93, 'Java': 82}
Name : Shyam      Marks : {'c': 82, 'Python': 89, 'Java': 73}
Name : Jadu       Marks : {'c': 77, 'Python': 90, 'Java': 85}
```

4.4.6 Dictionary Methods

Dictionaries also have some methods to do some specific jobs. We have already discussed some of them. Here we are discussing some other methods.

fromkeys(sequence [, value]): This method creates a new dictionary using the keys from the **sequence** and set values of all key to **value**. The default value of **value** is None.

copy( ): This method creates a new copy of a dictionary.

get(key[, d]): Returns the value of the **key** sent as argument. If **key** is not present, returns the default value, **d**.

setdefault(key[, d]): It also returns the value of the **key** sent as argument. But if the **key** is not present, it inserts the key with the default value, **d**.

Along with these methods dictionaries are also used with some of Python's basic functions like len(), str(), etc. The following example illustrates the operations of dictionary methods and functions:

Example 4.35: Write a program to show the use of dictionary methods.

```
new_dict=dict.fromkeys([1,3,5])
print("Dictionary created without default value : ", new_
```

```
                                                        dict)
new_dict=dict.fromkeys([1,3,5],0)
print("Dictionary created with default value 0: ", new_
                                                        dict)


square_dict={1:1, 2:4, 3:9, 4:16, 5:25}
print("\nDictionary with square values : ", square_dict)
print("Use of get() method :-")
val = square_dict.get(3)
print("Value of the key 3 is : ", val)
val = square_dict.get(7, 'Not Found')
print("Value of the key 7 is : ", val)

print("\nUse of setdefault() method :-")
val = square_dict.setdefault(3)
print("Value of the key 3 is : ", val)
val = square_dict.setdefault(7, 49)
print("Value of the key 7 is : ", val)
print("Final Dictionary : ", square_dict)

copied_dict = square_dict.copy()
print("Copied Dictionary : ", copied_dict)

elements = len(square_dict)
print("Number of elements in the dictionary:", elements)

print("Converting the dictionary into string: ",
                                    str(square_dict))
```

Output:

Dictionary created without default value:{1: None, 3: None, 5: None}
Dictionary created with default value 0: {1: 0, 3: 0, 5: 0}

Dictionary with square values : {1: 1, 2: 4, 3: 9, 4: 16, 5: 25}
Use of get() method :-
Value of the key 3 is : 9
Value of the key 7 is : Not Found

Use of setdefault() method :-
Value of the key 3 is : 9
Value of the key 7 is : 49

Final Dictionary : {1: 1, 2: 4, 3: 9, 4: 16, 5: 25, 7: 49}
Copied Dictionary : {1: 1, 2: 4, 3: 9, 4: 16, 5: 25, 7: 49}
Number of elements in the dictionary: 6
Converting the dictionary into string:{1:1, 2:4, 3:9, 4:16, 5:25, 7:49}

4.5   Comparative Study

In this chapter we have discussed four in-built data structures in Python. Now here is a comparative study of these data structures.

- Lists and tuples are ordered sets of elements, but the elements of sets and dictionaries are not ordered.

- Lists, sets, and dictionaries are mutable whereas a tuple is an immutable data structure.

- Lists and tuples allow duplicate elements but the elements of a set and the keys of dictionaries must be unique.

- To define a list, square bracket '[ ]' is used. To define a tuple and a set, parenthesis '( )' and curly brackets '{ }' respectively are used. To define a dictionary, curly brackets '{ }' are used but each key–value pair is separated by a colon ':'.

- Elements of a list and a tuple are accessed using index value but elements of a dictionary are accessed by keys.

- Slicing operation can be done on lists and tuples but not on sets and dictionaries.

- Lists, tuples and dictionaries can be nested but sets cannot be.

- By nature lists and tuples are sequences whereas dictionaries are mappings.

- A list is used as a dynamic data structure with heterogeneous collection of data, where elements are accessed sequentially as well as randomly. It is very helpful when elements are added, deleted or modified frequently. Tuples are similar to lists but are immutable. If we need a fixed set of elements that need not be updated, a tuple is the best option as it works fast. If we need an unordered collection of unique elements, a set is a better choice. Dictionaries are completely different in nature. It works as a lookup table.

4.6   Programming Examples

Here are some programming examples to understand the various operations that can be performed on lists, tuples, sets and dictionaries.

Program 4.1: Write a program to create a list whose elements are divisible by n but not divisible by n^2 for a given range.

```
#PRGD4_1 : Program to create a list whose elements are
#divisible by n but not divisible by n² for a given
#range.

st = int(input("Enter Starting Number: "))
end = int(input("Enter End Number: "))
n = int(input("Enter the value of n: "))
numList=[]
for i in range(st, end+1):
    if i%n==0 and i%(n*n)!=0:
        numList.append(i)

print(numList)
```

Sample Output:

Enter Starting Number: 10
Enter End Number: 50
Enter the value of n: 3
[12, 15, 21, 24, 30, 33, 39, 42, 48]

Program 4.2: Write a program to find the largest difference among a list of elements. Do not use library functions and traverse the list only once.

```
#PRGD4_2 : Program to find the largest difference among
#a list of elements. Do not use library functions and
#traverse the list only once.

n = int(input("Enter the number of elements: "))
numList=[]
for i in range(n):
    num = int(input("Enter any number: "))
    numList.append(num)

max=min=numList[0]
for i in range(1,n):
    if numList[i]>max:
        max=numList[i]
    elif numList[i]<min:
        min=numList[i]

print("Largest Difference =", max-min)
```

Sample Output:

Enter the number of elements: 6
Enter any number: 32
Enter any number: 47
Enter any number: 69
Enter any number: 98
Enter any number: -5
Enter any number: 27
Largest Difference = 103

Program 4.3: Write a program to find the average of list elements.

```
#PRGD4_3 : Program to find the average of list elements.

n = int(input("Enter the number of elements: "))
numList=[]
for i in range(n):
    num = int(input("Enter any number: "))
    numList.append(num)

sum=0
for i in numList:
    sum+=i
print("Average = ", sum/n)
```

Sample Output:

Enter the number of elements: 5
Enter any number: 45
Enter any number: 28
Enter any number: 77
Enter any number: 12
Enter any number: 10
Average = 34.4

Program 4.4: Write a program to find all occurrences of an inputted number in a list.

```
#PRGD4_4 : Program to find the all occurrences of an
#inputted number in a list.

def findNum(myList, num):
    l=len(myList)
```

```
        print(num, "present at index position ",end='')
        for i in range(l):
            if num==myList[i]:
                print(i, end=',')

n = int(input("Enter the number of elements: "))
numList=[]
for i in range(n):
    num = int(input("Enter any number: "))
    numList.append(num)

number = int(input("Enter the number to find: "))

findNum(numList, number)
```

Sample Output:

```
Enter the number of elements: 10
Enter any number: 2
Enter any number: 5
Enter any number: 7
Enter any number: 1
Enter any number: 3
Enter any number: 2
Enter any number: 1
Enter any number: 3
Enter any number: 2
Enter any number: 5
Enter the number to find: 2
2 present at index position 0,5,8,
```

Program 4.5: Write a program to create a list of n random integers between 1 to 100.

```
#PRGD4_5 : Program to create a list of n random integers
#between 1 to 100.

import random

n = int(input("Enter the number of elements: "))
randomList=[]
for i in range(n):
    num = random.randint(1,100)
    randomList.append(num)
```

```
print(randomList)
```

Sample Output:

Enter the number of elements: 10
[75, 25, 24, 73, 32, 46, 82, 17, 51, 1]

Program 4.6: Write a program to split a list containing odd and even numbers into two different lists so that one will contain odd numbers and the other will contain even numbers.

```
#PRGD4_6 : Program to split a list into two different odd
#and even lists

n = int(input("Enter the number of elements: "))
numList=[]
for i in range(n):
    num = int(input("Enter any number: "))
    numList.append(num)

oddList=[]
evenList=[]
for i in numList:
    if i%2==0:
        evenList.append(i)
    else:
        oddList.append(i)

print("List of Odd elements = ", oddList)
print("List of Even elements = ", evenList)
```

Sample Output:

Enter the number of elements: 10
Enter any number: 7
Enter any number: 34
Enter any number: 53
Enter any number: 87
Enter any number: 92
Enter any number: 53
Enter any number: 89
Enter any number: 6
Enter any number: 12
Enter any number: 73

List of Odd elements = [7, 53, 87, 53, 89, 73]
List of Even elements = [34, 92, 6, 12]

Program 4.7: Write a program to merge two sorted lists.

```
#PRGD4_7 : Program to merge two sorted lists.

def mergeList(m,n):
    l1=len(m)
    l2=len(n)
    i=j=0
    newList=[]
    while i<l1 and j <l2:
        if m[i]<n[j]:
            newList.append(m[i])
            i+=1
        else:
            newList.append(n[j])
            j+=1
    while i<l1:
        newList.append(m[i])
        i+=1
    while j<l2:
        newList.append(n[j])
        j+=1
    return newList

def inputList(lst):
    n = int(input("Enter the number of elements: "))
    for i in range(n):
        num = int(input("Enter element %d: "%(i+1)))
        lst.append(num)

numList1=[]
numList2=[]
print("Enter elements for 1st list:-")
inputList(numList1)
print("Enter elements for 2nd list:-")
inputList(numList2)

newList=mergeList(numList1,numList2)
print("Merged List : ", newList)
```

Sample Output:

```
Enter elements for 1st list:-
Enter the number of elements: 5
Enter element 1: 2
Enter element 2: 4
Enter element 3: 6
Enter element 4: 8
Enter element 5: 12
Enter elements for 2nd list:-
Enter the number of elements: 6
Enter element 1: 1
Enter element 2: 3
Enter element 3: 5
Enter element 4: 7
Enter element 5: 9
Enter element 6: 11
Merged List : [1, 2, 3, 4, 5, 6, 7, 8, 9, 11, 12]
```

Program 4.8: Write a program to create two sets such that one will contain the names of the students who have passed in Economics and the other will contain the names of those who have passed in Accountancy.

i.   Find the students who have passed in both subjects

ii. Find the students who have passed in at least one subject

iii. Find the students who have passed in one subject but not in both

iv. Find the students who have passed in Economics but not in Accountancy

v.   Find the students who have passed in Accountancy but not in Economics.

```python
#PRGD4_8 : Program on set operation

n = int(input("Enter the number of students who have
                                passed in Economics: "))
economics=set()
for i in range(n):
    name = input("Enter Name %d: "%(i+1))
    economics.add(name)

n = int(input("Enter the number of students who have
                                passed in Accountancy: "))
accountancy=set()
```

```
for i in range(n):
    name = input("Enter Name %d: "%(i+1))
    accountancy.add(name)

print("Students Passed in Economics:",economics)
print("Students Passed in Accountancy:",accountancy)
print("Students Passed in Both Subject:",economics &
                                        accountancy)
print("Students Passed in at least one Subject:",economics
                                      | accountancy)
print("Students Passed in one Subject but not in
                both:",economics ^ accountancy)
print("Students Passed in Economics but not in
            Accountancy:",economics - accountancy)
print("Students Passed in Accountancy but not in
            Economics:",accountancy - economics)
```

Sample Output:

Enter the number of students who have passed in Economics: 4

Enter Name 1: Shreya

Enter Name 2: Sriparna

Enter Name 3: Nandita

Enter Name 4: Sudeshna

Enter the number of students who have passed in Accountancy: 3

Enter Name 1: Shreya

Enter Name 2: Sriparna

Enter Name 3: Geetashree

Students Passed in Economics: {'Nandita', 'Sudeshna', 'Shreya', 'Sriparna'}

Students Passed in Accountancy: {'Geetashree', 'Shreya', 'Sriparna'}

Students Passed in Both Subject: {'Shreya', 'Sriparna'}

Students Passed in at least one Subject: {'Geetashree', 'Sudeshna', 'Nandita', 'Shreya', 'Sriparna'}

Students Passed in one Subject but not in both: {'Geetashree', 'Nandita', 'Sudeshna'}

Students Passed in Economics but not in Accountancy: {'Nandita', 'Sudeshna'}

Students Passed in Accountancy but not in Economics: {'Geetashree'}

Program 4.9: Write a program to create a dictionary that will contain all ASCII values and their corresponding characters.

```
#PRGD4_9 : Program to create a dictionary that will
#contain all ASCII values and their corresponding
#characters.
```

```
asciiDict={}
for i in range(256):
    asciiDict[i]=chr(i)
print(asciiDict)
```

Output:

{0: '\x00', 1: '\x01', 2: '\x02', 3: '\x03', 4: '\x04', 5: '\x05', 6: '\x06', 7: '\x07', 8: '\x08', 9: '\t', 10: '\n', 11: '\x0b', 12: '\x0c', 13: '\r', 14: '\x0e', 15: '\x0f', 16: '\x10', 17: '\x11', 18: '\x12', 19: '\x13', 20: '\x14', 21: '\x15', 22: '\x16', 23: '\x17', 24: '\x18', 25: '\x19', 26: '\x1a', 27: '\x1b', 28: '\x1c', 29: '\x1d', 30: '\x1e', 31: '\x1f', 32: ' ', 33: '!', 34: '"', 35: '#', 36: '$', 37: '%', 38: '&', 39: "'", 40: '(', 41: ')', 42: '*', 43: '+', 44: ',', 45: '-', 46: '.', 47: '/', 48: '0', 49: '1', 50: '2', 51: '3', 52: '4', 53: '5', 54: '6', 55: '7', 56: '8', 57: '9', 58: ':', 59: ';', 60: '<', 61: '=', 62: '>', 63: '?', 64: '@', 65: 'A', 66: 'B', 67: 'C', 68: 'D', 69: 'E', 70: 'F', 71: 'G', 72: 'H', 73: 'I', 74: 'J', 75: 'K', 76: 'L', 77: 'M', 78: 'N', 79: 'O', 80: 'P', 81: 'Q', 82: 'R', 83: 'S', 84: 'T', 85: 'U', 86: 'V', 87: 'W', 88: 'X', 89: 'Y', 90: 'Z', 91: '[', 92: '\\', 93: ']', 94: '^', 95: '_', 96: '`', 97: 'a', 98: 'b', 99: 'c', 100: 'd', 101: 'e', 102: 'f', 103: 'g', 104: 'h', 105: 'i', 106: 'j', 107: 'k', 108: 'l', 109: 'm', 110: 'n', 111: 'o', 112: 'p', 113: 'q', 114: 'r', 115: 's', 116: 't', 117: 'u', 118: 'v', 119: 'w', 120: 'x', 121: 'y', 122: 'z', 123: '{', 124: '|', 125: '}', 126: '~', 127: '\x7f', 128: '\x80', 129: '\x81', 130: '\x82', 131: '\x83', 132: '\x84', 133: '\x85', 134: '\x86', 135: '\x87', 136: '\x88', 137: '\x89', 138: '\x8a', 139: '\x8b', 140: '\x8c', 141: '\x8d', 142: '\x8e', 143: '\x8f', 144: '\x90', 145: '\x91', 146: '\x92', 147: '\x93', 148: '\x94', 149: '\x95', 150: '\x96', 151: '\x97', 152: '\x98', 153: '\x99', 154: '\x9a', 155: '\x9b', 156: '\x9c', 157: '\x9d', 158: '\x9e', 159: '\x9f', 160: '\xa0', 161: '¡', 162: '¢', 163: '£', 164: '¤', 165: '¥', 166: '¦', 167: '§', 168: '¨', 169: '©', 170: 'ª', 171: '«', 172: '¬', 173: '\xad', 174: '®', 175: '¯', 176: '°', 177: '±', 178: '²', 179: '³', 180: '´', 181: 'µ', 182: '¶', 183: '·', 184: '¸', 185: '¹', 186: 'º', 187: '»', 188: '¼', 189: '½', 190: '¾', 191: '¿', 192: 'À', 193: 'Á', 194: 'Â', 195: 'Ã', 196: 'Ä', 197: 'Å', 198: 'Æ', 199: 'Ç', 200: 'È', 201: 'É', 202: 'Ê', 203: 'Ë', 204: 'Ì', 205: 'Í', 206: 'Î', 207: 'Ï', 208: 'Ð', 209: 'Ñ', 210: 'Ò', 211: 'Ó', 212: 'Ô', 213: 'Õ', 214: 'Ö', 215: '×', 216: 'Ø', 217: 'Ù', 218: 'Ú', 219: 'Û', 220: 'Ü', 221: 'Ý', 222: 'Þ', 223: 'ß', 224: 'à', 225: 'á', 226: 'â', 227: 'ã', 228: 'ä', 229: 'å', 230: 'æ', 231: 'ç', 232: 'è', 233: 'é', 234: 'ê', 235: 'ë', 236: 'ì', 237: 'í', 238: 'î', 239: 'ï', 240: 'ð', 241: 'ñ', 242: 'ò', 243: 'ó', 244: 'ô', 245: 'õ', 246: 'ö', 247: '÷', 248: 'ø', 249: 'ù', 250: 'ú', 251: 'û', 252: 'ü', 253: 'ý', 254: 'þ', 255: 'ÿ'}

Program 4.10: Write a function to increment a day by one day.

```
#PRGD4_10 : Program to increment a day by one

import re
lastDate={1:31,2:28,3:31,4:30,5:31,6:30,7:31,8:31,9:30,
10:31,11:30,12:31}

def IncrementDay(date):
    dd,mm,yy=map(int,re.split('[./-]',date))
    sep=date[2]
    if yy%400==0 or (yy%100!=0 and yy%4==0):
        lastDate[2]=29
```

```
    if dd<lastDate[mm]:
        dd+=1
    else:
        dd=1
        mm+=1
        if mm==13:
            mm=1
            yy+=1
    return(str(dd)+sep+str(mm)+sep+str(yy))

dt= input("Enter any date(DD/MM/YYYY):")
incDt=IncrementDay(dt)
print("Next date of inputted date is:",incDt)
```

Sample Output:

Enter any date(DD/MM/YYYY):28/02/2000
Next date of inputted date is: 29/2/2000

Enter any date(DD/MM/YYYY): 31.12.2021
Next date of inputted date is: 1.1.2022

Enter any date(DD/MM/YYYY): 31-01-2020
Next date of inputted date is: 1-2-2020

Program 4.11: Define a dictionary to store names of students and marks in Python, OS and DBMS. Write a menu driven program to:

i.   Add new record in the dictionary.

ii. Modify an existing record in the dictionary.

iii. Delete an existing record from the dictionary.

iv. Find the highest marks for each subject.

v.   Print details of the students

```
#PRGD4_11 : Program to maintain students database

students={}

def addNew():
    name=input("Enter Name: ")
    python=int(input("Enter Marks in Python: "))
    os=int(input("Enter Marks in OS: "))
```

```
    dbms=int(input("Enter Marks in DBMS: "))
    students[name]={'Python':python,'OS':os,'DBMS':dbms}
    print("New record added successfully..")

def modify():
    name=input("Enter Name: ")
    if name not in students:
        print("Sorry!!", name, "not in database")
        return
    python=int(input("Enter Marks in Python: "))
    os=int(input("Enter Marks in OS: "))
    dbms=int(input("Enter Marks in DBMS: "))
    students[name]={'Python':python,'OS':os,'DBMS':dbms}
    print("Record modified successfully..")

def delete():
    name=input("Enter Name: ")
    if name not in students:
        print("Sorry!!", name, "not in database")
        return
    del students[name]
    print("Record deleted successfully..")

def findHighest():
    maxP=0
    maxO=0
    maxD=0
    for k,v in students.items():
        if v['Python']>maxP:
            maxP=v['Python']
        if v['OS']>maxO:
            maxO=v['OS']
        if v['DBMS']>maxD:
            maxD=v['DBMS']
    print("Highest marks in Python is =",maxP)
    print("Highest marks in OS     is =",maxO)
    print("Highest marks in DBMS   is =",maxD)

def display():
    print("\t\tStudent Details")
    print("---------------------------------------")
    print("Name              Python   OS   DBMS")
    print("---------------------------------------")
```

```
    for k,v in students.items():
        print("%-20s   %4d   %4d
                    3d"%(k,v['Python'],v['OS'],v['DBMS']))
    print("------------------------------------")
    print()

while(True):
    print("==========================================")
    print("1. Add new Student")
    print("2. Modify existing record of a student")
    print("3. Delete existing record of a student")
    print("4. Find the highest marks for each subject")
    print("5. Print Student Details")
    print("6. Exit")
    print("==========================================")
    choice=int(input("Enter your Choice : "))
    if choice==1 :
        addNew()
    elif choice==2 :
        modify()
    elif choice==3 :
        delete()
    elif choice==4 :
        findHighest()
    elif choice==5 :
        display()
    elif choice==6 :
        print("\nQuiting.......")
        break
    else:
        print("Invalid choice. Please Enter Correct
                                        Choice")
        continue
```

Sample Output:

```
==============================================
1. Add new Student
2. Modify existing record of a student
3. Delete existing record of a student
4. Find the highest marks for each subject
5. Print Student Details
6. Exit
==============================================
```

Enter your Choice : 1
Enter Name: Subrata Saha
Enter Marks in Python: 78
Enter Marks in OS: 92
Enter Marks in DBMS: 89
New record added successfully..
===
1. Add new Student
2. Modify existing record of a student
3. Delete existing record of a student
4. Find the highest marks for each subject
5. Print Student Details
6. Exit
===
Enter your Choice : 1
Enter Name: Gautam Dey
Enter Marks in Python: 67
Enter Marks in OS: 45
Enter Marks in DBMS: 69
New record added successfully..
===
1. Add new Student
2. Modify existing record of a student
3. Delete existing record of a student
4. Find the highest marks for each subject
5. Print Student Details
6. Exit
===
Enter your Choice : 1
Enter Name: Arijit Mitra
Enter Marks in Python: 90
Enter Marks in OS: 66
Enter Marks in DBMS: 82
New record added successfully..
===
1. Add new Student
2. Modify existing record of a student
3. Delete existing record of a student
4. Find the highest marks for each subject

5. Print Student Details

6. Exit

==

Enter your Choice : 5

Student Details

Name	Python	OS	DBMS
Arijit Mitra	90	66	82
Gautam Dey	67	45	69
Subrata Saha	78	92	89

==

1. Add new Student

2. Modify existing record of a student

3. Delete existing record of a student

4. Find the highest marks for each subject

5. Print Student Details

6. Exit

==

Enter your Choice : 4

Highest marks in Python is = 90

Highest marks in OS is = 92

Highest marks in DBMS is = 89

==

1. Add new Student

2. Modify existing record of a student

3. Delete existing record of a student

4. Find the highest marks for each subject

5. Print Student Details

6. Exit

==

Enter your Choice : 6

Quiting.......

Program 4.12: Write a function to test whether a variable is a list or a tuple or a set.

```
#Program 4_12 : Write a function to test whether a
#variable is a list or tuple or a set
```

```
def check(var):
    if type(var)==list:
        print(var, "is a List")
    elif type(var)==tuple:
        print(var, "is a Tuple")
    elif type(var)==set:
        print(var, "is a Set")

myList=[1,2,3]
myTuple=(1,2,3)
mySet={1,2,3}
check(myList)
check(myTuple)
check(mySet)
```

Output:

```
[1, 2, 3] is a List
(1, 2, 3) is a Tuple
{1, 2, 3} is a Set
```

Program 4.13: Write a program to sort a list of tuples by the second item.

```
#PRGD 4_13 : Program to sort a list of tuples by the
#second item

def usingLambda(myList):
    myList.sort(key=lambda x:x[1])

def usingBubbleSort(myList):
    n=len(myList)
    for i in range(n-1):
        for j in range(n-i-1):
            if myList[j][1]>myList[j+1][1]:
                myList[j],myList[j+1]=myList[j+1],myList[j]

list1=[(3,5),(7,9),(6,7)]
list2=[(3,9),(4,7),(2,8)]
usingLambda(list1)
print("Sorted list of Tuples:",list1)
usingBubbleSort(list2)
print("Sorted list of Tuples:",list2)
```

Output:

Sorted list of Tuples: [(3, 5), (6, 7), (7, 9)]
Sorted list of Tuples: [(4, 7), (2, 8), (3, 9)]

Python Data Structures at a Glance

- ✓ A list is a dynamic data structure with a heterogeneous collection of elements where elements are accessed sequentially as well as randomly.

- ✓ Lists are ordered, mutable and allow duplicate values.

- ✓ List is very helpful in programming when elements are added, deleted or modified frequently.

- ✓ Operations of list are similar to that of array, but arrays are homogeneous collections and lists are heterogeneous collections.

- ✓ Arrays are static, i.e., fixed in size but lists are dynamic, i.e., these can grow or sink as and when required.

- ✓ To define a list, square bracket '[ ]' is used.

- ✓ Tuples are ordered, immutable and allow duplicate values.

- ✓ To define a tuple, parenthesis '( )' is used. However, any comma separated values written without any brackets, which may be parenthesis, curly or square brackets, are treated as tuple.

- ✓ Both list and tuple elements are accessed with index values.

- ✓ Both list and tuple support both positive and negative index values.

- ✓ Both list and tuple support slicing operation.

- ✓ A set is a collection of elements that are separated by commas (,) inside curly brackets { }.

- ✓ Elements of a set are unordered and unique. However, we can add or remove elements from a set.

- ✓ Python allows all the basic mathematical operations on a set, like union, intersection, difference and symmetric difference, with the in-built set data structures.

- ✓ The membership operators are applicable for all the four above discussed data structures.

- ✓ Lists, tuples and dictionaries can be nested but sets cannot be.

Multiple Choice Questions

1. To create a list in Python _____ is used.

   a) ( )

   b) { }

   c) [ ]

   d) None of the above

2. Which method do we use to generate random numbers in Python?

   a) random.uniform( )

   b) random.randint()

   c) random.random()

   d) All of the above

3. What will be the output of the following Python code?

   list = ['a', 'b', 'c']

   list += 'de'

   print(list)

   a) ['a', 'b', 'c', 'd', 'e']

   b) ['a', 'b', 'c', 'de']

   c) ['ade', 'bde', 'cde']

   d) Error

4. What will be the output of the following Python code?

   ```
   even = [2, 4, 6, 8, 10]
   even[1:3] = [14, 16, 18]
   print (even)
   ```

   a) [2, 14, 16, 18, 10]

   b) [2, 14, 16, 18, 8, 10]

   c) [2, 14, 16, 18, 4, 6, 8, 10]

   d) Error

5. What will be the output of the following Python code?

   ```
   odd = [1, 3, 5]
   odd1= odd + [7, 9]
   print (odd1)
   ```

   a) [1, 3, 5, 7, 9]

   b) [1, 3, 5, [7, 9]]

c) Both are correct

d) None of the above

6. What will be the output of the following Python code?

```
odd = [ 3]
odd1= odd * 4
print(odd1)
```

a) [12]

b) [3, 3, 3, 3]

c) [[3], [3], [3], [3]]

d) None of the above

7. _var after executing the statement, my_var=max([sum([10,20]),min(abs(-30), 40)])

a) 0

b) 20

c) 30

d) 40

8. Which function constructs a list from those elements of the list for which a function returns True?

a) enumerate()

b) map()

c) reduce()

d) filter()

9. What will be the output of the following Python code?

```
odd = [1, 3, 5]
odd.append([7,9])
print(odd)
```

a) [1, 3, 5, [7, 9]]

b) [1, 3, 5, 7, 9]

c) 1, 3, 5, 7, 9

d) Error

10. If my_list = [1, 2, 3, 4, 5, 6], what will be the content of my_list after executing the statement, my_list.insert(-2,-2)

a) [1, -2, 2, 3, 4, 5, 6]

b) [1, 2, -2, 4, 5, 6]

c) [1, 2, 3, 4, -2, 5, 6]

d) Error as index position can't be negative

11. Which of the following statement removes the first element from any list, say my_list?

   a) my_list.remove(0)

   b) my_list.del(0)

   c) my_list.clear(0)

   d) my_list.pop(0)

12. Which data structure allows us to return multiple values from a function?

   a) List

   b) Tuple

   c) Dictionary

   d) Function cannot return multiple values

13. Which of these collections defines a TUPLE?

   a) ("Bca", "Mca", "Btech")

   b) {"Bca", "Mca", "Btech"}

   c) ["Bca", "Mca", "Btech"]

   d) {stream1:"Bca", stream2:"Mca"}

14. If d={1:4, 2:3, 3:2, 4:1}, then the statement `print (d[d[2]])` will print

   a) 2:3

   b) 2

   c) 3

   d) Error

15. Which of the following is not a declaration of the dictionary?

   a) {1: 'A', 2: 'B'}

   b) {1, "A", 2, "B"}

   c) dict([[1, "A"],[2,"B"]])

   d) {}

16. The statement `print ((10,20,30)< (20,30,10))` will print

   a) True

   b) False

   c) Equal

   d) Error

17. Which of the following is True for a Python set?

   a) Sets are unordered

   b) Set does not allow duplicate elements

   c) Sets are written within curly braces { }

   d) All of the above

18. What will be the output of the following code snippet?

```
mySet={1,3,5,7}
mySet.add(4)
mySet.add(5)
print(mySet)
```

a)   {1, 3, 5, 7, 4, 5}

b)   {1, 3, 4, 5, 7}

c)   Error

d)   None of the above

Review Exercises

1.   What are the properties of a list?

2.   What are the differences between an array and a list?

3.   What are the different ways by which a list can be created?

4.   'List items are ordered' – what does it mean?

5.   What will be the output of the following code snippet?

```
mylist=["Techno",[2,4,6,8]]
print(mylist[0])
print(mylist[1])
print(mylist[0][2])
print(mylist[1][2])
```

6.   Explain the slicing operation in a list.

7.   What will be the output of the following code snippet?

```
my_list = [1,2,3,4,5,6,7,8]
print(my_list[2:5])
print(my_list[:5])
print(my_list[5:])
print(my_list[:])
print(my_list[:-5])
print(my_list[-5:])
print(my_list[-2:-5:-1])
print(my_list[::-1])
```

8.   Is it possible to use slicing to modify list elements? What happens if we use slicing and provide less or more elements?

9. What will be the output of the following code snippet?

```
even = [2, 4, 6, 8, 10]
even[0] = 12
print(even)
even[1:4] = [14, 16, 18]
print(even)
even[1:4] = [22, 24, 26, 28]
print(even)
even[1:4] = [20, 25]
print(even)
```

10. Is it possible to add multiple items in a list in a single operation? Explain.

11. What are the different methods in Python by which elements can be added in a list?

12. What will be the output of the following code snippet?

```
my_list = [1,2,3,4]
my_list.insert(2,5)
print(my_list)
my_list.insert(0,7)
print(my_list)
my_list.insert(-2,9)
print(my_list)
```

13. How can we delete multiple items from a list? Explain with an example.

14. Explain different methods that are used to delete items from a list.

15. What is the difference between creating a new list using the '=' operator and the *copy( )* method?

16. Explain the properties of a tuple.

17. Differentiate between a list and a tuple.

18. Create a tuple containing only a single element.

19. What do you mean by packing and unpacking with respect to tuples?

20. What is the utility of a tuple?

21. Is it possible to modify any tuple element? What happens when the following statements are executed?

```
my_tuple = (5, 2, 6, [1, 3])
my_tuple[3][0] = 7
print(my_tuple)
```

22. Is it possible to sort tuple elements?

23. Is it possible to return multiple elements from any function? Explain with example.

24. What is a set in Python? What is its utility?

25. What are the operations that can be done on a set?

26. Differentiate between `discard()` and `remove()` methods.

27. What is the difference between `intersection()` and `intersection_update()` methods?

28. What is the difference between `difference()` and `symmetric_difference()` methods?

29. What is frozenset? Explain with example.

30. What is a dictionary in Python?

31. 'Dictionaries are not sequences, rather they are mappings.' Explain.

32. How can we add elements in a dictionary?

33. Explain different ways by which items can be removed from a dictionary?

34. Differentiate between `get()` and `setdefault()`.

35. What is the utility of the `update()` method in a dictionary?

36. Differentiate between set and dictionary data structures.

37. Explain nested dictionary with example.

Problems for Programming

1. Write a program to create a list containing the first n natural numbers.

2. Write a program to create a list containing odd numbers for a given range.

3. Write a program to create a list containing the first n Fibonacci numbers.

4. Write a program to count the odd and even numbers in a list.

5. Write a program to check whether an inputted number is present or not in a list. If present, print its index position.

6. Write a menu driven program to add, edit, delete and display operations on a list.

7. Write a program to remove all duplicate elements from a list.

8. Write a program to create a list of prime numbers for a given range.

9. Write a program to invert a dictionary, i.e., keys of a dictionary will be values in another dictionary and vice versa.

10. Write a program to find the frequency of each letter in a string.

11. Suppose a list containing duplicate values. Write a function to find the frequency of each number in the list.

12. Write a program to remove the elements from the first set that are also in the second set.

13. Write a program to split a list of tuples into individual lists.

14. Write a program to count the tuples in a list.

15. Write a program to merge two Python dictionaries into one.

16. Write a program to rename a key of a dictionary.

Strings

In the previous two chapters we have studied about arrays and other in-built data structures like lists, tuples, sets and dictionaries. In this chapter we will discuss another in-built data type/data structure of Python, and that is string. In programming languages, string handling is a very important task and in data structure we will learn about different algorithms for efficient string handling.

5.1 Introduction

A string is a sequence of characters allocated contiguously in memory where the characters may be letters of the alphabet, digits, punctuation marks, white spaces or any other symbols. In Python a string is implemented as an object of the in-built class `str`. To define a string constant we may use single quotation (' '), double quotation (" ") or triple quotation (''' '''). So, 'India', "India" and '''India''' – all three are valid string constants in Python. Apart from a normal string, there are two other types of strings. These are escape sequences and raw strings. Like C, C++ and Java programming, Python also supports escape sequences. An escape sequence is the combination of a backslash (\) and another character that together represent a specific meaning escaping from their original meaning when used individually. Table 5.1 shows some escape sequences in Python.

Table 5.1   Escape Sequences

Escape Characters	Represents
\b	Backspace
\f	Form feed
\n	New line
\r	Carriage return

Escape Characters	Represents
\t	Horizontal tab
\'	Single quotation mark
\"	Double quotation mark
\\	Backslash
\ooo	Octal value
\xhh	Hex value

The following example shows the use of escape sequences:

Example 5.1: Example to show the use of escape sequences.

```
print("Hello \nClass!!")
```

Output:
```
Hello
Class!!
```

```
print("Hello \tClass!!")
```

Output:
```
Hello        Class!!
```

```
print('Cat\rM')
```

Output:
```
Mat
```

```
print('Cat\b\bu')
```

Output:
```
Cut
```

```
print("Welcome to the world of \'Python\'")
```

Output:
```
Welcome to the world of 'Python'
```

```
print("\"India\" is great.")
```

Output:

"India" is great.

If a string is preceded by an 'r' or 'R', then it is called a raw string. Within a raw string, escape sequence do not work. They behave like a normal character. Consider the following example:

Example 5.2: Example to show the use of raw string.

```
print('Techno\nIndia')
```

Output:

Techno
India

```
print(r'Techno\nIndia')
```

Output:

Techno\nIndia

```
print('Techno\\India')
```

Output:

Techno\India

```
print(R'Techno\\India')
```

Output:

Techno\\India

5.2 Basic String Operations

Strings are immutable in Python. Hence, we cannot modify a string. But we can create a new string after manipulating an old string. We can extract an individual character or portion of a string. Characters within a string are accessed using the subscript operator and the index value. Index value starts from 0. Negative index is also supported by strings. The index value -1 represents the last character, -2 represents the last but one, and so on. Operations on strings include slicing, concatenation, multiplication and string repetition. There is a large set of methods and functions that can be used to manipulate strings. In this section we briefly discuss all these string operations.

5.2.1 Slicing Operations on String

Like lists, slicing operation can also be done on strings. We can extract a substring from a string using the slicing operation. The general format of slicing is:

```
String_name [ Start : End : Step ]
```

where `Start` is the starting index position from which the extraction operation begins. The extraction operation continues up to the `End - 1` index position and `Step` represents the incremented or decremented value needed to calculate the next index position to extract characters. If `Start` is omitted, the beginning of the string is considered, i.e., the default value of `Start` is 0. If `End` is omitted, the end of the string is considered and the default `Step` value is 1. If we use negative `Step` value, elements will be extracted in the reverse direction. Thus, for negative `Step` value, the default value of `Start` is -1 and that of `End` indicates the beginning of the string. The following example illustrates these concepts:

Example 5.3: Example to show the slicing operation on strings.

```
string = 'Python Programming'
print("string[0]        : ", string[0])
print("string[5]        : ", string[5])
print("string[7:14]     : ", string[7:14])
print("string[7:]       : ", string[7:])
print("string[:6]       : ", string[:6])
print("string[-1]       : ", string[-1])
print("string[-3]       : ", string[-3])
print("string[1:6:2]    : ", string[1:6:2])
print("string[:6:2]     : ", string[:6:2])
print("string[::2]      : ", string[::2])
print("string[:6:-1]    : ", string[:6:-1])
print("string[5::-1]    : ", string[5::-1])
print("string[::-1]     : ", string[::-1])
print("string[-2:-5:-1] : ", string[-2:-5:-1])
```

Output:

```
string[0]   : P
string[5]   : n
string[7:14] : Program
string[7:]  : Programming
string[:6]  : Python
string[-1]  : g
string[-3]  : i
```

```
string[1:6:2] : yhn
string[:6:2] : Pto
string[::2]  : Pto rgamn
string[:6:-1] : gnimmargorP
string[5::-1] : nohtyP
string[::-1] : gnimmargorP nohtyP
string[-2:-5:-1] : nim
```

5.2.2 Concatenation and Repeating Operation on Strings

The operator '+' is used to concatenate two or more strings. The resultant of this operation is a new string. The operator '*' is used to repeat a string a certain number of times. The order of the string and the number is not important. But generally string comes first. Consider the following example:

Example 5.4: Example to show the concatenation and repeating operation on string.

```
firstName = 'Subrata'
lastName  = 'Saha'
name = "Mr. "+firstName+" "+lastName    # Concatenation
print("Name : ", name)


print('-' * 24)         # Repetition of '-' 24 times
print(4 * "Hi !! " )    # Repetition of "Hi !! " 4 times
```

Output:

```
Name : Mr. Subrata Saha
------------------------
Hi !! Hi !! Hi !! Hi !!
```

5.3 Looping through a String

As strings are iterable like lists, we can iterate through a string very easily using the for loop. Consider the following example:

Example 5.5: Write a program to show how to iterate through a string using the for loop.

```
myString = 'Python'
for i in myString:
    print(i, end=' ')
```

Output:

```
Python
```

We can also iterate through a string using index values as follows,

Example 5.6: Write a program to show how to iterate through a string using the index value.

```
myString = 'Python'
for i in range(len(myString)):
    print(myString[i], end=' ')
```

Output:

```
Python
```

We can also use the `while` loop to iterate through a string when using index values. Consider the following example:

Example 5.7: Write a program to show how to iterate through a string using the `while` loop.

```
myString = 'Python'
i=0
while i < len(myString):
    print(myString[i], end=' ')
    i+=1
```

Output:

```
Python
```

5.4 String Methods

Python's `str` class provides several methods for properly handling strings. Here we discuss them briefly.

upper( ): This method converts the entire string into upper case.

lower( ): This method converts the entire string into lower case.

capitalize( ): This method converts the first character of the string into upper case.

casefold( ): This method converts the entire string into lower case. This is similar to lower() but it is more powerful as it able to converts more characters.

title( ): This method converts the first character of each word into upper case.

swapcase( ): This method converts each character into its reverse case, i.e., upper case letter is converted into to lower case and lower case letter into upper case.

center(width [, fillchar]): This method returns a center justified string of specified **width. fillchar** fills the extra positions. If **fillchar** is not specified, extra positions will be filled up with space.

ljust(width [, fillchar]): This method returns a left justified string of specified **width. fillchar** fills the extra positions. If **fillchar** is not specified, extra positions will be filled up with space.

rjust(width [, fillchar]): This method returns a right justified string of specified **width. fillchar** fills the extra positions. If **fillchar** is not specified, extra positions will be filled up with space.

zfill(width): This method returns a right justified string of specified **width** whose extra positions will be filled up with zeros. This method is used with digits.

lstrip( ): This method removes all leading white spaces.

rstrip( ): This method removes all trailing white spaces.

strip( ): This method removes both leading and trailing white spaces.

startswith(Prefix [, Start [, End]]): This method checks whether the string starts with the specified **Prefix.** If so, it returns True. Otherwise it returns False. We can restrict the search area by mentioning **start** and **end.**

endswith(Suffix [, Start [, End]]): This method checks whether the string ends with the specified **Suffix.** If so, it returns True. Otherwise it returns False. We can restrict the search area by mentioning **start** and **end.**

expandtabs(tabsize=8): This method returns a string with the specified **tabsize.** Default tabsize is 8.

count(Sub [, Start [, End]]): This method counts the occurrence of the substring **Sub** in the string. We can restrict the search area by mentioning **start** and **end.**

find(Sub [, Start [, End]]): This method searches the substring **Sub** within the string and returns the index position where it is found. It returns -1 if not found. We can restrict the search area by mentioning **start** and **end.**

rfind(Sub [, Start [, End]]): The operation of this method is the same as the find( ) method but it searches in reverse direction starting from the end.

index(Sub [, Start [, End]]): This method searches the substring **Sub** within the string and returns the index position where it is found. But it raises ValueError exception if not found. We can restrict the search area by mentioning **start** and **end.**

rindex(Sub [, Start [, End]]): Same as index( ) method but it searches in reverse direction starting from end.

replace(Old, New [, Count]): This method replaces the all occurrence of the substring **Old** with the substring **New**. **Count** restricts the maximum number of replacement.

join(Iterable): This method joins each element of the iterable using as delimiter the string for which it is invoked.

split(Sep, Maxsplit): This method splits the string based on the separator **Sep** and returns a list of substrings. If **Sep** is not specified, it splits on white space. Maxsplit restricts the maximum number of splitting.

rsplit(Sep, Maxsplit): This method is the same as split( ) but it starts splitting from right. If **Maxsplit** not specified, then it is the same as the split( ) method.

splitlines([Keepends]): This method splits the string based on the newline character and returns a list of substrings. If **Keepends** is True, the newline characters will be included with the split substring. By default, **Keepends** is False.

isalha( ): This method checks whether all the characters in the string are letters of the alphabet. If so, it returns True; otherwise it returns False.

isalnum( ): This method checks whether all the characters in the string are alphanumeric, i.e., either alphabet or numeric. If so, it returns True; otherwise it returns False.

isdigit( ): This method checks whether all the characters in the string are digits. If so, it returns True; otherwise it returns False.

isdecimal( ): This method checks whether all the characters in the string are decimal numbers. If so, it returns True; otherwise it returns False.

isnumeric( ): This method checks whether all the characters in the string are numeric digits. If so, it returns True; otherwise it returns False.

islower( ): If the string contains at least one letter of the alphabet and all the letters are in lower case, this method returns True; otherwise it returns False.

isupper( ): If the string contains at least one letter of the alphabet and all the letters are in upper case, this method returns True; otherwise it returns False.

isidentifier( ): If the string is a valid identifier, this method returns True; otherwise it returns False.

isspace( ): This method checks whether all the characters in the string are white spaces. If so, it returns True; otherwise it returns False.

istitle( ): If the string is in title case, this method returns True; otherwise it returns False.

Apart from these methods Python string supports some built-in functions also. Here are some of them:

len( ): This function returns the length of a string, i.e., number of characters in the string.

enumerate(iterable, Start=0): This function returns an enumerate object containing all the characters and their index position as a tuple. **Start** indicates the starting index position from which this operation will begin. To access the generated enumerated object, the `for` loop needs to be used or the enumerated object needs to be converted to a list using *list( )*.

sorted( ): This function returns a list containing the characters of the string in ascending order.

The following example shows the use of string methods and functions.

Example 5.8: Write a program to show the use of string methods and functions.

```
string='PYTHON programming'
print("String : ",string)
print("string.capitalize(): ", string.capitalize())
print("string.casefold()   : ", string.casefold())
print("string.upper()      : ", string.upper())
print("string.lower()      : ", string.lower())
print("string.title()      : ", string.title())
print("string.swapcase()   : ", string.swapcase())
print()

string='Python'
print("|String|                 : ",'|'+string+'|')
print("|string.center(10)|      : ",'|'+string.
                                      center(10)+'|')
print("|string.center(10,'*')|: ",'|'+string.
                                      center(10,'*')+'|')
print("|string.ljust(10)|       : ",'|'+string.
                                      ljust(10)+'|')
print("|string.rjust(10,'*')| : ",'|'+string.
                                      rjust(10,'*')+'|')
print("|string.zfill(10)|       : ",'|'+string.
                                      zfill(10)+'|')
print("string.startswith('Py'): ", string.
                                      startswith('Py'))
print("string.endswith('on')  : ", string.endswith('on'))
print()

string=' Python '
print("|String|                : ", '|'+string+'|')
print("|string.lstrip()| : ", '|'+string.lstrip()+'|')
```

```
print("|string.rstrip()| : ", '|'+string.rstrip()+'|')
print("|string.strip()|  : ", '|'+string.strip()+'|')

string='Python\tProgramming'
print("string.expandtabs()  : ", string.expandtabs())
print("string.expandtabs(10): ", string.expandtabs(10))
print()

string='Programming'
print("String             : ",string)
print("string.count('r' ) : ", string.count('r'))
print("string.find('r')   : ", string.find('r'))
print("string.rfind('r')  : ", string.rfind('r'))
print("string.index('r')  : ", string.index('r'))
print("string.rindex('r') : ", string.rindex('r'))
print("string.replace('r','R')  : ", string.
                                    replace('r','R'))
print("string.replace('r','R',1): ", string.
                                    replace('r','R',1))
print("string.join(['1','2','3']) : ", string.
                                    join(['1','2','3']))
print("' '.join(['1','2','3']) : ", '
                                    '.join(['1','2','3']))
print("string.split('r')    : ", string.split('r'))
print("string.split('r',1)  : ", string.split('r',1))
print("string.rsplit('r')   : ", string.rsplit('r'))
print("string.rsplit('r',1) : ", string.rsplit('r',1))
print()

string='World\nof\nPython'
print("string.splitlines() : ", string.splitlines())
print("string.splitlines(True) : ", string.
                                    splitlines(True))
print()

string='1234'
print("String : ", string)
print("string.isdecimal() : ", string.isdecimal())
print("string.isnumeric() : ", string.isnumeric())
print()

string='Python'
```

```
print("String : ", string)
print("string.isalpha() : ", string.isalpha())
print("string.isalnum() : ", string.isalnum())
print("string.isdigit() : ", string.isdigit())
print("string.islower() : ", string.islower())
print("string.isupper() : ", string.isupper())
print("string.isidentifier() : ", string.isidentifier())
print("string.isspace() : ", string.isspace())
print("string.istitle() : ", string.istitle())

print("len(string)        : ", len(string))
print("list(enumerate(string)): ",
                            list(enumerate(string)))
print("sorted(string)     : ", sorted(string))
```

Output:

```
String : PYTHON programming
string.capitalize(): Python programming
string.casefold() : python programming
string.upper()   : PYTHON PROGRAMMING
string.lower()   : python programming
string.title()   : Python Programming
string.swapcase() : python PROGRAMMING

|String|         : |Python|
|string.center(10)|  : | Python |
|string.center(10,'*')|: |**Python**|
|string.ljust(10)|   : |Python   |
|string.rjust(10,'*')| : |****Python|
|string.zfill(10)|   : |0000Python|
string.startswith('Py'): True
string.endswith('on') : True

|String|      : | Python |
|string.lstrip()| : |Python |
|string.rstrip()| : | Python|
|string.strip()|  : |Python|
string.expandtabs() : Python  Programming
string.expandtabs(10): Python    Programming
```

```
String        : Programming
string.count('r' ) : 2
string.find('r')  : 1
string.rfind('r') : 4
string.index('r') : 1
string.rindex('r') : 4
string.replace('r','R')  : PRogRamming
string.replace('r','R',1): PRogramming
string.join(['1','2','3']) : 1Programming2Programming3
' '.join(['1','2','3']) : 1 2 3
string.split('r')  : ['P', 'og', 'amming']
string.split('r',1) : ['P', 'ogramming']
string.rsplit('r')  : ['P', 'og', 'amming']
string.rsplit('r',1): ['Prog', 'amming']

string.splitlines() : ['World', 'of', 'Python']
string.splitlines(True) : ['World\n', 'of\n', 'Python']

String : 1234
string.isdecimal() : True
string.isnumeric() : True

String : Python
string.isalpha() : True
string.isalnum() : True
string.isdigit() : False
string.islower() : False
string.isupper() : False
string.isidentifier() : True
string.isspace() : False
string.istitle() : True
len(string)    : 6
list(enumerate(string)): [(0, 'P'), (1, 'y'), (2, 't'), (3, 'h'), (4, 'o'), (5, 'n')]
sorted(string)  : ['P', 'h', 'n', 'o', 't', 'y']
```

The Python string module also provides some useful string constants that help us in handling string. These are shown in Table 5.2. Remember, to use these constants first we need to import the string module.

Table 5.2 String constants

Constant Name	Value
ascii_lowercase	'abcdefghijklmnopqrstuvwxyz'
ascii_uppercase	'ABCDEFGHIJKLMNOPQRSTUVWXYZ'
ascii_letters	'ABCDEFGHIJKLMNOPQRSTUVWXYZabcdefghijklmnopqrstuvwxyz'
digits	'0123456789'
hexdigits	'0123456789abcdefABCDEF'
octdigits	'01234567'
punctuation	!"#$%&'()*+,-./:;<=>?@[\]^_`{|}~
whitespace	Includes space, new line, tab, linefeed and formfeed

5.5 String Comparison

Python allows us to compare two strings using the relational operators just like comparing numeric values. All the relational operators, i.e., >, <, >=, <=, == and != or <>, are used to compare strings. At the time of comparison, characters of corresponding index positions of two strings are compared. First, characters of 0th index positions of two strings are compared. If they are equal, characters of the next index positions are compared. When a mismatch occurs, ASCII values of the mismatched characters are compared. Suppose String1= "Anand" and String2 = "Anil". Here, the first two characters of both the strings are same. Mismatch occurs at index position 2. At this position String1 contains 'a' and String2 contains 'i'. As the ASCII value of 'a' is less than that of 'i', the condition String1<String2 will be True. Some other cases have been shown in the following example:

Example 5.9: Write a program to show string comparison.

```
print("'Java'>'Python' : ", 'Java'>'Python')
print("'Java'<'Python' : ", 'Java'<'Python')
print("'Anil'>='Anand' : ", 'Anil'>='Anand')
print("'Python'<='PYTHON' : ", 'Python'<='PYTHON')
print("'Python'=='Python' : ", 'Python'=='Python')
print("'Python'!='python' : ", 'Python'!='python')
```

Output:

'Java'>'Python': False
'Java'<'Python': True

'Anil'>='Anand' : True
'Python'<='PYTHON' : False
'Python'=='Python' : True
'Python'!='python' : True

5.6 Regular Expressions

Along with several methods for string handling, Python also provides a unique feature called RegEx or Regular Expression or simply RE, which is nothing but a sequence of characters and some meta-characters that forms a search pattern. Instead of searching a particular word, regular expressions help us to find a particular pattern in a text, code, file, log or spreadsheet, i.e., in any type of documents. For example, the string find() method helps us to search a particular email id; but if we want to find all the email ids in a document, Regular Expression is the solution. In Python this feature is available through the **re** module.

To avail this feature first we need to create a pattern. Within the pattern we may use several meta-characters and these meta-characters are shown in Table 5.3.

Table 5.3   Meta-characters in regular expression

Character	Description	Example
[]	A set of characters	"[aeiou]"
\	Signals a special sequence	"\d"
.	Any single character (except newline character)	".oo."
^	Starts with	"^hello"
$	Ends with	"world$"
*	Zero or more occurrences of the character left to it	"bel*"
?	Zero or one occurrence of the character left to it	"hel?o"
+	One or more occurrences of the character left to it	"hel+o"
{n}	Exactly the specified number of occurrences of the character left to it	"al{2}"
{n,}	specified or more number of occurrences of the character left to it	"al{2,}"
{n,m}	At least **n** and at most **m** number of occurrences of the character left to it	"al{2,4}"
|	Either or	"mca|btech"
()	Capture and group	"(B|C|M)at"

In the table of meta-characters the first column represents the character set. Table 5.4 shows the uses of the character set with some examples.

Table 5.4 Use of character set in meta-character

Character Set	Description
[aeiou]	Returns a match where one of the specified characters (a, e, i, o or u) is present
[a-e]	Returns a match for any lower case character which is alphabetically between a and e
[^aeiou]	Returns a match for any character EXCEPT a, e, i, o and u
[345]	Returns a match where any of the specified digits (3, 4 or 5) is present
[0-9]	Returns a match for any digit between 0 and 9
[0-5][0-9]	Returns a match for any two-digit number from 00 and 59
[a-zA-Z]	Returns a match for any alphabet character in lower case OR upper case
[+]	In character set, +, *, ., |, (), $,{} has no special meaning. Hence, [+] returns a match for any + character in the string

Different special sequences and their uses have been shown in Table 5.5.

Table 5.5 Special sequences in meta-character

Character	Description	Example
\A	Returns a match if the specified characters are at the beginning of the string	"\AThe"
\b	Returns a match where the specified characters are at the beginning or at the end of a word (the "r" in the beginning is to indicate that the string is being treated as a "raw string")	r"\baim" r"aim\b"
\B	Returns a match where the specified characters are present, but NOT at the beginning (or at the end) of a word (the "r" in the beginning is to indicate that the string is being treated as a "raw string")	r"\Baim" r"aim\B"
\d	Returns a match where the string contains digits (i.e., from 0 to 9)	"\d"
\D	Returns a match where the string DOES NOT contain any digit	"\D"
\s	Returns a match where the string contains any white space character	"\s"
\S	Returns a match where the string DOES NOT contain any white space character	"\S"

Character	Description	Example
\w	Returns a match where the string contains any word character (i.e., characters from a to Z, digits from 0 to 9, or the underscore ' _ ' character)	"\w"
\W	Returns a match where the string DOES NOT contain any word character	"\W"
\Z	Returns a match if the specified characters are at the end of the string	"aim\Z"

Now we will discuss the different functions that are used to search a pattern.

match( ): This function checks whether the pattern matches at the beginning of the given string or not. If so, it returns a match object; otherwise None. The general format of match() is:

```
re.match(Pattern, String, Flag=0)
```

where the first argument **Pattern** is to find the pattern in the **String**. The values of the **Flag** variable are discussed in Table 5.6.

Table 5.6 Option flags

Flags	Description
re.I or re.IGNORECASE	Performs matching operation ignoring case.
re.M or re.MULTILINE	Instead of only the end of the string, '$' matches the end of each line and instead of only the beginning of the string, '^' matches the beginning of any line.
re.S or re.DOTALL	Makes a dot (.) to match any character, including newline character.
re.L or re.LOCALE	Makes the flag \w to match all characters that are considered letters in the given current locale settings.
re.X	Ignores white space characters.

Consider the following example:

Example 5.10: Write a program to show the use of match().

```
import re

string = '15/08/1947 is the Independance day of India'
# Finding a date in the format DD/MM/YYYY
```

```
pattern = '\d{2}/\d{2}/\d{4}'
match = re.match(pattern, string)
if match:       # match variable contains a match object.
  print('The string contains a date')
else:
  print('The date pattern not found')
```

Output:

The string contains a date

The match object has different methods that provide us valuable information about the search. These are briefly described in Table 5.7.

Table 5.7   Methods of match object

Method	Description
group( )	Returns the string matched by any RE method
start( )	Returns the starting index position in the match string
end( )	Returns the ending index position in the match string
span()	Returns a tuple containing the (start, end) positions in the match string

Consider the following example which shows the use of methods of the match object:

Example 5.11: Write a program to show the use of methods of the match object.

```
import re

string = '15/08/1947 is the Independence day of India'
pattern = '\d{2}/\d{2}/\d{4}'
match = re.match(pattern, string)
if match:
    print("The matching String : ", match.group())
    print("Starting Index : ", match.start())
    print("End Index      : ", match.end())
    print("The span       : ", match.span())
else:
    print("The date pattern not found")
```

Output:

The matching String : 15/08/1947
Starting Index : 0
End Index   : 10
The span   : (0, 10)

We can also create a group by surrounding a portion of the regular expression using parentheses and hence easily extract the required information from that. Consider the following example:

Example 5.12: Write a program to show grouping in the regular expression.

```python
import re
string = '15/08/1947 is the Independence day of India'
pattern = '(\d{2})/(\d{2})/(\d{4})'
match = re.match(pattern, string)
if match:
    print("The matching String : ", match.group())
    print("Day    : ", match.group(1))
    print("Month  : ", match.group(2))
    print("Year   : ", match.group(3))
    print("Starting Index : ", match.start())
    print("End Index      : ", match.end())
    print("The span       : ", match.span())
else:
    print("the date pattern not found")
```

Output:

The matching String : 15/08/1947
Day : 15
Month : 08
Year : 1947
Starting Index : 0
End Index   : 10
The span   : (0, 10)

search( ): This method is almost same as `match()` but instead of searching only at the beginning of the string, it searches for a pattern anywhere in the given string and returns a match object on success. The general format of `search()` is:

```python
re.search(Pattern, String, Flag=0)
```

where the first argument **Pattern** is to find the pattern anywhere in the **String**. The values of the **Flag** variable are discussed in Table 5.6. Consider the following example:

Example 5.13: Write a program to show the use of search().

```
import re
string = "Contact number of Mr. Aniket Barua is 98345
                                                 23701 "
# Finding a mobile number in the format, 5 digits followed
# by a space followed by 5 digits
pattern = '\d{5} \d{5}'
match = re.search(pattern, string)
if match:
    print("Contact Number : ", match.group())
else:
    print("Contact Number not found")
```

Output:

Contact Number : 98345 23701

findall( ): findall () returns a list containing all matches found in the given string. The general format of findall () is:

re.findall(Pattern, String, Flag=0)

where the first argument **Pattern** is to find all occurrences of the pattern in the **String**. The values of the **Flag** variable are discussed in Table 5.6. Consider the following example:

Example 5.14: Write a program to show the use of findall().

```
import re
string = 'Today is 12/01/2022 - Birthday of Swami \
Vivekananda and the Independence day of India is \
15/08/1947.'
# Finding dates in the format DD/MM/YYYY
pattern = '\d{2}/\d{2}/\d{4}'
result = re.findall(pattern, string)
if result:
    print("Dates found are : ")
    for i in result:
        print(i)
else:
    print('The date pattern not found')
```

Output:

Dates found are :
12/01/2022
15/08/1947

finditer( ): This function finds all substrings where the regular expression matches and returns them as an iterator. If no match found, then also it returns an iterator. The general format of `finditer()` is:

```
re.finditer(Pattern, String, Flag=0)
```

where the first argument **Pattern** is to find the all occurrence of the pattern in the **String**. The values of the **Flag** variable are discussed in Table 5.6. Consider the following example:

Example 5.15: Write a program to show the use of `finditer()`.

```
import re
string = 'Today is 12/01/2022 - Birthday of Swami \
Vivekananda and the Independence day of India is \
15/08/1947.'
pattern = '\d{2}/\d{2}/\d{4}'
result = re.finditer(pattern, string)
for i in result:
    print('Date', i.group(), 'found at span', i.span())
```

Output:

Date 12/01/2022 found at span (9, 19)
Date 15/08/1947 found at span (89, 99)

split( ): This function splits the string into substrings based on the positions where the pattern matches in the original string and returns these substrings as a list. The general format of `split()` is:

```
re.split(Pattern, String, Flag=0)
```

where the first argument **Pattern** is to find all occurrences of the pattern in the **String** to split the string. The values of the **Flag** variable are discussed in Table 5.6. Consider the following example:

Example 5.16: Write a program to show the use of `split()`.

```
import re
string = 'This    is \tan\nexample'
```

```
pattern = '\s+'
result = re.split(pattern, string)
print(result)
```

Output:

['This', 'is', 'an', 'example']

sub( ): The sub() function substitutes all or a specified number of occurrences of the pattern in the string with the replacement substring. The general format of sub() is:

re.sub(Pattern, Repl, String, Max=0)

where the first argument **Pattern** is to find and replace with **Repl** in the **String** all or **Max** number of occurrences. Consider the following example:

Example 5.17: Write a program to show the use of sub() by replacing '/' or '–' with '.'

```
import re
string = 'Today is 12/01/2022, Birthday of Swami \
Vivekananda and the Independence day of India is \
15-08-1947.'
result1 = re.sub('[/-]', '.', string)
print("Replacing all occurrences : ", result1)
result2 = re.sub('[/-]', '.', string, 2)
print("\nReplacing first two occurrences : ", result2)
```

Output:

Replacing all occurrences : Today is 12.01.2022, Birthday of Swami Vivekananda and the Independence day of India is 15.08.1947.

Replacing first two occurrences : Today is 12.01.2022, Birthday of Swami Vivekananda and the Independence day of India is 15-08-1947.

5.7 Pattern Matching Algorithms

Pattern matching algorithms find a pattern or substring in a string. There are several pattern matching algorithms in computer science. The efficiency of these algorithms depends on the total number of comparisons in the algorithm. Here we will discuss two pattern matching algorithms: Brute Force pattern matching algorithm and Knuth Morris Pratt pattern matching algorithm.

5.7.1 Brute Force Pattern Matching Algorithm

The Brute Force pattern matching algorithm is the simplest pattern matching algorithm. It is a basic or naïve type search algorithm where the pattern is searched exhaustively in the main string. In this algorithm, starting from the first position of the main string each character of the pattern string is compared with each character of the main string. If all the characters of the pattern match with a certain portion of the main string, the algorithm returns the starting index position of the matched portion of the string. But if the match fails at any stage, the comparison starts again from the next index position of the current comparison's starting position of the main string. Consider the following example:

Example 5.18: Using the Brute Force pattern matching algorithm, find the pattern 'ABC' in the string 'ABDEABFAABC'.

Solution:

	0	1	2	3	4	5	6	7	8	9	10
String:	A	B	D	E	A	B	F	A	A	B	C
Pattern:	A	B	C								

The algorithm starts the comparison from the beginning of the main string, i.e., from the index position 0. Now the first two characters of both strings are the same but a mismatch occurs with the third character. So, searching again starts from index position 1 of the main string.

	0	1	2	3	4	5	6	7	8	9	10
String:	A	B	D	E	A	B	F	A	A	B	C
Pattern:		A									

But mismatch occurs. Hence, we start searching again from index position 2.

	0	1	2	3	4	5	6	7	8	9	10
String:	A	B	D	E	A	B	F	A	A	B	C
Pattern:			A								

Again mismatch occurs and we start searching from index position 3.

	0	1	2	3	4	5	6	7	8	9	10
String:	A	B	D	E	A	B	F	A	A	B	C
Pattern:				A							

Again mismatch occurs and we start searching from index position 4.

	0	1	2	3	4	5	6	7	8	9	10
String:	A	B	D	E	A	B	F	A	A	B	C
Pattern:					A	B	C				

Now, the first character of the pattern matches with the character of index position 4. So, we proceed to compare the second character of the pattern and the character of index position 5. They also match. So, we proceed again to compare the third character of the pattern and the character of index position 6. But this time mismatch occurs. Hence, we need to start searching again and it will be from index position 5 of the main string.

	0	1	2	3	4	5	6	7	8	9	10
String:	A	B	D	E	A	B	F	A	A	B	C
Pattern:					A						
Pattern:						A					
Pattern:							A	B			

Again mismatch occurs and we start searching from index position 6. Again mismatch occurs and search start from index position 7. This time matching occurs but the corresponding next characters are not the same. Thus, again we start searching from index position 8.

	0	1	2	3	4	5	6	7	8	9	10
String:	A	B	D	E	A	B	F	A	A	B	C
Pattern:									A	B	C

This time all the three characters of the pattern match with the eighth, ninth, and tenth characters of the main string correspondingly. Hence, the search operation becomes True and it returns 8 as the index position from where matching starts.

If the length of the string is n and the length of the pattern is m, in this algorithm we need to search the pattern almost n times, and in the worst case, mismatch will occur with the last character of the pattern. Hence, we need to compare $n \times m$ times in the worst case. So, we can say that the worst case time complexity is $O(nm)$. However, in the best case, by traversing the first m characters of the main string we can get the match and, hence, the best case time complexity can be calculated as $O(m)$.

Program 5.1: Write a program to demonstrate the Brute Force pattern matching algorithm.

```
# PRGD5_1: Brute Force pattern matching algorithm

def Brute_Force(s,p):
    l1 = len(s)
```

```
l2 = len(p)
for i in range(l1-l2+1):
    flag = True
    for j in range(l2):
        if (s[i+j]!=p[j]):
            flag = False
            break
    if flag:
        return i
return -1

string = input("Enter the String: ")
pattern = input("Enter the pattern: ")
index = Brute_Force(string, pattern)
if index!= -1:
    print("The pattern found at index position ", index)
else:
    print("Pattern not found")
```

Sample Output:

Enter the String: data structure in python

Enter the pattern: structure

The pattern found at index position 5

Enter the String: data structure in python

Enter the pattern: database

Pattern not found

5.7.2 Knuth Morris Pratt Pattern Matching Algorithm

The main disadvantage of the basic or naïve type search algorithms is that every time we have to compare each character of the pattern with the main string. If there is some repetition of the same sequence of characters within the pattern and that matches with the main string, the algorithm does not bother about it. But the Knuth Morris Pratt (KMP) pattern matching algorithm studies the pattern carefully and considers the repetitions, if any, and hence avoids the back tracking.

Before starting the discussion of this algorithm, first we need to know some keywords related to this algorithm. These are prefix, suffix and the π table. To find the prefix, we start from beginning of the string and take the subset by considering one, two, three, ... characters. For example, prefixes of the string 'ADCBEAD' are A, AD, ADC, etc. Similarly, the suffixes of this string are D, AD, EAD, etc. The idea behind the KMP algorithm is to find out if there is any common prefix and suffix within the string. This indicates that there may be situation where the searching operation may fail but the prefix of the pattern may match with the suffix of the portion of the original string. This helps us not to back track fully like the naïve approach; rather we may now continue from this position even if there is some overlapping portion in the main string. Next we need to find the π table or LPS (Longest Prefix that is also a Suffix) table. From the LPS table, we are able to find the index position of the repeating prefix. To construct the LPS table, we start searching from the second character (i.e., index position 1) and compare each and every character with the first character (i.e., character of the index position 0). If a match does not occur, we set the value as 0. But if match occurs, we set the corresponding value as 1 and check whether the next character also matches with the second character of the string. If so, we set the value 2 for the character to indicate the longest prefix size as 2. This process continues and we get the longest prefix in a word that is also repeated within that word. Here are some examples of a few words and their corresponding LPS table.

Example 5.19: Construct the LPS table for the following words.

   i.   CUCUMBER

  ii.   TOMATO

 iii.   TICTAC

Solution:

i.

	0	1	2	3	4	5	6	7
String:	C	U	C	U	M	B	E	R
LPS Table:	0	0	1	2	0	0	0	0

ii.

	0	1	2	3	4	5
String:	T	O	M	A	T	O
LPS Table:	0	0	0	0	1	2

iii.

	0	1	2	3	4	5
String:	T	I	C	T	A	C
LPS Table:	0	0	0	1	0	0

The Knuth Morris Pratt pattern matching algorithm works on the basis of this LPS table. In this algorithm, starting from the first position of the main string, each character of the pattern string is compared with each character of the main string. For both strings we need to take two different pointers/indicators to point at the character of the individual string. If the corresponding characters do not match, only the pointer of the main string proceeds to point at the next character. But if the corresponding characters do match, both pointers proceed to point at the next character of their corresponding string. After started matching if any mismatch occurs, instead of backtracking the entire pattern, pointer of the pattern string finds the corresponding value from the LPS table and move back only to that value so that common prefix need not traverse again. From this position both the pointers start comparing again. If the comparison fails again, the algorithm checks whether the pointer of the pattern string is at the beginning of the string or not. If it is at beginning of the string, pointer of the main string proceeds to point the next character of the string as there is no chance of overlapping pattern; otherwise the pointer of the pattern string moves back according to the corresponding value from the LPS table. When all the characters match with the portion of the main string, algorithm returns the starting index of the matched portion. But if the pointer of the main string reaches the end of the string and the pattern is not found, the algorithm returns -1. Following example illustrates this concept.

Example 5.20: Using the KMP pattern matching algorithm, find the pattern 'ABABC' in the string 'ABABDEABABABC'.

Solution: First we have to create the LPS table for the pattern 'ABABC'.

	0	1	2	3	4
Pattern:	A	B	A	B	C
LPS Table:	0	0	1	2	0

Now we initialize two variables as i = 0 and j = 0 and start comparison.

	0	1	2	3	4	5	6	7	8	9	10	11	12
String:	A	B	A	B	D	E	A	B	A	B	A	B	C
	i												
Pattern:	A	B	A	B	C								
	j													

As String[0] == Pattern[0] is True, both i and j will be incremented by 1. Hence, both i and j become 1. Again, String[1] == Pattern[1] is True. Hence, both i and j are incremented and become 2. Again, String[2] == Pattern[2] is True. Hence, both i and j are incremented and become 3. This time also, String[3] and Pattern[3] are same. Hence, both i and j are incremented to 4.

	0	1	2	3	4	5	6	7	8	9	10	11	12
String:	A	B	A	B	D	E	A	B	A	B	A	B	C
					i								
Pattern:	A	B	A	B	C								
					j									

Now, String[4] and Pattern[4] are not the same. So, we will check the LPS table for j-1 and find LPSTable[3] is 2. Hence, j will be reset to 2.

	0	1	2	3	4	5	6	7	8	9	10	11	12
String:	A	B	A	B	D	E	A	B	A	B	A	B	C
					i								
Pattern:	A	B	A	B	C								
				j									

Now the search process starts again and fails at immediate comparison as `String[4]` and `Pattern[2]` are not same. So, we again check LPS table for j-1 and find LPSTable[1] is 0. Hence, j will be reset to 0.

	0	1	2	3	4	5	6	7	8	9	10	11	12
String:	A	B	A	B	D	E	A	B	A	B	A	B	C
					i								
Pattern:	A	B	A	B	C								
	j												

Now the search process starts again and fails at immediate comparison as `String[4]` and `Pattern[0]` are not same. But now, value of j is 0. So, i will now be incremented.

	0	1	2	3	4	5	6	7	8	9	10	11	12
String:	A	B	A	B	D	E	A	B	A	B	A	B	C
						i							
Pattern:	A	B	A	B	C								
	j												

Now, `String[5]` is ≠ `Pattern[0]` and j is also 0. Hence, i will be incremented again.

	0	1	2	3	4	5	6	7	8	9	10	11	12
String:	A	B	A	B	D	E	A	B	A	B	A	B	C
							i						
Pattern:	A	B	A	B	C								
	j												

This time `String[6]` and `Pattern[0]` are equal. So, both i and j will be incremented by 1. Hence, i becomes 7 and j becomes 1.

	0	1	2	3	4	5	6	7	8	9	10	11	12
String :	A	B	A	B	D	E	A	B	A	B	A	B	C
								i					
Pattern:	A	B	A	B	C								
		j											

Again, `String[7]` and `Pattern[1]` are equal. So, both i and j will be incremented by 1 and i becomes 8 and j becomes 2. This is also true for next two comparisons. So, i becomes 10 and j becomes 4.

	0	1	2	3	4	5	6	7	8	9	10	11	12
String:	A	B	A	B	D	E	A	B	A	B	A	B	C
											i		
Pattern:	A	B	A	B	C								
					j								

But now, `String[10]` and `Pattern[4]` are not the same. So, we will check the LPS table for j-1 and find LPSTable[3] is 2. Hence, j will be reset to 2.

	0	1	2	3	4	5	6	7	8	9	10	11	12
String:	A	B	A	B	D	E	A	B	A	B	A	B	C
											i		
Pattern:	A	B	A	B	C								
			j										

Now, `String[10]` and `Pattern[2]` are equal. So, both i and j will be incremented by 1 and i becomes 11 and j becomes 3. This is also true for the next comparison. So, i becomes 12 and j becomes 4.

	0	1	2	3	4	5	6	7	8	9	10	11	12
String:	A	B	A	B	D	E	A	B	A	B	A	B	C
													i
Pattern:	A	B	A	B	C								
					j								

As j has reached the end of the pattern and still matching continues, we can now say that the pattern is found in the main string and it is at i-j, i.e., at index position 8.

The main advantage of this algorithm is that we need not move back in the main string. This is clear from the previous example as well, where the value of i never decreases or is reset to some lower value. It is always incremented and if there is some overlapping portion in the main string we need not set the pointer of the pattern to 0; we are continuing with the matched prefix of the pattern and the suffix of the main string. Hence we get the solution in linear time. If the size of the string is *n* and the size of the pattern is *m*, to construct the LPS table $O(m)$ running time is required and the KMP algorithm requires $O(n)$ time as generally *m* is very small in comparison to *n*. Hence, the overall time complexity of the KMP algorithm is $O(m+n)$.

The general algorithm of a KMP algorithm may be defined as follows:

```
KMP_Algorithm( String, Pattern)
```

Here String and Pattern are the two strings. Pattern is to be searched within String.

1. Set L1 = Length of String
2. Set L2 = Length of Pattern
3. Create LPS Table.
4. Set i = 0
5. Set j = 0
6. While i < L1, do
   a. If String[i] == Patter[j], then
      i. Set i = i + 1
      ii. Set j = j + 1
   b. Else
      i. If j != 0, then
         1. Set j = LPSTable[j-1]
      ii. Else,
         1. Set i = i + 1
   c. If j == L2, then
      i. Return i-j
7. Return -1

Here is a complete program to show the implementation of the KMP algorithm.

Program 5.2: Write a program to demonstrate the KMP pattern matching algorithm.

```
# PRGD5_2: Implementation of KMP Pattern Matching
# Algorithm

def createLpsTable(pattern):
    l = len(pattern)
    i=1
    j=0
    lpsTable = [0]* l
    while i < l:
        if pattern[i] == pattern[j]:
            lpsTable[i] = j+1
            j+=1
            i+=1
        else:
            if j != 0:
                j=lpsTable[j-1]
            else:
```

```
                    lpsTable[i] = 0
                    i+=1
        return lpsTable

def KMP(string, pattern):
    l1 = len(string)
    l2 = len(pattern)
    lpsTable=createLpsTable(pattern)
    i=0
    j=0
    while i < l1:
        if string[i] == pattern[j]:
            i+=1
            j+=1
        else:
            if j != 0:
                j=lpsTable[j-1]
            else:
                i+=1
        if j == l2:
            return(i-j)

    return -1

string = input("Enter the String: ")
pattern = input("Enter the pattern: ")
index = KMP(string, pattern)
if index!= -1:
    print("The pattern found at index position ", index)
else:
    print("Pattern not found")
```

Sample Output:

Enter the String: But Butter Is Bitter
Enter the pattern: Butter
The pattern found at index position 4

Enter the String: But Butter Is Bitter
Enter the pattern: Better
Pattern not found

5.8 Programming Example

Here are some programming examples to understand the various operations that can be performed on a string.

Program 5.3: Write a program to count the number of words in a string.

```
#PRGD5_3 : Program to count the number of words in a
#string.

string = input("Enter any string: ")
words=string.split()
count = len(words)
print("No. of words =", count)
```

Sample Output:

Enter any string: This is an   example.
No. of words = 4

Program 5.4: Write a program to count the number of non-space characters in a string.

```
#PRGD5_4 : Program to count the number of non space
#characters  in a string.

string = input("Enter any string: ")
c=0
for i in string:
    if i != ' ':
        c+=1

print("No. of non space characters =", c)
```

Sample Output:

Enter any string: His Roll number is 35.
No. of non space characters = 18

Program 5.5: Write a program to remove extra spaces between words in a string.

```
#PRGD5_5 : Program to remove extra spaces between words in
#a string.

string = input("Enter any string: ")
```

```
words  = string.split()
newStr = ' '.join(words)
print("After Removing Extra Spaces : ", newStr)
```

Sample Output:

Enter any string: This is   an   Example.
After Removing Extra Spaces : This is an Example.

Program 5.6: Write a program to count the number of vowels, consonants, digits and punctuation marks in a string.

```
#PRGD5_6 : Program to count the number of vowels,
#consonants, digits and punctuation marks in a string.

import string
strn = input("Enter any string: ")
v=0
c=0
d=0
p=0
for i in strn:
    ch=i.upper()
    if ch in  'AEIOU':
        v+=1
    elif ch.isalpha():
        c+=1
    elif ch.isdigit():
        d+=1
    elif (ch in string.punctuation):
        p+=1

print("No. of Vowels =", v)
print("No. of Consonants =", c)
print("No. of Digits =", d)
print("No. of Punctuation Marks =", p)
```

Sample Output:

Enter any string: Ram's date of birth is : 13/08/1997.
No. of Vowels = 6
No. of Consonants = 11
No. of Digits = 8
No. of Punctuation Marks = 5

Program 5.7: Write a program to check whether a string is a palindrome or not.

```
#PRGD 5_7 : Program to check whether a string is a
#palindrome or not.

string = input("Enter any String: ")
revString=string[::-1]
if string == revString:
    print("Palindrome")
else:
    print("Not a Palindrome")
```

Sample Output:

```
Enter any String: madam
Palindrome

Enter any String: Sir
Not a Palindrome
```

Program 5.8: Write a program that would sort a list of names in alphabetical order.

```
#PRGD 5_8 : Program to sort a list of names in
#alphabetical order.

names=[]
n=int(input("Enter number of Names: "))
for i in range(n):
    name = input("Enter Name %d: "%(i+1))
    names.append(name)

for i in range(n-1):
    for j in range(n-1-i):
        if names[j]>names[j+1]:
            temp = names[j]
            names[j]=names[j+1]
            names[j+1]=temp

print("\nSorted List of names:")
for i in names:
    print(i)
```

Sample Output:

Enter number of Names: 5
Enter Name 1: Bikram
Enter Name 2: Malini
Enter Name 3: Aanand
Enter Name 4: Dipesh
Enter Name 5: Aakash

Sorted List of names:
Aakash
Aanand
Bikram
Dipesh
Malini

Program 5.9: Write a program that will convert each character (only letters) of a string into the next letter of the alphabet.

```
#PRGD 5_9 : Program to convert each character(only
#letters) of a string into the next letter of the
#alphabet.

def encrypt(string):
    encStr=''
    for i in string:
        if i.isalpha():
            if i=='z':
                s=97
            elif i=='Z':
                s=65
            else:
                s=ord(i)+1
            encStr+=chr(s)
        else:
            encStr+=i
    return encStr

st=input("Enter any String: ")
newSt=encrypt(st)
print("Encrypted String:", newSt)
```

Sample Output:

Enter any String: Welcome to Zoo!!
Encrypted String: Xfmdpnf up App!!

Program 5.10: Write a program to find the partial abbreviation of a name.

```
#PRGD 5_10 : Program to find the partial abbreviation of a
#name.

def abbreviation(name):
    nameList=name. title().split()
    l=len(nameList)
    abbr=''
    for i in range(l-1):
        abbr+=nameList[i][0]+'.'
    abbr+=nameList[l-1]
    return abbr

name=input("Enter Your Name: ")
abbrName=abbreviation(name)
print("Your Abbreviated Name is :", abbrName)
```

Sample Output:

Enter Your Name: Vangipurapu Venkata Sai Laxman
Your Abbreviated Name is : V.V.S.Laxman

Program 5.11: Write a program to find the frequency of each word in a string.

```
#PRGD 5_11 : Program to find the frequency of each word in
#a string.

def countFrequency(string):
    wordDict={}
    words=string.split()
    for w in words:
        wordDict[w]=wordDict.get(w,0)+1
    return wordDict

st=input("Enter any String: ")
countDict=countFrequency(st)
print("Frequency of the words in the String:")
```

```
for k,v in countDict.items():
    print(k, ':', v)
```

Sample Output:

Enter any String: the boy is the best boy in the class
Frequency of the words in the String:
boy : 2
the : 3
is : 1
in : 1
best : 1
class : 1

Program 5.12: Write a program to convert a binary number to the equivalent decimal number.

```
#PRGD 5_12 :Program to convert a binary number to the equivalent
#decimal number.

def bin2dec(binary):
    dec=0
    length=len(binary)
    p=0
    for i in range(length-1,-1,-1):
        dec+=int(binary[i])*2**p
        p+=1
    return dec

binary=input("Enter any Binary Number: ")
dec=bin2dec(binary)
print("Equivalent decimal number is:", dec)
```

Sample Output:

Enter any Binary Number: 10110
Equivalent decimal number is: 22

Strings at a Glance

✓ A string is a sequence of characters allocated contiguously in memory where the characters may be letter of the alphabet, digits, punctuation marks, white spaces or any other symbols.

✓ In Python strings are implemented as an object of in-built class str.

✓ To define a string constant we may use single quotation (' '), double quotation (" ") or triple quotation (" " " ").

✓ An escape sequence is the combination of a backslash(\) and another character that together represent a specific meaning escaping from their original meaning when they are used individually.

✓ If a string is preceded by an 'r' or 'R', then it is called raw string. Within a raw string, escape sequences do not work.

✓ Strings support positive index as well as negative index.

✓ A positive index starts from 0 and is used to access a string from the beginning.

✓ A negative index starts from -1 and is used to access a string from end.

✓ Strings are immutable in python. However, we can create a new string from an old string.

✓ Using the slicing operation we can extract substrings from the original string.

✓ The operator '+' is used to concatenate two or more strings whereas the operator '*' is used to repeat a string a certain number of times.

✓ Relational operators can also be used to compare two strings.

✓ Python has a large number of functions to manipulate strings.

✓ Regular Expression is a unique feature of Python which helps to find a pattern instead of a fixed substring in a string.

✓ Brute Force Algorithm is a basic or naïve type pattern matching algorithm whose time complexity is $O(nm)$.

✓ Knuth Morris Pratt Algorithm is a very efficient pattern matching algorithm which searches a pattern in $O(m+n)$ running time.

Multiple Choice Questions

1. The `match()` function in re module
   a) determines if the RE matches at the beginning of the string
   b) determines if the RE matches at the end of the string
   c) determines if the RE matches anywhere within the string and returns match object
   d) determines if the RE matches anywhere within the string and returns its position in the original string

2. Which of the following prints the last word of the string?
   a) `print(re.match('\w{4}$', 'Python is easy'))`
   b) `print(re.search('\w*$', 'Python is easy'))`
   c) `print(re.findall('\w+$', 'Python is easy'))`
   d) None of these

3. What will be the output when the following statement is executed?
   `print(r'Hello\nStudents!!')`
   a) Syntax error
   b) Hello\nStudents!!
   c) Hello
      Students!!
   d) None of these

4. What will be the output of the following Python code?
   ```
   _ = '1 2 3 4 5 6'
   print(_)
   ```
   a) SyntaxError: EOL while scanning string literal
   b) SyntaxError: invalid syntax
   c) NameError: name '_' is not defined
   d) 1 2 3 4 5 6

5. What will be the output of the following Python code?
   ```
   a = '1 2 '
   print(a * 2, end=' ')
   print(a * 0, end=' ')
   print(a * -2)
   ```
   a) 1 2 1 2 0 -1 -2 -1 -2
   b) 1 2 1 2
   c) 2 4 0 -2 -4
   d) Error

6. What will be the output of the following Python code?

```python
word = "MAKAUT"
i = 0
while i in word:
        print('i', end = ". ")
```

a) no output

b) i i i i i i ...

c) M A K A U T

d) Error

7. What does the following statement return?

```python
'C' in "PYTHON"
```

a) Error

b) 0

c) 4

d) False

8. Which of the following would reverse a string, st?

i.   `st[::-1]`

ii.   `st.reverse()`

iii. `"".join(reversed(st))`

iv.   `"".join(sorted(st, reverse=True))`

a) i, ii

b) i, iii, iv

c) ii, iii, iv

d) All of the above

9. What does the following statement print?

```python
string = 'Python Programming'
print(string[5::-1])
```

a) n Programming

b) on Programming

c) gnimmargorP

d) nohtyP

10. What will be the output of the following Python code?

```python
def change(st):
        st[0]='X'
        return st
string ="Python"
```

```
print (change (string))
```

a) Xython

b) Python

c) XPython

d) None of these

11. What will be the output of the following Python code?

```
string='Python'
while i in string:
        print(i, end = " ")
```

a) P y t h o n

b) Python

c) P
   y
   t
   h
   o
   n

d) Error

12. Which of the following statement(s) is/are correct?

```
i.    s= 'Python'

ii.   s[2]='k'

iii. del s[1]

iv.   del  s
```

a) i, ii

b) i, iii, iv

c) i, iv

d) all of the above

13. Which function(s) is/are used to count the number of characters in a string?

a) `count ()`

b) `len ()`

c) both a and b

d) None of these

14. Which of the following function(s) converts/convert the string "python programming is easy" to "Python Programming Is Easy"?

a) `title()`

b) `capitalize()`

c) `capitalfirst()`

d) All of these

15. Identify the right way to write "Python Programming" in a file.

a) `write(file, "Python Programming")`

b) `write("Python Programming", file)`

c) `file.write("Python Programming")`

d) Both a and c

Review Exercises

1. What is string?

2. How a string be represented in Python?

3. What are the different types of strings in Python?

4. What is a raw string? What is its utility?

5. What are the operations that can be done on a string in Python?

6. Explain the slicing operation on a string in Python.

7. What is Regular Expression? How does Python handle it?

8. Differentiate between `match()` and `search()` in re module of Python.

9. What advantage do we get from `split()` of re module in comparison to `split()` method of string?

10. Write down the Brute Force pattern matching algorithm. What is the time complexity to find a pattern using this algorithm?

11. Using the Brute Force pattern matching algorithm, find the pattern 'Thu' in the string 'This Is The Thukpa'.

12. How can the LPS table be created from any pattern?

13. Construct the LPS table for the following words:

i. ABCDEAB

ii. ABABCAD

iii. XYXYZ

14. Using the KMP pattern matching algorithm, find the pattern 'cucumber' in the string 'cute cucumber'.

15. Using the KMP pattern matching algorithm, find the pattern 'pitpit' in the string 'picture of pipitpit'.

Problems for Programming

1. Write a program to find the full abbreviation of a name.

2. Write a program to count the number of letters in a string.

3. Write a program that will print a substring within a string. The program will take the input of the length of the substring and the starting position in the string.

4. Write a program to find the frequency of a particular word in an inputted string.

5. Write a program that will delete a particular word from a line of text.

6. Write a program that will replace a particular word with another word in a line of text.

7. Write a program to search a city among a set of cities.

8. Write a function to convert an amount into words. For example, 12345 should be printed as 'Twelve thousand three hundred forty five'.

9. Write a function to extract the day, month and year from any date. Assume that dates are in 'DDMMYYYY' format but the separator may be '/', '.' or '-'.

10. Write a program to check whether a string contains any email address.

11. Write a program to extract all product codes from a string where the product code is a 6-character string whose first 3 characters are letters in upper case and last 3 characters are numeric.

12. Write a program to extract all 10-digit phone numbers with a prefix of '+91'.

13. Write a program to check whether a string contains the word 'BCA' or 'MCA'.

14. Write a program to check whether an inputted string contains a particular pattern. The pattern consists of exactly 4 characters and may start with any character, but the last 3 characters should be 'all'.

15. Write a program to find all the words that end with the pattern 'tion' in a string.

Recursion

Recursion is a very important concept in programming technique. In programming there are situations where we may find that the solution of a problem can be achieved by solving smaller instances of that same problem. For example, in tree data structure, all the properties that comprise a tree also feature in its sub-trees. So, to get a solution for the tree first we need to get the solution of its sub-trees. Again to get the solution of a sub-tree we need to get the solution of the sub-trees of this sub-tree, and so on. This is the basis of recursion. This concept helps to solve many complex problems very easily.

6.1 Definition

In almost every programming language, a function or procedure may invoke other functions or procedures. Not only from other functions, a function may be invoked from within itself as well. When a function is invoked by itself, the function is called a recursive function. And the process is called recursion. Instead of direct invocation, it may happen that the first function invokes the second function and the second function again invokes the first function in turn. This is also recursion. So, we can define **recursion** as the process where a function is directly or indirectly invoked by itself. Though it is a comparatively more memory consuming process, it is very effective in implementation where the algorithm demands the same repetitive process but use of iteration is difficult.

For example, we can define factorial of **n** as **n! = n * (n-1)!**. So, to find the factorial of **n** we need to calculate factorial of **n-1** first. Again, to calculate the factorial of **n-1** we need to calculate factorial of **n-2**, and so on. But this process may not continue indefinitely. Stack will be overflowed in that case. Hence, we must impose some criteria based on which this invocation should be restricted. This is called **base criteria** or **base condition**. Thus, every recursive function must have a base condition. In the above example, we may set the base condition as: when the value of **n** is 0, instead of recursive call it directly returns 1. Hence, we can easily implement it using recursion as follows:

```
def factorial(num):
    if num == 0:
        return 1
    else:
        return num*factorial(num-1)
```

Here, if we want to calculate `factorial(4)`, the second return statement of the function will be executed as `return( 4 * factorial(3))`;but this statement cannot be executed until `factorial(3)` is executed. Again, for this function call `return( 3 * factorial(2));` – this statement will execute. This will continue until num becomes 1. Then `return(1)` statement will execute and return the control to its calling point. Then its previous return statement will return 2*1, i.e. 2. In this way, `factorial(4)` will be calculated as 4*3*2*1.

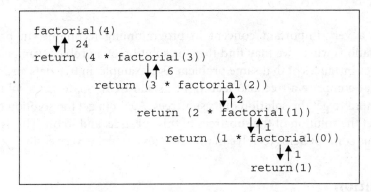

Figure 6.1   Execution of a recursive function

Here is the complete program:

Program 6.1: Write a program to find the factorial of a positive integer using recursive function.

```
#PRGD 6_1: Recursive function to find the factorial of a
#positive integer
def factorial(num):
    if num == 0:
        return 1
    else:
        return num*factorial(num-1)

n = int(input("Enter any number: "))
fact = factorial(n)
print("Factorial of %d is %d"%(n, fact))
```

6.2 Types of Recursion

Depending on the function call, recursion can be categorized into the following types:

1. Linear Recursion
2. Tail Recursion
3. Binary Recursion
4. Mutual Recursion
5. Nested Recursion

1. **Linear Recursion:** It is the simplest one. Here only a single recursive function call exists in the function to call its own self and a terminating condition to terminate.

2. **Tail Recursion:** It is a special form of linear recursion. When recursive call is the last statement of the function, the recursion is known as tail recursion. In most cases tail recursion can be easily converted to iteration. Instead of a recursive call, a loop can be used. Here is an example of tail recursion:

Program 6.2: Write a program to find a^b using tail recursion.

```
#PRGD 6_2: Program to find a^b using tail recursion
def power(a, b):
    if b == 0:
        return 1
    else:
        return a*power(a, b-1)

num = int(input("Enter any number: "))
exp = int(input("Enter Exponent: "))
result = power(num, exp)
print("%d^%d = %d"%(num, exp, result))
```

3. **Binary Recursion:** In this recursion, in place of once the function is called twice at a time. That is why its name is binary recursion. This type of recursion is found in the implementation of binary tree data structure, finding Fibonacci numbers, etc. Consider the following example:

Program 6.3: Write a program to find the nth Fibonacci number.

```
#PRGD 6_3: Program to find n-th Fibonacci number

def FibNum(n):
    if n < 1:
```

```
        return -1
    elif n == 1:
        return 0
    elif n == 2:
        return 1
    else:
        return FibNum(n - 1) + FibNum(n - 2)

term = int(input("Enter the term: "))
fib = FibNum(term)
print("The %dth term of the Fibonacci Series is :
                                %d"%(term, fib))
```

In the above function, at a time two recursive functions are called; that is why it is treated as **binary recursion**. As we know, the first two terms of the Fibonacci series is fixed and these are 0 and 1; the terminating condition is written as:

```
if n == 1:
    return 0
elif n == 2:
    return 1
```

Thus when the value of n will be 1 or 2, the function will return 1 and 0, respectively. Zero or negative value of **n** indicates invalid value, thus returns -1. The other terms of this series are generated by adding the two predecessor values of this series. So, to find the nth term of this series, we need to add $(n-1)^{th}$ and $(n-2)^{th}$ terms and the statement becomes:

```
return FibNum(n-1) + FibNum(n-2)
```

4. **Mutual Recursion:** A recursive function does not always call itself directly. Sometimes it may happen that the first function calls a second function, the second function calls a third function, and the third function calls the first function. In this way each function is called by its own self but not directly; rather via one or more functions. This is known as **mutual recursion.** So, it can be defined as an indirect form of recursion when one method calls another, which in turn calls the first.

The following example illustrates this:

Program 6.4: Write a program to check whether an inputted number is odd or even using the mutual recursive function.

```
#PRGD 6_4: Program to check odd or even number using mutual
#recursion
```

```
def iseven(n):
    if (n==0):
        return True
    else:
        return isodd(n-1)

def isodd(n):
    return not(iseven(n))

num = int(input("Enter the number: "))
if iseven(num):
    print("The number is Even")
else:
    print("The number is Odd")
```

In the above program both functions mutually call each other to check whether a number is even or odd. In the main function, instead of `iseven()`, `isodd()` can also be used.

5. **Nested Recursion:** If one of the arguments of any recursive call statement contains another recursive function call, then it is known as **nested recursion**. Implementation of the classical mathematical Ackermann's function is a good example of nested function.

Program 6.5: Write a program to implement the Ackermann function.

```
#PRGD 6_5: Program to implement the Ackermannn Function

def ackermann(m, n):
    if m == 0:
        return n+1
    elif n == 0:
        return ackermann(m-1,1)
    else:
        return ackermann(m-1,ackermann(m,n-1))

x = int(input("Enter any number: "))
y = int(input("Enter any number: "))
result = ackermann(x, y)
print("Result = ", result)
```

6.3   Recursion vs. Iteration

Both recursion and iteration do almost the same job. Both are used when some repetition of tasks is required. But the way of implementation is different. Now the question is which one is better or which one is better in which situation. We know that iteration explicitly uses a repetition structure, i.e. loop, whereas recursion achieves repetition through several function calls. If we think about time complexity, recursion is not a better choice. That is because we know there is a significant overhead always associated with every function call such as jumping to the function, saving registers, pushing arguments into the stack, etc., and in recursion these overheads are multiplied with each function call and, therefore, it slows down the process. But in iteration there is no such overhead. If we consider space complexity, with every function call all the local variables will be declared again and again, which consumes more and more space. But in case of iteration, a single set of variables are declared and they store different updated values for each iteration. Hence, the performance of iteration is much better than recursion when we think about space complexity. So, what is the utility of recursion? There are some situations where a complex problem can be easily implemented using recursion, such as implementation of trees, a sorting algorithm that follows the divide and conquer method, backtracking, top down approach of dynamic programming, etc.

6.4 Some Classical Problems on Recursion

Use of recursion to solve the problems on a tree is discussed in Chapter 10 and divide and conquer sorting algorithms are discussed in Chapter 13. In this section we will discuss some classical problems that are easily solved using recursion.

6.4.1 Towers of Hanoi Problem

Towers of Hanoi is a classical problem that can be solved easily using recursion. It is basically a puzzle of three rods and a set of disks. Initially all the disks are stacked into a rod maintaining ascending order of disk size. The objective of the puzzle is to move the entire stack of disks to another rod maintaining some simple rules:

1. At a time only a single disk can be moved.

2. Only the uppermost disk can be moved.

3. No disk can be placed on top of a smaller disk.

Though the puzzle can be played for n number of disks, here we are discussing the solution of this problem for three disks. To mention the rods and disks properly we are giving names of them. Initially all the disks are in rod X; we have to shift all disks from X to rod Z; the intermediate rod is Y. The disks are named 1, 2, and 3 in the increasing order of size. Now, to solve this problem, the following steps have to be followed:

1. Move Disk 1 from X to Z

2. Move Disk 2 from X to Y

3. Move Disk 1 from Z to Y

4. Move Disk 3 from X to Z

5. Move Disk 1 from Y to X

6. Move Disk 2 from Y to Z

7. Move Disk 1 from X to Z

Here is a complete program to implement the Towers of Hanoi problem:

Program 6.6: Write a program to implement the Towers of Hanoi problem using recursion.

```
#PRGD 6_6: Program to implement the Towers of Hanoi
#problem
def move_disk( p1, p2, p3, n):
        if n<=0:
            print("Invalid Entry")
        elif n==1:
            print ("Move disk from %c to %c"%(p1, p3))
        else:
            move_disk(p1,p3,p2,n-1)
            move_disk(p1,p2,p3,1)
            move_disk(p2,p1,p3,n-1)

num = int(input("Enter number of disks : "))
print("Towers of Hanoi for %d disks: "%(num))
move_disk('X','Y','Z',num)
```

Output:

Enter number of disks : 3
Towers of Hanoi for 3 disks:
Move disk from X to Z
Move disk from X to Y
Move disk from Z to Y
Move disk from X to Z
Move disk from Y to X
Move disk from Y to Z
Move disk from X to Z

6.4.2 Eight Queen Problem

Eight Queen Problem is another classical problem. It is a specific form of the general N-Queen problem. It is a puzzle of placing eight queens in an 8×8 chessboard so that no two queens threaten each other, which implies that no two queens are placed in a single row, column or diagonal.

To find the solution to this puzzle we may use Brute Force algorithm which exhaustively searches all the possibilities and hence takes more time. Here we are trying for a better solution that uses recursion:

Program 6.7: Write a program to implement the Eight Queen Problem using recursion.

```
#PRGD 6_7: Program to implement the Eight Queen Problem
#using recursion.
import numpy as np

def isPossible(board,x,y): #Checking for possibility to
                                          #place a queen
    l=len(board)
    for i in range(l):          #rowwise checking for queens
        if board[x][i]==1:
            return False
    for i in range(l):       #columnwise checking for queens
        if board[i][y]==1:
            return False

    for i in range(l):
        for j in range(l):
            if board[i][j]==1:
                if abs(i - x) == abs(j - y):
                                          #diagonal checking
                    return False
    return True

def getSolution(board):
    l=len(board)
    for i in range(l):
        for j in range(l):
            if board[i][j]==0:
                if isPossible(board,i,j):
                    board[i][j]=1       #Placing the queen
                    getSolution(board)
```

```
                    #passing for recursive Solution
           if sum(sum(a) for a in board)==1:
               return board
                             #returning final board
           board[i][j]=0
           #remove previously placed queen on failure

       return board

N=8
board=np.zeros([N,N],dtype=int)
print("Enter any position of a Queen:")
row=int(input("Row: "))
col=int(input("Column: "))
board[row, col]=1
board=board.tolist()

finalBoard = getSolution(board) #get the finalBoard
print(np.matrix(finalBoard)) #Print the Solution
```

Output:

Enter any position of a Queen:

Row: 2

Column: 3

```
[[1 0 0 0 0 0 0 0]
 [0 0 0 0 0 0 1 0]
 [0 0 0 1 0 0 0 0]
 [0 0 0 0 0 1 0 0]
 [0 0 0 0 0 0 0 1]
 [0 1 0 0 0 0 0 0]
 [0 0 0 0 1 0 0 0]
 [0 0 1 0 0 0 0 0]]
```

The above program can also be converted to N-Queen Problem by just changing the value of N. We may also take the value of N as input. In the above program we have taken the input of position of the first queen. Instead of taking input we may use a random number for a random position.

6.5 Advantages and Disadvantages of Recursion

Advantages: The advantages of recursion are as follows:

1. Reduces the code.

2. Helps in implementation of divide and conquer algorithm.

3. Helps in implementation where algorithms use stack.

4. Helps to reverse the order of some sequences.

Disadvantage: The major drawbacks of using recursion are as follows:

1. It is not as good as iteration regarding time and space complexity.

2. Recursion achieves repetition through repeated function calls.

In iteration the same set of variables are used. But in recursion, every time the function is called, the complete set of variables are allocated again and again. So, a significant space cost is associated with recursion.

Again there is also a significant time cost associated with recursion, due to the overhead required to manage the stack and the relative slowness of function calls.

6.6 Analysis of Recursive Algorithms

To analyze any recursive algorithm we may define the problem in terms of a recurrence relation. A recurrence relation is described by an equation where any term of the equation is defined in terms of its previous term. When we solve a recursive problem, we try to solve the smaller sub-problems and these solutions collectively solve the main problem. Hence the time complexity function of the entire problem is same as its sub-problems but the input size will vary and will be defined in terms of the input size of sub-problems. So, if a problem has k number of sub-problems, we may define:

$$T(n) = T(s1) + T(s2) + T(s3) + ... + T(sk) + \text{Time complexity of additional operations}$$

where T( ) is a time complexity function, n is the input size of the problem and s1, s2, ... are the input sizes of the sub-problem 1, sub-problem 2, ... sub-problem k. For example, in case of binary search in each step after one comparison the input size reduces to half. Hence, we may define:

Time complexity, $T(n) =$ Time complexity of n/2 size problem

$+$ Time complexity of comparison operation

$= T(n/2) + T(1)$

So, the recurrence relation of binary search is:

$$T(n) = T(n/2) + c \; ; \text{where } T(1) = c$$

Now to find the time complexity of any recursive algorithm we need to follow some simple steps. These are as follows:

1. Identify the input size of the original problem and smaller sub-problems.
2. Generate the recurrence relation for time complexity.
3. Solve the recurrence relation to find the time complexity.

The first two points have already been discussed briefly. Now to solve any recurrence relation we may follow the Recursion Tree Method or the Master Theorem.

In the **recursion tree** method, we need to follow the steps as given here:

1. The recursion tree of the recurrence relation has to be drawn first.
2. Determine the number of levels of the tree.
3. Calculate the cost of additional operations at each level which is the sum of the cost of all nodes of that level.
4. Next find the total cost by adding the cost of all levels.
5. Simplifying the above expression, find the complexity in terms of big O notation.

For example, we are considering the binary search method. In binary search, after each comparison, the input size of the sub-problem becomes half. If we consider the cost of each comparison is 1, the recurrence relation becomes:

$$T(n) = T(n/2) + 1$$

Hence, the recursion tree can be drawn as:

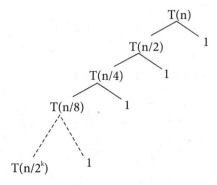

Now we have to determine the level.

Size of sub-problem at level 0 = $n/2^0$

Size of sub-problem at level 1 = $n/2^1$

Size of sub-problem at level 2 = $n/2^2$

.....

Size of sub-problem at level k = $n/2^k$

Suppose k^{th} level is the last level and at this level the size of the sub-problem will reduce to 1.

Thus,

$$n/2^k = 1$$

Or, $2^k = n$

Or, $\log_2 2^k = \log_2 n$ [Taking $\log_2$ in both side]

Or, $k \log_2 2 = \log_2 n$

Or, $k = \log_2 n$ $[\because \log_2 2 = 1]$

$\therefore$ Total number of levels in the recurrence tree is $\log_2 n + 1$

Now, we have to calculate the cost of all levels.

Cost at level 0 = T(n) = $T(n/2^0)$

Cost at level 1 = T(n/2) + 1 = $T(n/2^1) + 1$

Cost at level 2 = T(n/4) + 1 + 1 = $T(n/2^2) + 2$

Cost at level 3 = T (n/8) + 1 + 2 = $T(n/2^3) + 3$

.....

$\therefore$ Cost at level k = $T(n/2^k) + k$

$$= 1 + \log_2 n$$

[At k^{th} level, the size of the sub-problem becomes 1, $\therefore$ T(1) =1 and $k = \log_2 n$]

From the above equation, we can define the complexity of binary search as O ($\log_2 n$).

Master theorem is used in divide and conquer type algorithms where the recurrence relation can easily be transformed to the form T(n) = aT(n/b) + O(n^k), where a>=1 and b>1. Here **a** denotes the number of sub-problems, each of size(n/b). O(n^k) is the cost of dividing into sub-problems and combining results of all the components. There may be three cases:

1. If $k < \log_b(a)$, T(n) = O($n^{\wedge}\log_b(a)$)
2. If $k = \log_b(a)$, T(n) = O(n^k*logn)
3. If $k > \log_b(a)$, T(n) = O(n^k)

In case of binary search, the recurrence relation is: T(n) = T(n/2) + c.

Comparing with the transformed form, T(n) = aT(n/b) + O(n^k)

we get: a=1, b=2 and k=0 (c = 1 = n^k = n^0).

So, $\log_2(1) = 0$ = k which satisfies case 2.

Thus, time complexity T(n) = O(n^k*logn) = O(n^0*logn) = O(logn).

6.7 Programming Examples

Here are some programming examples to understand the various uses of recursion.

Program 6.8: Write a program to find the sum of the digits of a number using recursion.

```
#PRGD 6_8: Recursive function to find the Sum of the
#digits of a number.
def sumOfDigits(num):
    if num == 0:
        return 0
    else:
        return (num%10)+sumOfDigits(num//10)

n = int(input("Enter any number: "))
sod = sumOfDigits(n)
print("Sum of the digits of %d is %d"%(n, sod))
```

Output:

Enter any number: 3257
Sum of the digits of 3257 is 17

Program 6.9: Write a recursive function for GCD calculation.

```
#PRGD 6_9: Recursive function to find the GCD of two
#integers.

def gcd(n1, n2):
    if n1%n2 == 0:
        return n2
    else:
        return gcd(n2, n1%n2)

num1 = int(input("Enter any number: "))
num2 = int(input("Enter another number: "))
print("GCD of %d and %d is %d"%(num1, num2, gcd(num1,
                                                  num2)))
```

Sample Output:

```
Enter any number: 15
Enter another number: 25
GCD of 15 and 25 is 5
```

Program 6.10: Write a program to print Fibonacci series using recursion.

```
#PRGD 6_10 : Program to display first n Fibonacci number

def FibNum(n):
    if n < 1:
        return -1
    elif n == 1:
        return 0
    elif n == 2:
        return 1
    else:
        return FibNum(n - 1) + FibNum(n - 2)

def FibonacciSeries(num):
    if num > 0:
        fib = FibNum(num)
        FibonacciSeries(num-1)
        print(fib, end=' ')

term = int(input("Enter the term: "))
```

```
print("First %d Fibonacci numbers are : "%(term))
FibonacciSeries(term)
```

Sample Output:

Enter the term: 10
First 10 Fibonacci numbers are :
0 1 1 2 3 5 8 13 21 34

Program 6.11: Write a recursive function to convert a decimal number to its equivalent binary number.

```
#PRGD 6_11: Program to convert a decimal number to its
#binary equivalent

def d2b(num):
    if num == 0:
        return ''
    else:
        rem = num % 2
        return d2b(num // 2)+str(rem)

dec = int(input("Enter any number : "))
bin = d2b(dec)
print("Binary equivalent of %d is : %s"%(dec, bin))
```

Sample Output:

Enter any number : 10
Binary equivalent of 10 is : 1010

Recursion at a Glance

✓ Recursion is the process where a function is directly or indirectly invoked by itself.

✓ The advantage of recursion is that it not only reduces the lines of code but also helps to implement complex algorithm in easier method.

✓ Linear Recursion is the simplest form of recursion where only a single recursive function call exists in the function to call own self and a terminating condition to terminate.

✓ When a recursive call is the last statement of the function, the recursion is known as Tail Recursion.

✓ In Binary Recursion, in place of once the function is called twice at a time. That is why its name is binary recursion.

✓ Mutual Recursion can be defined as an indirect form of recursion when one method calls another, which in turn calls the first.

✓ If one of the arguments of any recursive call statement contains another recursive function call, then it is known as Nested Recursion.

✓ Though memory management and time management both are better in iteration, recursion helps to implement several complex algorithms like implementation of trees, sorting algorithm that follows the divide and conquer method, backtracking, top down approach of dynamic programming, etc.

Multiple Choice Questions

1. To execute recursive function compiler uses a
   a) Linked list
   b) Stack
   c) Queue
   d) Tree

2. Which of the following statements is false?
   a) Return statement is compulsory in a recursive function.
   b) Return statement may not be present in a recursive function.
   c) In a recursive function there may be multiple return statements.
   d) All of the above.

3. Which of the following statements is false?
   a) Base condition or terminating condition is compulsory in a recursive function.
   b) Base condition or terminating condition may not be present in a recursive function.
   c) In a recursive function there may be multiple base conditions or terminating conditions.
   d) There is no restriction on number of base condition or terminating condition.

4. Which of the following statements is true?
   a) The first statement of a recursive function should be the base condition or terminating condition.
   b) The last statement of a recursive function should be the recursive function call statement.

c) Recursive function should return a value.

d) None of these.

5. Tail recursive function is

a) A function where last statement is a recursive call

b) A nested function

c) A function with an infinite loop

d) None of these

6. Which of the following is true in case of recursion when it is compared with iteration?

a) Performance of recursion is relatively poor.

b) Much memory is required.

c) Any recursive program can also be written using iteration also.

d) All of the above.

7. What will be the output of the following Python code?

```python
i=0
def f(a, b):
    global i
    i+=1
    if(a<b):
        return(f(b,a))
    if (b==0):
        return(a)
    return(i)

a,b=11,12
print(f(a,b))
```

a) 11 12

b) 2

c) 11

d) 12

8. What will be the output of the following Python code?

```python
def sum(n):
    if n>0:
        return n+sum(n-1)
    else:
        return 0
```

```
print(sum(5))
```

a) Error

b) 9

c) 10

d) 15

9. What will be the output of the following Python code?

```
def func1(n):
    if n>0:
        return n*func2(n-1)
    else:
        return 1

def func2(n):
    if n>0:
        return n/func1(n-1)
    else:
        return 1
print(func1(5))
```

a) 13.333

b) 33.333

c) 3.333

d) 0.333

10. What will be the output of the following Python code?

```
def func(n):
    if n>0:
        return func(n//10)+1
    else:
        return 0

print(func(7007))
```

a) 0

b) 1

c) 2

d) 4

11. What will be the output of the following Python code?

```
def func1(n):
    if n>0:
        return n+func2(n//10)
    else:
        return 1

def func2(n):
    if n>0:
        return n-func1(n//10)
    else:
        return 1
print(func1(123))
```

a) 0

b) 123

c) 133

d) 134

Review Exercises

1. What do you mean by recursion? What are the advantages in its use?

2. Is there any disadvantage of using recursion?

3. Is recursion better than iteration? Justify your answer.

4. What do you mean by nested recursion?

5. What does the following function do?

```
def func(n):
    if n>0:
        if n%2:
            return func(n//10)+1
        else:
            return func(n//10)
    else:
        return 0

n=int(input("Enter N: "))
print("Result=",func(n))
```

6. Find the time complexity of the above code.

7. What is tail recursion? Explain with an example.

8. Explain mutual recursion with an example.

9. What do you mean by binary recursion? Explain with an example.

10. Explain nested recursion with an example.

Problems for Programming

1. Write a recursive function to count the number of zeroes in an integer.

2. Write a recursive function to find the sum of the first n natural numbers.

3. Write a recursive function to count the number of digits in an integer.

4. Write a recursive function to count the number of odd digits in an integer.

5. Write a recursive function to convert a decimal number to its equivalent number of any base.

6. Write a recursive function to find the length of a string.

7. Write a recursive function to count the number of digits in a string.

8. Write a recursive function to print a string in reverse order.

9. Write a recursive function to count the number of vowels in a string.

Linked List

We have already learned that to store a set of elements we have two options: array and Python's in-built list. Both provide easy and direct access to the individual elements. But when we handle a large set of elements there are some disadvantages with them. First of all, the allocation of an array is static. Thus we need to mention the size of the array before compilation and this size cannot be changed throughout the program. On the other hand, Python list may expand according to requirement but that does not come without a cost. Adding new elements into a list may require allocations of new block of memory into which the elements of the original list have to be copied. Again, if a very large array is required to be defined, then the program may face a problem of allocation. As an array is a contiguous allocation, for very large sized arrays, there may be a situation where even though the total free space is much larger than required, an array cannot be defined only due to those free spaces not being contiguous. Another problem related to arrays and lists is in insertion and deletion operations. If we want to insert an item at the front or at any intermediate position, it cannot be done very easily as the existing elements need to be shifted to make room. The same problem is faced in case of deleting an item. The solution to all these problems is to create a Linked List.

In a linked list we need not allocate memory for the entire list. Here only a single node is allocated at a time. This allocation takes place at runtime and as and when required. Thus, unlike an array, a large contiguous memory chunk is not allocated; instead very small memory pieces are allocated. When we need to store the first item, we have to allocate space for it only and it will store the data at this place. Next when the second item needs to be stored, we will again allocate space for the second item, and so on. As these memory spaces are not contiguous, to keep track of the memory addresses, along with the data part we have to store an extra piece information with each item and it is the address of the next item. Thus to store an item we have to store two things. One is the data part of the item and the other is the address part which stores the address of the next item. But Python does not provide the scope of direct access to memory; thus we will store the reference of the next item. So, we need to declare a class accordingly to implement it. In this chapter we discuss the representation of a linked list and various operations that can be done on it.

7.1 Definition

A linked list is a linear collection of data items that are known as nodes. Each node contains two parts – one is the data part that stores one or more data values and the other is the reference part which keeps the reference of the next node. The first node along with data values keeps the reference of the second node; the second node keeps the reference of the third node, and so on. And the last node contains None to indicate the end of the list. In this way each node is linked with the others to form a list. Thus this type of list is popularly known as linked list.

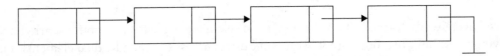

Figure 7.1   Linked list

7.2 Advantages of a Linked List

A linked list is a dynamic data structure. Hence the size of the linked list may increase or decrease at run time efficiently. We can create or delete a node as and when required. As a result, there is no chance of wastage of memory due to prior allocation. Similarly there is no chance of lack of memory either. Unlike arrays, we need not allocate a large contiguous memory chunk. Every time when an allocation is required, we will allocate only a single node. Thus, instead of a large contiguous memory chunk, a large set of very small memory chunks will be required. So, no matter how large our requirement, if total free space in memory supports it, then there will be no problem in allocation. Moreover, it provides flexibility in rearranging the items efficiently. It is possible to insert and/or delete a node at any point in the linked list very efficiently with only a few and constant number of operations. Here we need not shift items. What we have to do is just update some links.

7.3 Types of Linked Lists

There are different types of linked lists. They are as follows:

1.   Linear singly linked list

2.   Circular singly linked list

3.   Two way or doubly linked list

4.   Circular doubly linked list.

Linear singly linked list is the simplest type of linked list. Here each node points to the next node in the list and the last node contains None to indicate the end of the list. The problem of this type of list is that once we move to the next node, the previous node cannot be traversed again.

Circular singly linked list is similar to linear singly linked list except a single difference. Here also each node points to the next node in the list but the last node instead of containing None points to the first node of the list. The advantage of this list is that we can traverse circularly in this list. But the disadvantage is that to return to the previous node we have to traverse the total list circularly, which is time and effort consuming for large lists.

Two way or doubly linked list solves this problem. Here each node has two reference parts. One points to the previous node and the other points to the next node in the list. Both the ends of the list contain None. The advantage of this list is that we can traverse forward as well as backward according to our need. The disadvantage is that we cannot move circularly, i.e. to move from the last node to the first node we have to traverse the entire list.

Circular doubly linked list is the combination of doubly linked list and circular linked list. Here also each node has two reference parts. One points to the previous node and the other points to the next node in the list. But instead of containing None the first node points to last node and the last node points to the first node of the list. The advantage of this list is that we can move in any direction, i.e. forward, backward as well as circular. Figure 7.2 illustrates the different types of linked lists.

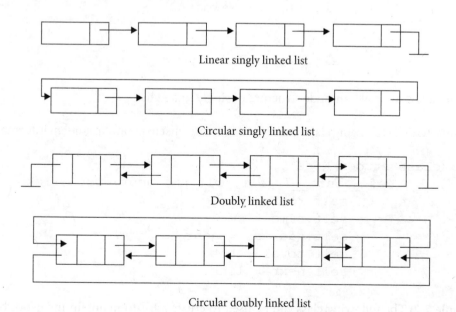

Linear singly linked list

Circular singly linked list

Doubly linked list

Circular doubly linked list

Figure 7.2   Different types of linked lists

7.4 Implementing a Singly Linked List

A linked list is a chain of elements or records called **nodes**. Each node has at least two members, one of which holds the data and the other points to the next node in the list. This is known as a single linked list because the nodes of this type of list can only point to the next node in the list but not to the previous. Thus, we can define the class to represent a node as following:

```
class Node :
       def __init__ ( self, Newdata, link ) :
           self.data = Newdata
           self.next = link
```

Here the first member of the class represents the data part and the other member, next, is a reference by which the node will point to the next node.

For simplicity the data part is taken as a single variable. But there may be more than one item with same or different data types. Thus the general form of a class to represent any node is as follows:

```
class Node :
     def __init__ ( self, Newdata1,Newdata2,..., link ) :
             self.data1 = Newdata1
             self.data2 = Newdata2
             self.data3 = Newdata3
             . . .
             . . .
             self.next = link
```

Here are a few examples of node structure of singly linked list:

Example 7.1: The following class can be used to create a list to maintain student information.

```
class studentNode :
       def __init__ ( self, rl, nm, addr, tot, link ) :
           self.roll = rl
           self.name = nm
           self.address = addr
           self.total = tot
           self.next = link
```

Example 7.2: The following class can be used to create a list to maintain the list of books in a library.

```
class bookNode :
        def __init__ ( self,acc_no,name,athr,rate,link ) :
                self.accession_no = acc_no
                self.title = name
                self.author = athr
                self.price = rate
                self.next = link
```

When a program is written on linked list we have to consider a variable (say, Head) which will be used to point to the first node of the list. When there is no node in the list it will contain None. By this variable we will access the list every time. Figure 7.3 illustrates the representation of a singly linked list.

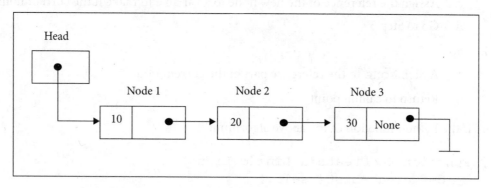

Figure 7.3   Representation of a singly linked list in memory

In Figure7.3, the linked list consists of three nodes. The data values of nodes are 10, 20, and 30 respectively. The Head variable contains a reference by which it points to the first node, i.e. **Node1**. Along with the data part, **Node1** contains a reference by which it points to **Node2** and similarly **Node2** points to **Node3**. As **Node3** is the last node of this list, its reference part contains None to indicate the end of the list.

7.5   Operations on Singly Linked List

In this section we will discuss various operations on singly linear linked lists, such as creating and traversing a list, inserting elements in a list, deleting elements from a list, etc. In all the subsequent cases we use the following class definition for the node.

```
class Node :
        def __init__ ( self, Newdata, link ) :
                self.data = Newdata
                self.next = link
```

7.5.1   Creating a Singly Linked List

To create a list we may follow the following algorithm:

1. Create a node.

2. Assign the reference of the node to a variable to make it the current node.

3. Take input for the data part and store it.

4. Take input for the option whether another node will be created or not.

5. If option is 'yes', then
    a. Create another new node.
    b. Assign the reference of the new node to the reference part of the current node.
    c. Assign the reference of the new node to a variable to make it the current node.
    d. Go to Step 3.

6. Else
    a. Assign None to the reference part of the current node.
    b. Return to calling point.

Here is the Python function of the above algorithm:

```
# Function to Create a Linked List
   def createList( self ) :
       self.Head = Node()
       cur = self.Head
       while True:
            cur.data=int(input("Enter Data : "))
            ch = input("Continue?(y/n): ")
            if ch.upper()=='Y':
                cur.next = Node()
                    # Current node pointing to new node
                cur = cur.next
          else:
                cur.next = None
       # Last node storing None at its reference part
                break
```

Here first a node is created and inputted data is assigned to its data part. Next a choice has been taken to decide whether another node will be created or not. If we want to create another node, a new node needs to be created and the next part of the current node will point to it otherwise None will be assigned to the next part of the current node to make it the end node.

7.5.2 Displaying a Singly Linked List

After creating a list we need to display it to see whether the values are stored properly. To display the list we have to traverse the list up to the end. The algorithm may be described as:

1. Start from the first node.

2. Print the data part of the node.

3. Move to next node.

4. If the control not reached at end of the list go to Step 2.

5. Otherwise return to calling point.

The corresponding function in Python is as follows:

```
# Function to display a linked list
    def display(self):
          curNode = self.Head
          while curNode is not None :
                print(curNode.data,end="->")
                curNode = curNode.next
          print("None")
```

In the above function the reference of the first node of the list, i.e. the content of Head, has been stored within a variable, curNode. Then it starts to print the data part of the current node and after printing each time it moves to the next node until the end of the list is reached. As to displaying the linked list we need to traverse the entire list starting from the first node, the time complexity to be calculated as O(n).

Here is a complete program that will create a linked list first and then display it:

Program 7.1: Write a program that will create a singly linked list. Also display its content.

```
#PRGD7_1: Program to create a singly linked list.

class Node :                    # Declaration of Node structure
    def __init__( self, Newdata=None, link=None ) :
          self.data = Newdata
          self.next = link

class singleLinkedList :
    def __init__( self ):
          self.Head = None

    def createList( self ) :
```

```
                         # Function to Create a Linked List
        self.Head = Node()
        cur = self.Head
        while True:
            cur.data=int(input("Enter Data : "))
            ch = input("Continue?(y/n): ")
            if ch.upper()=='Y':
                cur.next = Node()
                    # Current node pointing to new node
                cur = cur.next
            else:
                cur.next = None
            # Last node storing None at its reference part
                break

    def display(self):
        curNode = self.Head
        while curNode is not None :
            print(curNode.data,end="->")
            curNode = curNode.next
        print("None")

head=singleLinkedList()
head.createList()
                # head is the header node of linked list
print("\nThe List is : ")
head.display()
```

Sample output:

Enter Data : 10
Continue?(y/n): y
Enter Data : 20
Continue?(y/n): y
Enter Data :30
Continue?(y/n): n

The List is : 10->20->30->None

7.5.3   Inserting a New Element in a Singly Linked List

To insert a node in a linked list, a new node has to be created first and assigned the new value to its data part. Next we have to find the position in the list where this new node will be inserted. Then we have to update the reference part of predecessor and successor nodes (if any) and also the new node. The insertion in the list may take place :

- At the beginning of the list
- At the end of the list
- At any intermediate position of the list. It may be
  - o After the specified node
  - o Before the specified node

7.5.3.1 Inserting an Element at the Beginning of a List

As the element will be inserted at the beginning of the list, the content of the variable Head will be updated by the new node. Another argument of this function is the data part of the new node. We can omit it by taking the input from the function. But sending it as argument is better as it is more generalized, because input does not always come from keyboard; it may come from another list or from file, etc.

The general algorithm to insert an element at the beginning of the list may be defined as follows:

1. Create a new node.

2. Update its data part with the function argument.

3. Update its reference part with the content of Head variable which is also passed as argument.

4. Update the content of Head variable with the new node.

The following is the function of the above algorithm:

```
# Function to insert a node at the beginning of the list
class Node:
    def __init__( self, Newdata=None, link=None ) :
        self.data = Newdata
        self.next = link
class singleLinkedList :
    def insert_begin(self,newData):
        self.Head=Node(newData,self.Head)
```

Figure 7.4 shows the position of pointers after inserting a node at the beginning of a list. ------► line shows the old pointing path whereas ——► line shows the current pointing path.

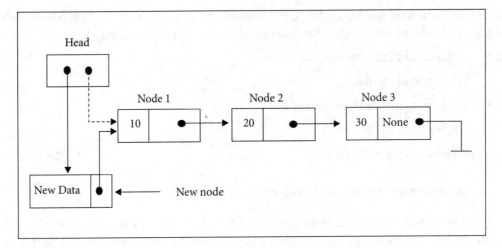

Figure 7.4 Inserting a node at the beginning of a list

In the above function, a new node will be created through the constructor. If the list is empty, the reference part of the new node will store None as Head contains None for empty lists. Otherwise it will store the reference of the node which was previously the first node. So, the new node becomes the first node and to point the first node of the list, Head will store the reference of the new node. As inserting a new node at the beginning of a linked list does need not traversing the list at all, but just updating some reference variables, the time complexity of inserting a new node at the beginning of a linked list is O(1).

7.5.3.2 Inserting an Element at the End of a List

When the node is inserted at the end, we may face two situations. First, the list may be empty and, second, there is an existing list. In the first case we have to update the Head variable with the new node. But in the second case, we need not update the Head variable as the new node will be appended at the end. For that we need to move to the last node and then update the reference part of the last node. To find the last node, we can check the reference part of the nodes. The node whose reference part contains None will be the last node. To insert a new node at the end of a list we need to traverse the entire list first, thus time complexity of this operation will be O(n).

The general algorithm to insert an element at the end of a list may be defined as follows:

1. Create a new node.

2. Update its data part with the function argument.

3. Update its reference part with None as it will be the last node.

4. If the content of Head variable is None then

    a. Update the content of Head variable with the new node.

5. Else

a. Move to last node

b. Update the reference part of last node with the new node.

Using the above algorithm we can write the following code.

```
# Function to insert a node at the end of the list
def insert_end(self,newData):
    newNode=Node(newData)
    if self.Head is None:
            # For Null list it will be the 1st Node
        self.Head=newNode
    else:
        curNode = self.Head
        while curNode.next is not None :
                            # Moving to last node
            curNode = curNode.next
        curNode.next=newNode
```

Figure 7.5 shows this insertion scheme.

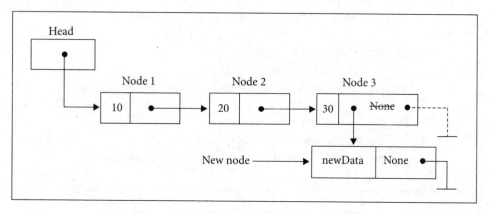

Figure 7.5   Inserting a node at the end of a list

7.5.3.3 Inserting a Node after a Specified Node

The specified node can be of two types. A node can be specified with the node number of the list, i.e. first node, second node,... n^{th} node, etc. Another way is to mention the data part, i.e. we need to match the supplied data with the data of each node. Here we discuss the algorithm for the first case. Another thing that we need to consider is what happens if the specified node is not in the list. In this situation we can abort the insertion operation by specifying that 'the node does not exist' or we can insert the new node at the end. Here we are considering the second case. The following algorithm describes how a new node can be inserted after the nth node.

1. Create a new node.

2. Update its data part with the function argument.

3. If the content of Head variable is None then

   a. Update the content of Head variable with the new node.

4. Else

   a. Move to the nth node

   b. If the specified node not exists, stay at last node and update the reference part of the last node with the new node.

   c. Update the reference part of the new node with the reference part of the nth node.

   d. Update the reference part of the nth node with the new node.

The following function shows how a node can be inserted after the nth node.

```
# Function to insert a node After Nth node
def insert_after_nth(self,newData,location):
    if self.Head is None :
        self.Head=Node(newData,self.Head)
    else:
        curNode = self.Head
        c=1
        while c<=location-1 and curNode.next is not None:
                                    # to Move to Nth node
            c+=1
            curNode = curNode.next
        curNode.next=Node(newData,curNode.next)
```

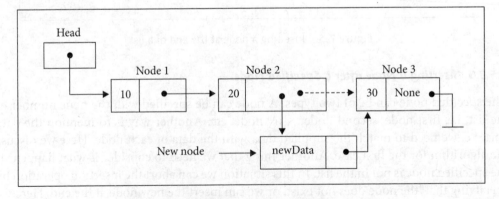

Figure 7.6 Inserting a node after the second node

To find the time complexity of this operation we need to know how many nodes to traverse or how many times we need to iterate. But here this depends on the position which is supplied at run time. Thus, in the best case, the position is 1 and we need not traverse at all. In this case, time complexity is O(1). But in the worst case, the node will be inserted at the end and we have to traverse the entire list. Then time complexity will be O(n).

7.5.3.4 Inserting a Node before a Specified Node

Here also, to mean a specified node we are considering the nth node. Thus our task is to insert a node before the nth node. In this case the new node may be inserted at the beginning of a list if is required to be inserted before the first node, otherwise it will be inserted in some intermediate position. But if the value of n is larger than the node count, the new node will be inserted at the end.

The following algorithm describes how a new node can be inserted before the nth node:

1. Create a new node.

2. Update its data part with the function argument.

3. If the content of Head variable is None or value of n is 1, then

    a. Update the reference part of the new node with the content of Head variable.

    b. Update the content of Head variable with the new node.

4. Else

    a. Move to the previous node of the nth node

    b. If the specified node does not exist, stay at the last node and update the reference part of the last node with the reference of the new node.

    c. Update the reference part of the new node with the reference part of the current node, i.e. $(n-1)^{th}$ node.

    d. Update the reference part of the current node with the new node.

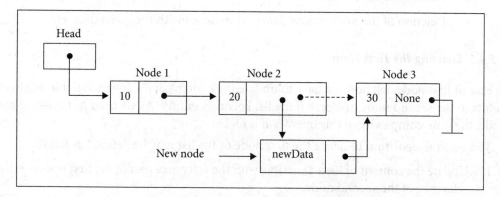

Figure 7.7 Inserting a node before the third node

The following function shows how a node can be inserted before the nth node.

```
# Function to insert a node before nth node
def insert_before_nth(self,newData,location):
    if self.Head is None or location==1:
        # If Null list or new node is inserted as 1st node
        self.Head=Node(newData,self.Head)
    else:
        curNode = self.Head
        c=1
        while c<=location-2 and curNode.next is not None :
                                        #to move to (n-1)th node
            c+=1
            curNode = curNode.next
        curNode.next=Node(num,curNode.next)
```

Here time complexity calculation is the same as in the previous and in the best case the time complexity is O(1) and in the worst case it is O(n).

7.5.4 Deleting a Node from a Singly Linked List

To delete a node from a linked list, first we have to find the node that is to be deleted. Next we have to update the reference part of the predecessor and successor nodes (if any) and finally de-allocate the memory spaces that are occupied by the node. Like insertion, there are several cases for deletion too. These may be :

- Deletion of the first node
- Deletion of the last node
- Deletion of any intermediate node. It may be
  o Deletion of the nth node or
  o Deletion of the node whose data part matches with the given data, etc.

7.5.4.1 Deleting the First Node

In case of first node deletion, we have to update the content of the Head variable as now it points to the second node or None if the list becomes empty. As we need not traverse any node, the time complexity of this operation is O(1).

The general algorithm to delete the first node of the list may be defined as follows:

1. Update the content of Head variable with the reference part of the first node, i.e. the reference of the second node.

2. De-allocate the memory of the first node.

Here is a function to delete the first node of a linked list:

```
# Function to delete the first node of a linked list
def delete_first(self):
    if self.Head is None:
        print("Empty List. Deletion not possible...")
    else:
        curNode = self.Head
        self.Head=self.Head.next
        del(curNode)
        print("Node Deleted Successfully...")
```

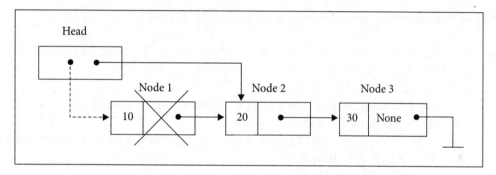

Figure 7.8   Deletion of the first node from a list

7.5.4.2 Deleting the Last Node

When we need to delete a node except the first node, first we have to move to the predecessor node of the node that will be deleted. So, to delete the last node we have to move to the previous node of the last node. Though our task is to delete the last node, the list may contain only a single node. Then deletion of this node makes the list empty and thus the content of the Head variable will be updated with None.

The general algorithm to delete the last node of the list may be defined as follows:

1. Check whether there is one or more nodes in the list.

2. If the list contains a single node only, update the content of Head variable with None and de-allocate the memory of the node.

3. Else
   a. Move to the previous node of the last node.
   b. De-allocate the memory of last node.

c. Update the reference part of current node with `None` as it will be the last node now.

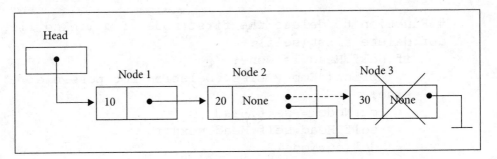

Figure 7.9 Deletion of the last node from a list

The following function shows how the last node can be deleted:

```
# Function to delete the last node of a linked list
def delete_last(self):
    if self.Head is None:
        print("Empty List. Deletion not possible...")
    elif self.Head.next is None:
                    #If the list contains single node only
        del(self.Head)
        self.Head=None
    else:
        curNode = self.Head
        while curNode.next.next is not None :
                #to Move to previous node of last node
            curNode = curNode.next
        del(curNode.next)
        curNode.next=None
        print("Node Deleted Successfully...")
```

If there are n number of nodes in a list, to delete the last node we need to traverse n-1 nodes. Thus to delete the last node of a list, the time complexity will be O(n).

7.5.4.3 *Deleting any Intermediate Node*

As we discussed that in the case of deletion of a node from any intermediate position, there may be several cases like the nth node deletion or deletion of the node whose data part matches with the given data. To delete the nth node, we have to move the predecessor node of the nth node. Next update the reference part of (n-1)th node with the reference part of the deleted node and then de-allocate the memory of the nth node.

But in the second case we have to compare each node with the argument data. In this case, the first node, the last node, or any intermediate node may be deleted. Again if the argument data does not match with any node, no node will be deleted.

The following algorithm describes how a node whose data part matches with the given data can be deleted:

1. Check the data of the first node with the given data.

2. If it matches, then

   a. Update the content of the Head variable with the reference part of first node, i.e. the reference of the second node.

   b. De-allocate the memory of the first node.

3. Else

   a. Check the data of each node against the given data.

   b. If searching fails, terminate operation mentioning appropriate message like "Node not found."

   c. If match occurs, then

      i. Stay at the previous node of the node whose data part matches with the given data.

      ii. Update the reference part of the current node with the reference part of the next node (i.e. the node to be deleted).

      iii. De-allocate the memory of the next node (i.e. the node to be deleted).

The following function shows how the node whose data part matches with the given data can be deleted:

```
# Function to Delete a node whose Data matches with the
#given Data
def delete_anynode(self,num):
    if self.Head is None:
        print("Empty List. Deletion not possible...")
    else:
        curNode = self.Head
        if curNode.data==num:                    # For 1st Node
            self.Head=self.Head.next
            del(curNode)
            print("Node Deleted Successfully...")
        else:                                    # For Others Node
```

```
flag=0
while curNode is not None:
    if  curNode.data == num:
        flag = 1
        break
    prev = curNode
# prev points to previous node of current node
    curNode = curNode.next
                # curNode points to current node
if flag == 0:
    print("Node Not Found...")
else:
    prev.next = curNode.next
    del(curNode)
    print("Node Deleted Successfully...")
```

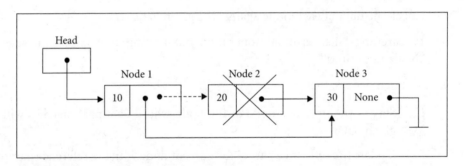

Figure 7.10 Deletion of an intermediate node (whose data value is 20) from a list

The time complexity calculation of this operation depends on the position of the node in the list. If we delete the first node, i.e. the best case, the time complexity is O(1). But if we delete the last node or the node is not found at all, that will be the worst case and we have to traverse the entire list. Then the time complexity will be O(n).

Here is a complete program to show the various operations of a linked list:

Program 7.2: Write a program to demonstrate the various operations of a singly linked list.

```
#PRGD7_2: Program to demonstrate Singly Linked List

class Node :                        # Declaration of Node class
    def __init__( self, Newdata=None, link=None ) :
        self.data = Newdata
        self.next = link


class singleLinkedList :
```

```python
def __init__( self ):
    self.Head = None
# Function to insert a node at the end of the list
def insert_end(self,newData):
    newNode=Node(newData)
    if self.Head is None:
        self.Head=newNode
    else:
        curNode = self.Head
        while curNode.next is not None :
                            #to Move to last node
            curNode = curNode.next
        curNode.next=newNode
# Function to insert a node at the beginning of the list
def insert_begin(self,newData):
    self.Head=Node(newData,self.Head)
# Function to insert a node before Nth node
def insert_before_nth(self,newData,location):
    if self.Head is None or location==1:
        self.Head=Node(newData,self.Head)
    else:
        curNode = self.Head
        c=1
        while c<=location-2 and curNode.next is not
                                         None :
                        #to move to (n-1)th node
            c+=1
            curNode = curNode.next
        curNode.next=Node(num,curNode.next)
# Function to insert a node After Nth node
def insert_after_nth(self,newData,location):
    if self.Head is None :
        self.Head=Node(newData,self.Head)
    else:
        curNode = self.Head
        c=1
        while c<=location-1 and curNode.next is not
                                         None :
                        # to Move to Nth node
            c+=1
            curNode = curNode.next
        curNode.next=Node(newData,curNode.next)
```

```
# Function to delete the first node of a linked list
def delete_first(self):
    if self.Head is None:
        print("Empty List. Deletion not possible...")
    else:
        curNode = self.Head
        self.Head=self.Head.next
        del(curNode)
        print("Node Deleted Successfully...")
# Function to delete the last node of a linked list
def delete_last(self):
    if self.Head is None:
        print("Empty List. Deletion not possible...")
    elif self.Head.next is None:
                #If the list contains single node only
        del(self.Head)
        self.Head=None
    else:
        curNode = self.Head
        while curNode.next.next is not None :
                #to Move to previous node of last node
            curNode = curNode.next
        del(curNode.next)
        curNode.next=None
        print("Node Deleted Successfully...")
# Function to Delete a node whose Data matches with the
# given Data
    def delete_anynode(self,num):
        if self.Head is None:
            print("Empty List. Deletion not possible...")
        else:
            curNode = self.Head
            if curNode.data==num:                    # For 1st Node
                self.Head=self.Head.next
                del(curNode)
                print("Node Deleted Successfully...")
            else:                                    # For Others Node
                flag=0
                while curNode is not None:
                    if  curNode.data == num:
                        flag = 1
                        break
```

```
                prev = curNode
# prev points to previous node of current node
                curNode = curNode.next
                    # curNode points to current node
            if flag == 0:
                print("Node Not Found...")
            else:
                prev.next = curNode.next
                del(curNode)
                print("Node Deleted Successfully...")
# Function to display the entire linked list
  def display(self):
        if self.Head is None:
            print("Empty List.")
        else:
            curNode = self.Head
            while curNode is not None :
                print(curNode.data,end="->")
                curNode = curNode.next
            print("None")


head=singleLinkedList()
while True:
    print("\nPROGRAM TO IMPLEMENT SINGLE LINKED LIST ")
    print("=====================================")
    print("1.Create / Appending The List")
    print("2.Insert Node At Begining")
    print("3.Insert Node Before Nth node")
    print("4.Insert Node After Nth node")
    print("5.Delete First Node")
    print("6.Delete Last Node")
    print("7.Delete the Node whose Data matches with given
                                        Data")
    print("8.Displaying the list")
    print("9.Exit")
    print("=====================================")
    choice=int(input("Enter your Choice : "))
    if choice==1 :
        opt='Y'
        while opt.upper()=='Y':
            num=int(input("Enter the Data: "))
            head.insert_end(num)
```

```
            opt=input("Enter more (y/n) :")
    elif choice==2 :
        num=int(input("Enter the Data: "))
        head.insert_begin(num)
    elif choice==3 :
        loc=int(input("Enter The Node number Before which
                        new node will be inserted :"))
        num=int(input("Enter the Data: "))
        head.insert_before_nth(num,loc)
    elif choice==4 :
        loc=int(input("Enter The Node number After which
                        new node will be inserted :"))
        num=int(input("Enter the Data: "))
        head.insert_after_nth(num,loc)
    elif choice==5 :
        head.delete_first()
    elif choice==6 :
        head.delete_last()
    elif choice==7 :
        num=int(input("Enter The Data You Want To Delete :
                                                        "))
        head.delete_anynode(num)
    elif choice==8 :
        head.display()
    elif choice==9 :
        print("\nQuiting.......")
        break
    else:
        print("Invalid choice. Please Enter Correct Choice")
        continue
```

7.6 Applications of a Singly Linked List

A linked list is an important data structure in computer programming. It is used in a wide variety of programming applications, such as implementing various data structures like stack, queue, graph, etc., implementing sparse matrix, performing arithmetic operation on large integers, etc. Polynomials can also be represented using singly linked lists.

The advantage of using a linked list is that the size of a polynomial may grow or shrink as all the terms are not present always. Again if the size of the polynomial is very large, then also it can fit into the memory very easily as, instead of the total polynomial, each term will be allocated individually. The general form of a polynomial of degree n is:

$$f(x) = a_n x^n + a_{n-1} x^{n-1} + a_{n-2} x^{n-2} + \ldots\ldots + a_1 x + a_0$$

where a_n, a_{n-1}, ... , a_1, a_0 are the coefficients and n, n-1, n-2,…. are the exponents or powers of the each term of the polynomial. Thus we can easily implement it using a singly linked list whose each node will consist of three elements: coefficient, power, and a link to the next term. So, the class definition will be:

```
class Node :
    def __init__(self,newCoef=None,newPower=None,link=No
                                                      ne):
        self.coef = newCoef
        self.pwr  = newPower
        self.next = link
```

Suppose a polynomial is $f(x) = 3x^6 + 5x^3 + 9x + 2$. It will be represented as follows:

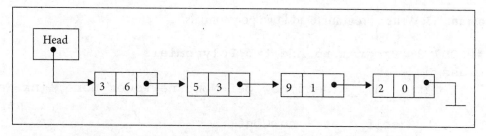

Figure 7.11   Representation of a polynomial using a linked list

To create the polynomial we can use a function similar to the `insert_end` function, which inserts a node at the end of a list. But if we use this function we have to assume that the user will give the input in descending order of power of the terms. Alternatively we can write a function that will insert nodes in descending order of power. But for simplicity we are following the `insert_end` function. Thus the functions to create a polynomial will be as follows:

```
#Function to insert a node at end of a list to create a
Polynomial
    def insert_end(self,newCoef,newPower):
        newNode=Node(newCoef,newPower)
        if self.Head is None:
            self.Head=newNode
        else:
            curNode = self.Head
            while curNode.next is not None :
                curNode = curNode.next
            curNode.next=newNode
```

By repetitively calling the above function we can create a polynomial.

```
# Function to create a Polynomial
def create_poly(self):
        while True:
                cof=int(input("Enter Coefficient : "))
                pr=int(input("Enter Power : "))
                self.insert_end(cof,pr)
                ch=input("Continue?(y/n): ")
                if ch.upper()=='N':
                        break
```

Now using the above functions we will write a complete program that will create two polynomials, display them, add these two polynomials, and finally display the resultant polynomial.

Program 7.3: Write a program to add two polynomials.

```
#PRGD7_3: Program to Add two Polynomials
class Node :
        def __init__(self,newCoef=None,newPower=None,link=No
                                                        ne):
                self.coef = newCoef
                self.pwr  = newPower
                self.next = link

class polynomial:
        def __init__( self ):
                self.Head = None
#Function to insert a node at end of a list to create a
#Polynomial
        def insert_end(self,newCoef,newPower):
                newNode=Node(newCoef,newPower)
                if self.Head is None:
                        self.Head=newNode
                else:
                        curNode = self.Head
                        while curNode.next is not None :
                                curNode = curNode.next
                        curNode.next=newNode
        # Function to create a Polynomial
        def create_poly(self):
```

```
        while True:
                cof=int(input("Enter Coefficient : "))
                pr=int(input("Enter Power : "))
                self.insert_end(cof,pr)
                ch=input("Continue?(y/n): ")
                if ch.upper()=='N':
                        break
    # Function to display the Polynomial
    def display(self):
        if self.Head is None:
            print("Empty List.")
        else:
            curNode = self.Head
            while curNode is not None :
                print(str(curNode.coef)
                        +"x^"+str(curNode.pwr), end="+")
                curNode = curNode.next
            print("\b ")


# Function to Add two Polynomials
def add_poly(p1, p2):
    pol1=p1.Head
    pol2=p2.Head
    pol3=polynomial()
    while pol1 is not None and pol2 is not None:
        if pol1.pwr > pol2.pwr :
            pol3.insert_end(pol1.coef,pol1.pwr)
            pol1=pol1.next
        elif pol1.pwr < pol2.pwr :
            pol3.insert_end(pol2.coef,pol2.pwr)
            pol2=pol2.next
        else:
            pol3.insert_end(pol1.coef+pol2.coef,pol1.
                                                    pwr)
            pol1=pol1.next
            pol2=pol2.next
    while pol1 is not None:
        pol3.insert_end(pol1.coef,pol1.pwr)
        pol1=pol1.next
    while pol2 is not None:
        pol3.insert_end(pol2.coef,pol2.pwr)
        pol2=pol2.next
    return pol3
```

```
poly1=polynomial()
poly2=polynomial()
print("Enter values for 1st Polynomials:-")
poly1.create_poly()
print("Enter values for 2nd Polynomials:-")
poly2.create_poly()
poly3=add_poly(poly1, poly2)
print("\n1st Polynomial : ",end="")
poly1.display()
print("2nd Polynomial : ",end="")
poly2.display()
print("Resultant Polynomial : ",end="")
poly3.display()
```

Sample output:

Enter values for 1st Polynomials:-
Enter Coefficient : 6
Enter Power : 4
Continue?(y/n): y
Enter Coefficient : 2
Enter Power : 3
Continue?(y/n): n
Enter values for 2nd Polynomials:-
Enter Coefficient : 5
Enter Power : 3
Continue?(y/n): y
Enter Coefficient : 4
Enter Power : 1
Continue?(y/n): n

1st Polynomial : 6x^4+2x^3
2nd Polynomial : 5x^3+4x^1
Resultant Polynomial : 6x^4+7x^3+4x^1

If the first polynomial contains m nodes and the second polynomial contains n nodes, the time complexity to add the two polynomials would be $O(m+n)$ as we need to traverse both lists exactly once.

7.7 Implementing a Circular Singly Linked List

The main problem associated with a singly linked list is that once we move to the next node, the previous nodes cannot be traversed again. One solution to this problem is the **circular singly linked list**, or simply **circular linked list**, which is similar to the linear singly linked list except for a single difference. Here also each node points to the next node in the list but the last node, instead of containing None, points to the first node of the list. The advantage of this list is that we can traverse circularly in this list.

So, to implement a circular linked list we can use the same class that is used to implement a singly linked list. Figure 7.12 illustrates the representation of a circular singly linked list.

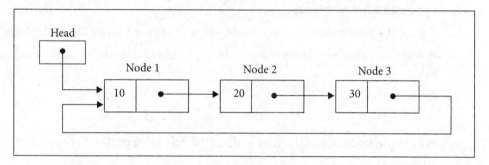

Figure 7.12   Representation of a circular singly linked list in memory

In Figure 7.12, the linked list consists of three nodes. The data values of nodes are 10, 20, and 30 respectively. As Node1 is the first node in the list, Head contains the reference of Node1 and in the list, Node1 points to Node2, and Node2 points to Node3. Node3 is the last node of this list. This will point to the first node of the list, i.e. Node1.

7.8 Operations on a Circular Singly Linked List

All the operations that can be done on a singly linked list can also be done on a circular linked list. In this section we will discuss these operations on a circular singly linked list, such as creating and traversing a list, inserting elements in a list, deleting elements from a list, etc. As to implementing a circular singly linked list, the same class is required. In all the following cases we follow the following class definition for the node:

```
class Node :
    def __init__ ( self, Newdata=None, link=None ) :
        self.data = Newdata
        self.next = link
```

7.8.1   Creating a Circular Singly Linked List

To create a list we may follow the following algorithm.

1. Create a node.

2. Update the Head field with this node to make it the first node.

3. Assign the reference of the node to a variable to make it the current node.

4. Take input for the data part and store it.

5. Take input for the option whether another node will be created or not.

6. If option is 'yes', then
    a.   Create another new node.
    b.   Assign the reference of the new node to the reference part of the current node.
    c.   Assign the reference of the new node to the current node to make it current node.
    d.   Go to Step 3.

7. Else
    a.   Assign the reference of the first node to the reference part of the current node.
    b.   Return to calling point.

Here is a function in Python for the above algorithm.

```python
# Function to Create a circular Linked List
def createList( self ) :
        self.Head = Node()
        cur = self.Head
        while True:
                cur.data=int(input("Enter Data : "))
                ch = input("Continue?(y/n): ")
                if ch.upper()=='Y':
                    cur.next = Node()
                    cur = cur.next
                else:
                    cur.next = self.Head
                            # Last node pointing to firstNone
                    break
```

In the above function, like in singly linked list creation, first a node is created and inputted data is assigned to its data part. Next a choice has been taken to decide whether another node will be created or not. If we want to create another node, a new node will be created and the next part of the current node will point to it, otherwise the reference of the first node will be assigned to the next part of the current node to make it circular.

7.8.2 Displaying a Circular Singly Linked List

After creating a list we need to display it to see whether the values are stored properly. To display the list we have to traverse the list up to the end. The algorithm may be described as:

1. Start from the first node.

2. Make a copy of the first node.

3. Print the data part of the node.

4. Move to the next node.

5. If the control has not reached the first node of the list, go to Step 3.

6. Otherwise return to calling point.

The corresponding Python function is as follows:

```
# Function to Display a Circular Linked List
    def display(self):
            curNode = self.Head
            while curNode.next != self.Head :
                print(curNode.data,end="->")
                curNode = curNode.next
            print(curNode.data)
```

In the above function the reference of the first node of the list, i.e. the content of Head, has been stored within a variable, curNode. Then it starts to print the data part of the current node and after printing each time it moves to the next node until it traverses back to the first node. Like a single linear linked list, to display the circular linked list we need to traverse the entire list. Thus, time complexity of this operation is to be calculated as O(n).

Here is a complete program that will create a circular linked list first and then display it:

Program 7.4: Write a program that will create a circular linked list. Also display its content.

```
#PRGD7_4: Program to create a circular linked list.
class Node :
      def __init__( self,Newdata=None,link=None) :
            self.data = Newdata
            self.next = link

class circularLinkedList :
      def __init__( self ) :
```

```python
        self.Head = None
# Function to Create a circular Linked List
    def createList( self ) :
        self.Head = Node()
        cur = self.Head
        while True:
            cur.data=int(input("Enter Data : "))
            ch = input("Continue?(y/n): ")
            if ch.upper()=='Y':
                cur.next = Node()
                cur = cur.next
            else:
                cur.next = self.Head
                        # Last node pointing to firstNone
                break

    def display(self):
        curNode = self.Head
        while curNode.next != self.Head :
            print(curNode.data,end="->")
            curNode = curNode.next
        print(curNode.data)

head=circularLinkedList()
head.createList()
print("\nThe List is : ",end="")
head.display()
```

Sample output:

Enter Data : 10

Continue?(y/n): y

Enter Data : 20

Continue?(y/n): y

Enter Data :30

Continue?(y/n): n

The List is : 10->20->30

7.8.3 Inserting a New Element in a Circular Linked List

Similar to a singly linked list, to insert a node in a circular linked list too, a new node has to be created first and its data part has to be assigned the new value. Next we have to find the position in the list where this new node will be inserted. Then we have to update the reference part of the predecessor and successor nodes (if any) and also the new node. The insertion in the list can take place:

- At the beginning of the list
- At the end of the list
- At any intermediate position of the list. It may be
    - After the specified node
    - Before the specified node

7.8.3.1 Inserting an Element at the Beginning of a Circular Linked List

As the element will be inserted at the beginning of the list, the content of the Head variable will be updated by the new node and the new node will point to the existing first node. Finally, we need to move to the last node to update the reference part of the last node by the new node.

The general algorithm to insert an element at the beginning of the circular linked list may be defined as follows:

1. Create a new node.
2. Update its data part with the function argument.
3. If the content of the Head variable is None, then
    a. Update the reference part of the new node with its own reference.
4. Else
    a. Move to the last node
    b. Update the reference part of the last node with the new node.
    c. Update the reference part of the new node with the reference of the first node.
5. Update the content of the Head variable with the new node.

Figure 7.13 shows the position of pointers after inserting a node at the beginning of a list. [------➤ line shows the old pointing path whereas ———➤ line shows the current pointing path.]

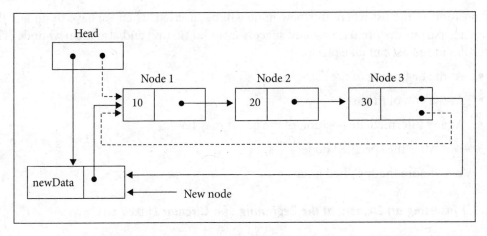

Figure 7.13   Inserting a node at the beginning of a list

The following is the function of the above algorithm:

```
# Function to insert a node at the beginning of the list
def insert_begin(self,newData):
    newNode=Node(newData,self.Head)
    curNode = self.Head
    if self.Head is None:
        newNode.next=newNode
    else:
        while curNode.next!=self.Head:
            curNode=curNode.next
        curNode.next=newNode
    self.Head=newNode
```

In the above function, if the list is empty, the new node will point to itself. So, the reference part of the new node will store its own reference. Otherwise, the new node will point to the existing first node and the last node will point to the new node. Thus we need to move to the last node first. Then the reference of this last node will store the reference of the new node to point to it and the reference part of the new node will store the reference of the existing first node to become the first node. As the new node becomes the first node, Head will now store the reference of the new node.

Though we are inserting the new node at the beginning of the list, we need to reach the end node traversing all the intermediate nodes. Thus time complexity to insert a node at the beginning of a circular linked list would be O(n).

7.8.3.2 Inserting an Element at the End of a List

When the node is inserted at the end, we may face two situations. First, the list may be empty and, second, there is an existing list. In the first case we have to update the Head variable with the new node. But in the second case, we need not update the Head variable as the new node will be appended at the end. For that we need to move to the last node and then have to update the reference part of the last node. To find the last node, we can check the reference part of the nodes. The node whose reference part contains the reference of the first node will be the last node.

The general algorithm to insert an element at the end of a circular list may be defined as follows:

1. Create a new node.

2. Update its data part with the function argument.

3. If the content of the Head variable is None, then

    a.   Update the reference part of the new node with its own reference.

    b.   Update the content of the Head variable with the reference of the new node.

4. Else

    a.   Move to the last node

    b.   Update the reference part of the last node with the new node.

    c.   Update the reference part of the new node with the first node.

Figure 7.14 shows this insertion scheme.

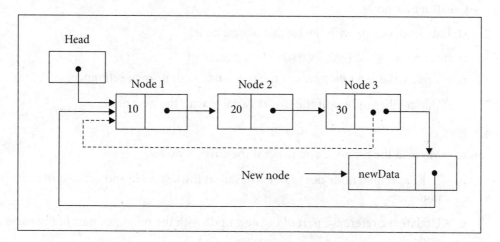

Figure 7.14   Inserting a node at the end of a list

Using the above algorithm we can write the following code:

```
# Function to insert a node at the end of the list
def insert_end(self,newData):
    newNode=Node(newData)
    if self.Head is None:
        self.Head=newNode
        newNode.next=newNode
    else:
        curNode = self.Head
        while curNode.next!=self.Head:
            curNode = curNode.next
        curNode.next=newNode
        newNode.next=self.Head
```

If we consider the time complexity of inserting a new node at the end of a circular list, it would be O(n) as we have to traverse the entire list.

7.8.3.3 Inserting a Node after a Specified Node

Here also, to mean a specified node we are considering the nth node. Thus our task is to insert a node after the nth node. This algorithm is also similar to the singly linked list. Move to the nth node. If the specified node is not in the list, stay at the last node. This node will point to the new node and the new node will point to the next node.

The following algorithm describes how a new node can be inserted after the nth node:

1. Create a new node.

2. Update its data part with the function argument.

3. If the content of the Head variable is None, then

    a. Update the reference part of the new node with its own reference.

    b. Update the content of the Head variable with the new node.

4. Else

    a. Move to the nth node and make it the current node

    b. If the specified node does not exist, stay at the last node and make it the current node.

    c. Update the reference part of the new node with the reference part of the current node.

    d. Update the reference part of the current node with the new node.

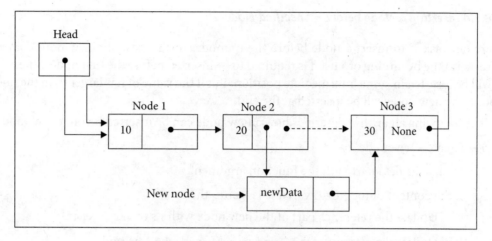

Figure 7.15   Inserting a node after the second node

The following function shows how a node can be inserted after the nth node:

```
# Function to insert a node After Nth node
def insert_after_nth(self,newData,location):
    newNode=Node(newData)
    if self.Head is None :
        self.Head=newNode
        newNode.next=newNode
    else:
        curNode = self.Head
        c=1
        while c<=location-1 and curNode.next!=self.
                                                Head:
            c+=1
            curNode = curNode.next
        newNode.next=curNode.next
        curNode.next=newNode
```

Time complexity of this operation depends on the position where the node will be inserted. If it inserts after first node, that will be the best case as we need not traverse the list at all and the time complexity will be O(1). But in worst case the new node will be inserted at the end of the list. In that case we have to traverse all the nodes to reach the last node and time complexity will be O(n).

7.8.3.4 Inserting a Node before a Specified Node

Here our task is to insert a node before the nth node. In this case the new node may be inserted at the beginning of a list if is required to be inserted before the first node, otherwise it will be inserted in some intermediate position. But if the value of n is larger than the node count, the new node will be inserted at the end.

The following algorithm describes how a new node can be inserted before the nth node.

1. Create a new node.

2. Update its data part with the function argument.

3. If the content of the Head variable is None, then

   a. Update the reference part of the new node with its own reference.

   b. Update the content of the Head variable with the new node.

4. Else if the value of n is 1, then

   a. Move to the last node

   b. Update the reference part of the last node with the new node.

   c. Update the reference part of the new node with the first node.

   d. Update the content of Head variable with the new node.

5. Else

   a. Move to the previous node of nth node, i.e. (n-1)[th] node and make it the current node.

   b. If the specified node does not exist, stay at the last node and make it the current node.

   c. Update the reference part of the new node with the reference part of the current node.

   d. Update the reference part of the current node with the new node.

The following function shows how a node can be inserted before the nth node:

```
# Function to insert a node before Nth node
def insert_before_nth(self,newData,location):
    newNode=Node(newData)
    if self.Head is None :
        self.Head=newNode
        newNode.next=newNode
    elif location==1:
        curNode = self.Head
        while curNode.next!=self.Head:
```

```
            curNode=curNode.next
        curNode.next=newNode
        newNode.next=self.Head
        self.Head=newNode
    else:
        curNode = self.Head
        c=1
        while c<=location-2 and curNode.next!=self.Head:
            c+=1
            curNode = curNode.next
        newNode.next=curNode.next
        curNode.next=newNode
```

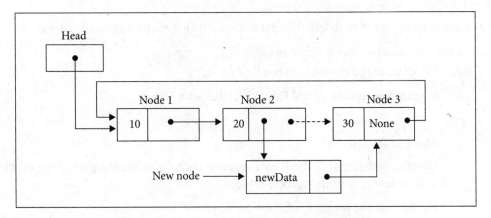

Figure 7.16   Inserting a node before the third node

Time complexity of this operation also depends on the position where the node will be inserted. But as it inserts before any node and if it inserts before the first node, we will need to update the reference part of the last node. Thus we need to move to the last node, which increments the time complexity to O(n). In this operation we will get the best case situation when the node will be inserted before the second node. In that case we need not update any other node except the first node and the new node, and the time complexity will be calculated as O(1). If a node is inserted before the last node, the time complexity will be again O(n) as we need to traverse the entire list.

7.8.4   Deleting a Node from a Circular Singly Linked List

Deletion of a node from a circular linked list is almost similar to a singly linked list. Here also first we have to find the node that is to be deleted. Next we have to update the reference part of the predecessor and successor nodes (if any) and finally de-allocate the memory spaces that are occupied by the node. Different cases what we are discussing here are:

- Deletion of the first node
- Deletion of the last node
- Deletion of any intermediate node. It may be
    - o   Deletion of the nth node or
    - o   Deletion of the node whose data part matches with the given data, etc.

7.8.4.1 Deleting the First Node

In case of first node deletion, we have to update the content of the Head variable as now it points to the second node as well as update the reference part of the last node to point to the existing second node, which will be now the first node. But if the list contains only a single node, the Head variable will contain None.

The general algorithm to delete the first node of the list may be defined as follows:

1. If the list contains only a single node
    a.   De-allocate the memory of the first node.
    b.   Update the content of the Head variable with None.

2. Else
    a.   Move to the last node
    b.   Update the content of the Head variable with the reference part of the existing first node, i.e. with the second node.
    c.   De-allocate the memory of the first node.
    d.   Update the reference part of the last node with the content of the Head variable.

Here is a function to delete the first node of a circular linked list.

```
# Function to delete the first node of a circular linked
# list
    def delete_first(self):
        if self.Head is None:
            print("Empty List. Deletion not possible...")
        else:
            curNode = self.Head
            if curNode.next==curNode:
                self.Head=None
                del(curNode)
            else:
                while curNode.next!=self.Head:
                    curNode=curNode.next
                self.Head=self.Head.next
```

```
del(curNode.next)
curNode.next=self.Head
print("Node Deleted Successfully...")
```

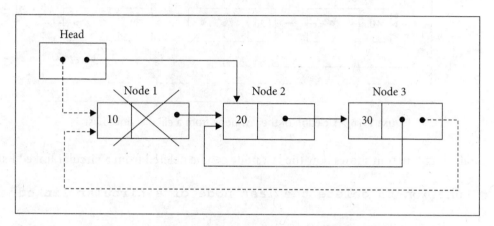

Figure 7.17 Deletion of first node from a circular linked list

Though we are deleting the first node, we have to update the reference part of the last node. Thus, we have to traverse the entire list and time complexity will be O(n).

7.8.4.2 Deleting the Last Node

As we know, to delete a node except the first node, first we have to move to the predecessor node of the node that will be deleted. So, to delete the last node we have to move at the previous node of the last node. Though our task is to delete the last node, the list may contain only a single node. Then deletion of this node makes the list empty and thus the content of the Head variable will be updated with the None value.

The general algorithm to delete the last node of the list may be defined as follows:

1. Check whether there is one or more nodes in the list.

2. If the list contains only a single node, update the content of the Head variable with None and de-allocate the memory of the node.

3. Else

   a. Move to the previous node of the last node.

   b. De-allocate the memory of the last node.

   c. Update the reference part of the current node with the first node as it will be the last node now.

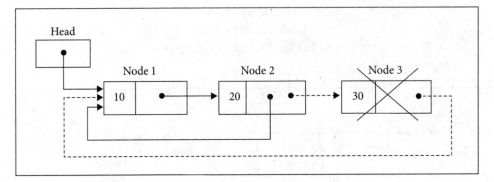

Figure 7.18   Deletion of the last node from a circular linked list

The following function shows how the last node can be deleted from a circular linked list:

```
# Function to delete the last node of a circular linked
# list
    def delete_last(self):
        if self.Head is None:
            print("Empty List. Deletion not possible...")
        else:
            curNode = self.Head
            if curNode.next==curNode:
                self.Head=None
                del(curNode)
            else:
                while curNode.next.next!=self.Head:
                    curNode=curNode.next
                del(curNode.next)
                curNode.next=self.Head
            print("Node Deleted Successfully...")
```

The time complexity to delete the last node of a circular linked list is O(n) as we need to traverse the entire list to reach the last node.

7.8.4.3 Deleting any Intermediate Node

As we discussed, in the case of deletion of a node from any intermediate position, there may be several cases such as the nth node deletion or deletion of the node whose data part matches with the given data. To delete the nth node, we have to move to the predecessor node of the nth node. Next, update the reference part of the $(n-1)^{th}$ node with the reference part of the deleted node and then de-allocate the memory of the nth node.

But in the second case we have to compare each node with the argument data. In this case, the first node, the last node, or any intermediate node may be deleted. Again, if the argument data does not match with any node, no node will be deleted.

The following algorithm describes how a node whose data part matches with the given data can be deleted:

1. Check the data of the first node with the given data.

2. If it matches, then

    a. If the list contains only a single node

        i. De-allocate the memory of the first node.

        ii. Update the content of the Head variable with None.

    b. Else

        i. Move to the last node

        ii. Update the content of the Head variable with the reference part of the existing first node, i.e. with the second node.

        iii. De-allocate the memory of the first node.

        iv. Update the reference part of the last node with the content of the Head variable.

3. Else

    a. Check the data of each node against the given data and store the reference of the current node to a variable, named 'previous', before moving to next node.

    b. If searching fails, terminate operation mentioning appropriate message like "Node not found."

    c. If match occurs, then

        i. Update the reference part of the previous node with the reference part of the current node (i.e. the node to be deleted).

        ii. De-allocate the memory of the current node (i.e. the node to be deleted).

The following function shows how the node whose data part matches with the given data can be deleted:

```
#Function to Delete a node whose Data matches with the
#given Data
def delete_anynode(self,num):
    if self.Head is None:
        print("Empty List. Deletion not possible...")
```

```
else:
    curNode = self.Head
    if curNode.data==num:                    # For 1st Node
        if curNode.next==curNode:
            self.Head=None
            del(curNode)
        else:
            while curNode.next!=self.Head:
                curNode=curNode.next
            self.Head=self.Head.next
            del(curNode.next)
            curNode.next=self.Head
            print("Node Deleted Successfully...")
    else:                                     # For Others Node
        while curNode.next!=self.Head:
            if  curNode.data == num:
                break
            prev = curNode
            curNode = curNode.next
        if curNode.data!=num:
            print("Node Not Found...")
        else:
            prev.next = curNode.next
            del(curNode)
            print("Node Deleted Successfully...")
```

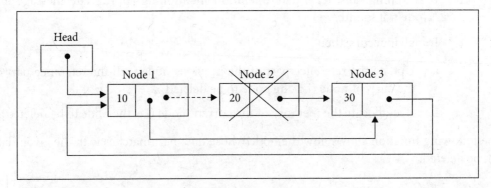

Figure 7.19   Deletion of an intermediate node (whose data value is 20) from a circular list

Time complexity of this operation also depends on the position from where the node will be deleted. If the first node is deleted, we need to update the reference part of the last node. Thus we need to move to the last node which increases the time complexity to O(n). Time complexity will be the same if the last node is deleted as then also we need to traverse the entire list. We will get the best case situation if the second node is deleted. In that case we need not move anywhere and the time complexity will be calculated as O(1).

Here is a complete program to show the various operations of a circular singly linked list:

Program 7.5: Write a program to demonstrate the various operations of circular singly linked list.

```
#PRGD7_5: Program to demonstrate Circular Linked List
class Node :
      def __init__( self,Newdata=None,link=None):
          self.data = Newdata
          self.next = link


class circularLinkedList :
      def __init__( self ):
          self.Head = None
      # Function to insert a node at the end of the list
      def insert_end(self,newData):
          newNode=Node(newData)
          if self.Head is None:
              self.Head=newNode
              newNode.next=newNode
          else:
              curNode = self.Head
              while curNode.next!=self.Head:
                  curNode = curNode.next
              curNode.next=newNode
              newNode.next=self.Head
     # Function to insert a node at the beginning of the list
      def insert_begin(self,newData):
          newNode=Node(newData,self.Head)
          if self.Head is None:
              newNode.next=newNode
          else:
              curNode = self.Head
              while curNode.next!=self.Head:
                  curNode=curNode.next
              curNode.next=newNode
          self.Head=newNode
      # Function to insert a node before Nth node
      def insert_before_nth(self,newData,location):
```

```
        newNode=Node(newData)
        if self.Head is None :
            self.Head=newNode
            newNode.next=newNode
        elif location==1:
            curNode = self.Head
            while curNode.next!=self.Head:
                curNode=curNode.next
            curNode.next=newNode
            newNode.next=self.Head
            self.Head=newNode
        else:
            curNode = self.Head
            c=1
            while c<=location-2 and curNode.next!=self.
                                                    Head:
                c+=1
                curNode = curNode.next
            newNode.next=curNode.next
            curNode.next=newNode
# Function to insert a node After Nth node
    def insert_after_nth(self,newData,location):
        newNode=Node(newData)
        if self.Head is None :
            self.Head=newNode
            newNode.next=newNode
        else:
            curNode = self.Head
            c=1
            while c<=location-1 and curNode.next!=self.
                                                    Head:
                c+=1
                curNode = curNode.next
            newNode.next=curNode.next
            curNode.next=newNode
#Function to delete the first node of a circular linked
#list
    def delete_first(self):
        if self.Head is None:
            print("Empty List. Deletion not possible...")
        else:
            curNode = self.Head
```

```
                if curNode.next==curNode:
                    self.Head=None
                    del(curNode)
            else:
                while curNode.next!=self.Head:
                    curNode=curNode.next
                self.Head=self.Head.next
                del(curNode.next)
                curNode.next=self.Head
            print("Node Deleted Successfully...")
#Function to delete the last node of a circular linked
#list
    def delete_last(self):
        if self.Head is None:
            print("Empty List. Deletion not possible...")
        else:
            curNode = self.Head
            if curNode.next==curNode:
                self.Head=None
                del(curNode)
            else:
                while curNode.next.next!=self.Head:
                    curNode=curNode.next
                del(curNode.next)
                curNode.next=self.Head
            print("Node Deleted Successfully...")
# Function to Delete a node whose Data matches with the
# given Data
    def delete_anynode(self,num):
        if self.Head is None:
            print("Empty List. Deletion not possible...")
        else:
            curNode = self.Head
            if curNode.data==num:            # For 1st Node
                if curNode.next==curNode:
                    self.Head=None
                    del(curNode)
                else:
                    while curNode.next!=self.Head:
                        curNode=curNode.next
                    self.Head=self.Head.next
                    del(curNode.next)
```

```
                    curNode.next=self.Head
             print("Node Deleted Successfully...")
        else:                              # For Others Node
            while curNode.next!=self.Head:
                if  curNode.data == num:
                    break
                prev = curNode
                curNode = curNode.next
            if curNode.data!=num:
                print("Node Not Found...")
            else:
                prev.next = curNode.next
                del(curNode)
                print("Node Deleted Successfully...")
    # Function to display the entire linked list
    def display(self):
        if self.Head is None:
            print("Empty List.")
        else:
            curNode = self.Head
            while curNode.next != self.Head :
                print(curNode.data,end="->")
                curNode = curNode.next
            print(curNode.data)

head=circularLinkedList()
while True:
    print("\nPROGRAM TO IMPLEMENT CIRCULAR LINKED LIST ")
    print("====================================")
    print("1.Create / Appending The List")
    print("2.Insert Node At Begining")
    print("3.Insert Node Before Nth node")
    print("4.Insert Node After Nth node")
    print("5.Delete First Node")
    print("6.Delete Last Node")
    print("7.Delete the Node whose Data matches with given
                                            Data")
    print("8.Displaying the list")
    print("9.Exit")
    print("====================================")
    choice=int(input("Enter your Choice : "))
    if choice==1 :
```

```
        opt='Y'
        while opt.upper()=='Y':
            num=int(input("Enter the Data: "))
            head.insert_end(num)
            opt=input("Enter more (y/n) :")
    elif choice==2 :
        num=int(input("Enter the Data: "))
        head.insert_begin(num)
    elif choice==3 :
        loc=int(input("Enter The Node number Before which
                          new node will be inserted :"))
        num=int(input("Enter the Data: "))
        head.insert_before_nth(num,loc)
    elif choice==4 :
        loc=int(input("Enter The Node number After which
                          new node will be inserted :"))
        num=int(input("Enter the Data: "))
        head.insert_after_nth(num,loc)
    elif choice==5 :
        head.delete_first()
    elif choice==6 :
        head.delete_last()
    elif choice==7 :
        num=int(input("Enter The Data You Want To Delete :
                                               "))
        head.delete_anynode(num)
    elif choice==8 :
        head.display()
    elif choice==9 :
        print("\nQuiting.......")
        break
    else:
        print("Invalid choice. Please Enter Correct Choice")
        continue
```

7.9 Applications of a Circular Singly Linked List

A circular linked list is a very important data structure in computer programming where we need to access data circularly or repeatedly. Though its use is not as broad as a singly linear linked list, yet sometimes it shows its efficiency in implementing data structures such as queues. As in a queue insertion takes place at one end and deletion takes place at the other end, to implement a queue using a singly linked list we need two pointers. But if we use a circular linked list, only one pointer is sufficient. (Details given in Chapter 9.)

Implementation of waiting and context switch uses queues in an operating system. When there are multiple processes running on an operating system and limited time slots are provided for each process, the waiting process can form a circular linked list. The task at head of the list is given CPU time; once the time allocated finishes, the task is taken out and added to the list again at the end and it continues.

Circular lists are useful in applications to repeatedly go around the list. We can implement the Josephus Problem – a classical problem in data structure.

Josephus Problem: The Josephus Problem is a counting-out game problem. People will stand in a circle. Counting begins from a specified position in the circle and proceeds around the circle. After skipping a specified number of people, the next person will be eliminated from the circle. This process will continue for the remaining people, starting with the person next to the eliminated person, until only one person remains and is freed.

Program 7.6: Write a program to implement the Josephus problem.

```
#PRGD7_6: Program to implement Josephus Problem.

class Node :
     def __init__( self, Newdata=None, link=None ) :
          self.data = Newdata
          self.next = link


class circularLinkedList :
     def __init__( self ):
          self.Head = None
     # Function to Create a circular Linked List
     def createList( self ) :
        self.Head = Node()
        cur = self.Head
        while True:
             cur.data=input("Enter Name : ")
             ch = input("Continue?(y/n): ")
             if ch.upper()=='Y':
                 cur.next = Node()
                 cur = cur.next
             else:
                 cur.next = self.Head
                 break

Jlist=circularLinkedList()
```

```
Jlist.createList()
ptr=Jlist.Head
n=int(input("Enter any number: "))
while ptr.next!=ptr:
    for i in range(1,n):
          prev=ptr
          ptr=ptr.next
    prev.next=ptr.next
    ptr=prev.next
print(ptr.data,"will be freed")
```

Sample output:

Enter Name : Subrata
Continue?(y/n): y
Enter Name : Gautam
Continue?(y/n): y
Enter Name : Arijit
Continue?(y/n): y
Enter Name : Dibyendu
Continue?(y/n): n
Enter any number: 3
Subrata will be freed

7.10 Implementing a Doubly Linked List

In a singly linked list, once we move to the next node, the previous nodes cannot be traversed again. This problem can be solved partially using a circular linked list. But the disadvantage with this is that to return to the previous node we have to traverse the entire list circularly, which is time and effort consuming for large lists. In situations where we need to traverse nodes in both directions frequently it is really a problem. To solve this we can implement a **doubly linked list** by implementing a minor modification in the node structure. It is similar to a linear singly linked list but here each node contains an extra member to store the reference of the previous node. As each node contains both the reference of the previous and successor nodes, we can traverse the list in both directions. The disadvantage of a doubly linked list is that it requires extra spaces. So, it needs to be used extremely judiciously on the specific situations where traversing in both directions is frequently required.

So, to implement a doubly linked list we have to declare a node with at least three members, one of which holds the data and the other two point to the previous and next nodes respectively in the list. Thus we can define the class to represent the node of a doubly linked list as follows:

```
class DNode :
    def __init__(self,Newdata=None,plink=None,nlink=No
                                                      ne):
        self.previous = plink
        self.data = Newdata
        self.next = nlink
```

Figure 7.20 illustrates the representation of a doubly linked list.

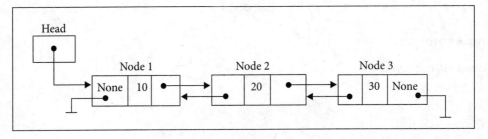

Figure 7.20   Representation of a doubly linked list in memory

In the Figure7.20, the linked list consists of three nodes. The data values of the nodes are 10, 20, and 30 respectively. Node1 is the first node in the list; thus its previous part contains None as there is no node before it and the next part contains the reference of its successor node, i.e. Node2. Similarly the previous and next parts of Node2 contain references of Node1 and Node3 respectively as they are the predecessor and successor nodes of it. Node3 is the last node of this list. Thus next part of Node3 also contains None and its previous part contains the reference of Node2.

7.11 Operations on a Doubly Linked List

All the operations that can be done on a singly linked list or on a circular linked list can also be done on a doubly linked list. To reduce the monotonousness of the discussion, here we implement some of these. In all the subsequent cases we use the following class definition for the node.

```
class DNode :
    def __init__(self,Newdata=None,plink=None,nlink=No
                                                      ne):
        self.previous = plink
        self.data = Newdata
        self.next = nlink
```

7.11.1 Inserting an Element at the Beginning of a Doubly Linked List

As the element will be inserted at the beginning of the list, the content of the Head variable will be updated by the new node. The previous part of the new node will contain None as there is no node before it and next part will contain the reference of the existing first node. The previous part of the existing first node will contain the reference of the new node.

The general algorithm to insert an element at the beginning of a doubly linked list may be defined as follows:

1. Create a new node.
2. Update its data part with the function argument.
3. Update its previous part with None.
4. Update its next part with the content of the Head variable.
5. Update the previous part of the existing first node, if any, with the new node.
6. Update the content of the Head variable with the new node.

Figure 7.21 shows the position of pointers after inserting a node at the beginning of a doubly linked list.

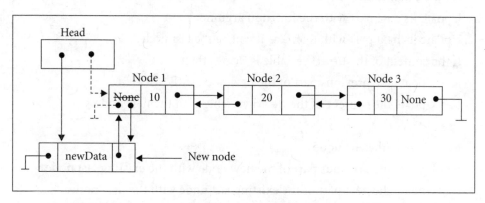

Figure 7.21   Inserting a node at the beginning of a doubly linked list

The following is the function of above algorithm:

```
# Function to insert a node at the beginning of the list
    def insert_begin(self,newData):
        newNode=DNode(newData,None,self.Head)
        if self.Head is not None:
            self.Head.previous=newNode
        self.Head=newNode
```

In the above function, if the list is empty, both the previous and next parts of the new node will store None as it is the only node in the list. Otherwise the previous part of the new node will contain None and the next part will store the reference of the existing first node. So, the new node becomes the first node, and to point to the first node of the list, Head will store the reference of the new node. The previous first node, if it exists, now becomes the second node; so its previous part will point to the new node.

Time complexity calculation in case of a doubly linked list is the same as in a single linear linked list as the basic logic is the same for both. Here we only need to take extra care of the previous part of the node. Thus time complexity to insert a node at the beginning of a doubly linked list is O(1).

7.11.2 Inserting an Element at the End of a Doubly Linked List

This operation is almost similar to a single linked list. Here also we have to move to the last node and then have to update the next part of the last node with the new node. The only difference is here the new node that will be inserted at the end will also point to the existing last node. The time complexity of this operation is O(n).

The general algorithm to insert an element at the end of a list may be defined as follows:

1. Create a new node.
2. Update its data part with the function argument.
3. Update its next part with None as it will be the last node.
4. If the content of the Head variable is None, then
    a. Update the previous part of the new node with None.
    b. Update the content of the Head variable with the new node.
5. Else
    a. Move to the last node
    b. Update the previous part of the new node with the existing last node.
    c. Update the next part of the existing last node with the new node.

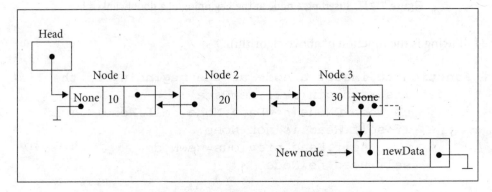

Figure 7.22   Inserting a node at the end of a doubly linked list

Figure 7.22 shows the position of pointers after inserting a node at the end of a doubly linked list.

Using the above algorithm we can write the following code:

```
# Function to insert a node at the end of the list
def insert_end(self,newData):
    newNode=DNode(newData)
    if self.Head is None:
        self.Head=newNode
    else:
        curNode = self.Head
        while curNode.next is not None :
            curNode = curNode.next
        curNode.next=newNode
        newNode.previous=curNode
```

As the new node will be inserted at the end, its next part should be initialized with None first. If the list is empty initially, the previous part of the new node will also store None. Otherwise, move to the last node by checking whether the next part is None. Update the previous part of the new node with the existing last node as it will also point to the last node and update the next part of the existing last node with the new node.

7.11.3 Inserting a Node at a Specified Position in a Doubly Linked List

In case of singly linked and circular linked lists we inserted a node before and after a particular node. In case of a double linked list the same type of function can be written following the same algorithm. Here we will see almost the same function but in a slightly different form. Now we will insert a node at a specified position. If we want to insert a node at the nth position, the new node may be inserted at any position – it may be the beginning of a list, the end of a list, or any intermediate position. But if the value of n is larger than the node count, what will happen? We have two options. We can reject the insertion operation mentioning an error message that sufficient nodes are not present in the list or simply a new node can be inserted at the end. Here we opt for the latter option.

The following algorithm describes how a new node can be inserted at the nth position.

1. Create a new node.

2. Update its data part with the function argument.

3. If the content of the Head variable is None or the value of n is 1, then

    a. Update the previous part of the new node with None.

    b. Update the next part of the new node with the content of the Head variable.

c. Update the previous part of the existing first node, if any, with the reference of the new node.

d. Update the content of the Head variable with the reference of the new node.

4. Else

a. Move to the previous node of the nth node and make it the current node.

b. If the specified node does not exist, stay at the last node and make it the current node.

c. Update the next part of the new node with the next part of the current node.

d. Update the previous part of the new node with the current node.

e. Update the next part of the current node with the new node.

f. Update the previous part of the next to current node, if any, with the new node.

Using the above algorithm we can write the following code.

```python
# Function to insert a node at Nth position, i.e. before
# Nth node
    def insert_before_nth(self,newData,location):
        newNode=DNode(newData)
        if self.Head is None or location==1:
            if self.Head is not None:
                self.Head.previous=newNode
            newNode.next=self.Head
            self.Head=newNode
        else:
            curNode = self.Head
            c=1
            while c<=location-2 and curNode.next is not
                                                None :
                c+=1
                curNode = curNode.next
            newNode.next=curNode.next
            newNode.previous=curNode
            if curNode.next!=None:
                curNode.next.previous=newNode
            curNode.next=newNode
```

Figure 7.23 shows the position of nodes and their references after inserting a node at the third position in a doubly linked list.

In this algorithm as the new node is inserted at the nth position the time complexity calculation depends on the value of n. When n = 1, we are inserting at the first position. Thus we need not traverse any node except the first one. So, the time complexity is O(1). This is the best case. But if n denotes the last node, we have to traverse all the nodes. Then the time complexity would be O(n).

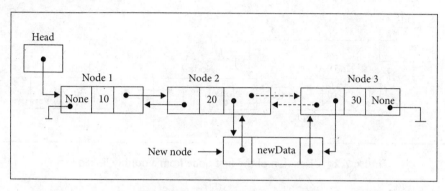

Figure 7.23   Inserting a node at the third position in a doubly linked list

7.11.4 Deleting a Node from a Doubly Linked List

Deletion of a node from a doubly linked list is also similar to a singly linked list. Only we have to take extra care of the previous part of the next node, if any. Here also first we have to find the node that is to be deleted. Next we have to update the previous and next parts of the predecessor and/or successor nodes and finally need to de-allocate the memory spaces that are occupied by the node. Different cases of what we are discussing here are:

- Deletion of the first node
- Deletion of the last node
- Deletion of any intermediate node

7.11.4.1 Deleting the First Node

In case of first node deletion, here also we have to update the content of the Head variable as now it will point to the second node, and the previous part of the second node, if any exists, will point to None as it becomes the first node. But if the list contains only a single node, the Head variable will contain None. The time complexity of deletion of the first node is O(1).

The general algorithm to delete the first node of the list may be defined as follows:

1. Update the content of the Head variable with the reference part of the first node, i.e. with the second node.

2. If the second node exists, update its previous part with None as it will be the first node now.

3. De-allocate the memory of the first node.

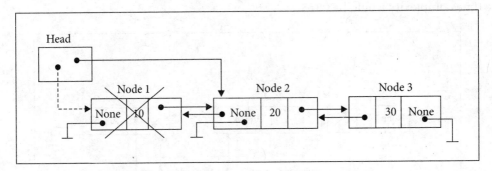

Figure 7.24   Deletion of the first node from a doubly linked list

Here is a function to delete the first node of a linked list.

```
# Function to delete the first node of a linked list
def delete_first(self):
    if self.Head is None:
        print("Empty List. Deletion not possible...")
    else:
        curNode = self.Head
        self.Head=self.Head.next
        if self.Head is not None:
            self.Head.previous=None
        del(curNode)
        print("Node Deleted Successfully...")
```

7.11.4.2 Deleting the Last Node

As a doubly linked list contains the references of both previous and next nodes, to delete the last we can move to the last node as well as its previous node. From both positions we can delete the last node. Though our task is to delete the last node, the list may contain only a single node. Then deletion of this node makes the list empty and thus the content of the Head variable will be updated with the None value. The time complexity of the deletion of the last node is O(n).

The general algorithm to delete the last node of the list may be defined as follows:

1. Check whether there is one or more nodes in the list.

2. If the list contains only a single node, update the content of the Head variable with None and de-allocate the memory of the node.

3. Else

   a. Move to the previous node of the last node.

   b. De-allocate the memory of the last node.

   c. Update the next part of the current node with None as it will be the last node now.

Here is a function to delete the last node of a linked list:

```
# Function to delete the last node of a linked list
    def delete_last(self):
        if self.Head is None:
            print("Empty List. Deletion not possible...")
        elif self.Head.next is None:
                    #If the list contains single node only
            del(self.Head)
            self.Head=None
        else:
            curNode = self.Head
            while curNode.next.next is not None :
                curNode = curNode.next
            del(curNode.next)
            curNode.next=None
            print("Node Deleted Successfully...")
```

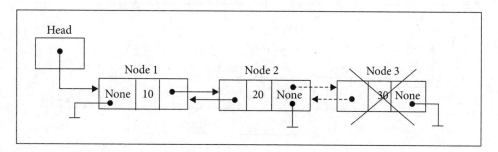

Figure 7.25 Deletion of last node from a doubly linked list

7.11.4.3 Deleting any Intermediate Node

In case of singly linked and circular linked lists we discussed the deletion of a node whose data part matched with the given data. In case of a doubly linked list the same algorithm can be followed with the necessary extra pointer adjustment for the previous part. Here we will discuss the nth node deletion as an intermediate node deletion. To delete the nth node, we have to consider two cases. It may be the first node or any other node. If it is the first node, the operations are similar to the deletion of the first node. But in second case we may move to the nth node or its previous node. From both positions we can delete the specified node.

The general algorithm to delete the nth node of the list may be defined as follows:

1. If n = 1, then

     a.   Update the content of the Head variable with the reference part of first node, i.e. with the second node.

     b.   If the second node exists, update its previous part with None as it will be the first node now.

     c.   De-allocate the memory of the first node.

2. Else

     a.   If there is less than n number of nodes, terminate operation mentioning appropriate message like "Node not found."

     b.   Otherwise, move to the $(n-1)^{th}$ node and make it the current node.

     c.   Update the reference part of the current node with the reference part of the next node (i.e. the nth node).

     d.   If the reference part of the nth node is not None, i.e. if the $(n+1)^{th}$ node exists, update the previous part of the $(n+1)^{th}$ node with the current node.

     e.   De-allocate the memory of the next node (i.e. the nth node).

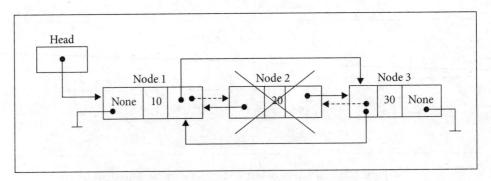

Figure 7.26   Deletion of the second node from a doubly linked list

Here is a function to delete the nth node of a linked list:

```
# Function to Delete N-th node
def delete_nth(self,posn):
```

```
        if self.Head is None:
            print("Empty List. Deletion not possible...")
        else:
            curNode = self.Head
            if posn==1:                    # For 1st Node
                self.Head=curNode.next
                del(curNode)
                if self.Head is not None:
                    self.Head.previous=None
                print("Node Deleted Successfully...")
            else:                          # For Others Node
                c=1
                while c<=posn-2 and curNode.next is not
                                                    None :
                    c+=1
                    curNode = curNode.next
                if curNode.next is None:
                    print("Node Not Found...")
                else:
                    temp=curNode.next
                    curNode.next=temp.next
                    if temp.next is not None:
                        temp.next.previous=curNode
                    del(temp)
                    print("Node Deleted Successfully...")
```

The time complexity calculation of this operation depends on the position of the node in the list. If we delete the first node, that is the best case and the time complexity is O(1). But if we delete the last node or the node is not found at all, that will be the worst case and we have to traverse the entire list. Then the time complexity will be O(n).

Here is a complete program to show the various operations of a doubly linked list:

Program 7.7: Write a program to demonstrate the various operations of a doubly linked list.

```
#PRGD7_7: Program to demonstrate Doubly Linked List

class DNode :
    def __init__(self,Newdata=None,plink=None,nlink=No
                                                    ne):
        self.data = Newdata
        self.previous = plink
```

```
            self.next = nlink

class doublyLinkedList :
     def __init__( self ):
          self.Head = None
     # Function to insert a node at the end of the list
     def insert_end(self,newData):
          newNode=DNode(newData)
          if self.Head is None:
              self.Head=newNode
          else:
              curNode = self.Head
              while curNode.next is not None :
                   curNode = curNode.next
              curNode.next=newNode
              newNode.previous=curNode
# Function to insert a node at the beginning of the list
     def insert_begin(self,newData):
          newNode=DNode(newData,None,self.Head)
          if self.Head is not None:
               self.Head.previous=newNode
          self.Head=newNode
# Function to insert a node at Nth position, i.e. before
# Nth node
     def insert_before_nth(self,newData,location):
          newNode=DNode(newData)
          if self.Head is None or location==1:
               if self.Head is not None:
                   self.Head.previous=newNode
               newNode.next=self.Head
               self.Head=newNode
          else:
               curNode = self.Head
               c=1
               while c<=location-2 and curNode.next is not
                                                      None :
                   c+=1
                   curNode = curNode.next
               newNode.next=curNode.next
               newNode.previous=curNode
               if curNode.next!=None:
                   curNode.next.previous=newNode
```

```
            curNode.next=newNode
# Function to insert a node after Nth node
def insert_after_nth(self,newData,location):
    newNode=DNode(newData)
    if self.Head is None:
        self.Head=newNode
    else:
        curNode = self.Head
        c=1
        while c<=location-1 and curNode.next is not
                                            None :
            c+=1
            curNode = curNode.next
        newNode.next=curNode.next
        newNode.previous=curNode
        if curNode.next!=None:
            curNode.next.previous=newNode
        curNode.next=newNode
# Function to delete the first node of a linked list
def delete_first(self):
    if self.Head is None:
        print("Empty List. Deletion not possible...")
    else:
        curNode = self.Head
        self.Head=self.Head.next
        if self.Head is not None:
            self.Head.previous=None
        del(curNode)
        print("Node Deleted Successfully...")
# Function to delete the last node of a linked list
def delete_last(self):
    if self.Head is None:
        print("Empty List. Deletion not possible...")
    elif self.Head.next is None:
        del(self.Head)
        self.Head=None
    else:
        curNode = self.Head
        while curNode.next.next is not None :
            curNode = curNode.next
        del(curNode.next)
        curNode.next=None
```

```python
            print("Node Deleted Successfully...")
# Function to Delete N-th node
def delete_nth(self,posn):
    if self.Head is None:
        print("Empty List. Deletion not possible...")
    else:
        curNode = self.Head
        if posn==1:                      # For 1st Node
            self.Head=curNode.next
            del(curNode)
            if self.Head is not None:
                self.Head.previous=None
            print("Node Deleted Successfully...")
        else:                            # For Others Node
            c=1
            while c<=posn-2 and curNode.next is not
                                              None :
                c+=1
                curNode = curNode.next
            if curNode.next is None:
                print("Node Not Found...")
            else:
                temp=curNode.next
                curNode.next=temp.next
                if temp.next is not None:
                    temp.next.previous=curNode
                del(temp)
                print("Node Deleted Successfully...")
# Function to display the entire linked list
def display(self):
    if self.Head is None:
        print("Empty List.")
    else:
        curNode = self.Head
        print("None<=>",end="")
        while curNode is not None :
            print(curNode.data,end="<=>")
            curNode = curNode.next
        print("None")
# Function to display in reverse order
def rev_display(self):
    if self.Head is None:
```

```
                    print("Empty List.")
            else:
                curNode = self.Head
                print("None<=>",end="")
                while curNode.next is not None :
                    curNode = curNode.next
                while curNode is not None :
                    print(curNode.data,end="<=>")
                    curNode = curNode.previous
                print("None")


head=doublyLinkedList()
while True:
    print("\nPROGRAM TO IMPLEMENT DOUBLY LINKED LIST ")
    print("=====================================")
    print(" 1.Create / Appending The List")
    print(" 2.Insert Node At Begining")
    print(" 3.Insert Node at Nth position")
    print(" 4.Insert Node After Nth node")
    print(" 5.Delete First Node")
    print(" 6.Delete Last Node")
    print(" 7.Delete Nth Node")
    print(" 8.Displaying the list")
    print(" 9.Displaying the list in Reverse Order")
    print("10.Exit")
    print("=====================================")
    choice=int(input("Enter your Choice : "))
    if choice==1 :
        opt='Y'
        while opt.upper()=='Y':
            num=int(input("Enter the Data: "))
            head.insert_end(num)
            opt=input("Enter more (y/n) :")
    elif choice==2 :
        num=int(input("Enter the Data: "))
        head.insert_begin(num)
    elif choice==3 :
        loc=int(input("Enter The Node number Before which
                            new node will be inserted :"))
        num=int(input("Enter the Data: "))
        head.insert_before_nth(num,loc)
    elif choice==4 :
```

```
        loc=int(input("Enter The Node number After which
                        new node will be inserted :"))
        num=int(input("Enter the Data: "))
        head.insert_after_nth(num,loc)
    elif choice==5 :
        head.delete_first()
    elif choice==6 :
        head.delete_last()
    elif choice==7 :
        num=int(input("Enter The Node Number You Want To
                                            Delete:"))
        head.delete_nth(num)
    elif choice==8 :
        head.display()
    elif choice==9 :
        head.rev_display()
    elif choice==10:
        print("\nQuiting.......")
        break
    else:
        print("Invalid choice. Please Enter Correct
                                            Choice")

        continue
```

7.12 Implementation of a Circular Doubly Linked List

A circular doubly linked list is basically a combination of a circular list and a doubly linked list. It is similar to a linear doubly linked list with a single exception. Here, instead of storing None values in the previous part of the first node and the next part of the last node, the two parts point to the last node and the first node respectively. The advantage of this list is that we can traverse in any direction, i.e. forward, backward, or circularly, in this list.

To implement a circular doubly linked list we can use the same class that is used to implement a doubly linked list. Whatever change we need to do have to be done programmatically. Figure 7.27 illustrates the representation of a circular doubly linked list.

In Figure 7.27, the linked list consists of three nodes. The data values of the nodes are 10, 20, and 30 respectively. Node1 is the first node in the list; thus its previous part points to the last node of the list, i.e. here Node3, and the next part points to its successor node, i.e. Node2. Similarly the previous and next parts of Node2 point to Node1 and Node3 respectively as they are its predecessor and successor nodes. Node3 is the last node of this list. Thus the next part of Node3 also contains the reference of the first node, i.e. Node1, and its previous part contains the reference of Node2.

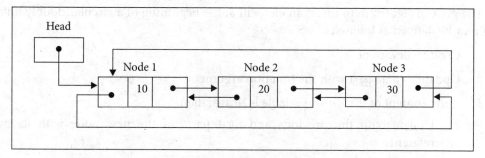

Figure 7.27　Representation of a circular doubly linked list in memory

7.13 Operations on a Circular Doubly Linked List

Similar to other linked lists, here also we can implement all operations such as insertion of node at the beginning or at the end or at any intermediate position and deletion of the first node, last node, or any intermediate node. In case of a circular doubly linked list we can traverse the list in forward direction, backward direction as well as circularly. In this section we will discuss some of these operations. As to implementing a circular doubly linked list, the same class of doubly linked list is required; in all the subsequent cases we use the following class definition for the node:

```
class DNode :
    def __init__(self,Newdata=None,plink=None,nlink=No
                                                    ne):
        self.data = Newdata
        self.previous = plink
        self.next = nlink
```

7.13.1 Inserting an Element at the Beginning of a Circular Doubly Linked List

To insert an element at the beginning of the list, the content of the Head variable will be updated by the reference of the new node. The previous part of the new node will contain the reference of the last node as it will be the first node and the next part of the new node will contain the reference of the existing first node. The previous part of the existing first node will contain the reference of the new node like a linear doubly linked list. The next part of the last node will contain the reference of the new node as the list becomes circular.

The advantage of a circular doubly linked list is that when we insert an element at the beginning of a list, unlike a single circular list, we need not move to the end of a list to update the last node. We can access the last node staying at the first node. That is why the time complexity to insert a node at the beginning of a circular doubly linked list is O(1).

The general algorithm to insert an element at the beginning of a circular doubly linked list may be defined as follows:

1. Create a new node.

2. Update its data part with the function argument.

3. If the content of the `Head` variable is `None`, then

   a. Update both the previous and next parts of the new node with its own reference.

4. Else

   a. Point the last node from the first node as it is the previous node of the first node.

   b. Update the previous part of the new node with the last node.

   c. Update the next part of the new node with the reference of the existing first node.

   d. Update the previous part of the existing first node with the new node.

   e. Update the next part of the last node with the new node.

5. Update the content of the `Head` variable with the new node.

Figure 7.28 shows the position of pointers after inserting a node at the beginning of a circular doubly linked list.

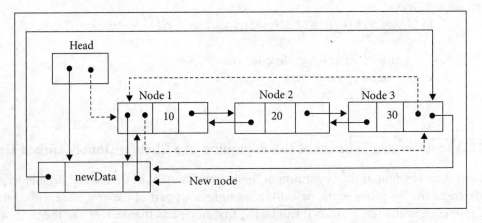

Figure 7.28   Inserting a node at the beginning of a circular doubly linked list

The following function describes the above algorithm:

```
# Function to insert a node at the beginning of the list
def insert_begin(self,newData):
        newNode=DNode(newData,None,self.Head)
        if self.Head is None:
```

```
        newNode.next=newNode
        newNode.previous=newNode
else:
        curNode = self.Head
        lastNode=curNode.previous
        newNode.previous=lastNode
        newNode.next=curNode
        curNode.previous=newNode
        lastNode.next=newNode
self.Head=newNode
```

7.13.2 Inserting an Element at the End of a Circular Doubly Linked List

To insert a node at the end of a circular doubly linked list, we may face two situations. First, the list may be empty and, second, there is an existing list. For an empty list we have to update the Head variable with the new node, and the previous and next parts of the new node will point to itself. But in the second case, we need not update the Head variable as the new node will be appended at the end. We just need to move to the last node and then update both the next part of the last node and the previous part of the first node with the new node. The previous and next parts of the new node will be updated with the existing last node and first node respectively.

The time complexity to insert a node at the end of a circular doubly linked list is also $O(1)$ as we can access the last node staying at the first node. We need not traverse the entire list.

The general algorithm to insert an element at the end of a circular doubly linked list may be defined as follows:

1. Create a new node.

2. Update its data part with the function argument.

3. If the content of the Head variable is None, then

    a. Update both the previous and next parts of the new node with its own reference.

    b. Update the content of the Head variable with the new node.

4. Else

    a. Point to the last node from the first node as it is the previous node of the first node.

    b. Update the previous part of the new node with the existing last node.

    c. Update the next part of the new node with the first node.

    d. Update the previous part of the first node with the new node.

    e. Update the next part of the existing last node with the new node.

Using the above algorithm we can write the following code:

```python
# Function to insert a node at the end of the list
def insert_end(self,newData):
    newNode=DNode(newData)
    if self.Head is None:
        self.Head=newNode
        newNode.next=newNode
        newNode.previous=newNode
    else:
        curNode = self.Head
        lastNode=curNode.previous
        newNode.previous=lastNode
        newNode.next=curNode
        curNode.previous=newNode
        lastNode.next=newNode
```

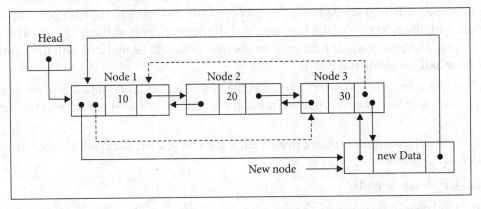

Figure 7.29   Inserting a node at the end of a circular doubly linked list

Figure 7.29 shows the position of pointers after inserting a node at the end of a circular doubly linked list.

7.13.3 Deleting the First Node from a Circular Doubly Linked List

In case of first node deletion, here also we have to update the content of the Head variable as now it will point to the second node, and the previous part of the second node, if any exists, will point to the last node as it becomes the first node. The next part of the last node now points to this existing second node. But if the list contains only a single node, the Head variable will contain None.

The time complexity to delete the first node from a circular doubly linked list is also O(1) as we can access the last node staying at the first node. We need not traverse the entire list.

The general algorithm to delete the first node from a circular doubly linked list may be defined as follows:

1. If the list contains only a single node

    a. Update the content of the Head variable with None.

2. Else

    a. Move to the last node by getting the reference of the last node from the previous part of the first node.

    b. Update the content of the Head variable with the next part of the first node, i.e. with the existing second node.

    c. Update the previous part of the existing second node (which has now become the first node) with the last node.

    d. Update the next part of the last node with the existing second node.

3. De-allocate the memory of the first node.

Figure 7.30 shows the position of pointers after deleting the first node from a circular doubly linked list.

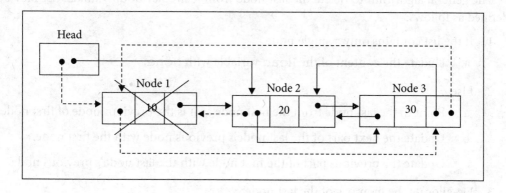

Figure 7.30 Deletion of the first node from a circular doubly linked list

Here is a function to delete the first node of a circular doubly linked list:

```
# Function to delete the first node of a linked list
def delete_first(self):
    if self.Head is None:
        print("Empty List. Deletion not possible...")
    else:
        curNode = self.Head
        if curNode.next==curNode:
```

```
                self.Head=None
        else:
                lastNode=curNode.previous
                self.Head=self.Head.next
                self.Head.previous=lastNode
                lastNode.next=self.Head
        del(curNode)
        print("Node Deleted Successfully...")
```

7.13.4 Deleting the Last Node from a Circular Doubly Linked List

As a doubly linked list contains the references of both the previous and next nodes, to delete the last node we may move to the last node as well as its previous node. From both positions we can delete the last node. We have to update only the next part of the last node's previous node and the previous part of the first node.

As in a circular doubly linked list we can access the last node staying at the first node, we need not traverse the entire list. Thus the time complexity to delete the last node is also O(1).

The general algorithm to delete the last node from a circular doubly linked list may be defined as follows:

1. If the list contains only a single node

    a. Update the content of the Head variable with None.

2. Else

    a. Point to the last node from the first node as it is the previous node of first node.

    b. Update the next part of the last node's previous node with the first node.

    c. Update the previous part of the first node with the last node's previous node.

3. De-allocate the memory of the last node.

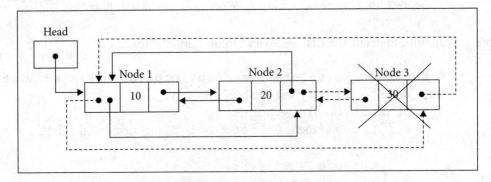

Figure 7.31   Deletion of the last node from a circular doubly linked list

Figure 7.31 shows the position of pointers after deleting the last node from a circular doubly linked list.

Here is a function to delete the last node of a circular doubly linked list:

```
# Function to delete the last node of a linked list
def delete_last(self):
    if self.Head is None:
        print("Empty List. Deletion not possible...")
    else:
        curNode = self.Head
        if curNode.next==curNode:
            self.Head=None
            del(curNode)
        else:
            lastNode=curNode.previous
            lastNode.previous.next=curNode
            curNode.previous=lastNode.previous
            del(lastNode)
        print("Node Deleted Successfully...")
```

For a circular doubly linked list, we have discussed the insertion operation at the beginning and the end of a list and the deletion operation of the first and last nodes. Insertion of a node at any intermediate position and deletion of any intermediate node can also be written similarly. To remove monotonousness we are not discussing these operations but the code of these functions is given in the Program 7.8.

Here is a complete program to show the various operations of circular doubly linked list:

Program 7.8: Write a program to demonstrate the various operations of circular doubly linked list.

```
#PRGD7_8: Program to demonstrate Circular Doubly Linked List

class DNode :
    def __init__(self,Newdata=None,plink=None,nlink=No
                                                    ne):
        self.data = Newdata
        self.previous = plink
        self.next = nlink

class doublyLinkedList :
    def __init__( self ):
        self.Head = None
```

```python
# Function to insert a node at the end of the list
def insert_end(self,newData):
    newNode=DNode(newData)
    if self.Head is None:
        self.Head=newNode
        newNode.next=newNode
        newNode.previous=newNode
    else:
        curNode = self.Head
        lastNode=curNode.previous
        newNode.previous=lastNode
        newNode.next=curNode
        curNode.previous=newNode
        lastNode.next=newNode
# Function to insert a node at the beginning of the list
def insert_begin(self,newData):
    newNode=DNode(newData,None,self.Head)
    if self.Head is None:
        newNode.next=newNode
        newNode.previous=newNode
    else:
        curNode = self.Head
        lastNode=curNode.previous
        newNode.previous=lastNode
        newNode.next=curNode
        curNode.previous=newNode
        lastNode.next=newNode
    self.Head=newNode
#Function to insert a node at Nth position, i.e. before
#Nth node
def insert_before_nth(self,newData,location):
    newNode=DNode(newData)
    if self.Head is None or location==1:
        if self.Head is None:
            newNode.next=newNode
            newNode.previous=newNode
        else:
            curNode = self.Head
            lastNode=curNode.previous
            newNode.previous=lastNode
            newNode.next=curNode
            curNode.previous=newNode
```

```
                  lastNode.next=newNode
            self.Head=newNode
      else:
            curNode = self.Head
            c=1
            while c<=location-2 and curNode.next is not
                                                  None :
                  c+=1
                  curNode = curNode.next
            newNode.next=curNode.next
            newNode.previous=curNode
            curNode.next.previous=newNode
            curNode.next=newNode
# Function to insert a node after Nth node
def insert_after_nth(self,newData,location):
      newNode=DNode(newData)
      if self.Head is None:
            self.Head=newNode
            newNode.next=newNode
            newNode.previous=newNode
      else:
            curNode = self.Head
            c=1
            while c<=location-1 and curNode.next is not
                                                  None :
                  c+=1
                  curNode = curNode.next
            newNode.next=curNode.next
            newNode.previous=curNode
            curNode.next.previous=newNode
            curNode.next=newNode
# Function to delete the first node of a linked list
def delete_first(self):
      if self.Head is None:
            print("Empty List. Deletion not possible...")
      else:
            curNode = self.Head
            if curNode.next==curNode:
                  self.Head=None
            else:
                  lastNode=curNode.previous
                  self.Head=self.Head.next
```

```
                    self.Head.previous=lastNode
                    lastNode.next=self.Head
            del(curNode)
            print("Node Deleted Successfully...")
# Function to delete the last node of a linked list
def delete_last(self):
    if self.Head is None:
        print("Empty List. Deletion not possible...")
    else:
        curNode = self.Head
        if curNode.next==curNode:
            self.Head=None
            del(curNode)
        else:
            lastNode=curNode.previous
            lastNode.previous.next=curNode
            curNode.previous=lastNode.previous
            del(lastNode)
        print("Node Deleted Successfully...")
# Function to Delete N-th node
def delete_nth(self,posn):
    if self.Head is None:
        print("Empty List. Deletion not possible...")
    else:
        curNode = self.Head
        if posn==1:
            if curNode.next==curNode:
                self.Head=None
            else:
                lastNode=curNode.previous
                self.Head=self.Head.next
                self.Head.previous=lastNode
                lastNode.next=self.Head
            del(curNode)
            print("Node Deleted Successfully...")
        else:
            c=1
            while c<=posn-2 and curNode.next!=self.
                                                Head:
                c+=1
                curNode = curNode.next
            if curNode.next==self.Head:
```

```
                print("Node Not Found...")
            else:
                temp=curNode.next
                curNode.next=temp.next
                temp.next.previous=curNode
                del(temp)
                print("Node Deleted Successfully...")
    # Function to display the entire linked list
    def display(self):
        if self.Head is None:
            print("Empty List.")
        else:
            curNode = self.Head
            while curNode.next != self.Head :
                print(curNode.data,end="<=>")
                curNode = curNode.next
            print(curNode.data)
    # Function to display in reverse order
    def rev_display(self):
        if self.Head is None:
            print("Empty List.")
        else:
            firstNode = self.Head
            curNode=lastNode=firstNode.previous
            while curNode.previous!=lastNode:
                print(curNode.data,end="<=>")
                curNode = curNode.previous
            print(curNode.data)


head=doublyLinkedList()
while True:
    print("\nPROGRAM TO IMPLEMENT CIRCULAR DOUBLY LINKED
                                            LIST ")
    print("=====================================")
    print(" 1.Create / Appending The List")
    print(" 2.Insert Node At Begining")
    print(" 3.Insert Node at Nth position")
    print(" 4.Insert Node After Nth node")
    print(" 5.Delete First Node")
    print(" 6.Delete Last Node")
    print(" 7.Delete Nth Node")
    print(" 8.Displaying the list")
```

```
print(" 9.Displaying the list in Reverse Order")
print("10.Exit")
print("====================================")
choice=int(input("Enter your Choice : "))
if choice==1 :
    opt='Y'
    while opt.upper()=='Y':
        num=int(input("Enter the Data: "))
        head.insert_end(num)
        opt=input("Enter more (y/n) :")
elif choice==2 :
    num=int(input("Enter the Data: "))
    head.insert_begin(num)
elif choice==3 :
    loc=int(input("Enter The Node number Before which
                    new node will be inserted :"))
    num=int(input("Enter the Data: "))
    head.insert_before_nth(num,loc)
elif choice==4 :
    loc=int(input("Enter The Node number After which
                    new node will be inserted :"))
    num=int(input("Enter the Data: "))
    head.insert_after_nth(num,loc)
elif choice==5 :
    head.delete_first()
elif choice==6 :
    head.delete_last()
elif choice==7 :
    num=int(input("Enter The Node Number You Want To
                                     Delete : "))
    head.delete_nth(num)
elif choice==8 :
    head.display()
elif choice==9 :
    head.rev_display()
elif choice==10:
    print("\nQuiting.......")
    break
else:
    print("Invalid choice. Please Enter Correct
                                     Choice")

    continue
```

7.14 Header Linked List

A header linked list is a linked list with an extra node that contains some useful information regarding the entire linked list. This node is known as the header node and may contain any information such as reference of the first node and/or last node, largest element and/or smallest element in the list, total number of nodes, mean value of the data elements of the nodes, etc. As there is no restriction on how many elements there will be or what elements can be stored, there is no specific structure of the header node. It may vary from program to program depending on the requirement of the problem.

There are some variations of the header linked list:

- **Grounded header linked list:** The header node points to the first node of the linked list and the reference part of the last node points to None.

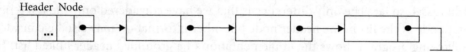

Figure 7.32   Grounded header linked list

- **Circular header linked list:** The header node points to the first node of the linked list and the reference part of the last node points to the header node.

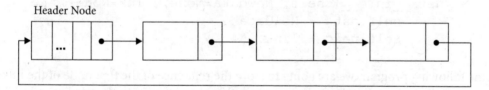

Figure 7.33   Circular header linked list

- **Two-way header linked list:** The header node points to the first node as well as the last node of the linked list, and the previous part of the first node and the next part of the last node both point to None.

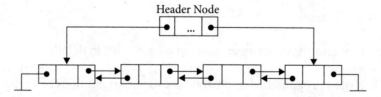

Figure 7.34   Two-way header linked list

- **Two-way circular header linked list:** The header node points to both the first node and the last node of the linked list and the previous part of first node and next part of last node both point to the header node.

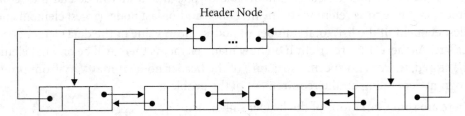

Figure 7.35   Two-way circular header linked list

The implementation of a header linked list is almost the same as a normal linked list we have discussed so far. The only difference is that we have considered only the reference of the first node of the list in the header node but other information may also be considered. The following program shows the implementation of a grounded header linked list. Here two classes have been defined. One is for the node of a single linear linked list that contains the data part and the reference part, and other one for the header node. So, the definition of the node of the linked list may be the following:

```
class Node :
    def __init__( self, Newdata=None, link=None ) :
        self.data = Newdata
        self.next = link
```

In the following program we are going to store the reference of the first node of the linked list, the total number of nodes, and the largest element of the list in the header node. Thus the header node can be defined as:

```
class groundedHeaderList :
    def __init__( self ):
        self.Head = None
        self.count=0
        self.max=None
```

The following program shows the operations of a header list in detail:

Program 7.9: Write a program to demonstrate the various operations of a grounded header linear linked list.

```
#PRGD7_9: Program to demonstrate Grounded Header Linked List

class Node :                                    # Declaration of Node
    def __init__ ( self, Newdata=None, link=None ) :
        self.data = Newdata
        self.next = link


class groundedHeaderList :        # Declaration of Header Node
    def __init__ ( self ):
        self.Head = None
        self.count=0
        self.max=None
    # Function to insert a node at the end of the list
    def insert_end(self,newData):
        newNode=Node(newData)
        if self.Head is None:
            self.Head=newNode
            self.max=newData
        else:
            curNode = self.Head
            while curNode.next is not None :
                curNode = curNode.next
            curNode.next=newNode
            if newData>self.max:
                self.max=newData
        self.count+=1
  # Function to insert a node at the beginning of the list
    def insert_begin(self,newData):
        self.Head=Node(newData,self.Head)
        if self.count==0:
            self.max=newData
        else:
            if newData>self.max:
                self.max=newData
        self.count+=1
    # Function to insert a node at Nth node
    def insert_nth(self,newData,location):
        if self.Head is None or location==1:
            self.Head=Node(newData,self.Head)
        else:
            curNode = self.Head
            c=1
```

```
                    while c<=location-2 and curNode.next is not
                                                    None :
                c+=1
                curNode = curNode.next
            curNode.next=Node(num,curNode.next)
        if self.count==0:
            self.max=newData
        else:
            if newData>self.max:
                self.max=newData
        self.count+=1
# Function to delete the first node
def delete_first(self):
    if self.Head is None:
        print("Empty List. Deletion not possible...")
    else:
        firstNode = self.Head
        if self.count==1:
            self.max=None
        else:
            if self.max==firstNode.data:
                curNode=firstNode.next
                self.max=curNode.data
                while curNode is not None:
                    if curNode.data>self.max:
                        self.max=curNode.data
                    curNode = curNode.next
        self.Head=self.Head.next
        del(firstNode)
        self.count-=1
        print("Node Deleted Successfully...")
# Function to delete the last node
def delete_last(self):
    if self.Head is None:
        print("Empty List. Deletion not possible...")
    elif self.Head.next is None:
        del(self.Head)
        self.Head=None
        self.max=None
        self.count=0
    else:
        curNode = self.Head
```

```
        self.max=curNode.data
        while curNode.next is not None :
            if curNode.data>self.max:
                self.max=curNode.data
            prevNode=curNode
            curNode = curNode.next
        del(curNode)
        prevNode.next=None
        self.count-=1
        print("Node Deleted Successfully...")
```
#Function to Delete a node whose Data matches with the
#given Data
```
    def delete_anynode(self,num):
        if self.Head is None:
            print("Empty List. Deletion not possible...")
        else:
            curNode = self.Head
            if curNode.data==num:                # For 1st Node
                firstNode = self.Head
                if self.count==1:
                    self.max=None
                else:
                    if self.max==firstNode.data:
                        curNode=firstNode.next
                        self.max=curNode.data
                        while curNode is not None:
                            if curNode.data>self.max:
                                self.max=curNode.data
                            curNode = curNode.next
                self.Head=self.Head.next
                del(firstNode)
                self.count-=1
                print("Node Deleted Successfully...")
            else:                                # For Others Node
                flag=0
                newMax=curNode.data
                while curNode is not None:
                    if  curNode.data == num:
                        flag = 1
                        break
                    if curNode.data>newMax:
                        newMax=curNode.data
```

```python
                        prev = curNode
                        curNode = curNode.next
                if flag == 0:
                        print("Node Not Found...")
                else:
                        prev.next = curNode.next
                        temp=curNode.next
                        if self.max==curNode.data:
                                while temp is not None:
                                        if temp.data>newMax:
                                                newMax=temp.data
                                        temp = temp.next
                                self.max=newMax
                        del(curNode)
                        self.count-=1
                        print("Node Deleted Successfully...")
        # Function to display the entire linked list
        def display(self):
                if self.Head is None:
                        print("Empty List.")
                else:
                        curNode = self.Head
                        while curNode is not None :
                                print(curNode.data,end="->")
                                curNode = curNode.next
                        print("None")


head=groundedHeaderList()
while True:
    print("\nPROGRAM TO IMPLEMENT GROUNDED HEADER LIST ")
    print("=============================================")
    print("1.Create / Appending The List")
    print("2.Insert Node At Begining")
    print("3.Insert Node at Nth Position")
    print("4.Delete First Node")
    print("5.Delete Last Node")
    print("6.Delete the Node whose Data matches with given
                                        Data")
    print("7.Displaying the list")
    print("8.Count the number of Nodes")
    print("9.Find Largest element in the List")
    print("10.Exit")
```

```python
    print("=========================================")
    choice=int(input("Enter your Choice : "))
    if choice==1 :
        opt='Y'
        while opt.upper()=='Y':
            num=int(input("Enter the Data: "))
            head.insert_end(num)
            opt=input("Enter more (y/n) :")
    elif choice==2 :
        num=int(input("Enter the Data: "))
        head.insert_begin(num)
    elif choice==3 :
        loc=int(input("Enter Node number in which position
                        new node will be inserted :"))
        num=int(input("Enter the Data: "))
        head.insert_nth(num,loc)
    elif choice==4 :
        head.delete_first()
    elif choice==5 :
        head.delete_last()
    elif choice==6 :
        num=int(input("Enter The Data You Want To Delete :
                                                        "))
        head.delete_anynode(num)
    elif choice==7 :
        head.display()
    elif choice==8 :
        print("Total number of Nodes in the List is:
                                        ",head.count)
    elif choice==9 :
        if head.count>0:
            print("The Largest Element in the List is: ",
                                        head.max)
        else:
            print("Null List")
    elif choice==10:
        print("\nQuiting.......")
        break
    else:
        print("Invalid choice. Please Enter Correct
                                        Choice")
        continue
```

In the above program every time a node is inserted or deleted, the header node is updated correspondingly. Thus, to access these pieces of information, we need not traverse the list. They are available at the header node. Thus, to count the number of nodes or to find the largest element, the time complexity reduces from O(n) to O(1).

In the next program, operations on a two-way header list have been shown. Here the header node points to the first node as well as the last node. So, we can insert or delete a node from both ends very easily without traversing the list. For a two-way list we are using the same class that has been used in the program of a double linked list, i.e.

```python
class DNode :
    def __init__(self,Newdata=None,plink=None,nlink=None):
        self.previous = plink
        self.data = Newdata
        self.next = nlink
```

The header node contains the references of the first node and the last node. Here also we are storing the total number of nodes and the largest element of the list. Thus the class to represent the header node will be

```python
class twoWayHeaderList :
    def __init__( self ):
        self.Head = None
        self.count= 0
        self.max  = None
        self.Tail = None
```

A complete program showing the details operations on two-way header list is given here:

Program 7.10: Write a program to demonstrate the various operations of a two-way header linked list.

```python
#PRGD7_10: Program to demonstrate Two way Header Linked List

class DNode :
    def __init__(self,Newdata=None,plink=None,nlink=No
                                                     ne):
        self.previous = plink
        self.data = Newdata
        self.next = nlink


class twoWayHeaderList :
    def __init__( self ):
```

```python
        self.Head = None
        self.count= 0
        self.max  = None
        self.Tail = None

    # Function to insert a node at the end of the list
    def insert_end(self,newData):
        newNode=DNode(newData)
        if self.Head is None:
            self.Head=newNode
            self.Tail=newNode
            self.max=newData
        else:
            newNode.previous=self.Tail
            self.Tail.next=newNode
            self.Tail=newNode
            if newData>self.max:
                self.max=newData
        self.count+=1
    # Function to insert a node at the beginning of the list
    def insert_begin(self,newData):
        newNode=DNode(newData,None,self.Head)
        if self.Head is None:
            self.Tail=newNode
            self.max=newData
        else:
            self.Head.previous=newNode
            if newData>self.max:
                self.max=newData
        self.Head=newNode
        self.count+=1
    # Function to insert a node at Nth position
    def insert_nth(self,newData,location):
        newNode=DNode(newData)
        if self.Head is None or location==1:
            if self.Head is not None:
                self.Head.previous=newNode
            else:
                self.Tail=newNode
            newNode.next=self.Head
            self.Head=newNode
        else:
```

```
            curNode = self.Head
            c=1
            while c<=location-2 and curNode.next is not
                                                    None :
                c+=1
                curNode = curNode.next
            newNode.next=curNode.next
            newNode.previous=curNode
            if curNode.next!=None:
                curNode.next.previous=newNode
            else:
                self.Tail=newNode
            curNode.next=newNode
        if self.count==0:
            self.max=newData
        else:
            if newData>self.max:
                self.max=newData
        self.count+=1
# Function to delete the first node
def delete_first(self):
    if self.Head is None:
        print("Empty List. Deletion not possible...")
    else:
        firstNode = self.Head
        if self.count==1:
            self.Tail=None
            self.max=None
        else:
            if self.max==firstNode.data:
                curNode=firstNode.next
                self.max=curNode.data
                while curNode is not None:
                    if curNode.data>self.max:
                        self.max=curNode.data
                    curNode = curNode.next
        self.Head=self.Head.next
        if self.Head is not None:
            self.Head.previous=None
        del(firstNode)
        self.count-=1
        print("Node Deleted Successfully...")
```

```python
# Function to delete the last node
def delete_last(self):
    if self.Head is None:
        print("Empty List. Deletion not possible...")
    elif self.Head.next is None:
                #If the list contains single node only
        del(self.Head)
        self.Head=None
        self.max=None
        self.count=0
        self.Tail=None
    else:
        if self.max==self.Tail.data:
            curNode = self.Head
            self.max=curNode.data
            while curNode.next is not None :
                if curNode.data>self.max:
                    self.max=curNode.data
                curNode = curNode.next
        lastNode=self.Tail
        self.Tail=self.Tail.previous
        self.Tail.next=None
        del(lastNode)
        self.count-=1
        print("Node Deleted Successfully...")
# Function to Delete N-th node
def delete_nth(self,posn):
    if self.Head is None:
        print("Empty List. Deletion not possible...")
    elif posn>self.count:
        print("Node not found..")
    else:
        curNode = self.Head
        if posn==1:                    # For 1st Node
            if self.count==1:
                self.Head=None
                self.max=None
                self.count=0
                self.Tail=None
            else:
                self.Head=curNode.next
                self.Head.previous=None
```

```
                        if self.max==curNode.data:
                            flag=1
                        self.count-=1
                else:                           # For Others Node
                    c=1
                    while c<=posn-1:
                        c+=1
                        curNode = curNode.next
                    if self.Tail==curNode:
                        self.Tail=curNode.previous
                        self.Tail.next=None
                    else:
                        curNode.previous.next=curNode.next
                        curNode.next.previous=curNode.
                                                    previous
                    if self.max==curNode.data:
                        flag=1
                    self.count-=1
            if flag==1:
                temp=self.Head
                self.max=temp.data
                while temp is not None:
                    if temp.data>self.max:
                        self.max=temp.data
                    temp=temp.next
            del(curNode)
            print("Node Deleted Successfully...")
# Function to display the entire linked list
def display(self):
    if self.Head is None:
        print("Empty List.")
    else:
        curNode = self.Head
        print("None<=>",end="")
        while curNode is not None :
            print(curNode.data,end="<=>")
            curNode = curNode.next
        print("None")
# Function to display in reverse order
def rev_display(self):
    if self.Head is None:
        print("Empty List.")
```

```
        else:
            curNode = self.Tail
            print("None<=>",end="")
            while curNode is not None :
                print(curNode.data,end="<=>")
                curNode = curNode.previous
            print("None")

head=twoWayHeaderList()
while True:
    print("\nPROGRAM TO IMPLEMENT TWO WAY HEADER LIST")
    print("========================================")
    print(" 1.Create / Appending The List")
    print(" 2.Insert Node At Begining")
    print(" 3.Insert Node at Nth position")
    print(" 4.Delete First Node")
    print(" 5.Delete Last Node")
    print(" 6.Delete Nth Node")
    print(" 7.Displaying the list")
    print(" 8.Displaying the list in Reverse Order")
    print(" 9.Count the number of Nodes")
    print("10.Find Largest element in the List")
    print("11.Exit")
    print("========================================")
    choice=int(input("Enter your Choice : "))
    if choice==1 :
        opt='Y'
        while opt.upper()=='Y':
            num=int(input("Enter the Data: "))
            head.insert_end(num)
            opt=input("Enter more (y/n) :")
    elif choice==2 :
        num=int(input("Enter the Data: "))
        head.insert_begin(num)
    elif choice==3 :
        loc=int(input("Enter Node number in which position
                        new node will be inserted :"))
        num=int(input("Enter the Data: "))
        head.insert_nth(num,loc)
    elif choice==4 :
        head.delete_first()
    elif choice==5 :
```

```
        head.delete_last()
    elif choice==6 :
        num=int(input("Enter The Node Number You Want To
                                        Delete : "))
        head.delete_nth(num)
    elif choice==7 :
        head.display()
    elif choice==8 :
        head.rev_display()
    elif choice==9 :
        print("Total number of Nodes in the List is:
                                    ",head.count)
    elif choice==10:
        if head.count>0:
            print("The Largest Element in the List is: ",
                                    head.max)
        else:
            print("Null List")
    elif choice==11:
        print("\nQuiting.......")
        break
    else:
        print("Invalid choice. Please Enter Correct
                                        Choice")
        continue
```

7.15 Advantages of a Header Linked List

The basic disadvantage of any type of linked list is that only sequential access is possible on a linked list. Thus, to find any information from the linked list, we need to traverse the entire list. This is time consuming. But if we store the pieces of information that are required frequently in the header list, the problem can be easily solved. For example, if the reference of last node is stored within the header node, to insert a node at the end or to delete the last node we need not traverse the entire list. We can reach directly the end of the list and operate accordingly. These are the advantages of a header linked list.

7.16 Disadvantages of a Linked List

Though there are several advantages of using a linked list, there are also a few disadvantages. The disadvantage of a linked list is that it consumes extra space if compared to an array as each node in the list along with the data must contain the reference of the next node. If the data part of the node is very small in size, this extra space is really a headache. For example, if it contains a single integer, then to store a single item we need to allocate double space. To allocate 2 bytes, we have to allocate 4 bytes (2 bytes for integer data and 2 bytes for the reference). But if the size of the data part is large or if it contains many items, then this wastage is negligible. For example, if we want to store data about students like roll number, name, father's name, local address, permanent address, fees paid, etc., and suppose the size of this record structure is 300 bytes, then to store this 300 bytes we have to allocate 302 bytes, which is negligible.

Another disadvantage is we can perform only sequential access on a linked list. But an array supports sequential access as well as random access.

7.17 Programming Examples

Here are some programming examples to understand the various operations that can be performed on different types of linked lists. The following functions are written considering that they are the member functions of the class **singleLinkedList** that we have already seen in this chapter.

Program 7.11: Write a function to count the number of nodes in a singly linked list.

```
#    Function to count the node in a list
    def count(self):
        c=0
        curNode = self.Head
        while curNode is not None :
            c+=1
            curNode = curNode.next
        return(c)
```

Program 7.12: Write a function to find the sum of the data part in a singly linked list.

```
#    Function to find the sum of data part in a list
    def calc_sum(self):
        sum=0
        curNode = self.Head
        while curNode is not None :
            sum+=curNode.data
            curNode = curNode.next
        return(sum)
```

Program 7.13: Write a function to find a node with the given data in a singly linked list.

```
#    Function to search a node in a list
     def search(self,num):
          curNode = self.Head
          while curNode is not None :
               if curNode.data==num:
                    return curNode
               curNode = curNode.next
          return (None)
```

Program 7.14: Write a function to find the largest node in a singly linked list.

```
#    Function to find the largest node in a list
     def largest_node(self):
          if self.Head is None:
               return (None)
          maxNode = curNode = self.Head
          max = curNode.data
          while curNode is not None :
               if curNode.data > max:
                    max = curNode.data
                    maxNode = curNode
               curNode = curNode.next
          return (maxNode)
```

Program 7.15: Write a function to physically reverse a singly linked list.

```
#    Function to reverse a list physically
     def reverse_list(self):
          curNode = self.Head
          nxtNode = curNode.next;
          prevNode = None;
          curNode.next = None;
          while nxtNode is not None:
               prevNode = curNode
               curNode  = nxtNode
               nxtNode  = curNode.next
               curNode.next = prevNode
          self.Head = curNode
```

Program 7.16: Write a function to insert a node at the proper position in a previously sorted linked list.

```
#     Function to insert a node in a previously sorted list
      def insert_proper(self, newData):
          newNode=Node(newData)
          if self.Head is None:
             self.Head=newNode
          else:
             curNode = self.Head
             if curNode.data > newData:
                 newNode.next = curNode
                 self.Head=newNode
             else:
                 while curNode != None:
                     if curNode.data > newData:
                         break
                     prevNode = curNode
                     curNode = curNode.next
                 newNode.next = curNode
                 prevNode.next = newNode
```

The following functions are written considering that they are the member functions of the class **circularLinkedList** that we have already seen in this chapter.

Program 7.17: Write a function to count the number of nodes in a circular linked list.

```
# Function to count number of nodes in the list
def countNode(self):
    if self.Head is None:
       return 0
    else:
        c=1
        curNode = self.Head
        while curNode.next != self.Head :
            c+=1
            curNode = curNode.next
    return c
```

Program 7.18: Write a function to find the node with the smallest value in a circular linked list.

```
# Function to find smallest node in the list
def smallestNode(self):
    if self.Head is None:
```

```
                    return None
            else:
                    curNode = self.Head
                    min=curNode.data
                    temp=curNode
                    curNode = curNode.next
                    while curNode != self.Head :
                            if curNode.data < min:
                                    min=curNode.data
                                    temp=curNode
                            curNode = curNode.next
            return temp
```

Program 7.19: Write a function to delete the nth node from a circular linked list.

```
# Function to Delete n-th node
def delete_nth(self,posn):
    if self.Head is None:
        print("Empty List. Deletion not possible...")
    else:
        curNode = self.Head
        if posn==1:                    # For 1st Node
            if curNode.next==curNode:
                self.Head=None
                del(curNode)
            else:
                while curNode.next!=self.Head:
                    curNode=curNode.next
                self.Head=self.Head.next
                del(curNode.next)
                curNode.next=self.Head
            print("Node Deleted Successfully...")
        else:                          # For Others Node
            c=self.countNode()
            if posn>c:
                print("Node Not Found...")
            else:
                c=1
                while c<=posn-1:
                    c+=1
                    prev = curNode
                    curNode = curNode.next
```

```
prev.next = curNode.next
del(curNode)
print("Node Deleted Successfully...")
```

The following functions are written considering that they are the member functions of the class **doublyLinkedList** that we have already seen in this chapter.

Program 7.20: Write a function to find the largest difference among the elements of a doubly linked list.

```
# Function to find Largest Difference
def largestDifference(self):
    if self.Head is None:
        return 0
    else:
        curNode = self.Head
        max=min=curNode.data
        while curNode is not None :
            if curNode.data>max:
                max=curNode.data

            elif curNode.data<min:
                min=curNode.data
            curNode = curNode.next
        return max-min
```

Program 7.21: Write a function to insert a node at the proper position in a previously sorted doubly linked list.

```
# Function to insert a node in a previously sorted list
    def insert_proper(self, newData):
        newNode=DNode(newData)
        if self.Head is None:
            self.Head=newNode
        else:
            curNode = self.Head
            if curNode.data > newData:
                newNode.next = curNode
                curNode.previous=newNode
                self.Head=newNode
            else:
                while curNode != None:
```

```
                    if curNode.data > newData:
                        break
                    prevNode = curNode
                    curNode = curNode.next
                newNode.next = curNode
                newNode.previous=prevNode
                prevNode.next = newNode
                if curNode is not None:
                    curNode.previous = newNode
```

Program 7.22: Write a function to remove all nodes from a doubly linked list.

```
#    Function to remove all nodes
    def remove_all(self):
        if self.Head is None:
            print("Empty List.")
        else:
            self.Head=None
```

Program 7.23: Write a function to find the average of the data elements of a circular doubly linked list.

```
    # Function to find the average
    def average(self):
        if self.Head is None:
            return 0
        else:
            curNode = self.Head
            sum=curNode.data
            c=1
            curNode=curNode.next
            while curNode != self.Head :
                sum+=curNode.data
                c+=1
                curNode = curNode.next
        return sum/c
```

Program 7.24: Write a function to remove nodes with negative elements from a circular doubly linked list.

```
    # Function to remove nodes with negative elements
    def delNegative(self):
```

```
        if self.Head is None:
            print("Empty List. Deletion not possible...")
        else:
            curNode = self.Head
            while curNode is not None and curNode.data<0:
                if curNode.next==curNode:
                    self.Head=None
                    return
                else:
                    lastNode=curNode.previous
                    self.Head=self.Head.next
                    self.Head.previous=lastNode
                    lastNode.next=self.Head
                    nextNode=curNode.next
            del(curNode)
            print("delete")
            curNode=nextNode
        curNode=curNode.next
        while curNode != self.Head :
            print(curNode.data)
            if curNode.data<0:
                prevNode=curNode.previous
                prevNode.next=curNode.next
                curNode.next.previous=prevNode
                temp=curNode
                curNode=curNode.next
                del(temp)
            else:
                curNode = curNode.next
```

Linked List at a Glance

✓   A linked list is a linear collection of data items which is known as nodes.

✓   Linked list is a dynamic data structure. Hence the size of the linked list
     may increase or decrease at run time, i.e. we can add or delete node as and
     when required.

✓   In contrast to array it does not possess the problems of wastage of memory
     nor the lack of memory.

✓   Linked list provides flexibility in rearranging the items efficiently instead
     of allocating a large contiguous memory chunk.

✓ Insertion and deletion of nodes at any point in the list is very simple and require some pointer adjustment only.

✓ In linear singly linked list each node points to the next node in the list and the last node contains None to indicate the end of list.

✓ In circular singly linked each node points to the next node in the list but the last node instead of containing None it points to the first node of the list.

✓ In two way or doubly linked list each node has two reference parts. One points to the previous node and the other points to the next node in the list. Both the ends of the list contain None.

✓ In circular doubly linked list each node has two reference parts. One points to the previous node and the other points to the next node in the list. But instead of containing None the first node points to last node and the last node points to the first node of the list.

✓ Linked list is used to represent polynomials, to implement various data structures, sparse matrix, to perform arithmetic operation on large integers, etc.

✓ The disadvantage of linked list is that it consumes extra space since each node contains the reference of the next item in the list and the nodes of the list can be accessed sequentially only.

✓ Header linked list is a linked list with an extra node which contain some useful information regarding the entire linked list.

Multiple Choice Questions

1. What kind of data structure do you prefer for implementation of polynomials?
   a) Array
   b) Tree
   c) Graph
   d) Linear Linked List

2. The address of the fifth element in a linked list of integers is 1000. Then the address of the eighth element is
   a) 1006
   b) 1004
   c) 1008
   d) Cannot Say

3. Linked lists are not suitable for implementing

   a) Insertion Sort

   b) Binary Search

   c) Polynomial Manipulation

   d) Radix Sort.

4. What is the worst case time complexity to search for an element from the following logical structure?

   a) O(n)

   b) O(1)

   c) O(n²)

   d) O(n log n)

5. Which of the following is True?

   a) One can traverse through a doubly linked list in both directions.

   b) Singly linked list requires less space than a doubly linked list.

   c) Singly linked list requires less time than a doubly linked list for both insertion and deletion operations.

   d) All of the above.

6. Consider a single circular linked list with a tail pointer. Which of the following operations requires O(1) time?

   i. Insert a node at the beginning of a list

   ii. Delete the first node

   iii. Insert a node at the end of a list

   iv. Delete the last node

   a) I and II only

   b) I, II and III only

   c) II and III only

   d) I, II, III and IV

7. Consider a two way header list containing references of first and last node. Which of the following operations cannot be done in O(1) time?

   a) Insert a node at the beginning

   b) Insert a node at the end

   c) Delete the last node

   d) Delete the first node

8. Which of the following is not true when a linked list is compared with an array?

   a) As an array has better cache locality, its performance is better in comparison to linked list.

   b) Insertion and deletion operations are easy and less time consuming in linked lists

   c) Random access is not allowed in case of linked lists

   d) Access of elements in linked list takes less time than compared to arrays

9. Suppose we have two reference variables, Head and Tail, to refer to the first and last nodes of a singly linked list. Which of the following operations is dependent on the length of the linked list?

   a) Add a new element at the end of the list

   b) Insert a new element as a first element

   c) Delete the first element of the list

   d) Delete the last element of the list

10. Which of the following applications makes use of a circular linked list?

    a) Recursive function calls

    b) Implementation of hash tables

    c) Allocating CPU to resources

    d) Undo operation in a text editor

11. Which of the following statements is true?

    a) Linked list is a static data structure

    b) Linked list is a dynamic data structure

    c) Linked list is a non-linear data structure

    d) None of these

12. To insert a node at the beginning of a single circular linked list how many pointers/ reference fields are needed to be adjusted?

    a) 1

    b) 2

    c) 3

    d) 4

13. To delete an intermediate node from a double linked list how many pointers/ reference fields are needed to be adjusted?

    a) 1

    b) 2

    c) 3

    d) 4

14. What is the time complexity to delete the first node of a circular linked list?

    a) O(log₂n)

    b) O(nlogn)

    c) O(n)

    d) O(1)

15. What is the time complexity to insert a node at the second position of a double linked list?

    a) O(log₂n)

    b) O(nlogn)

    c) O(n)

    d) O(1)

16. Suppose we have to create a linked list to store some data (roll no., name, and fees paid) of students. Which of the following is a valid class design in Python for this purpose?

```
a) class student :
        roll=0
        name= None
        fees_paid=0.0
b) class student :
        int roll
        char name[30]
        float fees_paid
c) class student :
        def __init__(self, mroll, mname, mfees):
            roll=mroll
            name= mname
            fees_paid=mfees
d) class student :
        def __init__(self, roll, name, fees_paid):
            self.roll=roll
            self.name= name
            self.fees_paid=fees_paid
```

17. Consider the following Python code.

```
class Node :
        def __init__( self, Newdata=None, link=None ) :
            self.data = Newdata
            self.next = link
```

```
class X :
    def __init__( self ):
        self.Head = None
    def func(self, newData):
        self.Head=Node(newData, self.Head)
```

What does the method func of class X do?

a) Creates a object for the class X

b) Inserts a node at the beginning of a linked list

c) Inserts a node at the end of a linked list

d) Inserts a node in a circular linked list

18. To represent a polynomial how many member fields are required in a node structure?

a) 2

b) 3

c) 4

d) 5

Review Exercises

1. What is a linked list?

2. Why is a linked list called a dynamic data structure?

3. What are the advantages of using linked lists over arrays?

4. Is there any disadvantage of linked lists?

5. What are the different types of linked lists?

6. Is it possible to apply binary search algorithm on a linked list? Explain.

7. How many reference adjustments are required to insert a new node at any intermediate position in a single linked list?

8. How many reference adjustments are required to delete a node from any intermediate position of a single linked list?

9. What is the time complexity to insert a node at the end of a single linked list?

10. What is a circular linked list? What advantage do we get from a circular linked list?

11. What is the time complexity to insert a node at the beginning of a circular linked list?

12. What is a head pointer reference? What is a tail pointer reference?

13. What happened if we use tail pointer reference for a single linear linked list?

14. Compare and contrast between a single linked list and a doubly linked list.

15. Compare and contrast between a single circular linked list and a doubly linked list.

16. Compare and contrast between a single circular linked list and a circular doubly linked list.

17. What is a header list? What is its utility?

18. How many reference adjustments are required to insert a new node in a circular doubly linked list?

19. How many reference adjustments are required to delete a node from a circular doubly linked list?

20. Discuss some applications of a linked list.

Problems for Programming

1. Write a function to find the smallest element in a singly linked list.

2. Write a function to find the average of the data part in a singly linked list.

3. Write a function to insert a node before a node whose data matches with given data in a singly linked list.

4. Write a function to insert a node after a node whose data matches with given data in a singly linked list.

5. Write a function to delete a node before a specified node from a singly linked list.

6. Write a function to delete a node after a specified node from a singly linked list.

7. Write a function to sort a singly linked list.

8. Write a function to merge two sorted singly linked lists.

9. Write a function that will split a singly linked list into two different lists, one of which will contain odd numbers and other will contain even numbers.

10. Write a function to multiply two polynomials.

11. Write a function to remove alternate elements from a linked list.

12. Write a function to delete an entire list.

13. Write a function to count the number of nodes in a circular linked list.

14. Write a function to insert a node before a node whose data matches with given data in a circular singly linked list.

15. Write a function to insert a node after a node whose data matches with given data in a circular singly linked list.

16. Write a function to delete the nth node from a circular singly linked list.

17. Write a program to create a circular linked list using the tail pointer. Define the necessary functions to add a new node, delete a node, and display the list.

18. Write a function to insert a node before a node whose data matches with given data in a doubly linked list.

19. Write a function to insert a node after a node whose data matches with given data in a doubly linked list.

20. Write a function to delete the node whose data matches with given data in a doubly linked list.

21. Write a function to insert a node before a node whose data matches with given data in a circular doubly linked list.

22. Write a function to insert a node after a node whose data matches with given data in a circular doubly linked list.

23. Write a function to delete the node whose data matches with given data in a circular doubly linked list.

24. Write a function to implement a circular header linked list.

25. Write a program to implement a circular linked list such that insert at end and delete from beginning operation executes with O(1) time complexity.

26. Write a function to split a circular doubly linked list into two single circular linked lists, one of which will contain positive numbers and other will contain negative numbers.

27. Write a function to remove alternate elements from a circular doubly linked list.

Stack

A stack is a very important data structure. We find its application in various situations in computer science. In this chapter we will discuss the operations related to stacks, how a stack is represented in memory, various areas of applications where stacks are used, etc.

8.1 Definitions and Concept

A stack is a linear data structure in which both insertion and deletion operations occur only at one end. The insertion operation is commonly known as PUSH and the deletion operation is known as POP. As both the operations occur at one end, when the elements are pushed into a stack the elements are stored one after another and when the elements are popped only the topmost element can be removed first and then the next element gets the scope to be popped. In real life also we can see various analogies of this structure, such as a stack of coins, stack of plates, stack of boxes, etc. (Figure 8.1). Suppose, in a stack of coins, if we want to place a new coin, it should be placed at the top of the stack, and if we want to get a coin from that stack, we should remove the topmost coin from the stack. Since in a stack always the element that was inserted last is removed first, it is known as a LIFO (Last In First Out) data structure.

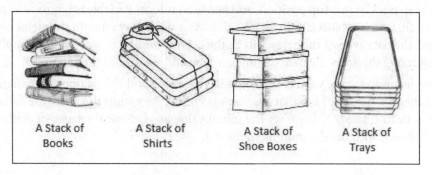

A Stack of Books   A Stack of Shirts   A Stack of Shoe Boxes   A Stack of Trays

Figure 8.1   Examples of stack

8.2   Operations Associated with Stacks

The basic operations related to a stack are the following:.

- Push: Insert an element into a stack.
- Pop: Retrieve an element from a stack.

Apart from these two basic operations, to use a stack efficiently we need to add the following functionalities:

- Peek: Get the top element of the stack without removing it.
- Isempty: To check whether the stack is empty or not.
- Isfull: To check whether the stack is full or not.

All these operations execute with the time complexity O(1).

In some situations we need to check the top element without removing it. That is why the peek operation is required. Again, if a stack is full, the push operation cannot be done on the stack. Similarly, pop and peek operations cannot be performed on an empty stack. Thus, before these operations we need to check whether the stack is full or empty.

8.3 Representation of a Stack

As a stack is a linear data structure consisting of a set of elements, it can be represented in memory using an array as well as a linked list. But Python does not support traditional arrays. Python's array is dynamic and much similar to its list data structure. In the following section we will theoretically discuss traditional array representation and implementation of two very common approaches: Python's built-in data structure **list** and linked list representation.

8.3.1 Array Representation

To store a set of elements in computer memory a linear array is needed and as all the operations related to a stack, i.e. push, pop, and peek, occur at the topmost position, we have to keep track of this **top** position, and hence an integer variable is required to store the top position, which is basically an array index. As a stack may contain the elements of any data type, the data type of the array will be the corresponding type. Here for simplicity we are considering the array elements as integer type and the size of the array as 5.

Before using the stack we have to initialize the stack and this is done by assigning the value of the **top** -1 to indicate that the stack is empty. As within the array the value of the top varies from 0 to SIZE-1, we set the initial value as -1. Now the basic operations on a stack are shown with the diagram in Figure 8.2.

Operation	top	array				
Initial state	-1					
		0	1	2	3	4
Push 5	0	5				
		0	1	2	3	4
Push 10	1	5	10			
		0	1	2	3	4
Push 15	2	5	10	15		
		0	1	2	3	4
Pop	1	5	10			
		0	1	2	3	4
Pop	0	5				
		0	1	2	3	4

Figure 8.2   Operations on a stack using an array

Considering the above example we can write the algorithm of the push operation as:

```
1.  If top = SIZE - 1, Then
    a. Print "Stack Overflow"
    b. Go to Step3
2.  Else
    a.top = top + 1
    b. array[top] = new element
3.  End
```

The algorithm of pop operation can be written as:

```
1.  If top = -1, Then
    a. Print "Stack Underflow"
    b. Go to Step3
2.  Else
    a. Element = array[top]
    b. top = top - 1
    c. Return Element
3.  End
```

8.3.2 Python List Representation

Though Python does not support traditional arrays, yet the above concept can be easily implemented using Python's in-built **list** data structure. We already find that all the operations related to stack, i.e. push, pop, and peek, occur at the topmost position. So, we have to decide which end of the list will be considered as top. Though we can use any end for pushing the elements into the stack, appending, i.e. pushing the elements from back end, is more efficient as it operates with O(1) time complexity whereas inserting an element through the front end requires time complexity of O(n). So, obviously we will consider the end of the list as the top of the stack. The list method `append()` will help us to push an element into a stack and the method `pop()` will help us in the stack's pop operation.

Now the basic operations on stack are shown with the diagram in Figure 8.3.

Operation	arr
Initial state	Empty Stack
Push 5	5 0
Push 10	5 10 0 1
Push 15	5 10 15 0 1 2
Pop	5 10 0 1
Pop	5 0

Figure 8.3 Operations on a stack using list data structure

Considering the given example now we are able to write `push()` and `pop()`. To write the `push()` operation, our algorithm appends a new element in the list. Thus, the `push()` can be written as:

```
def push(self, item):
    self.items.append(item)
```

Again, to remove the last element from the list we have the list function `pop()`. So, we will write the `pop()` function as:

```
def pop(self):
    return self.items.pop()
```

The peek() function is similar to pop(). The difference is that here the element will not be removed from the stack. Only the top element will be returned. Here is the function:

```
def peek(self):
    return self.items[len(self.items)-1]
```

But before invoking these functions from our main program we need to write some other functions for efficient use of stacks in the program. When we want to push an element into a stack it is necessary to check whether the stack is full or not. If the stack is full it is not possible to insert more items and this situation is known as 'Stack Overflow'. But we are using the **list** data structure and list grows dynamically as long as memory supports. So, we need not check this overflow condition.

Similarly, when we want to pop or peek any element we have to check whether the stack is empty or not. This empty situation is known as 'Stack Underflow'. This can be easily implemented by checking whether the list is empty or not. Here is the function:

```
def isEmpty(self):
    return self.items == []
```

Now, we will be able to invoke these functions efficiently. To pop an element from the stack, s, the code will be:

```
if s.isEmpty() :
    print("Stack Underflow")
else :
    num=s.pop();
    print("Popped Item = ",num)
```

Similarly, to peek an element from the stack, s, the code will be:

```
if s.isEmpty() :
    print("Stack Underflow")
else :
    num=s.peek()
    print("Item at top of stack = ",num)
```

The following menu-driven program demonstrates the various operations of a stack as well as the positions of elements in the stack:

Program 8.1: Write a program to demonstrate the various operations of a stack using list.

```python
# PRGD 8_1:  Program to implement Stack

class Stack:
    def __init__(self):
        self.items = []

    def isEmpty(self):
        return self.items == []

    def push(self, item):
        self.items.append(item)

    def pop(self):
        return self.items.pop()

    def peek(self):
        return self.items[len(self.items)-1]

    def size(self):
        return len(self.items)

    def display(self):
        top=len(self.items)-1
        print()
        for i in range(top,-1,-1):
            print('  |',format(self.items[i],'>3'),'|')
        print("  -------");

s=Stack()
while(True):
    print("\nPROGRAM TO IMPLEMENT STACK ")
    print("=============================")
    print("\t1. Push")
    print("\t2. Pop")
    print("\t3. Peek")
    print("\t4. Display")
    print("\t5. Exit")
    print("===========================")
    choice=int(input("Enter your Choice : "))
    if choice==1 :
```

```
            num=int(input("Enter the Data: "))
            s.push(num)
        elif choice==2 :
            if s.isEmpty() :
                print("Stack Underflow")
            else :
                num=s.pop();
                print("Popped Item = ",num)
        elif choice==3 :
            if s.isEmpty() :
                print("Stack Underflow")
            else :
                num=s.peek()
                print("Item at top of stack = ",num)
        elif choice==4 :
            if s.isEmpty() :
                print("Stack is Empty")
            else :
                s.display()
        elif choice==5 :
            print("\nQuiting.......")
            break
        else:
            print("Invalid choice. Please Enter Correct
                                            Choice")
            continue
```

8.3.3 Linked Representation

The implementation of a stack using a list is quite easy. But it suffers from some problems. List has a few shortcomings. If the number of elements in the stack is large, then to accommodate the elements in a list Python may have to reallocate memory. Then push() and pop() may require O(n) time complexities. Thus to implement a stack, the choice of a linked list is always better. As the operation of a stack occurs in just one end and need not traverse the entire list, singly linked list is the better option to implement a stack.

To use a linked list, again we have to decide how to design the stack structure. Though we designed the end of the list as the top of the stack in case of Python list representation, yet in case of linked list representation it would be efficient if we considered the front of the list as the top of the stack as the head points to the first element. To push an element we just insert a node at the beginning of a list and to pop an element we delete the first node. Both operations require O(1) time.

As each element of the stack will be represented by the nodes of the linked list, first we will define a class to represent a node.

```
class stackNode :
          def __init__( self, Newdata, link ) :
                 self.data = Newdata
                 self.next = link
```

To implement a stack using linked list we will define another class which will contain a reference of the above `stackNode` class, say `top`, to point to the top element of the stack. At the very beginning as there is no element in the stack, there will be no node in the list and the reference of the stack class, `top` will contain `None`.

In case of linked representation there is no chance of overflow condition as any linked list can grow until the computer's memory is fully allocated. Thus we need not check the overflow condition. However, the underflow condition can be easily checked by checking whether the reference, `top`, is `None` or not. The `isEmpty()` function for a linked stack can be written as:

```
def isEmpty( self ):
          return self.top is None
```

To write the `push()` operation we can insert the new element at any end of the list. If we insert it at the end, we need to traverse the entire list each time, which leads to the complexity of `push()` being O(n). But if we insert the new element at the beginning of the list, we need not move at all and the complexity is reduced to O(1). Thus to implement `push()` we should follow the second option, i.e. element should be inserted at the beginning of the list. The following function represents this:

```
def push( self, Newdata ) :
      self.top = stackNode( Newdata, self.top )
```

Here, first a new node is created. Its data part will be updated by the new element and the reference part, `top`, will store the reference of the first node in the list.

As the last element is inserted at the beginning of the list, to implement `pop()` the element will be removed from the beginning of the list. First we will store the reference of the first node to a temporary variable. Then the `top` pointer points to the next node of the list, if it exists. Finally, the data part of the temporary variable will be returned to the calling point. Here is the function:

```
def pop( self ):
      node = self.top
      self.top = self.top.next
```

```
      return node.data
```

Now here is a complete program to demonstrate the operations of a stack using linked list:

Program 8.2: Write a program to demonstrate the various operations of a stack using linked list.

```
# PRGD8_2: Implementation of the Stack using a singly
# linked list.

class stackNode :              # Declaration of Node structure
    def __init__( self, Newdata, link ) :
        self.data = Newdata
        self.next = link

class Stack :
    def __init__( self ):      # Creates an empty stack
        self.top = None

    def isEmpty( self ):
        return self.top is None

    def peek( self ):
# Returns the top element on the stack without removing it
        return self.top.data

    def pop( self ):
# Removes and returns the top data from the stack
        node = self.top
        self.top = self.top.next
        return node.data

    def push( self, Newdata ) :
    # Pushes new element onto top of the stack.
        self.top = stackNode( Newdata, self.top )

    def display(self):   # Display the content of stack
        curNode = self.top
        print()
        while curNode is not None :
            print('   |',format(curNode.data,'>3'),'|')
            print("   -------");
```

```python
                curNode = curNode.next

s=Stack()
while(True):
    print("\nPROGRAM TO IMPLEMENT STACK ")
    print("============================")
    print("\t1. Push")
    print("\t2. Pop")
    print("\t3. Peek")
    print("\t4. Display")
    print("\t5. Exit")
    print("============================")
    choice=int(input("Enter your Choice : "))
    if choice==1 :
        num=int(input("Enter the Data: "))
        s.push(num)
    elif choice==2 :
        if s.isEmpty() :
            print("Stack Underflow")
        else :
            num=s.pop();
            print("Popped data = ",num)
    elif choice==3 :
        if s.isEmpty() :
            print("Stack Underflow")
        else :
            num=s.peek()
            print("data at top of stack = ",num)
    elif choice==4 :
        if s.isEmpty() :
            print("Stack is Empty")
        else :
            s.display()
    elif choice==5 :
        print("\nQuiting.......")
        break
    else:
        print("Invalid choice. Please Enter Correct
                                        Choice")

        continue
```

8.4 Multiple Stacks

In case of traditional array representation of a stack, it is found that we need to predict the size of the array in advance to allocate memory for it. But it is very difficult to predict the exact size. If the size of the array is small, frequent overflow condition may occur. On the other hand, if we declare the array as large, there is a chance of huge wastage of memory.

One solution to this problem is to use multiple stacks in the same array to share the common space. Figure 8.4 shows this concept.

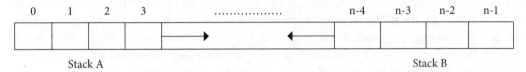

Figure 8.4   Representation of two stacks using a single array

In Figure 8.4, it is shown that we may implement two stacks, stack A and stack B, within a single array. Stack A will grow from left to right and stack B will grow from right to left. Within stack A, the first element will be stored at the zeroth position, next element at the index position 1, then at the index position 2, and so on. Whereas within stack B, the first element will be stored at the $(n-1)^{th}$ position, next element at $(n-2)^{th}$ position, then at $(n-3)^{th}$ position, and so on. The advantage of this scheme is that the intermediate space in between two stacks is common for both and may be used by any one of them. Suppose the array size is 10 and in a particular situation stack B contains three elements. At this position, stack A is free to expand up to array index 6 in the array. Similarly stack B is also able to expand up to the top of stack A.

Extending this concept, it is possible to accommodate any number of stacks within a single array. For each stack an equal amount of space will be allocated and if there is **n** number of stacks, each stack will be bounded by s[n] and e[n]. Figure 8.5 illustrates this concept.

Figure 8.5   Representation of multiple stacks

8.5 Applications of a Stack

A stack is a very important data structure that is used in various situations in our program. Knowingly or unknowingly we use stacks in our programs. For example, when a function is called internally, a stack is used. We can get its essence especially when a nested call of functions is used. For example, if f1 function calls f2 function and in turn f2 function calls f3 function, f1 function will be pushed first into the stack and then f2 function will be pushed on top of the f1 function. After completion of all tasks of f3 function, f2 function will be popped from the stack and the remaining task of f2 function will get executed. Similarly, when the execution of f2 function is over, f1 function will be popped from the stack and get executed. Thus the stack maintains the order of execution in between different function calls. Another programming situation where a stack is used is recursion where the same function is called again and again until a certain condition is satisfied. Each function call is pushed into a stack and after achieving the terminating condition all the function calls are popped from the stack one by one but in reverse order of calls as stacks follow the LIFO order. We can also use stack in our program in some situations like to reverse a list, to reverse the order of a set of elements, traversing another two important data structures – tree and graph – and many more. Here we will discuss some of them.

8.5.1 Parenthesis Checking Problem

To check whether an algebraic expression is properly parenthesized or not, a stack can be used. Generally there are three type of parenthesis used: ( ), { }, and [ ]. Properly parenthesized means all the opening brackets have the corresponding closing brackets and they are properly nested. For example, A + [B * { (C – D) / E }] is a valid expression whereas A + [B * { (C – D) / E] } or A + [B * { C – D) / E }] is an invalid expression.

The following algorithm can be used to solve this problem:

1. Create a stack
2. Read each character of the inputted string until end of string
    a. If the read character is an opening bracket, i.e. (, {, or [, then

        push it into the stack

    b. Else

        If the read character is an closing bracket, i.e.), }, or], then
        i. If the stack is empty, then

            Terminate operation mentioning appropriate Error message like "No matching opening bracket"

        ii. Else
            a. **Pop** from stack and store in a variable, ch
            b. If the read character not corresponding to ch, then
            c. Terminate operation mentioning appropriate error message like "Improper nesting of brackets"

3. If the stack is empty, then

    Print the success message like "Expression is well parenthesized"

4. Else

    Print error message like "No matching closing bracket"

The above algorithm can be implemented by the following function:

```
def chk_parenthesis(expr):
    st=Stack()
    for ch in expr :
        if (ch=='(' or ch=='{' or ch=='[') :
            st.push(ch)
        elif (ch==')' or ch=='}' or ch==']') :
            if st.isEmpty():
                print("No matching opening
                                        parenthesis")
                return
            else:
                if(getmatch(ch) != st.pop()):
                    print("Improper nesting of
                                        Parenthesis")
                    return
    if not st.isEmpty():
        print("No matching closing parenthesis")
    else:
        print("Expression is well parenthesized")
```

In the above function getmatch() is used to get the opening parenthesis of the corresponding closing parenthesis. It is defined below:

```
def getmatch(chr):
    if chr==')' :
        return '('
    elif chr=='}' :
        return '{'
    elif chr==']' :
        return('[')
```

Here is a complete program:

Program 8.3: Write a program to check whether an expression is properly parenthesized or not.

```
#PRGD8_3: Program to check whether an expression is well
#parenthesized
```

```python
class stackNode :
    def __init__( self, Newdata, link ) :
        self.data = Newdata
        self.next = link

class Stack :
    def __init__( self ) :
        self.top = None

    def isEmpty( self ) :
        return self.top is None

    def peek( self ) :
        return self.top.data

    def pop( self ) :
        node = self.top
        self.top = self.top.next
        return node.data

    def push( self, Newdata ) :
        self.top = stackNode( Newdata, self.top )

    def display(self) :
        curNode = self.top
        print()
        while curNode is not None :
            print('   |',format(curNode.data,'>3'),'|')
            print("   -------");
            curNode = curNode.next

def chk_parenthesis(expr):
    st=Stack()
    for ch in expr :
        if (ch=='(' or ch=='{' or ch=='[') :
            st.push(ch)
        elif (ch==')' or ch=='}' or ch==']') :
            if st.isEmpty():
                print("No matching opening
                                parenthesis")
                return
```

```
            else:
                if(getmatch(ch)!= st.pop()):
                    print("Improper nesting of
                                    Parenthesis")
                    return
        if not st.isEmpty():
            print("No matching closing parenthesis")
        else:
            print("Expression is well parenthesized")

    def getmatch(chr):
        if chr==')' :
            return '('
        elif chr=='}' :
            return '{'
        elif chr==']' :
            return('[')

    exp=input("Enter any expression: ")
    chk_parenthesis(exp)
```

8.5.2 Conversion and Evaluation of Different Arithmetic Expressions

Arithmetic expressions are represented using different notations. We can also convert them from one notation to another. Stacks are extensively used in these conversion procedures and to evaluate these expressions. Before conversion first we may get an idea about different notations.

8.5.2.1 Different Notations of Arithmetic Expressions

There are three types of notation used in representing an arithmetic expression. These are the following:

- Infix Notation
- Prefix Notation
- Postfix Notation

The most common notation is infix notation. In this notation the operator is placed in between two operands. Examples are:

A + B

X * Y – Z

A + (B – C) / D, etc.

Though we are much familiar with these expressions, it is very difficult for the computer to parse this type of expressions as the evaluation of an infix expression depends on the precedence and associativity of the operators. The associativity of arithmetic operators is left to right. So, for same priority, evaluation is performed from left to right, and for different priorities, based on priority. Again, brackets override these priorities. On the other hand, prefix and postfix notations are completely bracket-free notations and to evaluate need not to bother about the operator precedence. Thus these notations are much easier to evaluate for the computer.

In **prefix notation** the operator is placed before the operands. It is also known as **Polish notation** (PN), normal Polish notation (NPN), Łukasiewicz notation, Warsaw notation, or Polish prefix notation. It was invented by Polish mathematician Jan Lukasiewicz in the year of 1920 to simplify the expression and to have parenthesis-free expressions so that the computer can parse the expression easily. In prefix notations, the infix notation A + B is written as +AB. Here the order of evaluation is right to left.

To convert an infix expression to its prefix notation, obviously we follow the precedence rules and each operation will be enclosed within brackets ([ ]) to indicate the partial translation. The following example illustrates this:

Example 8.1: Convert the following infix expressions into its equivalent prefix expressions:

a) A + B * C − D
b) A + (B − C * D) / E

Solution: a) A + B * C − D
⇒ A + [*BC] − D
⇒ [+ A*BC] − D
⇒ − + A*BCD

b) A + (B − C * D) / E
⇒ A + (B − [*CD]) / E
⇒ A + [− B*CD] / E
⇒ A + [/ − B*CDE]
⇒ + A / − B*CDE

In **postfix notation** the operator is placed after the operands. Thus, the infix notation A + B is written as AB+ in postfix notation. Here the order of evaluation is left to right. Postfix notation is also known as **reverse Polish notation** (RPN) or Polish postfix notation.

The following example illustrates how an infix expression can be converted into a postfix expression:

Example 8.2: Convert the following infix expressions into its equivalent postfix expressions:

a) A + B * C – D

b) A + (B – C * D) / E

Solution: a) A + B * C – D

$\Rightarrow$ A + [BC*] – D

$\Rightarrow$ [ABC*+] – D

$\Rightarrow$ ABC*+ D –

b) A + (B – C * D) / E

$\Rightarrow$ A + (B – [CD*]) /E

$\Rightarrow$ A + [BCD* –] / E

$\Rightarrow$ A + [BCD* – E /]

$\Rightarrow$ ABCD* – E / +

8.5.2.2 Conversion of an Infix Expression into a Postfix Expression

Any infix expression may contain operators, operands, and opening and closing brackets. For simplicity we are considering only binary arithmetic operators, such as +, –, *, /, and %. Operands may be any variable or digits. For simplicity we are considering that the operands are of single character. To convert an infix expression to its equivalent postfix expression we need a stack. The following algorithm describes the procedure. The algorithm takes the infix expression as source string and produces the postfix expression as target string.

1. Create a stack

2. Read each character from source string until End of string is reached

    a. If the scan character is '(', Then

       Push it into the stack

    b. If the scan character is ')', Then

       i. Pop from stack and send to target string until '(' is encountered

       ii. Pop '(' from stack but do not send to target string

    c. If the scan character is an operand, Then

       Send it to target string

    d. If the scan character is an operator, Then

       i. While stack is not empty or the Top element of stack is not '(' or Priority of Top element of stack >= Priority of scan character

Pop from stack and send to target string

[End of while]

ii. Push the scan character into the stack

3. Pop from stack and send to target string until the stack becomes empty

The following example illustrates the above example:

Example 8.3: Convert the following infix expression into its equivalent postfix expression:

A + (B – C * D) / E

Solution: Source string: A + (B – C * D) / E

Scan Character	Stack	Target String
A		A
+	+	A
(	+ (	A
B	+ (	A B
–	+ (–	A B
C	+ (–	A B C
*	+ (– *	A B C
D	+ (– *	A B C D
)	+	A B C D * –
/	+ /	A B C D * –
E	+ /	A B C D * – E
End of string		A B C D * – E / +

Thus the equivalent postfix expression is: A B C D * – E / +

Here is the implementation of the above algorithm:

```python
def infixToPostfix(source):
    target=""
    st=Stack()
    for ch in source:
        if ch=='(':
            st.push(ch)
```

```
            elif ch==')':
                while(not st.isEmpty() and st.peek()!='('):
                    target+=st.pop()
                st.pop()
              # Pop from stack but not send to target string
            elif ch.isdigit() or ch.isalpha():
                target+=ch
            elif ch=='+' or ch=='-' or ch=='*' or ch=='/' or
                                                    ch=='%' :
                while (not st.isEmpty() and st.peek()!='('
            and getPriority(st.peek())>=getPriority(ch)):
                    target+=st.pop()
                st.push(ch)
        while(not st.isEmpty()):
            target+=st.pop()
        return target
```

The above function uses a user-defined function `getPriority()` to check the priority of the operators. Its coding is given below:

```
def getPriority(opr):
    if (opr=='*' or opr=='/' or opr=='%'):
        return 1
    else:
        return 0
```

Program 8.4: Write a program to convert an infix expression into its equivalent postfix expression.

```
#PRGD8_4: Program to convert an infix expression into
#Postfix expression

class stackNode :
    def __init__( self, Newdata, link ) :
        self.data = Newdata
        self.next = link

class Stack :
    def __init__( self ):
        self.top = None
    def isEmpty( self ):
```

```
                return self.top is None
        def peek( self ):
                return self.top.data
        def pop( self ):
                node = self.top
                self.top = self.top.next
                return node.data
        def push( self, Newdata ) :
                self.top = stackNode( Newdata, self.top )

def infixToPostfix(source):
        target=""
        st=Stack()
        for ch in source:
                if ch=='(':
                        st.push(ch)
                elif ch==')':
                        while(not st.isEmpty() and st.peek()!='('):
                                target+=st.pop()
                        st.pop()
                        # Pop from stack but not send to target string
                elif ch.isdigit() or ch.isalpha():
                        target+=ch
                elif ch=='+' or ch=='-' or ch=='*' or ch=='/' or
                                        ch=='%' :
                        while (not st.isEmpty() and st.peek()!='('
                        and getPriority(st.peek())>=getPriority(ch)):
                                target+=st.pop()
                        st.push(ch)
        while(not st.isEmpty()):
                target+=st.pop()
        return target

def getPriority(opr):
        if (opr=='*' or opr=='/' or opr=='%'):
                return 1
        else:
                return 0

infix=input("Enter an Infix Expression: ")
postfix=infixToPostfix(infix)
```

```
print("The Equivalent Postfix Expression is : ")
print(postfix)
```

8.5.2.3 Evaluation of a Postfix Expression

To evaluate any postfix expression again the data structure `Stack` is required. As it is discussed earlier that the order of evaluation for postfix expressions is left to right, we need to scan each character of a postfix expression from left to right. A postfix expression is a parenthesis-free expression. So it contains operand and operators only. The algorithm to evaluate a postfix expression is given below:

1. Create a stack
2. Read each character of the postfix expression until end of string is reached
    a. If the scan character is an operand, Then
        i. Push it into the stack
    b. If the scan character is an operator, say OP, Then
        i. Pop from stack and store into A
        ii. Pop from stack and store into B
        iii. Evaluate as B OP A and push the result into the stack
3. Pop from stack and return as a result

To understand the algorithm clearly let us consider the infix expression $4 - (9 + 3 * 2) / 5$.

So, the equivalent postfix expression will be $4\ 9\ 3\ 2\ * + 5\ / -$. Following the above algorithm let us try to evaluate the expression.

Example 8.4: Evaluate the following postfix expression:

$4\ 9\ 3\ 2\ * + 5\ / -$

Solution:

Scan Character	Stack	Intermediate Operations
4	4	
9	4 9	
3	4 9 3	
2	4 9 3 2	

Scan Character	Stack	Intermediate Operations
*	4 9 6	A = 2 B = 3 C = 3 * 2 = 6
+	4 15	A = 6 B = 9 C = 9 + 6 = 15
5	4 15 5	
/	4 3	A = 5 B = 15 C = 15 / 5 = 3
−	1	A = 3 B = 4 C = 4 − 3 = 1
End of string		Return (1)

Thus the value of the above postfix expression is 1.

Here is the implementation of the above algorithm:

```python
def evaluatePostfix(source):
    st=Stack()
    for ch in source:
        if ch==' ' or ch=='\t':
            continue
        if(ch.isdigit()):
            st.push(int(ch))
        else:
            a=st.pop()
            b=st.pop()
            if ch=='+':
                c = b + a
            elif ch=='-':
                c = b - a
            elif ch=='*':
                c = b * a
            elif ch=='/':
                c = b / a
            elif ch=='%':
```

```
                    c = int(b) % int(a)
               st.push(c)
        return st.pop()
```

Program 8.5: Write a program to evaluate a postfix expression.

```
#PRGD8_5: Program to evaluate a Postfix expression

class stackNode :
    def __init__( self, Newdata, link ) :
        self.data = Newdata
        self.next = link

class Stack :
    def __init__( self ):
        self.top = None
    def isEmpty( self ):
        return self.top is None
    def peek( self ):
        return self.top.data
    def pop( self ):
        node = self.top
        self.top = self.top.next
        return node.data
    def push( self, Newdata ) :
        self.top = stackNode( Newdata, self.top )

def evaluatePostfix(source):
    st=Stack()
    for ch in source:
        if ch==' ' or ch=='\t':
            continue
        if(ch.isdigit()):
            st.push(int(ch))
        else:
            a=st.pop()
            b=st.pop()
            if ch=='+':
                c = b + a
            elif ch=='-':
                c = b - a
            elif ch=='*':
```

```
                    c = b * a
          elif ch=='/':
                    c = b / a
          elif ch=='%':
                    c = int(b) % int(a)
          st.push(c)
    return st.pop()

postfix=input("Enter a postfix Expression: ")
result=evaluatePostfix(postfix)
print("The Evaluated value of the Postfix Expression is :
                                    ",result)
```

8.5.2.4 Conversion of a Postfix Expression into an Infix Expression

Making some slight modification on the above algorithm, i.e. on the algorithm to evaluate a postfix expression, we can get the algorithm to convert a postfix expression into an infix expression. Instead of evaluating the result if we create a string of the operation enclosed within the parenthesis, we will get the corresponding infix expression. The following algorithm describes this.

Algorithm to convert a postfix expression into an infix expression:

1. Create a stack
2. Read each character of the postfix expression until end of string is reached
   a. If the scan character is an operand, Then
      i. Push it into the stack
   b. If the scan character is an operator, say OP, Then
      i. Pop from stack and store into A
      ii. Pop from stack and store into B
      iii. Concatenate '(' and B
      iv. Concatenate the resultant string and OP
      v. Concatenate the resultant string and A
      vi. Concatenate the resultant string and ')'
      vii. Push the resultant string into the stack
3. Pop from stack and return as a result

The following example illustrates the above example:

Example 8.5: Convert the following postfix expression into infix expression:

4 9 3 2 * + 5 / −

Solution:

Scan Character	Stack	Intermediate Operations
4	4	
9	4 9	
3	4 9 3	
2	4 9 3 2	
*	4 9 (3*2)	A = 2 B = 3 C = (3*2)
+	4 (9+(3*2))	A = (3*2) B = 9 C = (9+(3*2))
5	4 (9+(3*2)) 5	
/	4 ((9+(3*2))/5)	A = 5 B = (9+(3*2)) C = ((9+(3*2))/5)
–	(4–((9+(3*2))/5))	A = ((9+(3*2))/5) B = 4 C = (4–((9+(3*2))/5))
End of string		Return (4–((9+(3*2))/5))

Thus the resultant infix expression is: (4–((9+(3*2))/5)).

The implementation of the above algorithm is left as an exercise for the readers.

8.5.2.5 Conversion of an Infix Expression into a Prefix Expression

There are several algorithms for conversion of an infix expression into its equivalent prefix expression. Here we are using a simple one. The advantage of this algorithm is that we can use the same algorithm of infix to postfix conversion with a very minor modification and just two extra steps. The modification is that when the scan character is an operator, then elements will be popped first only if priority of the top element of stack is greater than (not >=) the priority of the scan character. Thus the algorithm can be described as:

1. Create a stack
2. Reverse the infix string. While reversing, we need to remember that the left parenthesis will be converted to the right parenthesis and the right parenthesis will be converted to the left parenthesis.

3. Read each character from source string until End of string is reached

   a. If the scan character is '(', Then

      Push it into the stack

   b. If the scan character is ')', Then

      i. Pop from stack and send to target string until '(' is encountered

      ii. Pop '(' from stack but do not send to target staring

   c. If the scan character is an operand, Then

      Send it to target string

   d. If the scan character is an operator, Then

      i. While stack is not empty or the Top element of stack is not '(' or Priority of Top element of stack > Priority of scan character

         Pop from stack and send to target string

      [End of while]

      ii. Push the scan character into the stack

4. Pop from stack and send to target string until the stack becomes empty.

5. Reverse the target string to get the required prefix expression.

The following example illustrates the above example:

Example 8.6: Convert the following infix expression into its equivalent prefix expression:

$$A + (B - C * D) / E$$

Solution: Source string: $A + (B - C * D) / E$

              Reversed string: $E / (D * C - B) + A$

Scan Character	Stack	Target String
E		E
/	/	E
(	/ (	E
D	/ (	E D
*	/ (*	E D
C	/ (*	E D C
–	/ (–	E D C *
B	/ (–	E D C * B

Scan Character	Stack	Target String
)	/	E D C * B –
+	+	E D C * B – /
A	+	E D C * B – / A
End of string		E D C * B – / A +

Required Prefix expression: + A / – B * C D E

Program 8.6: Write a program to convert an infix expression into its equivalent prefix expression.

```
#PRGD8_6:  Program to convert an infix expression into
#Prefix expression

class stackNode :
    def __init__( self, Newdata, link ) :
        self.data = Newdata
        self.next = link

class Stack :
    def __init__( self ):
        self.top = None
    def isEmpty( self ):
        return self.top is None
    def peek( self ):
        return self.top.data
    def pop( self ):
        node = self.top
        self.top = self.top.next
        return node.data
    def push( self, Newdata ) :
        self.top = stackNode( Newdata, self.top )

def getPriority(opr):
    if (opr=='*' or opr=='/' or opr=='%'):
        return 1
    else:
        return 0

def infixToPrefix(source):
    source=reverse(source)
```

```
        target=""
        st=Stack()
        for ch in source:
            if ch=='(':
                st.push(ch)
            elif ch==')':
                while(not st.isEmpty() and st.peek()!='('):
                    target+=st.pop()
                st.pop()
               # Pop from stack but not send to target string
            elif ch.isdigit() or ch.isalpha():
                target+=ch
            elif ch=='+' or ch=='-' or ch=='*' or ch=='/' or
                                                ch=='%' :
                while (not st.isEmpty() and st.peek()!='('
                and getPriority(st.peek())>getPriority(ch)):
                    target+=st.pop()
                st.push(ch)
        while(not st.isEmpty()):
            target+=st.pop()
        target=reverse(target)
        return target


def reverse( str1):
    str2=""
    j=len(str1)-1
    while(j>=0):
        if str1[j]=='(':
            str2+=')'
        elif str1[j]==')':
            str2+='('
        else:
            str2+=str1[j]
        j=j-1
    return str2

infix=input("Enter an Infix Expression: ")
prefix=infixToPrefix(infix)
print("The Equivalent Prefix Expression is : ",prefix)
```

8.5.3 Reversing any Sequence

To reverse the sequence of elements in a list, whether the elements are in an array or a linked list, a stack can be used. Read each element from the list and push them one by one into a stack. After storing all elements pop each element from the stack and restore within the list. The following example illustrates this:

Program 8.7: Write a program to reverse the elements of an array.

```
# PRGD8_7 Program to reverse the elements of an array

class Stack:
    def __init__(self):
        self.items = []
    def isEmpty(self):
        return self.items == []
    def push(self, item):
        self.items.append(item)
    def pop(self):
        return self.items.pop()
    def peek(self):
        return self.items[len(self.items)-1]
    def size(self):
        return len(self.items)

import array as arr
numbers=arr.array('i', [])
st=Stack()
for i in range(0, 10):
    n=int(input("Enter element: "))
    numbers.append(n)
print("\nElements are in inputted order : ")
for i in range(0, 10):
        print(numbers[i])
for i in range(0, 10):        # Pushing Array elements into
                                              #stack
        st.push(numbers[i])
for i in range(0, 10):      # Retrieving back elements from
                                        #stack to array
        numbers[i]=st.pop()
print("\nElements are in reversed order : ")
for i in range(0, 10):
        print(numbers[i])
```

Not only an array, we can reverse the elements of a linked list also. Consider the following program:

Program 8.8: Write a program to reverse the elements of a linked list.

```python
#Program 8_8: Write a program to reverse the elements of a
#linked list.

class Stack:
    def __init__(self):
        self.items = []
    def isEmpty(self):
        return self.items == []
    def push(self, item):
        self.items.append(item)
    def pop(self):
        return self.items.pop()

class Node :
    def __init__( self, Newdata, link ):
        self.data = Newdata
        self.next = link

class SLList :
    def __init__( self ):
        self.head = None
    def display( self ):
        current=self.head
        while current != None:
            print(current.data," ")
            current=current.next
    def addNode( self, Newdata ) :
        if self.head == None:
            self.head = Node(Newdata, None)
        else:
            current=self.head
            while current.next != None:
                current=current.next
            current.next=Node(Newdata, None)

def reverse(lst):
    st=Stack()
```

```
        ptr1=lst.head
        ptr2=ptr1
        while (ptr1):
            st.push(ptr1.data)
            ptr1 = ptr1.next
        while (ptr2):
            ptr2.data=st.pop()
            ptr2 = ptr2.next;

st=Stack()
newList=SLList()
for i in range(0, 4):
    n=int(input("Enter element: "))
    newList.addNode(n)
print("The List is : ")
newList.display()
reverse(newList)
print("The Reversed List is : ")
newList.display()
```

8.5.4 Recursion

We already discussed that when a function is called internally a stack is used. Thus we find the application of stacks in implementing recursion also. Though to write any recursive function we need not declare any stack directly, yet the compiler internally maintains a stack. If we go through any recursive function it will be clear to us. Consider the following example:

```
def factorial(n):
    if n==0:
        return 1
    else:
        return n * factorial(n-1)

num=int(input("Enter any number: "))
fact=factorial(num)
print("Factorial of ",num," is ",fact)
```

Suppose, the above function is called for n=4. So, the first call of this function will be pushed into the stack since to evaluate the return statement it will call factorial(3).

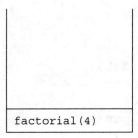

Similarly to evaluate the corresponding return statement it will further call `factorial(2)`, and `factorial(3)` will be pushed into the stack.

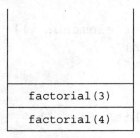

From the function `factorial(2)`, `factorial(1)` will be called and `factorial(2)` will be pushed into the stack. Finally, when `factorial(1)` will be executed, `factorial(0)` will be called and `factorial(1)` will be pushed into the stack.

factorial(1)
factorial(2)
factorial(3)
factorial(4)

Now n becomes 0 and from this function call 1 will be returned. Now `factorial(1)` will be popped from the stack and will return 1*1, i.e. 1.

factorial(2)
factorial(3)
factorial(4)

Next `factorial(2)` will be popped and return 2*1, i.e. 2.

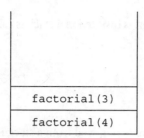

This process will continue and `factorial(3)` and `factorial(4)` will be popped from the stack respectively and finally we get the result as 24.

Stack at a Glance

✓ A stack is a linear data structure in which both the insertion and deletion operations occurs only at one end.

✓ The insertion operation is commonly known as PUSH and the deletion operation is known as POP.

✓ Stack is a LIFO (Last In First Out) data structure.

✓ In memory, a stack can be represented using an array as well as a linked list.

✓ Infix notation, prefix notation, and postfix notation are three notations used to represent any algebraic expression.

✓ The prefix notation is also known as Polish notation and the postfix notation is known as reverse Polish notation.

✓ In case of array representation, instead of using two or more separate stacks, use of multiple stacks is more memory efficient.

✓ Stack is implicitly used in function calls.

✓ Stack is used in various programming situations like checking whether parentheses are well balanced in an expression, conversion of infix expression to postfix or prefix expression or vice versa, evaluating infix, prefix, or postfix expressions, reversing the order of a list, etc.

Multiple Choice Questions

1. The process by which an element is inserted in a stack is called
   a) Create
   b) Insert
   c) Push
   d) Pop

2. The process by which an element is removed from a stack is called
   a) Delete
   b) Remove
   c) Push
   d) Pop

3. When an element is tried to be removed from an empty stack, it is called
   a) Underflow
   b) Overflow
   c) Empty collection
   d) Garbage Collection

4. When an element is tried to be pushed into a stack that is already full, it is called
   a) Underflow
   b) Overflow
   c) User flow
   d) Full flow

5. Which of the following is not an application of stack?
   a) Tracking of local variables at run time
   b) A parentheses balancing program
   c) Syntax analyzer of a compiler
   d) Data transfer between two asynchronous processes

6. Consider the parenthesis checking algorithm. If the input string is '((())()(()))', what is the maximum number of parentheses that may appear in a stack?
   a) 5
   b) 4
   c) 3
   d) 2

7. Consider the parenthesis checking algorithm. If the number of left and right parentheses in the input string is 2 and 3, respectively, what is the maximum number of parentheses that may be found in the stack?

   a) 5

   b) 2

   c) 3

   d) Cannot say

8. What will be the result when the postfix expression 7 2 3 4 + – * is evaluated?

   a) 24

   b) -24

   c) 35

   d) -35

9. Suppose the infix expression 5 + 2 / (8 / 4 – 6) is evaluated using stack. At any one time, maximum how many number of symbols may appear on the stack?

   a) 1

   b) 2

   c) 3

   d) 4

10. The postfix form of the expression (P- Q)*(R*S+ T)*U / V is

    a) P Q – R S * T + U V / * *

    b) P Q – R S * T + U * * V /

    c) P Q – R S * T + * U * V /

    d) P Q – R S T * + * U * V /

11. Which data structure is required to check whether the parentheses are properly placed in an expression?

    a) Array

    b) Stack

    c) Queue

    d) Tree

12. When a recursive algorithm is implemented non-recursively, which data structure is most likely used?

    a) Tree

    b) Linked list

    c) Queue

    d) Stack

13. The postfix form of A/B-C*D is
    a) /AB*CD-
    b) AB/CD*-
    c) A/BC-*D
    d) ABCD-*/

14. Which data structure is required when an infix expression is converted to postfix expression?
    a) Linked List
    b) Stack
    c) Queue
    d) Tree

15. The prefix form of A+B/ (C * D % E) is
    a) +A/B%*CDE
    b) /+AB%*CDE
    c) +A/B*C%DE
    d) +A/BC*%DE

16. The prefix form of an infix expression (A + B) – (C * D) is
    a) + AB – *CD
    b) – +ABC * D
    c) – +AB * CD
    d) – + * ABCD

17. Which data structure is used for implementing recursion?
    a) Array
    b) Queue
    c) Stack
    d) List

18. The result of evaluating the postfix expression 5 2 4 + * 4 6 3 / + * is
    a) 180
    b) 368
    c) 140
    d) 375

19. Convert the following infix expressions into its equivalent postfix expressions.
    (X + Y ^ Z) / (P + Q) – R
    a) X Y Z ^ + P Q + / R –
    b) X Y Z + ^ P Q + / R –

c) X Y Z ^ + P Q / + R −

d) X Y Z P Q + ^ / + R −

20. Which of the following statements is not True?

a) Python list data structure may be used for implementing stack.

b) Linked list may be used for implementing stack.

c) NumPy array cannot be used to implement stack.

d) All of the above

21. If the following operation is performed in sequence on a stack, after completion of execution how many elements will be in the stack?

```
Push ('+')
Push ('-')
Pop ()
Push ('*')
Push ('/')
Pop ()
Pop ()
Pop ()
Push ('%')
```

a) 0

b) 1

c) 2

d) 3

22. Which of the following is not an inherent application of stack?

a) Job scheduling

b) Reversing a string

c) Implementation of recursion

d) Evaluation of postfix expression

23. If the elements "A", "B", "C" and "D" are pushed in a stack and then popped one by one, what will be the order of popping?

a) ABCD

b) ABDC

c) DCAB

d) DCBA

24. If the following postfix expression is evaluated using a stack, after the first * is evaluated the top two elements of the stack will be

    4 2 2 ^ / 3 2 * + 1 5 * -

    a) 6, 1

    b) 7, 5

    c) 3, 2

    d) 1, 5

25. Which one of the following is an application of stack data structure?

    a) Managing function calls

    b) The stock span problem

    c) Arithmetic expression evaluation

    d) All of these

26. How many stacks are needed to implement a queue? Assume no other data structure like an array or linked list is available.

    a) 1

    b) 2

    c) 3

    d) 4

27. The postfix equivalent of the prefix * − P Q + R S is

    a) P Q − R S + *

    b) P Q R S − + *

    c) P Q − R S * +

    d) P Q − + R S *

28. The postfix expression for the infix expression a*(b+c)/(e-f) is

    a) a b c + * e f - /

    b) a b c + e / f - *

    c) a b c + e / * f -

    d) None of these

Review Exercises

1. What is a stack?

2. Why is a stack called a LIFO data structure?

3. What are the operations associated with stack? Explain with example.

4. What do you mean by 'Stack Overflow' and 'Stack Underflow'?

5. Compare and contrast between array representation, list representation, and linked list representation of stack.

6. Write algorithm of PUSH( ) and POP( ) operation in stack.

7. Convert the following infix expressions to their prefix equivalent using stack:

   a. A + B * C – D

   b. (A – B + C) * D

   c. (A + B) / (C – D) * (E % F)

   d. 4 + 3 * 1 / 6 + 7 - 4 / 2 + 5 * 3

   e. A + (B * C – (D / E * F) * G) * H

8. Convert the following infix expressions to their postfix equivalent using stack:

   a. A + B * C – D

   b. (A – B + C) * D

   c. (A + B) / (C – D) * (E % F)

   d. 4 + 3 * 1 / 6 + 7 - 4 / 2 + 5 * 3

   e. A + (B * C – (D / E * F) * G) * H

9. Convert the following postfix expressions into infix expressions:

   a. A B C * + D –

   b. A B + C D – / E F % *

   c. A B C * D – E F G % + / –

10. Evaluate the following postfix expressions:

    a. 5 3 – 2 + 4 *

    b. 9 3 + 6 4 – / 7 2 % *

    c. 3 5 2 * + 4 –

11. Convert the following postfix expressions into prefix expressions:

    a. A B C * + D –

    b. A B + C D – / E F % *

    c. A B C * D – E F G % + / –

Problems for Programming

1. Write a menu-driven program to implement array representation of stack.

2. Write a menu-driven program to implement a stack using linked list.

3. Write a program to convert an infix expression to its equivalent postfix expression.

4. Write a program to convert an infix expression to its equivalent prefix expression.

5. Write a program to convert a postfix expression to its equivalent infix expression.

6. Write a program to convert a postfix expression to its equivalent prefix expression.

7. Write a program to convert a prefix expression to its equivalent postfix expression.

8. Write a program to reverse the order of a list of strings.

9. Write a program to reverse a string using stack.

10. Write a program to implement multiple stacks using a single list.

Queue

Another important data structure is queue. Queues are also exhaustively used in various situations in computer science. In this chapter we will discuss the operations related to queues; how a queue is represented in memory, both array and linked representation of queues, different types of queues and various applications of queues.

9.1 Definitions and Concept

A queue is a linear data structure in which insertion and deletion operations take place at two different ends. The insertion operation is commonly known as ENQUEUE and the deletion operation is known as DEQUEUE. These two operations take place at two different ends. The end at which elements are inserted is known as the **rear** end and the other end at which elements are deleted from the queue is known as the **front** end. Elements are inserted through the **rear** end and removed through the **front** end following the First-In-First-Out (FIFO) order, i.e. in the order the elements entered the queue they will leave the queue maintaining the same order. In real life we are very familiar with queues. We can see several queues in our surroundings. For example, passengers standing in front of a railway ticket booking counter. The passenger who stands at the first position gets the ticket first and when a new passenger comes, he joins the queue at the end. The same can be seen when passengers wait at a bus stop, people standing in front of a ticket counter in a cinema hall, luggage moving through conveyor belt, cars passing through single lane in a one-way road, etc.

Figure 9.1   Example of a queue

9.2 Operations Associated with Queues

The basic operations related to a queue are as follows:

- Enqueue: Insert an element into a queue.
- Dequeue: Retrieve an element from a queue.

Apart from these basic two operations, to use a queue efficiently we need to add the following functionalities:

- Peek: Get the front element of a queue without removing it.
- Isempty: To check whether a queue is empty or not.
- Isfull: To check whether a queue is full or not.

All these operations execute with the time complexity O(1).

Like in stack, the peek operation is required to check the front element of the queue without removing it. And if a queue is full, the enqueue operation cannot be done on the queue. Similarly, dequeue and peek operations cannot be performed on an empty queue. Thus before these operations, we need to check whether the queue is full or empty.

9.3 Representation of a Queue

A queue is also a linear data structure consisting of a set of elements. Thus it can be represented in memory using an array as well as a linked list. In the following section, we will discuss traditional array representation as well as implementation of two very common approaches of queue representation, i.e. using Python's built-in **list** data structure and using linked list.

9.3.1 Array Representation of a Queue

To represent a queue in computer memory using a traditional array we have to point to the front and rear positions within the array. As these positions are basically the array indices, two integer variables are required for this purpose. As any queue may contain the elements of any data type, the data type of the array will be the corresponding type. For simplicity we are considering the array elements as integer type, and to show the essence of a traditional array the size of the array has been consider as fixed. Thus to represent a queue in memory we may define the class as:

```
import array as array
class Queue:
    def __init__(self,size):
        self.front=-1
        self.rear =-1
        self.arr=array.array('i', [0]*size)
```

Like stack before using the queue we have to initialize the queue and this is done by assigning the value -1 both to the **front** and **rear** to indicate that the queue is empty. As within the array the value of the **front** and **rear** varies from 0 to SIZE-1, we set the initial value as -1. Now the basic operations on queue are shown with the diagram in Figure 9.2.

Operation	front	rear	arr
Initial state	-1	-1	(empty array) 0 1 2 3 4
Enqueue 5	0	0	5 | | | | ; f↑0↑r 1 2 3 4
Enqueue 10	0	1	5 | 10 | | | ; f↑0 1↑r 2 3 4
Enqueue 15	0	2	5 | 10 | 15 | | ; f↑0 1 2↑r 3 4

Operation	front	rear	arr
Dequeue	1	2	`[ , 10, 15, , ]` indices 0, f↑1, 2↑r, 3, 4
Dequeue	2	2	`[ , , 15, , ]` indices 0, 1, f↑2↑r, 3, 4
Dequeue	-1	-1	`[ , , , , ]` indices 0, 1, 2, 3, 4
Enqueue 20	0	0	`[20, , , , ]` indices f↑0↑r, 1, 2, 3, 4
Enqueue 25	0	1	`[20, 25, , , ]` indices f↑0, 1↑r, 2, 3, 4
Enqueue 30	0	2	`[20, 25, 30, , ]` indices f↑0, 1, 2↑r, 3, 4
Dequeue	1	2	`[ , 25, 30, , ]` indices 0, f↑1, 2↑r, 3, 4
Enqueue 35	1	3	`[ , 25, 30, 35, ]` indices 0, f↑1, 2, 3↑r, 4
Dequeue	2	3	`[ , , 30, 35, ]` indices 0, 1, f↑2, 3↑r, 4
Enqueue 40	2	4	`[ , , 30, 35, 40]` indices 0, 1, f↑2, 3, 4↑r

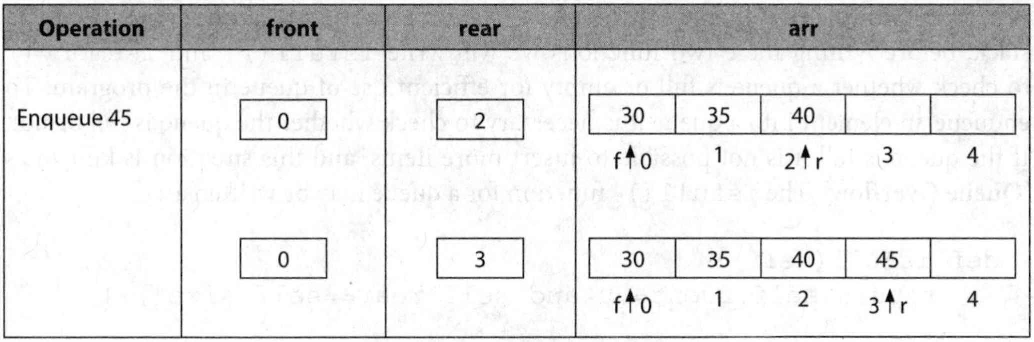

Operation	front	rear	arr				
Enqueue 45	0	2	30	35	40		
			f↑0	1	2↑r	3	4
	0	3	30	35	40	45	
			f↑0	1	2	3↑r	4

Figure 9.2 Operations on a queue

Considering the above example we can write the algorithm of the Enqueue operation as:

```
1.  If front = 0 And rear = SIZE - 1, Then
    a. Print "Queue Overflow"
    b. Go to Step4
2.  Else
    a. If rear = -1, Then
       i. front = rear = 0
    b. Else
       i. If rear = SIZE - 1, Then
          1. Shift the elements towards front
          2. Set front = 0
          3. Adjust rear accordingly
      ii. Else
          1. rear = rear + 1
3.  arr[rear] = new element
4.  End
```

The algorithm of the Dequeue operation can be written as:

```
1.  If front = -1, Then
    a. Print "Queue Underflow"
    b. Go to Step3
2.  Else
    a. Element = arr[front]
    b. If front = rear, Then
          i. front = rear = -1
    c. Else
          i. front = front + 1
    d. Return Element
3.  End
```

Based on these algorithms now enqueue() and dequeue() can be written. Like in stack, before writing these two functions we will write isfull() and isempty() to check whether a queue is full or empty for efficient use of queue in the program. To enqueue an element into a queue it is necessary to check whether the queue is full or not. If the queue is full it is not possible to insert more items, and this situation is known as **'Queue Overflow'**. The isfull() function for a queue may be written as:

```
def isFull(self):
    return self.front==0 and self.rear==self.size()-1
```

To check whether a queue is full or not, only inspecting the value of **rear** is not sufficient. There may be situations when **rear** will point to the end of the array but still the queue is not full (consider the example in Figure 9.2 after enqueueing 40). There may be some vacant place at the front side of the queue. At these positions **front** will point to some position except 0. Thus we need to check the value of **front** as well as **rear.**

Similarly, when we want to dequeue or peek at any element we have to check whether the queue is empty or not. This empty situation is known as **'Queue Underflow'**. We can write the isempty() for a queue as:

```
def isEmpty(self):
    return self.front == -1
```

When a queue is empty the value of the **front** and **rear** should be **-1** and in other cases the value of the **front** is the array index where the first element of the queue resides and the value of the **rear** stores the array index of the last element of the queue. So to write isempty(), we can check only **front** or only **rear** or can check both. Thus all the following versions work the same as above:

```
def isEmpty(self):
    return self.rear == -1
```

Or

```
def isEmpty(self):
    return self.front == -1 and self.rear==-1
```

Or

```
def isEmpty(self):
    return self.front == -1 or self.rear==-1
```

Now, we will write the enqueue() function. Based on the algorithm written above we will write the following function:

```
def enqueue(self, item):
        j=0
        if self.rear==-1:
                self.front=self.rear=0
        elif self.rear==self.size()-1:
                for i in range(self.front,self.rear+1):
                        self.arr[j] = self.arr[i]
                        j=j+1
                self.front = 0
                self.rear = j
        else:
                self.rear+=1
        self.arr[self.rear]=item
```

In the above function, first the value of **rear** is checked. If it is -1, it indicates the queue is empty and both **front** and **rear** are set to zero. In its **else** part it is checked whether rear==SIZE-1. If it is true, the situation is that **rear** points to the end of the queue but still the queue is not full (consider the example in Figure 9.3 when enqueueing 45). There are some vacant places at the front side of the queue. So, we need to shift the elements towards the front side. Shifting is started from the position which is pointed to by **front** and up to the end of the array, i.e. the position which is pointed to by **rear**. These shifted elements are stored consecutively starting from zeroth position in the array. As now all the elements have shifted to front side of the array, **front** is set to 0 and **rear** points to the next position of the last element in the array. When both the above conditions are false, **rear** will point to the next position in the array. Finally, the new element is stored at this newly set **rear** position.

In case of dequeue(), first we assign the front element to a temporary variable and then increment the value of **front** by 1 except when the queue contains a single element. This situation is achieved only when **front** and **rear** point to the same position. As on dequeueing this element, the queue becomes empty, we need to set both **front** and **rear** to -1. Finally, the temporary variable is returned. The dequeue() function can be written as:

```
def dequeue(self):
        temp = self.arr[self.front]
        if self.front==self.rear:
                self.front=self.rear=-1
        else:
                self.front+=1
        return temp
```

The following program demonstrates the various operations of a queue:

Program 9.1: Write a program to demonstrate the various operations of a queue using an array.

```python
# PRGD9_1: Program to implement Queue using fixed size Array

import array as array
class Queue:
    def __init__(self,size):
        self.front=-1
        self.rear =-1
        self.arr=array.array('i', [0]*size)
    def isEmpty(self):
        return self.front == -1
    def isFull(self):
        return self.front == 0 and self.rear== self.size()-1
    def enqueue(self, item):
        j=0
        if self.rear==-1:
            self.front=self.rear=0
        elif self.rear==self.size()-1:
            for i in range(self.front,self.rear+1):
                self.arr[j] = self.arr[i]
                j=j+1
            self.front = 0
            self.rear = j
        else:
            self.rear+=1
        self.arr[self.rear]=item

    def dequeue(self):
        temp = self.arr[self.front]
        if self.front==self.rear:
            self.front=self.rear=-1
        else:
            self.front+=1
        return temp
    def peek(self):
        return self.arr[self.front]
    def size(self):
        return len(self.arr)
    def display(self):
```

```
            print(self.arr)
            print("------"*self.size()+"-")
            print("|      "*(self.front),end="")
            for i in range(self.front,self.rear+1):
                print('|',format(self.arr[i],'>3'), end=" ")
            print("|      "*(self.size()-(self.
                                            rear+1)),end="")
            print("|")
            print("------"*self.size()+"-")

size=int(input("Enter the size of the Queue"))
q=Queue(size)
while(True):
    print("\nPROGRAM TO IMPLEMENT QUEUE ")
    print("=============================")
    print("\t1. Enqueue")
    print("\t2. Dequeue")
    print("\t3. Peek")
    print("\t4. Display")
    print("\t5. Exit")
    print("=============================")
    choice=int(input("Enter your Choice : "))
    if choice==1 :
        if q.isFull() :
            print("Queue Overflow")
        else :
            num=int(input("Enter the Data: "))
            q.enqueue(num)
    elif choice==2 :
        if q.isEmpty() :
            print("Queue Underflow")
        else :
            num=q.dequeue()
            print("Item dequeued = ",num)
    elif choice==3 :
        if q.isEmpty() :
            print("Queue Underflow")
        else :
            num=q.peek()
            print("Item at the front of the Queue = ",num)
    elif choice==4 :
        if q.isEmpty() :
```

```
            print("Queue is Empty")
        else :
            q.display()
    elif choice==5 :
        print("\nQuiting.......")
        break
    else:
        print("Invalid choice. Please Enter Correct
                                            Choice")

        continue
```

9.3.2 Circular Queue

The major drawback in array representation of a queue is that at the time of enqueuing, there may be a situation when the **rear** will point to the end of the array but still the queue is not full (consider the example in Figure 9.2 when enqueueing 45). There are some vacant places at the front side of the queue. So, we need to shift the elements towards the front side so that we can make space to accommodate new elements. But it is very time consuming, especially for large queues.

To solve this problem we can imagine the array to be bent so that the position next to the last position of the array becomes the first position, just like in Figure 9.3.

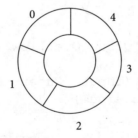

Figure 9.3   Circular queue

So, the linear queue now becomes the circular queue. The advantage of this concept is that we need not shift elements to **enqueue** a new element when the queue is not full but **rear** reaches the end of the queue (i.e. SIZE-1 position). We can simply store the new element at the next position, i.e. the zeroth position of the array. In case of **dequeue** also after removing the element at position SIZE-1, **front** will point to the zeroth position of the array. In the next section we will see the various operations on a circular queue and the position of the elements within the array.

9.3.2.1 Operations on a Circular Queue

A circular queue is implemented in the same way a normal queue, i.e. a linear queue, is implemented. Like linear queues, the front and rear should be initialized with -1. Other operations are also similar to those in a linear queue. The only difference is that at the time of **enqueue**, when **rear** reaches the end of the array, instead of shifting the elements, **rear** points to the zeroth position, and at the time of **dequeue**, after removing the last element of the array, **front** points to the zeroth position of the array. Figure 9.4 shows the basic operations on a circular queue.

Operation	front	rear	arr
Initial state	-1	-1	
Enqueue 5	0	0	
Enqueue 10	0	1	

Operation	front	rear	arr
Enqueue 15	0	2	
Dequeue	1	2	
Dequeue	2	2	
Dequeue	-1	-1	
Enqueue 20	0	0	

Operation	front	rear	arr
Enqueue 25	0	1	
Enqueue 30	0	2	
Dequeue	1	2	
Enqueue 35	1	3	
Dequeue	2	3	

Operation	front	rear	arr
Enqueue 40	2	4	
Enqueue 45	2	0	

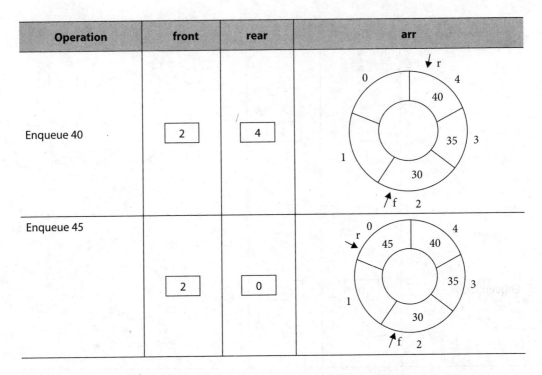

Figure 9.4 Operations on a circular queue

Considering the above example we can write the algorithm of an `enqueue` operation for a circular queue as:

```
1.  If (front=0 And rear=SIZE - 1)Or(front=rear + 1), Then
    a. Print "Queue Overflow"
    b. Go to Step4
2.  Else
    a. If rear = -1, Then
          i. front = rear = 0
    b. Else
          i. If rear = SIZE - 1, Then
                1. rear = 0
         ii. Else
                1. rear = rear + 1
3.  arr[rear] = new element
4.  End
```

The algorithm of a `dequeue` operation for a circular queue can be written as :

```
1.  If front = -1, Then
    a. Print "Queue Underflow"
```

```
   b. Go to Step3
2: Else
   a. Element = arr[front]
   b. If front = rear, Then
         i. front = rear = -1
   c. Else
         i. If front = SIZE - 1, Then
               1. front = 0
        ii. Else
               1. front = front + 1
   d. Return Element
3. End
```

Based on these algorithms now we will write isfull(), isempty(), enqueue(), and dequeue() for circular queue. isempty() is exactly that same as that of a linear queue. But in case of isfull() we have to consider an extra situation when the front moves forward from the zeroth position and the rear rounds back with the array reaching the front. Thus the function will be as follows:

```
def isFull(self):
    return (self.front==0 and self.rear==self.size()-1) or
                        (self.front==self.rear+1)
```

The enqueue() function can be written as:

```
def enqueue(self, item):
    if self.rear==-1:
        self.front=self.rear=0
    elif self.rear==self.size()-1:
        self.rear = 0
    else:
        self.rear+=1
    self.arr[self.rear]=item
```

Or in short:

```
def enqueue(self, item):
    if self.rear==-1:
        self.front=self.rear=0
    else:
        self.rear=(self.rear+1)%self.size()
    self.arr[self.rear]=item
```

The above enqueue () function is almost similar to enqueue () of a linear queue but when the value of **rear** becomes SIZE – 1, we set **rear** =0.

Similarly the dequeue () function for a circular queue will be as follows:

```python
def dequeue(self):
        temp = self.arr[self.front]
        if self.front==self.rear:
            self.front=self.rear=-1
        elif self.front==self.size()-1:
            self.front=0
        else:
            self.front+=1
        return temp
```

Or in short:

```python
def dequeue(self):
    temp = self.arr[self.front]
    if self.front==self.rear:
        self.front=self.rear=-1
    else:
        self.front=(self.front+1)%self.size()
    return temp
```

The following program demonstrates the various operations of a circular queue.

Program 9.2: Write a program to demonstrate the various operations of a circular queue.

```python
# PRGD9_2: Program to implement Circular Queue

import array as array
class Queue:
    def __init__(self,size):
        self.front=-1
        self.rear =-1
        self.arr=array.array('i', [0]*size)
    def isEmpty(self):
        return self.front == -1
    def isFull(self):
        return (self.front == 0 and self.rear== self.
                    size()-1) or (self.front==self.rear+1)

    def enqueue(self, item):
```

```python
            if self.rear==-1:
                self.front=self.rear=0
            elif self.rear==self.size()-1:
                self.rear = 0
            else:
                self.rear+=1
            self.arr[self.rear]=item

    def dequeue(self):
        temp = self.arr[self.front]
        if self.front==self.rear:
            self.front=self.rear=-1
        elif self.front==self.size()-1:
            self.front=0
        else:
            self.front+=1
        return temp

    def peek(self):
        return self.arr[self.front]
    def size(self):
        return len(self.arr)
    def display(self):
        print("------"*self.size()+"-")
        if(q.front<=q.rear):
            print("|      "*(self.front),end="")
            for i in range(self.front,self.rear+1):
                print('|',format(self.arr[i],'>3'),
                                            end="  ")
            print("|      "*(self.size()-(self.
                                    rear+1)),end="")
        else:
            for i in range(0,self.rear+1):
                print('|',format(self.arr[i],'>3'),
                                        end="  ")
            print("|      "*(self.front-(self.
                                    rear+1)),end="")
            for i in range(self.front,self.size()):
                print('|',format(self.arr[i],'>3'),
                                        end="  ")
        print("|")
        print("------"*self.size()+"-")
```

```python
size=int(input("Enter the size of the Queue"))
q=Queue(size)
while(True):
    print("\nPROGRAM TO IMPLEMENT CIRCULAR QUEUE ")
    print("====================================")
    print("\t1. Enqueue")
    print("\t2. Dequeue")
    print("\t3. Peek")
    print("\t4. Display")
    print("\t5. Exit")
    print("====================================")
    choice=int(input("Enter your Choice : "))
    if choice==1 :
        if q.isFull() :
            print("Queue Overflow")
        else :
            num=int(input("Enter the Data: "))
            q.enqueue(num)
    elif choice==2 :
        if q.isEmpty() :
            print("Queue Underflow")
        else :
            num=q.dequeue()
            print("Item dequeued = ",num)
    elif choice==3 :
        if q.isEmpty() :
            print("Queue Underflow")
        else :
            num=q.peek()
            print("Item at the front of the Queue = ",num)
    elif choice==4 :
        if q.isEmpty() :
            print("Queue is Empty")
        else :
            q.display()
    elif choice==5 :
        print("\nQuiting.......")
        break
    else:
        print("Invalid choice. Please Enter Correct
                                            Choice")
        continue
```

9.3.3 Python List Representation of a Queue

As Python's in-built **list** data structure grows and shrinks dynamically, we can implement the queue data structure much easily. The front end of the list may be treated as **front** and the back end will be then treated as **rear**. So, to enqueue an element into the queue we can use the list method append() and to dequeue an element from the queue we can use pop(0). In this representation, the time complexity of the enqueue operation is O(1) but for the dequeue operation it will be O(n).

The basic operations on a queue are shown in Figure 9.5 when it is implemented using list.

Operation	Arr
Initial state	Empty Queue
Enqueue 5	5 0
Enqueue 10	5 10 0 1
Enqueue 15	5 10 15 0 1 2
Dequeue	10 15 0 1
Dequeue	15 0

Figure 9.5 Operations on queue using list data structure

Program 9.3: Write a program to demonstrate the various operations of a queue using list.

```
# PRGD9_3: Program to implement Queue using list

class Queue:
    def __init__(self):
        self.items = []
    def isEmpty(self):
```

```
            return self.items == []
    def enqueue(self, item):
        self.items.append(item)
    def dequeue(self):
        return self.items.pop(0)
    def peek(self):
        return self.items[0]
    def size(self):
        return len(self.items)
    def display(self):
        rear=len(self.items)
        print("------"*rear+"-")
        for i in range(rear):
            print('|',format(self.items[i],'>3'), end="
                                                      ")

        print("|")
        print("------"*rear+"-")

q=Queue()
while(True):
    print("\nPROGRAM TO IMPLEMENT QUEUE ")
    print("=============================")
    print("\t1. Enqueue")
    print("\t2. Dequeue")
    print("\t3. Peek")
    print("\t4. Display")
    print("\t5. Exit")
    print("============================")
    choice=int(input("Enter your Choice : "))
    if choice==1 :
        num=int(input("Enter the Data: "))
        q.enqueue(num)
    elif choice==2 :
        if q.isEmpty() :
            print("Queue Underflow")
        else :
            num=q.dequeue()
            print("Item dequeued = ",num)
    elif choice==3 :
        if q.isEmpty() :
            print("Queue Underflow")
        else :
```

```
                num=q.peek()
                print("Item at the front of the Queue = ",num)
        elif choice==4 :
            if q.isEmpty() :
                print("Queue is Empty")
            else :
                q.display()
        elif choice==5 :
            print("\nQuiting.......")
            break
        else:
            print("Invalid choice. Please Enter Correct
                                                    Choice")

        continue
```

9.3.4 Linked Representation of a Queue

Implementation of a queue using a traditional fixed size array suffers from the basic problem of wastage of memory or lack of memory. On the other hand, if it is implemented using the built-in list data structure, the time complexity of the dequeue operation increases to O(n). The solution of these problems is linked list representation.

As the operation of a queue occurs just at two ends, we need not traverse the entire list. Thus a singly linked list is the better option to implement a queue. The linked list representation of a queue can be done efficiently in two ways.

1. With the header list representation and

2. Using a single circular linked list with a single tail pointer.

9.3.4.1 Using a Header List

We can represent a queue very efficiently with the help of a header linked list. Here the header node of the linked list will consist of two pointers to point to the **front** and **rear** nodes of the queue (i.e. the first node and last node of the list). Figure 9.6 illustrates this.

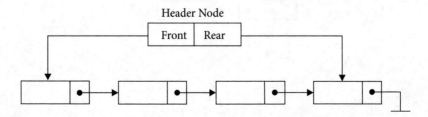

Figure 9.6 Linked representation of a queue

From Figure 9.6 we can see that to implement it we have to declare two different classes – one for the nodes of a single linked list and another for the header node. Nodes of the single linked list represent each element in the queue and the header node keeps track of the front position and the rear position. For the nodes of a single linked list the class can be defined as:

```
class Node :
    def __init__( self, Newdata, link ) :
        self.data = Newdata
        self.next = link
```

And the header node can be defined as:

```
class Queue :
    def __init__( self ):
        self.front=None
        self.rear =None
```

The basic operations on a queue using linked list are shown in Figure 9.7.

Initial State:

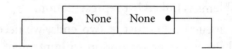

Enqueue 5:

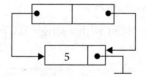

Enqueue 10:

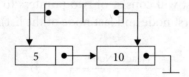

Enqueue 15:

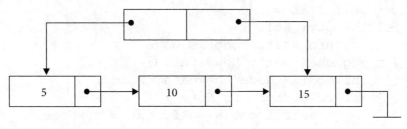

Dequeue :

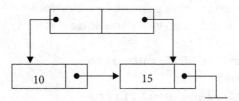

Figure 9.7 Operations on a linked queue

Initially when the queue is empty there will be no nodes in the linked list. Thus **front** and **rear** both contain None. Next **5** is inserted into the queue. So, a node is created containing 5 and both **front** and **rear** point to that node. Next operation is **Enqueue 10**. Again a new node is created containing 10 and this node is inserted after the first node in the linked list. As now it becomes the last node in the list, **rear** points to this new node. Similarly, in case of **Enqueue 15**, a new node is inserted at the end of the list and **rear** points to the new node. Thus for the enqueue operation, we need not traverse the list and the time complexity of this operation is O(1). When the dequeue operation is done, as the front points to the first node of the list, the content of this node, i.e. 5, is returned and the node is deleted from the list. The front pointer now points to the next node of the list. Thus the time complexity of dequeue is also O(1).

Here is a complete program to demonstrate the various operations of a queue using linked list:

Program 9.4: Write a program to demonstrate the various operations of a queue using linked list.

```
#PRGD9_4: Implementation of Queue using linked list.

class Node :                              # Declaration of Node
    def __init__( self, Newdata, link ) :
        self.data = Newdata
        self.next = link


class Queue :
    def __init__( self ):             # Creates an empty Queue
```

```python
        self.front=None
        self.rear =None
    def isEmpty( self ):
        return self.front is None
    def enqueue( self, Newdata ) :
        newNode = Node( Newdata, None )
        if self.front is None :
            self.front = self.rear = newNode
        else:
            self.rear.next = newNode
            self.rear = newNode
    def peek( self ):
        return self.front.data
    def dequeue( self ):
        frontNode = self.front
        if self.front==self.rear :
            self.front = self.rear = None
        else:
            self.front = frontNode.next
        return frontNode.data
    def display(self):
        curNode = self.front
        print()
        while curNode is not None :
            print(curNode.data,'-> ',end="")
            curNode = curNode.next
        print("None");

q=Queue()
while(True):
    print("\nPROGRAM TO IMPLEMENT QUEUE ")
    print("=============================")
    print("\t1. Enqueue")
    print("\t2. Dequeue")
    print("\t3. Peek")
    print("\t4. Display")
    print("\t5. Exit")
    print("=============================")
    choice=int(input("Enter your Choice : "))
    if choice==1 :
        num=int(input("Enter the Data: "))
        q.enqueue(num)
```

```
            elif choice==2 :
                if q.isEmpty() :
                    print("Queue Underflow")
                else :
                    num=q.dequeue()
                    print("Item dequeued = ",num)
            elif choice==3 :
                if q.isEmpty() :
                    print("Queue Underflow")
                else :
                    num=q.peek()
                    print("Item at the front of the Queue = ",num)
            elif choice==4 :
                if q.isEmpty() :
                    print("Queue is Empty")
                else :
                    q.display()
            elif choice==5 :
                print("\nQuiting.......")
                break
            else:
                print("Invalid choice. Please Enter Correct
                                                    Choice")
                continue
```

9.3.4.2 Using a Single Circular Linked List with a Single Tail Pointer

Instead of using a header node, a queue can be implemented using a single circular linked list. But instead of a head pointer, here a tail pointer is required. The advantage of this implementation is that instead of two pointers, **front** and **rear,** a single pointer is sufficient. The following program illustrates this:

Program 9.5: Write a program to demonstrate the operations of a queue using a circular linked list with a single tail pointer.

```
#PRGD9_5: Implementation of Queue using a circular linked
#list and a tail pointer

class Node :                          # Declaration of Node
    def __init__( self, Newdata, link ) :
        self.data = Newdata
        self.next = link
```

```python
class Queue :
    def __init__( self ):          # Creates an empty Queue
        self.tail=None
    def isEmpty( self ):
        return self.tail is None
    def enqueue( self, Newdata ) :
        newNode = Node( Newdata, None )
        if self.tail is None :
            newNode.next = newNode
        else:
            newNode.next = self.tail.next
            self.tail.next = newNode
        self.tail = newNode
    def peek( self ):
        return self.tail.next.data
    def dequeue( self ):
        frontNode = self.tail.next
        if frontNode.next==frontNode :
            self.tail = None
        else:
            self.tail.next = frontNode.next
        return frontNode.data
    def display(self):
        curNode = self.tail.next
        print()
        while curNode is not self.tail :
            print(curNode.data,'-> ',end="")
            curNode = curNode.next
        print(curNode.data)

q=Queue()
while(True):
    print("\nPROGRAM TO IMPLEMENT QUEUE ")
    print("============================")
    print("\t1. Enqueue")
    print("\t2. Dequeue")
    print("\t3. Peek")
    print("\t4. Display")
    print("\t5. Exit")
    print("============================")
    choice=int(input("Enter your Choice : "))
    if choice==1 :
```

```
        num=int(input("Enter the Data: "))
        q.enqueue(num)
    elif choice==2 :
        if q.isEmpty() :
            print("Queue Underflow")
        else :
            num=q.dequeue()
            print("Item dequeued = ",num)
    elif choice==3 :
        if q.isEmpty() :
            print("Queue Underflow")
        else :
            num=q.peek()
            print("Item at the front of the Queue = ",num)
    elif choice==4 :
        if q.isEmpty() :
            print("Queue is Empty")
        else :
            q.display()
    elif choice==5 :
        print("\nQuiting.......")
        break
    else:
        print("Invalid choice. Please Enter Correct
                                            Choice")
        continue
```

9.4 Multiple Queues

Like in stacks, in case of queues also in traditional array representation it is very difficult to predict the size of the array in advance. If the size of the array is small, frequent overflow condition may occur. On the other hand, if we declare the array as large, there is a chance of a huge wastage of memory. So, there needs to be a trade-off between frequent overflow and wastage of memory.

One solution to this problem is to use multiple queues in the same array to share the common space. Figure 9.8 shows this concept.

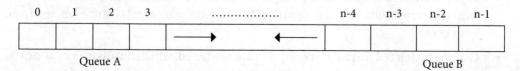

Queue A   Queue B

Figure 9.8   Representation of two queues using a single array

In Figure 9.8, it is shown that we may implement two queues, queue A and queue B, within a single array. Queue A will grow from left to right and queue B will grow from right to left. Within queue A, the first element will be stored at the zeroth position, the next element at the index position 1, then at the index position 2, and so on. Whereas within the queue B, the first element will be stored at the $(n-1)^{th}$ position, the next element at the $(n-2)^{th}$ position, then at $(n-3)^{th}$ position, and so on. The advantage of this scheme is that the intermediate space in between two queues is common for both and may be used by any one of them. Suppose the array size is 10 and in a particular situation queue B contains three elements. Thus for queue B, the **front** will point to 9 and the **rear** will point to 7. At this position, queue A is free to expand up to array index 6 in the array. Similarly, queue B is also able to expand up to the **rear** position of queue A.

Extending this concept, it is possible to accommodate any number of queues within a single array. For each queue an equal amount of space will be allocated and if there is n number of queues, each queue will be bounded by s[n] and e[n]. Figure 9.9 illustrates this concept.

| s[0] | e[0] | s[1] | e[1] | .... | s[n-2] | e[n-2] | s[n-1] | e[n-1] |

| Queue 1 | Queue 2 | ...... | Queue n-1 | Queue n |

Figure 9.9 Representation of multiple queues

9.5 Special Queues

In data structure we find some variations of a queue. These can be considered as special queues. In the following section we will discuss them.

9.5.1 DEQue

The full form of DEque is Double Ended Queue. It is a special type of queue where elements can be inserted or deleted from either end. But insertion or deletion is not allowed in the middle or any intermediate position. Thus the operations related to deque are: insert from left, insert from right, delete from left, and delete from right.

There are two variations of deque. Those are:

- **Input restricted deque**: In this deque inputs are restricted, which means elements will be inserted only through a particular end but the elements can be deleted from both ends.

- **Output restricted deque**: Here outputs are restricted, which means elements can be deleted only from a particular end but can be inserted through both ends.

In Python, the deque module is a part of the collections library. It contains several methods to operate on it. Table 9.1 describes some of its functions.

Table 9.1 Python methods of deque

Methods	Description
append ( )	Inserts a element to the right
appendleft ( )	Inserts a element to the left
pop ( )	Removes an element from right
popleft ( )	Removes an element from left
remove (n)	Remove the first occurrence of n
clear ( )	Removes all elements from a deque
count (n)	Counts the number of elements equal to n
reverse ( )	Reverse the elements of a deque

The following program shows the basic operations of a deque:

Program 9.6: Write a program to demonstrate the different operations on deque.

```
#PRGD9_6: Different operations on Deque

from collections import deque
dq = deque()
print("Empty deque created")
print(dq)
dq.append("Sachin")
print("Added at right")
print(dq)
dq.append("Sunil")
print("Added at right")
print(dq)
dq.appendleft("Paji")
print("Added at left")
print(dq)
name=dq.pop()
print("Removed from right")
print(name+" popped")
```

```
print(dq)
name=dq.popleft()
print("Removed from left")
print(name+" popped")
print(dq)
dq.append("Sourav")
dq.append("Sehwag")
dq.append("Sachin")
print("New 3 elements added at right")
print(dq)
c=dq.count("Sachin")
print(c,"'Sachin' is here")
dq.remove("Sachin")
print("First 'Sachin' is removed")
print(dq)
print("Members are reversed")
dq.reverse()
print(dq)
dq.clear()
print(dq)
```

Output of the above program:

```
Empty deque created
deque([])
Added at right
deque(['Sachin'])
Added at right
deque(['Sachin', 'Sunil'])
Added at left
deque(['Paji', 'Sachin', 'Sunil'])
Removed from right
Sunil popped
deque(['Paji', 'Sachin'])
Removed from left
Paji popped
deque(['Sachin'])
New 3 elements added at right
deque(['Sachin', 'Sourav', 'Sehwag', 'Sachin'])
2 'Sachin' is here
First 'Sachin' is removed
```

deque(['Sourav', 'Sehwag', 'Sachin'])
Members are reversed
deque(['Sachin', 'Sehwag', 'Sourav'])
deque([])

9.5.2 Priority Queue

A priority queue is a special type of queue where each element is associated with a priority and the element with the highest priority will leave the queue first. But within the same priority elements, FIFO order will be followed, i.e. it will act as a normal queue. An example of use of priority queue is in implementation of the priority scheduling algorithm of CPU scheduling where the higher priority job get the CPU first. Priority queue can be implemented in several ways:

- **Using single queue:** To implement a priority queue we can maintain a sorted list based on the priority of the element. When a new element is inserted it will be inserted at the proper position of the sorted list. But within the same priority it will act like a normal queue, i.e. the new element will be inserted after the elements of the same priority. Generally, lower priority value is considered as higher priority. For example, if a queue contains elements having priority 3 and 5, a new element with priority 4 will be inserted in between the elements of priority 3 and 5. However, a new element with priority 3 will be inserted after all the elements of priority 3 but before the first element having priority 5. In this implementation, the dequeue operation is the same as a normal queue. As element with highest priority will always be at **front** position. Thus the time complexity of the enqueue operation will be $O(n)$ whereas that of dequeue is $O(1)$.

  On the other hand, we can insert a new element always at the end of the list following the normal enqueue operation. At the time of dequeue, the element with highest priority will be searched and removed. Here the time complexity of the enqueue operation will be $O(1)$ but that of dequeue is $O(n)$.

  Like a normal queue, a priority queue can also be represented using a traditional array, list, or linked list. In Python, array representation and list representation are quite the same. For both representations we have to create an array or list of objects where each object will contain the data part and the priority value of the element. For linked list representation the node structure will contain the data part, the priority value of the element, and the reference of the next node.

  In the following program, a priority queue is implemented using the list data structure. As deletion of any element from the end of the list requires time complexity of $O(1)$, here the end of the list has been considered as the front. So, in this implementation, the time complexity of the dequeue operation is $O(1)$ and that of enqueue is $O(n)$.

Program 9.7: Write a program to demonstrate the operations of a priority queue.

```
# PRGD9_7: Program to implement Priority Queue Using List

class Node :
    def __init__( self, Newdata, NewPriority ) :
        self.data = Newdata
        self.priority= NewPriority

class priorityQueue:
    def __init__(self):
        self.items = []
    def isEmpty(self):
        return self.items == []
    def enqueue(self, item):
        rear=len(self.items)
        for i in range(rear):
            if item.priority>=self.items[i].priority :
                self.items.insert(i,item)
                break
        else:
            self.items.append(item)
    def dequeue(self):
        return self.items.pop()
    def peek(self):
        return self.items[self.size()-1]
    def size(self):
        return len(self.items)
    def display(self):
        rear=len(self.items)
        print("---------"*rear+"-")
        for i in range(rear):
            print('|',format(str(self.items[i].data)
    +"("+str(self.items[i].priority)+")",'>6'), end=" ")
        print("|")
        print("---------"*rear+"-")

q=priorityQueue()
while(True):
    print("\nPROGRAM TO IMPLEMENT PRIORITY QUEUE ")
    print("=====================================")
    print("\t1. Enqueue")
```

```
print("\t2. Dequeue")
print("\t3. Peek")
print("\t4. Display")
print("\t5. Exit")
print("====================================")
choice=int(input("Enter your Choice : "))
if choice==1 :
    num=int(input("Enter the Data: "))
    prio=int(input("Enter Priority value: "))
    newNode=Node(num,prio)
    q.enqueue(newNode)
elif choice==2 :
    if q.isEmpty() :
        print("Queue Underflow")
    else :
        popNode=q.dequeue()
        print("Item dequeued = ",popNode.data," with
                            Priority ", popNode.priority)
elif choice==3 :
    if q.isEmpty() :
        print("Queue Underflow")
    else :
        popNode=q.peek()
        print("Item at the front of the Queue =
    ",popNode.data," with Priority ",popNode.priority)
elif choice==4 :
    if q.isEmpty() :
        print("Queue is Empty")
    else :
        q.display()
elif choice==5 :
    print("\nQuiting.......")
    break
else:
    print("Invalid choice. Please Enter Correct
                                    Choice")
    continue
```

- **Using multiple queues:** We can implement priority queues using multiple queues also. For each priority value, a separate queue can be maintained, and all these individual queues together form the general priority queue. This implementation can also be done using an array, list, or linked list. For array/list representation a 2D array/list is a better choice where each row will be treated as a different queue of different priority. We need not store the priority values with the data part. The zeroth row maintains the queue having priority value 0, the first row maintains the queue having priority value 1, the second row maintains the queue having priority value 2, and so on. For linked list representation, each queue of different priorities is implemented by different linked lists, and a linked list will contain the priority and address of the fist node of each list.

- **Using heap:** It will be discussed in Chapter 11.

9.6 Applications of a Queue

A queue is a very important data structure and is used in various applications of computer science. We find its use in implementation of various aspects of the operating system as well. Some of the applications of queue are as follows:

- Linear queue is used in FCFS and Round Robin scheduling of CPU scheduling.
- Priority queue is used in priority scheduling of CPU scheduling.
- Queue is used in implementation of multilevel queue scheduling.
- Used in implementation of multilevel feedback queue scheduling.
- Used for serving request on single shared resources like printer, disk, etc.
- Used as buffers to maintain playlist for music system.
- Used to implement level order traversal of a tree data structure.
- Used to implement BFS algorithm to traverse a graph data structure.
- Used on call center phone systems to hold calls of customer in an order until any service representative is free.
- Simulation of some real-world queue like traffic control system, etc.
- And many more…

Queue at a Glance

✓ A queue is a linear data structure in which insertion and deletion operations take place at two different ends.

✓ The insertion operation is commonly known as ENQUEUE and the deletion operation is known as DEQUEUE.

✓ A queue is a FIFO (First In First Out) data structure.

✓ In memory, a queue can be represented using an array as well as a linked list.

✓ A circular queue is the same as a linear queue with the only difference being that it is considered to be bent so that the position next to the last position of the queue becomes the first position. By this consideration the enqueue operation never requires shifting.

✓ DEque or Double Ended Queue is a special type of a queue where elements can be inserted or deleted from either end. But insertion or deletion is not allowed in the middle or any intermediate position.

✓ In case of array representation, instead of using two or more separate queues, use of multiple queues is more memory efficient.

✓ Queues are used in various programming situations like CPU scheduling, maintaining buffer list, traversing tree, graph, implementing several real-world scenarios, etc.

Multiple Choice Questions

1. In which data structure can insertion take place at one end (rear) and deletion done from other end (front)?

    a) Linked list

    b) Stack

    c) Queue

    d) Tree

2. Which data structure is required for Breadth First Traversal on a graph?

    a) Array

    b) Stack

    c) Queue

    d) Tree

3. Suppose the four elements 20, 10, 40 and 30 are inserted one by one in a linear queue. Now if all the elements are dequeued from the queue, what will be the order?

   a) 20, 10, 40, 30

   b) 10, 20, 30, 40

   c) 40, 30, 20, 10

   d) 30, 40, 10, 20

4. In which of the following data structures can elements be inserted at both ends, deletion done from both ends, but neither insertion nor deletion done in the middle?

   a) Priority Queue

   b) Circular Queue

   c) Deque

   d) Linear Queue

5. Suppose a linear queue is implemented using a traditional array and the size of the array is SIZE. Which of the following conditions becomes True when the queue becomes full?

   a) Rear == SIZE-1

   b) Rear == (Front+1) mod SIZE

   c) Front == SIZE-1

   d) Front == (Rear+1) mod SIZE

6. If a circular queue is implemented using an array of size SIZE, it may get full when

   a) Rear = Front + 1

   b) Front = (Rear + 1) mod SIZE

   c) Front = Rear + 1

   d) Rear = Front

7. Which of the following is true when a queue contains only a single element?

   a) Rear = Front + 1

   b) Front = (Rear + 1) mod SIZE

   c) Front = Rear + 1

   d) Rear = Front

8. Queues can be used to implement

   a) Recursion

   b) Depth first search

   c) Quick sort

   d) Radix sort

9. Queues use the following strategy:

   a) First In First Out

   b) First In Last Out

c) Last In First Out

d) None of these.

10. The initial configuration of a queue is 10, 20, 30, 40 (10 is at the front end). To get the configuration 40, 30, 20, 10 one needs a minimum of

a) 2 deletions and 3 additions

b) 3 deletion and 2 additions

c) . 3 deletion and 3 additions

d) 3 deletion and 4 additions

11. Circular queue uses which of the following strategies?

a) FIFO

b) LIFO

c) Both (a) and (b)

d) None of these

12. If the elements 'A','B','C', and 'D' are inserted in a priority queue with the priority 5, 3, 5, 6 respectively and then removed one by one, in which order will the elements be removed? Consider higher value indicates higher priority.

a) ABCD

b) ACBD

c) DACB

d) DCAB

Review Exercises

1. What is a queue? How does it differ from a stack?

2. Why is a queue called a FIFO data structure?

3. What are the operations associated with a queue? Explain with example.

4. What is a circular queue? What is its advantage over a linear queue?

5. Compare and contrast between traditional array representation, list representation, and linked list representation of queues.

6. How can you implement a queue using only stack?

7. Is it possible to implement a stack using only a queue? Explain.

8. What is a priority queue? What is its use?

9. Write a short note on Double Ended queue.

10. Is it possible to implement a stack of queues? Explain how.

11. Implement a queue of stacks and queue of queues.

12. What is a multiple queue? What are the different ways by which a multiple queue can be implemented programmatically in Python?

13. Show the position of a queue of size 5 when implemented using an array for the following operations. Assume initially the queue is empty.
    a. Enqueue 23 and 75
    b. Dequeue twice
    c. Enqueue 58, 75, 46
    d. Dequeue
    e. Enqueue 83, 55 and 9

14. Show the position of a circular queue of size 5 for the following operations. Assume initially the queue is empty.
    a. Enqueue 23 and 75
    b. Dequeue twice
    c. Enqueue 58, 75, 46
    d. Dequeue
    e. Enqueue 83, 55 and 9
    f. Dequeue twice
    g. Enqueue 10
    h. Deque

15. Show the position of a priority queue of size 5 for the following operations. Assume initially the queue is empty and higher value is higher priority.
    a. Enqueue 23 and 75 with priority 5
    b. Dequeue
    c. Enqueue 58 with priority 7, 75 with priority 3, 46 with priority 5
    d. Dequeue

Problems for Programming

1. Write a menu-driven program to implement array representation of a queue.
2. Write a menu-driven program to implement a circular queue.
3. Write a menu-driven program to implement a queue using the list data structure of Python.
4. Write a menu-driven program to implement a queue using a linked list.
5. Write a menu-driven program to implement a priority queue using a 2D list.
6. Write a menu-driven program to implement a queue using only stack.
7. Write a menu-driven program to implement a stack using only queue.
8. Write a menu-driven program to implement a queue of queues.

9. Write a menu-driven program to implement a priority queue which will contain Job no, Duration, and Priority of each Job.

10. Write a menu-driven program to implement a multiple queue of different priorities.

Trees

So far we have discussed different linear data structures like arrays, linked lists, stacks, queues, etc. These are called linear data structures because elements are arranged in linear fashion, i.e. one after another. Apart from these there are also some non-linear data structures. Trees and graphs are the most common non-linear data structures. In this chapter we will discuss the tree data structure. A tree structure is mainly used to store data items that have a hierarchical relationship among them. In this chapter we will discuss the different types of trees, their representation in memory, and recursive and non-recursive implementation.

10.1 Definition and Concept

A tree is a non-linear data structure that is used to represent hierarchical relationship among data items. Basically a tree is an acyclic and connected graph. It consists of some **nodes** and these nodes are connected by **edges**. The topmost node or starting node is known as **root**. Zero or more nodes can be connected with this root node through edges. The structure of a tree is recursive by its nature. Each node connected with the root node may be further considered as a root node with which some other nodes can be connected to form a sub-tree. Thus, a **tree**, T, can be defined as a finite non-empty set of elements among whose one is root and others are partitioned into trees known as sub-trees of T. Figure 10.1 shows a sample tree structure.

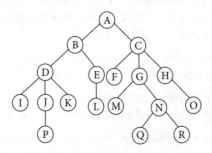

Figure 10.1 Tree

10.2 Terminology

In this section we will know about the basic terminologies of trees considering Figure 10.1.

Node: It is the main component of a tree. It contains the data elements and the links to other nodes. In the above tree, A, B, C, D, etc. are the nodes.

Root Node: The topmost node or starting node is known as the **root** node. Here A is the root node.

Edge: It is the connecter of two nodes. In Figure 10.1, the line between any two nodes can be considered as an edge. As every two nodes are connected by a single edge only, there should be exactly n-1 edges in a tree having n nodes.

Parent Node: The immediate predecessor node of a node is called its parent node. It is also known as its ancestor node. Here A is the parent node of B and C. Again B is the parent node of D and E.

Child Node: The immediate successor node of a node is called its child node. It is also known as its descendant. Here B and C are the child nodes of A; I, J, and K are the child nodes of D.

Siblings: All the child nodes of a particular parent node are called siblings. Thus B and C are siblings; F, G, and H are siblings; etc.

Leaf Node: A node that does not have any child node is known as a leaf node, or terminal node, or external node. I, P, K, L, F, M, etc. are the leaf nodes.

Internal Node: A node that has any child node is known as an internal node or non-terminal node. All the nodes except the leaf nodes in a tree are internal nodes. B, D, E, J, etc. are internal nodes.

Degree: The number of child nodes of a node is called the degree of that node. Thus the degree of any leaf node is always 0. In the tree in Figure 10.1, the degree of A is 2, degree of D is 3, degree of E is 1, etc. The highest degree among all nodes in a tree is the degree of that tree. Thus the degree of the above tree is 3. In other words, the degree or the order of a tree implies the maximum number of possible child nodes of a particular node. If the degree or order of a tree is **n**, the nodes of this tree have a maximum of **n** number of children.

Level: Positions of nodes in the hierarchy are considered as levels. In tree structure it is considered that the root node is at level 0; the immediate children of the root node are at level 1; their immediate children are at level 2, and so on.

Path: The sequence of consecutive edges between two given nodes is known as the path. The path between A to M can be shown as A → C → G → M.

Depth: The length of a path starting from the root to a particular node is called the depth of that node. Here the depth of P is 4 whereas the depth of E is 2.

Height: The height of a tree is the number of nodes on the path starting from the root to the deepest node. In other words, total number of levels in a tree is the height of that tree. The height of the above tree is 5.

10.3 Types of Trees

There are several types of trees. Here we will discuss some of them:

- General Tree
- Forest
- Binary Tree
- Strictly Binary Tree
- Complete Binary Tree
- Full Binary Tree
- Extended Binary Tree
- Binary Search Tree
- Expression Tree

10.3.1 General Tree

By the term **tree** we actually mean general tree. Thus it starts with the root node and this root node may have zero or any number of sub-trees. Except the root node, every node must have a parent node, and except the leaf node, every node possesses one or more child nodes. As there is no specific order or degree of this tree it is treated as a general tree and represented as an Abstract Data Type (ADT).

10.3.2 Forest

A forest is a collection of trees. It can be defined as a union of several disjoint trees. As a tree is an acyclic graph, it is better represented by graphs (discussed in a later chapter). It is a graph containing multiple sub-graphs that are not connected to each other. Thus the omission of some edges turns a graph or tree into a forest. Similarly, if we connect the trees of a forest with each other or with a particular node, the forest becomes a tree. Figure 10.2 (a) shows a tree and Figure 10.2 (b) shows its corresponding forest.

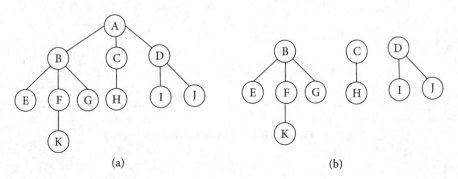

(a)   (b)

Figure 10.2   Tree and its corresponding forest

10.3.3 Binary Tree

A binary tree is a tree of degree 2, i.e. each node of this tree can have a maximum of two children. It is either empty or consists of a root node and zero or one or two binary trees as children of the root. These are known as left sub-tree and right sub-tree. The starting node of each sub-tree is considered as their root node and can have further left sub-tree and right sub-tree, if any. Figure 10.3 shows a binary tree.

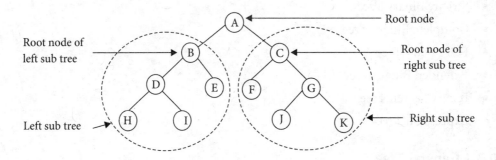

Figure 10.3   Binary tree

Here, A is the root node and the nodes B, D, E, H, and I form the left sub-tree and the nodes C, F, G, J, and K form the right sub-tree. Again B is the root node of this left sub-tree whose left sub-tree consists of D, H, and I nodes and the right sub-tree consists of a single node, E, and so on. If any node does not have left sub-tree and/or right sub-tree, it means it consists of empty sub-trees.

10.3.4 Strictly Binary Tree

If each node of a binary tree has exactly zero (in case of leaf node) or two non-empty children, the binary tree is known as a strictly binary tree or 2-tree. Figure 10.4 shows a strictly binary tree.

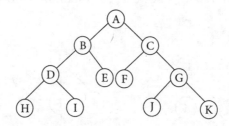

Figure 10.4   Strictly binary tree

10.3.5 Complete Binary Tree

A complete binary tree is a binary tree whose all levels, except possibly the last level, have the maximum number of nodes and at the last level all the nodes appear as far left as possible. Figure 10.5 shows some complete binary trees.

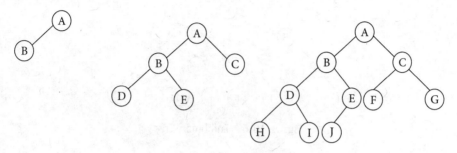

Figure 10.5 Complete binary trees

10.3.6 Full Binary Tree

A binary tree whose all levels have the maximum number of nodes is called a full binary tree. Thus except the leaf nodes all nodes have exactly two child nodes. In a full binary tree, the total number of nodes at the first level is 1, i.e. 2^0, at the second level it is 2, i.e. 2^1, at the third level it is 4, i.e. 2^2, and so on. Thus at the dth level the total number of nodes will be 2^{d-1} and the total number of nodes in a full binary tree of height h can be calculated as:

$$\mathbf{n} = 2^0 + 2^1 + 2^2 + 2^3 + \ldots\ldots + 2^h = \sum 2^{h-1} = \mathbf{2^h - 1}$$

From this equation we can also find the height of a full binary tree.

$$n = 2^h - 1$$

or, $$2^h = n + 1$$

or, $$\log_2 2^h = \log_2 (n + 1)$$

or, $$h \log_2 2 = \log_2 (n + 1)$$

or, $$h = \log_2 (n + 1)$$

Thus, the height of a full binary tree having n nodes is: $\mathbf{h = \log_2 (n + 1)}$

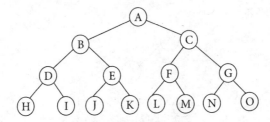

Total number of nodes in a full binary tree of height h is $n = 2^h - 1$

The height of a full binary tree having n nodes is $h = \log_2 (n + 1)$

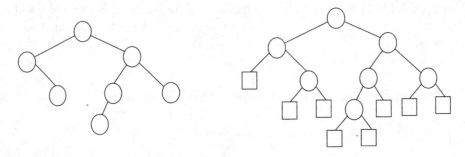

Figure 10.6 Full binary tree

10.3.7 Extended Binary Tree

It is a transformation of a binary tree. When every null sub-tree in a binary tree is replaced by some special nodes, it is known as an extended binary tree. The newly added special nodes are known as external nodes, whereas the nodes of the original tree are known as internal nodes. Generally, external nodes are represented with squares and internal nodes are represented with circles as shown in Figure 10.7.

Figure 10.7 A binary tree and its corresponding extended binary tree

10.3.8 Binary Search Tree (BST)

A binary search tree is an ordered binary tree. It is either empty or must maintain the order in between the root node and its child nodes. The key values in the left sub-tree always possess less value than its root node and the key values in the right sub-tree always possess larger value than its root node. The left and right sub-trees also maintain the same rules and form a binary search tree. Figure 10.8 shows a binary search tree.

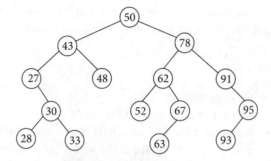

Figure 10.8 Binary search tree

10.3.9 Expression Tree

An expression tree is used to represent algebraic expressions. Basically it is a binary tree whose internal nodes are used to store any operator and its leaf nodes store the operands. These operands are either constants or variables. To construct an expression tree from any expression, we have to follow the precedence and associativity rules of the operators. Suppose we have an expression A + (B − C) * D. In this expression, (B − C) will be evaluated first. So, first we have to draw the expression sub-tree for B − C as:

Next, * will be evaluated. So, in the next step * will be the root, the above sub-tree will be the left sub-tree, and D will be the right sub-tree.

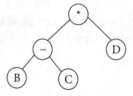

Finally, + will be evaluated and we will get the following tree:

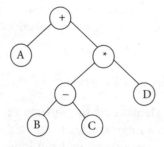

Figure 10.9 Expression tree of the expression A + (B − C) * D

Similarly to get back the expression from an expression tree, we have to proceed from the bottom. First, we will get (B – C), then ((B – C) * D), and, finally, A + ((B – C) * D).

10.3.10 Tournament Tree

In a tournament, especially in case of a knock-out tournament, a set of team/player participates to play. In the first round, every two teams play against each other and one becomes the winner. All the winner teams of the first round move to the second round and participate in the second round match. Again, in the second round, every two winner teams of the first round play against each other and the winner teams of this second round move to the next round. This process continues and finally one team becomes the winner of the tournament. This concept can be easily represented by the tournament tree. In this tree, all the leaf nodes represent all the participated team/player of the tournament and internal nodes are the winners of the child node teams/players. Figure 10.10 shows a tournament tree of eight teams.

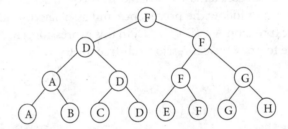

Figure 10.10   Tournament tree of eight teams

In the tournament tree shown in Figure 10.10, the first match was played between A and B, and A was the winner. Similarly between C and D, E and F, and G and H, the respective winners were D, F, and G. In the next round, D and F were the winners and finally F was the winner of the tournament.

10.4 Representation of a Binary Tree

Similar to other data structures, a binary tree can also be represented in memory in two ways. One is using an array and other is using a linked list. Here we will discuss both of them.

10.4.1 Array Representation of a Binary Tree

In array representation, each element of the binary tree would be stored in an array maintaining a specific rule. We can start storing from the zeroth index position or from the index position 1. For simplicity we are starting from index position 1. So, the root will be stored at the index position 1, and the position of immediate left and right children of the root will be calculated as:

Position of left child = 2 * Position of root

Position of right child = 2 * Position of root + 1

These rules are applicable for sub-trees also. Consider the following example:

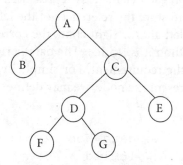

Figure 10.11   Binary tree

As the height of the above binary tree is four, the required size of the array is $(2^4 - 1) + 1$ (as we decided to skip the zeroth index position), i.e. 16. Now, the root element A will be stored at index position 1. The immediate left child, B, will be stored at position 2*1, i.e. at index position 2, and the immediate right child, C, will be stored at position 2*1+1, i.e. at index position 3 of the array. The node B does not have any child. So, we proceed to the next node, C, which has two children, D and E. The index position of D will be 3*2, i.e. 6, and that of E will be 3*2+1=7. Similarly, the positions of F and G will be 12 and 13 respectively and we will get the following array:

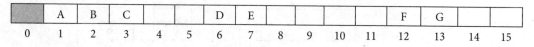

	A	B	C			D	E					F	G		
0	1	2	3	4	5	6	7	8	9	10	11	12	13	14	15

Figure 10.12   Array representation of binary tree of Figure 10.11

From Figure 10.12, we can find that there are several vacant places in the array and thus producing wastage of memory. This representation is effective in case of a full tree or at least a complete tree. Otherwise there will be wastage. Especially in case of a skew tree the wastage is huge. The solution to this problem is linked list representation.

10.4.2 Linked list Representation of a Binary Tree

Similar to other data structure, in case of a tree also linked list representation is much more efficient in comparison to array representation. Here we need not allocate memory for the nodes that are not currently present. As and when a new node is needed to be inserted, we can allocate memory dynamically for the node and insert it into the tree. This is true for deletion also. And this insertion and deletion operations are much more efficient than array representation, because here we need not shift items; only a few pointer operations are required. The only disadvantage is that to store the reference of left and right children, extra space is required for each node. But this would be negligible if the number of data items is large.

In linked list representation each element is represented by a node that has one data part and two reference parts to store the references of the left child and the right child. If any node does not have any left and/or right child, the corresponding reference part will contain NULL (in case of python it is None). The data part may contain any number of data members according to the requirement. For simplicity, we are considering a single data member here. So, to represent the node, we may define the class as:

```python
class TreeNode :
    def __init__(self,Newdata=None,lchild=None,rchild=None):
        self.left  = lchild
        self.data  = Newdata
        self.right = rchild
```

Now we can diagrammatically represent the linked list representation of the binary tree of Figure 10.11 as:

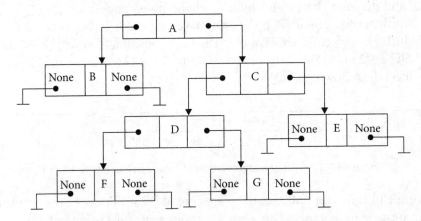

Figure 10.13   Linked list representation of the binary tree of Figure 10.11

10.5 Binary Tree Traversal

Once a binary tree is created, we need to traverse the tree to access the elements in the tree. It is the way by which each node of the tree is visited exactly once in a systematic manner.

Based on the way nodes of a tree are traversed, the traversal technique can be classified mainly into three categories. These are as follows:

1. **Preorder traversal (VLR):** In this traversal technique the root is visited before its child. The order is:

    i.   Visit the Root

    ii. Visit the left sub-tree in preorder fashion

    iii. Visit the right sub-tree in preorder fashion

2. **Inorder traversal (LVR):** In this traversal technique the left sub-tree is visited first, then the root, and then the right sub-tree. The order is:

    i.   Visit the left sub-tree in inorder fashion

    ii. Visit the root

    iii. Visit the right sub-tree in inorder fashion

3. **Postorder traversal (LRV):** In this traversal technique the root is visited after traversing both its children. The order is:

    i.   Visit the left sub-tree in postorder fashion

    ii. Visit the right sub-tree in postorder fashion

    iii. Visit the root

The preorder, inorder, and postorder traversal paths of the binary tree of Figure 10.11 are as follows:

Preorder: A B C D F G E

Inorder: B A F D G C E

Postorder: B F G D E C A

Apart from these three traversal techniques, there is another traversal technique, named **level order traversal**. In this technique, nodes are visited level by level starting from the root, and in each level from left to right. So, the level order traversal path of the binary tree of Figure 10.11 is A B C D E F G.

10.5.1 Preorder Traversal of a Binary Tree

As the definition of preorder traversal is inherently recursive in nature, the programmatic implementation of this traversal using recursive function is very easy. We may define the function as the following:

```
#Recursive function to implement preorder traversal of
#binary tree
def preorder_rec(curNode):
```

```
if curNode is not None:
    print(curNode.data,end=" ")
    preorder_rec(curNode.left)
    preorder_rec(curNode.right)
```

Though it is very easy to write the code, we may also write the above function in an iterative way. For iterative implementation, a stack is required. Here is a general algorithm to implement a non-recursive or iterative approach of preorder traversal technique of a binary tree:

1. Create a stack.

2. Push None to the stack.

3. Set curNode = Root

4. While curNode is not None, do

   a. Print data part of curNode

   b. If curNode have a right child, then

      i. Push the right child reference of curNode into stack.

   c. If curNode have a left child, then

      i. Set left child of curNode as curNode

   d. Otherwise,

      i. Pop from stack and set the reference as curNode

Based on the above algorithm, the following non-recursive function may be written:

```
#Non-Recursive function to implement preorder traversal of
#binary tree
```

```
def preorder(self):
    st=Stack()
    st.push(None)
    curNode=self.Root
    while curNode is not None:
        print(curNode.data, end=" ")
        if curNode.right:
            st.push(curNode.right)
        if curNode.left:
            curNode=curNode.left
        else:
            curNode=st.pop()
```

10.5.2 Inorder Traversal of a Binary Tree

Similarly, we may implement the inorder traversal technique of a binary search tree easily. The recursive function to implement inorder traversal may be defined as:

```
#Recursive function to implement inorder traversal of
#binary tree

def inorder_rec(curNode):
    if curNode is not None:
        inorder_rec(curNode.left)
        print(curNode.data,end=" ")
        inorder_rec(curNode.right)
```

For iterative implementation of inorder traversal, a stack is also required. The general algorithm to implement a non-recursive or iterative approach to inorder traversal technique of a binary tree may be defined as:

1. Create a stack.

2. Push None to the stack.

3. Set curNode = Root

4. While curNode is not None, do

   a. While curNode is not None, do

      i. Push curNode into stack.

      ii. Set left child of curNode as curNode

   b. Pop from stack and set to curNode

   c. Set flag as True

   d. While curNode is not None and flag is True, do

      i. Print data part of curNode

      ii. If curNode have a right child, then

         1. Set right child of curNode as curNode

         2. Set flag as False

      iii. Otherwise,

         1. Pop from stack and set to curNode

Here is a non-recursive function to implement inorder traversal of a binary tree:

```
#Non-Recursive function to implement inorder traversal of
#binary tree .
```

```
def inorder(self):
    st=Stack()
    st.push(None)
    curNode=self.Root
    while curNode is not None:
        while curNode is not None:
            st.push(curNode)
            curNode=curNode.left
        curNode=st.pop()
        flag = True
        while curNode and flag is True:
            print(curNode.data, end=" ")
            if curNode.right:
                curNode=curNode.right
                flag=False
            else:
                curNode=st.pop()
```

10.5.3 Postorder Traversal of a Binary Tree

Like preorder and inorder traversal, by definition the postorder traversal is also inherently recursive in nature. Thus, the programmatic implementation of this traversal using recursive function is very easy and also almost similar to the previous two algorithms. We may define the function as the following:

```
#Recursive function to implement postorder traversal of
#binary tree
```

```
def postorder_rec(curNode):
    if curNode is not None:
        postorder_rec(curNode.left)
        postorder_rec(curNode.right)
        print(curNode.data,end=" ")
```

Iterative implementation of a postorder traversal is little bit tougher than iterative preorder and inorder traversal, as the root has been popped twice – first after visiting the left sub-tree and the second time after visiting the right sub-tree. The general algorithm to implement a non-recursive or iterative approach to postorder traversal technique of a binary tree may be defined as:

1. Create a stack.

2. Set curNode = Root

3. While `True`, do

   a. While `curNode` is not `None`, do

      i.   If `curNode` has a right child, then

         1.   Push the right child of `curNode` into stack

      ii.   Push `curNode` into stack

      iii.   Set left child of `curNode` as `curNode`

   b.   Pop from stack and set to `curNode`

   c.   If `curNode` has a right child and top of stack is also the reference of right child of `curNode`, then

      i.   Pop from stack

      ii.   Push `curNode` into stack

      iii.   Set right child of `curNode` as `curNode`

   d.   Otherwise,

      i.   Print data part of `curNode`

      ii.   Set `None` to `curNode`

   e.   If stack is empty, then

      i.   Exit from the loop

The non-recursive function to implement postorder traversal of a binary tree may be defined as follows:

```python
#Non-recursive function to implement postorder traversal
#of binary tree
    def postorder(self):
        st=Stack()
        curNode=self.Root
        if curNode is None:
            return
        while True:
            while curNode is not None:
                if curNode.right:
                    st.push(curNode.right)
                st.push(curNode)
                curNode=curNode.left
            curNode=st.pop()
            if curNode.right and st.peek()==curNode.
                                                right:
                st.pop()
```

```
            st.push(curNode)
            curNode=curNode.right
        else:
            print(curNode.data, end=" ")
            curNode=None
    if st.isEmpty():
        break
```

10.5.4 Level Order Traversal of a Binary Tree

In level order traversal, all the nodes at a particular level are traversed before going to the next level. To implement level order traversal, instead of stack we need a queue. The following algorithm shows how a binary tree can be traversed level wise.

1. Create a queue.

2. Enqueue root node into the queue

3. While the queue is not empty, do

    a. Dequeue from queue and set to curNode

    b. If curNode has a left child, then

        i. Enqueue the left child of curNode into queue

    c. If curNode has a right child, then

        i. Enqueue the right child of curNode into queue

    d. Print data part of curNode

The non-recursive function to implement level order traversal of a binary tree may be defined as follows:

```
def levelorder(rootNode):
    q=Queue()
    q.enqueue(rootNode)
    while not q.isEmpty():
        curNode= q.dequeue()
        if curNode.left is not None:
            q.enqueue(curNode.left)
        if curNode.right is not None:
            q.enqueue(curNode.right)
        print(curNode.data, end=" ")
```

10.6 Construction of a Binary Tree from the Traversal Path

If we have the traversal path, we can reconstruct the binary tree. But a single path is not sufficient to draw the tree. We need the inorder path and either the preorder or the postorder path. Purpose of both the preorder and the postorder paths is same. They identify the root. For the preorder path, the left-most element is the root, whereas in the postorder path, the right-most element is the root. Once the root is identified either from the preorder or the postorder path, the inorder path shows the elements of the left sub-tree and the right sub-tree. Elements in the left side of the root in the inorder path will be in the left sub-tree and the elements in the right side of the root in the inorder path will be in the right sub-tree. The following example illustrates this:

Example 10.1: Consider the following sequence of binary tree traversals:

> **Preorder :** A B C D F G E
>
> **Inorder :** B A F D G C E

Construct the binary tree.

Solution: Preorder : Ⓐ B C D F G E

The left-most element of the preorder path is the root. So, A is the root here. Now marking A as the root in the inorder path, we can easily identify that the left sub-tree consists of only a single node, B, and the right sub-tree consists of F, D, G, C, and E.

> Inorder : B Ⓐ F D G C E

Now, partially we can construct the tree as:

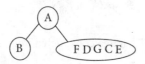

Figure 10.14 Partially constructed tree

In the left sub-tree, there is a single element, B. So, we have nothing to do. Now we concentrate on the right sub-tree. To construct the right sub-tree we have to follow the same technique.

> Preorder : Ⓒ D F G E

> Inorder : F D G Ⓒ E

From preorder we are getting C as the root, and identifying C in the inorder path we get F, D, and G in the left sub-tree and E in right sub-tree. So, the tree becomes:

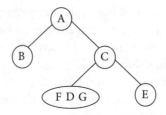

Figure 10.15   Partially constructed tree

Finally, considering the remaining portion:

Preorder : $\boxed{D}$ F G

Inorder : F $\boxed{D}$ G

Now, it is clear that D is the root and F will be in the left sub-tree and G will be in the right sub-tree and the final tree will be:

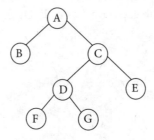

Figure 10.16   Final tree constructed from the traversal path

Here we consider the preorder and the inorder paths. It is also possible to reconstruct a binary tree from its postorder and inorder paths. The algorithm is the same; the only difference is that the root will be the right-most element in the postorder path.

10.7 Conversion of a General Tree to a Binary Tree

It is possible to create a binary tree from a general tree. For this conversion we need to follow three simple rules:

1. Set the root of the general tree as the root of the binary tree.
2. Set the left-most child of any node in the general tree as the left child of that node in the binary tree.
3. Set the right sibling of any node in the general tree as the right child of that node in the binary tree.

Example 10.2: Construct a binary tree from the following general tree.

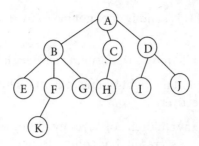

Solution :

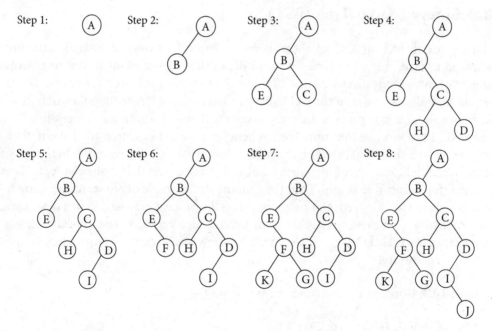

Figure 10.17   Steps to construct a binary tree from a general tree

Explanation: To convert the given general tree to a binary tree, we have to apply the above-mentioned three rules one by one.

1. As the root of the general tree is A, first we have to set A as the root of the binary tree.

2. The left-most child of A is B. Set B as the left child of A. As there is no siblings of A, there is no right child of A.

3. The left-most child of B is E and the right sibling of B is C. Thus the left and right children of B are E and C respectively.

4. Similarly, as the left child of C is H and the right sibling of C is D, the left and right children of C are H and D respectively.

5. The left-most child of D is I and D does not have any right siblings. Thus D has only left child, I.

6. E does not have any child but its right sibling is F. So, E has only right child F.

7. K is the left child of F and the right sibling of F is G. Thus the left and right children of F are K and G respectively.

8. G and H neither have any children nor have any siblings. I does not have any children but its right sibling is J. As a result, I has only a right child, J. Node J also neither has any children nor any siblings. So, we get the final tree.

10.8 Binary Search Tree (BST)

A binary search tree, or BST in short, is a very important non-linear data structure in computer science. It is an ordered tree and thus searching an element in a BST is much faster. We have already discussed that all the nodes in the left sub-tree have values less than the root and all the nodes in the right sub-tree have values larger than the root. The left and right sub-trees also possess the same property. Thus to search an element in a binary tree we need not traverse the entire tree. Whenever we want to search an element, first we compare with the root and based on the comparison we need to move either in the left sub-tree or in the right sub-tree. Thus we are able to bypass almost half of the elements. This is again true for its sub-tree as well. Thus the running time complexity to search an element in a BST is reduced to $O(\log_2 n)$. Not only searching, the process of insertion of a new element and/or deletion of an existing element from a BST is also very fast. The time complexity of these operations is also $O(\log_2 n)$. Now we learn how a BST can be constructed. Consider the following example:

Example 10.3: Construct a binary search tree from the following data:

'14 15 4 9 7 18 3 5 16 20 17

Solution:

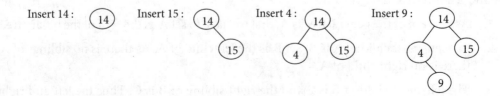

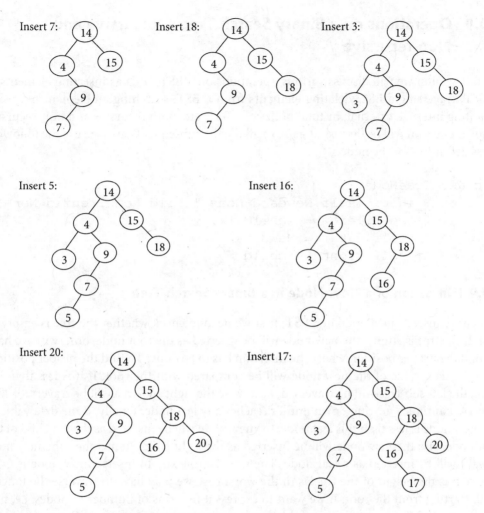

Figure 10.18 Steps to construct a binary search tree

Explanation: The first element is 14. So, it would be the root. The next element is 15. As it is larger than the root it is inserted as the right child. Next comes 4; it is smaller than the root and is inserted as the left child of 14. The next element is 9. Comparison always starts from the root. So, first it would be compared with 14. As it is less than the root we move towards the left sub-tree and find 4. Now 9 is greater than 4, thus 9 will be inserted as the right child of 4. The next element is 7. Again first it would be compared with 14. As it is less than 14, we move to the left sub-tree and find 4. Now 7 is greater than 4; we move to the right sub-tree of 4 and find 9. As 7 is less than 9, it is inserted as the left child of 9. The next element is 18. It is larger than 14 and also larger than 15. Thus, it is inserted as the right child of 15. The next element is 3. It is smaller than 14 as well as 4. So, it is inserted as the left child of 4. In this way the rest of the elements are processed and we get the final tree.

10.9 Operations on a Binary Search Tree – Recursive and Non-recursive

In this section we will discuss various operations on a BST, such as inserting elements in a BST, traversing a BST, deleting elements from a BST, searching an element in a BST, counting internal, external, or total nodes of a BST, etc. Both recursive and non-recursive implementation will be discussed here. In all the the subsequent cases we use the following class definition for the node:

```
class TreeNode :
  def __init__(self,Newdata=None,lchild=None,rchild=None):
        self.left  = lchild
        self.data  = Newdata
        self.right = rchild
```

10.9.1 Insertion of a New Node in a Binary Search Tree

When we insert a new node in a BST, first we need to check whether the tree is empty or not. If the tree is empty, the new node will be inserted as the root node, otherwise we have to find the proper position where the insertion has to be done. To find the proper position, first the data value of the new node will be compared with the root. If it is less than the root, the left sub-tree will be traversed, otherwise the right sub-tree will be traversed. This process continues moving down until it reaches any leaf node. Finally, if the data value of the new node is less than this leaf node, the new node will be inserted as the left child of the leaf node, else the new node will be inserted as the right child. Remember, the new node always will be inserted as a leaf node. The time complexity to insert a new node is O(h) where h is the height of the tree as in the worst case we may have to traverse the longest path starting from the root. If we want to express it in terms of number of nodes, i.e. n, it would be O(n) in the worst case (if the tree is a skew tree) but on average $O(\log_2 n)$.

The general algorithm to insert a new node in a BST may be defined as follows:

1. Create a new node.

2. Update its data part with the function argument.

3. Update both the reference parts of the left child and the right child with None.

4. If the Root is None, then

    a. Update the Root with new node

5. Else

    a. Set current node = Root

    b. Set parent node = None

    c. While current node is not None, do

    i.   Parent node = current node

    ii. If the data value of new node is less than data value of current node, then

        Set left child of current node as current node

    iii. Otherwise,

        Set right child of current node as current node

  d. If the data value of new node is less than data value of parent node, then

     Set the new node as left child of parent node

  e. Otherwise,

     Set the new node as right child of current node

Using the above algorithm we can write the following code:

```python
# Function to insert a new node in a Binary Search Tree
    def insert(self,newData):
        newNode=TreeNode(newData)
        if self.Root is None:
            self.Root=newNode
        else:
            curNode = self.Root
            parentNode = None
            while curNode is not None :
                parentNode=curNode
                if newData<curNode.data:
                    curNode = curNode.left
                else:
                    curNode = curNode.right
            if newData<parentNode.data:
                parentNode.left=newNode
            else:
                parentNode.right=newNode
```

As the operation on a BST is recursive in nature, the above function may also be implemented using a recursive function as follows:

```python
# Recursive Function to insert a new node in a BST
def insert_rec(curNode,newData):
    if curNode is None:
        return TreeNode(newData)
    elif newData<curNode.data:
        curNode.left=insert_rec(curNode.left, newData)
    else:
```

```
        curNode.right=insert_rec(curNode.right, newData)
    return curNode
```

10.9.2 Searching a Node in a Binary Search Tree

Searching a node means we have to check whether a particular node is present in the BST or not. Before starting the search operation, first we need to check whether the tree is empty or not. If it is empty, there is no scope of finding the element and the process terminates with an appropriate message, otherwise the search process is started. The search process always starts from the root. First the data value of the root node is compared with the key value to be searched. If both values are the same, the process terminates signaling true. Otherwise, if the key value is less than the data value of the root we need to move to the left sub-tree, else the right sub-tree. This process continues until we get the node or reach None. The time complexity of the search operation is also O(n) in the worst case and O(log$_2$ n) in the average case.

The general algorithm to insert a new node in a binary search tree may be defined as follows:

1. Set current node = root

2. While current node is not None, do

    a. If the key value to be searched is equal to the data value of the current node, then
        Return the node

    b. Else, If the key value is less than the data value of current node, then
        Set left child of current node as current node

    c. Else, Set right child of current node as current node

3. Return False

Using the above algorithm we can write the following code:

```
# Function to search an element in a Binary Search Tree
    def search(self, key):
        curNode= self.Root
        while curNode is not None:
            if key == curNode.data :
                return curNode
            elif key < curNode.data :
                curNode = curNode.left
            else:
                curNode = curNode.right
        return curNode
```

The recursive function to implement the search operation may be defined as:

```
# Recursive Function to search an element in a BST
def search_rec(curNode, key):
    if curNode is None or curNode.data==key:
        return curNode
    elif key<curNode.data:
        return search_rec(curNode.left, key)
    else:
        return search_rec(curNode.right, key)
```

10.9.3 Traversing a Binary Search Tree

Traversing a binary search tree is exactly the same as traversing any binary tree. That means we may follow the following traversal techniques:

- Preorder traversal
- Inorder traversal
- Postorder traversal, and
- Level order traversal

All the algorithms and functions that were discussed for the traversal of a binary tree are applicable exactly the same way for a BST.

10.9.4 Deletion of a Node from a Binary Search Tree

To delete a node from any BST we have to take care of two things. First, only the required node will be deleted; no other node will be lost. Second, after deletion the tree that remains possesses the properties of a BST. Thus we need to consider following three cases:

1. **No-child case:** This case is very simple. Delete the node and set None to the left pointer of its parent if it is a left child of its parent, otherwise set None to the right pointer. Consider the following example. Suppose we want to delete the node with value 17.

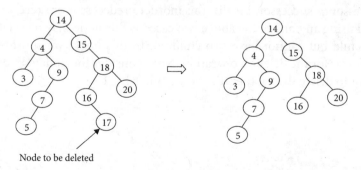

Node to be deleted

Figure 10.19 Deletion of a node with no child

2. **One-child case:** In this case, as the specified node has only one child – either left child or right child – the corresponding left or right reference of parent would be updated by the left or right child (whichever exists) of the node to be deleted. That means if the node that is going to be deleted is the left child of its parent, the left pointer of its parent will be updated by the reference of the child node of the node to be deleted, and if it is the right child of its parent, the right pointer of the parent will be updated by the reference of child node of the node to be deleted. Consider the updated tree and suppose now we want to delete the node with value 9.

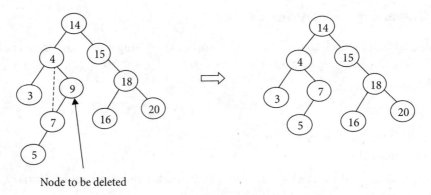

Node to be deleted

Figure 10.20   Deletion of node with one child

The node with value 9 is the right child of the node with value 4 and has only a left sub-tree but no right child, i.e. it is a case of one child. So, after deletion, the left sub-tree of the node with value 9 will be the right sub-tree of the node with value 4.

3. **Two-children case:** This type of case cannot be handled directly. We have to solve it in two steps. First, we have to find the inorder predecessor (i.e. the largest node of the left sub-tree) or the inorder successor (i.e. the smallest node of the right sub-tree) of the node to be deleted. Next, update the node's value with the value of the inorder predecessor or successor. Finally, this inorder predecessor or successor node will be deleted using any one of the above two cases as this node may have either one child or no child but cannot have two children. In this book, we consider the inorder predecessor for the deletion operation. Now, consider the updated tree and suppose we want to delete the root, i.e. the node with value 14.

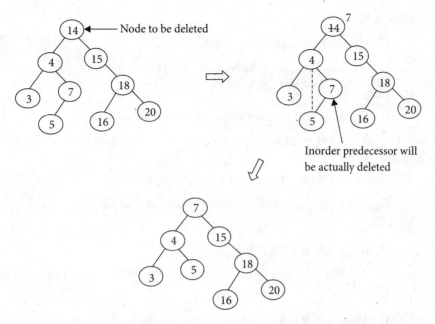

Figure 10.21   Deletion of a node with two children

As the root have both right sub-tree and left sub-tree, first we find the inorder predecessor of the root and it is the node with value 7. Now, 14 will be replaced by 7 and the predecessor node will be deleted physically. From Figure 10.21 we can find that it is a case of one child and thus the right child reference of its parent (i.e. the node with value 4) has been updated with the left child of the predecessor node.

Considering the above two cases now we are able to write the algorithm for the deletion of a node. The general algorithm to delete a node from a BST may be defined as follows:

1. Find the node to be deleted along with its parent

2. If search ends with `None`, terminate the function with appropriate message like "Node not found."

3. Otherwise,

    a. Set `current` node as current

    b. Set `parent` node as parent

4. If both the left child and the right child of `current` is None (i.e. node has no child), then

    a. If `parent` is None, i.e. tree has only `Root` node, then

        i. Update `Root` with None

b. Else,

i. If current is a left child, then

I. Update left child reference of parent with None

ii. Else,

II. Update right child reference of parent with None

5. Else, If either the left child or right child of current is None (i.e. node has only one child), then

a. If parent is None, i.e. Root has only one child, then

i. Update Root with child node reference of current

b. Else,

i. If current is a left child, then

II. Update left child reference of parent with the child of current

ii. Else,

II. Update right child reference of parent with the child of current

6. Else (i.e. node has only two children),

a. Find the largest node in the left sub-tree along with its parent

b. Replace the value of the node to be deleted with the value of this largest node

c. Delete this largest node following steps 4 and 5.

Based on the above algorithm we may write the following code.

```python
# Function to find the node to be deleted along with its
# parent
    def findNodeWithParent(self, key):
        parent = None
        curNode= self.Root
        while curNode is not None:
            if key == curNode.data :
                return (parent, curNode)
            elif key < curNode.data :
                parent = curNode
                curNode = curNode.left
            else:
                parent = curNode
                curNode = curNode.right
        return (parent, curNode)
```

```python
# Function to delete a node from BST non-recursively
    def delete(self, key):
        parent, curNode = self.findNodeWithParent(key)
        if curNode is None:
            print("Node not Found")
        elif curNode.left is None and curNode.right is
                                                    None:
                                            #No child case
            if parent is not None:
                if parent.right is curNode:
                    parent.right = None
                else:
                    parent.left = None
            else:
                self.Root = None
            del(curNode)
        elif curNode.left is None or curNode.right is
                                                    None:
                                            #One child case
            if curNode.left is None:
                childNode = curNode.right
            else:
                childNode = curNode.left
            if parent is not None:
                if parent.left is curNode:
                    parent.left = childNode
                else:
                    parent.right= childNode
            else:
                self.Root = childNode
            del(curNode)
        else:                               #Two children case
            parentLeft = curNode
            largestLeft = curNode.left
            while largestLeft.right is not None:
                    # finding largest node of left subtree
                parentLeft = largestLeft
                largestLeft = largestLeft.right
            curNode.data = largestLeft.data
            if parentLeft.right == largestLeft:
                parentLeft.right = largestLeft.left
            else:
```

```
                parentLeft.left = largestLeft.left
            del(largestLeft)
```

The recursive function to implement the deletion operation may be defined as:

```
# Recursive function to delete a node from BST
def delete_rec(curNode, key):
    if curNode is None:
        print("Node not found...")
    elif key<curNode.data:
        curNode.left=delete_rec(curNode.left, key)
    elif key>curNode.data:
        curNode.right=delete_rec(curNode.right, key)
    else:
        if curNode.left is None:
            return curNode.right
        elif curNode.right is None:
            return curNode.left
        else:
            temp = findLargest_rec(curNode.left)
            curNode.data=temp.data
            curNode.left=delete_rec(curNode.left, temp.
                                                    data)
    return curNode
```

To delete a node first we have to search the node. For that the running time complexity is $O(\log_2 n)$. Next, to delete the node, if the node has 0 or 1 child, time complexity would be $O(1)$ as a constant number of operations is required. So, the time complexity to delete a node for this case is $O(\log_2 n)$. But if it is a case of two children, then again we need to find the largest node. But this total searching time (i.e. first finding the node to delete + finding the largest node in the left sub-tree) cannot be larger than the height of the tree. Thus in all cases, the average time complexity to delete a node from a BST is $O(\log_2 n)$.

10.9.5 Find the Largest Node from a Binary Search Tree

In a BST the value in the right sub-tree is larger than its root. Thus the largest element in a binary search tree would be the right-most element in the tree. So, to find the largest element we need not compare elements but have to move to the right sub-tree always until the right sub-tree of any node is None. Thus the time complexity to find the largest node is also $O(\log_2 n)$.

The general algorithm to find the largest node in a BST may be defined as follows:

1. Set current node = Root

2.   While right child reference of current node is not None, do

    a.   Set right child of current node as current node

3.   Return current node

The non-recursive implementation of the above algorithm is as follows:

```
# Non-recursive function to find the largest node from a BST
    def findLargestNode(self):
            largestNode = self.Root
            while largestNode.right is not None:
                largestNode = largestNode.right
            return largestNode
```

And the recursive implementation is:

```
# Recursive function to find the largest node from a BST
def findLargest_rec(curNode):
    if curNode is None or curNode.right is None:
        return curNode
    else:
        return findLargest_rec(curNode.right)
```

10.9.6 Finding the Smallest Node from a Binary Search Tree

Similarly, as in a BST the value in the left sub-tree is smaller than its root, the smallest element in a BST would be the left-most element in the tree. Thus, to find the smallest element we need to move to the left sub-tree always until the left sub-tree of any node is None. Here also the time complexity would be $O(\log_2 n)$.

The general algorithm to find the smallest node in a BST is as follows:

1.   Set current node = Root

2.   While left child reference of current node is not None, do

    a.   Set left child of current node as current node

3.   Return current node

The non-recursive implementation of the above algorithm is as follows:

```
# Non-recursive function to find the Smallest node from a
BST
    def findSmallestNode(self):
            smallestNode = self.Root
            while smallestNode.left is not None:
                smallestNode = smallestNode.left
```

```
        return smallestNode
```

The recursive function to find the smallest node in a BST may be defined as:

```
# Recursive function to find the Smallest node from a BST
def findSmallest_rec(curNode):
    if curNode is None or curNode.left is None:
        return curNode
    else:
        return findSmallest_rec(curNode.left)
```

10.9.7 Counting the Total Number of Nodes in a Binary Search Tree

If we want to count the total number of nodes in a BST we have to traverse the entire tree using any of the three traversal techniques – preorder, inorder, or postorder traversal – and have to count each node. But in recursive technique, the calculation is very easy. It may be defined as:

Total number = number of nodes in left child + number of nodes in right child + 1(for root)

Thus we may define the recursive function as:

```
# Recursive function to count number of nodes in a BST
def countNode(curNode):
    if curNode is None:
        return 0
    else:
        return countNode(curNode.left)+countNode(curNode.
                                            right)+1
```

10.9.8 Counting the Number of External Nodes in a Binary Search Tree

External nodes are leaf nodes, i.e. the nodes with no children. Thus, we have to count those nodes whose both left and right references are None. We may calculate the number of external nodes as:

Total number of external nodes = number of external nodes in left child + number of external nodes in right child

Thus we may define the recursive function as:

```
# Recursive function to count number of External nodes in
# a BST
```

```
def countExternal(curNode):
    if curNode is None:
        return 0
    elif curNode.left is None and curNode.right is None:
        return 1
    else:
        return countExternal(curNode.left)+
                        countExternal(curNode.right)
```

10.9.9 Counting the Number of Internal Nodes in a Binary Search Tree

Internal nodes are the nodes that have at least one child. Thus, we have to count those nodes whose left child reference or right child reference or both are not None. We may calculate the number of internal nodes as:

Total number of internal nodes = number of internal nodes in left child + number of internal nodes in right child + 1

Thus we may define the recursive function as:

```
# Recursive function to count number of Internal nodes in
# a BST
def countInternal(curNode):
    if curNode is None or
        (curNode.left is None and curNode.right is None):
        return 0
    else:
        return countInternal(curNode.left)+
                        countInternal(curNode.right)+1
```

10.9.10 Finding the Height of a Binary Search Tree

To find the height of a BST, we have to first find the height of the left sub-tree and the right sub-tree and have to consider the greater one. With this greater value, add 1 (for the root) to get the final height of the tree.

The recursive function to find the height of a binary tree may be defined as:

```
# Recursive function to find the height of a BST
def findHeight(curNode):
    if curNode is None:
        return 0
    else:
        heightLeft =findHeight(curNode.left)
```

```
        heightRight=findHeight(curNode.right)
        if heightLeft > heightRight:
            return heightLeft+1
        else:
            return heightRight+1
```

10.9.11 Finding the Mirror Image of a Binary Search Tree

The mirror image of a BST can be obtained by interchanging the left child and right child references of each and every node. The following recursive function shows how the mirror image of a BST can be obtained:

```
# Recursive function to find the Mirror image of a BST
def findMirrorImage(curNode):
    if curNode is not None:
        findMirrorImage(curNode.left)
        findMirrorImage(curNode.right)
        curNode.left, curNode.right = curNode.right,
                                            curNode.left
```

Here is a complete program to show the various operations on a BST:

Program 10.1: Write a program to demonstrate the various operations on a binary search tree.

```
#PRGD10_1: Program to demonstrate Binary Search Tree (Non-
#recursive)

class Stack:                          #Stack class
    def __init__(self):
        self.items = []

    def isEmpty(self):
        return self.items == []

    def push(self, item):
        self.items.append(item)

    def pop(self):
        return self.items.pop()

    def peek(self):
        if self.isEmpty():
```

```
                return -1
            return self.items[len(self.items)-1]

class TreeNode :    # Declaration of Node of a Binary Tree
     def __init__(self,Newdata=None,lchild=None,rchild=No
                                                    ne):
          self.left  = lchild
          self.data  = Newdata
          self.right = rchild

class BST :                      # class to represent BST
     def __init__( self ):
          self.Root = None


     def insert(self,newData):
          newNode=TreeNode(newData)
          if self.Root is None:
               self.Root=newNode
          else:
               curNode = self.Root
               parentNode = None
               while curNode is not None :
                    parentNode=curNode
                    if newData<curNode.data:
                         curNode = curNode.left
                    else:
                         curNode = curNode.right
               if newData<parentNode.data:
                    parentNode.left=newNode
               else:
                    parentNode.right=newNode


def preorder(self):
          st=Stack()
          st.push(None)
          curNode=self.Root
          while curNode is not None:
               print(curNode.data, end=" ")
               if curNode.right:
                    st.push(curNode.right)
               if curNode.left:
                    curNode=curNode.left
```

```python
        else:
            curNode=st.pop()

    def inorder(self):
        st=Stack()
        st.push(None)
        curNode=self.Root
        while curNode is not None:
            while curNode is not None:
                st.push(curNode)
                curNode=curNode.left
            curNode=st.pop()
            flag = True
            while curNode and flag is True:
                print(curNode.data, end=" ")
                if curNode.right:
                    curNode=curNode.right
                    flag=False
                else:
                    curNode=st.pop()


    def postorder(self):
        st=Stack()
        curNode=self.Root
        if curNode is None:
            return
        while True:
            while curNode is not None:
                if curNode.right:
                    st.push(curNode.right)
                st.push(curNode)
                curNode=curNode.left
            curNode=st.pop()
            if curNode.right and st.peek()==curNode.\
                                                right:
                st.pop()
                st.push(curNode)
                curNode=curNode.right
            else:
                print(curNode.data, end=" ")
                curNode=None
            if st.isEmpty():
```

```
            break

    def findNodeWithParent(self, key):
        parent = None
        curNode= self.Root
        while curNode is not None:
            if key == curNode.data :
                return (parent, curNode)
            elif key < curNode.data :
                parent = curNode
                curNode = curNode.left
            else:
                parent = curNode
                curNode = curNode.right
        return (parent, curNode)

    def delete(self, key):
        parent, curNode = self.findNodeWithParent(key)
        if curNode is None:
            print("Node not Found")
        elif curNode.left is None and curNode.right is
                                                    None:
                                            #No child case
            if parent is not None:
                if parent.right is curNode:
                    parent.right = None
                else:
                    parent.left = None
            else:
                self.Root = None
            del(curNode)
        elif curNode.left is None or curNode.right is
                                                    None:
                                            #One child case
            if curNode.left is None:
                childNode = curNode.right
            else:
                childNode = curNode.left
            if parent is not None:
                if parent.left is curNode:
                    parent.left = childNode
                else:
```

```
                    parent.right= childNode
            else:
                self.Root = childNode
            del(curNode)
        else:                              #Two children case
            parentLeft = curNode
            largestLeft = curNode.left
            while largestLeft.right is not None:
                    # finding largest node of left subtree
                parentLeft = largestLeft
                largestLeft = largestLeft.right
            curNode.data = largestLeft.data
            if parentLeft.right == largestLeft:
                parentLeft.right = largestLeft.left
            else:
                parentLeft.left = largestLeft.left
            del(largestLeft)


    def search(self, key):
        curNode= self.Root
        while curNode is not None:
            if key == curNode.data :
                return curNode
            elif key < curNode.data :
                curNode = curNode.left
            else:
                curNode = curNode.right
        return curNode


    def findLargestNode(self):
        largestNode = self.Root
        while largestNode.right is not None:
            largestNode = largestNode.right
        return largestNode


    def findSmallestNode(self):
        smallestNode = self.Root
        while smallestNode.left is not None:
            smallestNode = smallestNode.left
        return smallestNode


bst=BST()
```

```
while True:
    print("\nPROGRAM TO IMPLEMENT BINARY SEARCH TREE")
    print("=====================================")
    print("1.Insert Node")
    print("2.Preorder Traversal")
    print("3.Inorder Traversal")
    print("4.Postorder Traversal")
    print("5.Delete a Node")
    print("6.Search an element")
    print("7.Find Largest Node")
    print("8.Find smallest Node")
    print("9.Exit")
    print("=====================================")
    choice=int(input("Enter your Choice : "))
    if choice==1 :
        num=int(input("Enter the Data: "))
        bst.insert(num)
    elif choice==2 :
        print("Preorder : ", end = ' )
        bst.preorder()
    elif choice==3 :
        print("Inorder : ", end = ' ')
        bst.inorder()
    elif choice==4 :
        print("Postorder : ", end = ' ')
        bst.postorder()
    elif choice==5 :
        num=int(input("Enter The Data You Want To Delete : "))
        bst.delete(num)
    elif choice==6 :
        num=int(input("Enter The Data You Want To Search : "))
        findNode=bst.search(num)
        if findNode is None:
            print("Node not found")
        else:
            print("Node found")
    elif choice==7 :
        if bst is None:
            print("Null Tree")
        else:
            max=bst.findLargestNode()
            print("Largest element: ",max.data)
    elif choice==8 :
```

```
        if bst is None:
            print("Null Tree")
        else:
            min=bst.findSmallestNode()
            print("Smallest element: ",min.data)
    elif choice==9 :
        print("\nQuiting.......")
        break
    else:
        print("Invalid choice. Please Enter Correct
                                    Choice")
        continue
```

The following program shows the implementation of a BST using recursive functions:

Program 10.2: Write a program to demonstrate the various operations on a binary search tree using recursive functions.

```
#PRGD10_2: Program to demonstrate Binary Search Tree using
#recursive functions

class TreeNode :
    def __init__(self,Newdata=None,lchild=None,rchild=No
                                    ne):
        self.left  = lchild
        self.data  = Newdata
        self.right = rchild

def insert_rec(curNode,newData):
    if curNode is None:
        return TreeNode(newData)
    elif newData<curNode.data:
        curNode.left=insert_rec(curNode.left, newData)
    else:
        curNode.right=insert_rec(curNode.right, newData)
    return curNode

def preorder_rec(curNode):
    if curNode is not None:
        print(curNode.data,end=" ")
        preorder_rec(curNode.left)
        preorder_rec(curNode.right)
```

```python
def inorder_rec(curNode):
    if curNode is not None:
        inorder_rec(curNode.left)
        print(curNode.data,end=" ")
        inorder_rec(curNode.right)

def postorder_rec( curNode):
    if curNode is not None:
        postorder_rec(curNode.left)
        postorder_rec(curNode.right)
        print(curNode.data,end=" ")

def delete_rec(curNode, key):
    if curNode is None:
        print("Node not found...")
    elif key<curNode.data:
        curNode.left=delete_rec(curNode.left, key)
    elif key>curNode.data:
        curNode.right=delete_rec(curNode.right, key)
    else:
        if curNode.left is None:
            return curNode.right
        elif curNode.right is None:
            return curNode.left
        else:
            temp = findLargest_rec(curNode.left)
            curNode.data=temp.data
            curNode.left=delete_rec(curNode.left, temp.data)
    return curNode

def search_rec(curNode, key):
    if curNode is None or curNode.data==key:
        return curNode
    elif key<curNode.data:
        return search_rec(curNode.left, key)
    else:
        return search_rec(curNode.right, key)

def findLargest_rec(curNode):
    if curNode is None or curNode.right is None:
        return curNode
    else:
        return findLargest_rec(curNode.right)
```

```python
def findSmallest_rec(curNode):
    if curNode is None or curNode.left is None:
        return curNode
    else:
        return findSmallest_rec(curNode.left)

def countNode(curNode):
    if curNode is None:
        return 0
    else:
        return countNode(curNode.left)+countNode(curNode.
                                                right)+1

def countExternal(curNode):
    if curNode is None:
        return 0
    elif curNode.left is None and curNode.right is None:
        return 1
    else:
        return countExternal(curNode.
                        left)+countExternal(curNode.right)

def countInternal(curNode):
    if curNode is None or (curNode.left is None and curNode.
                                            right is None):
        return 0
    else:
        return countInternal(curNode.
                    left)+countExternal(curNode.right)+1

def findHeight(curNode):
    if curNode is None:
        return 0
    else:
        heightLeft =findHeight(curNode.left)
        heightRight=findHeight(curNode.right)
        if heightLeft > heightRight:
            return heightLeft+1
        else:
            return heightRight+1

def findMirrorImage(curNode):
```

```python
        if curNode is not None:
            findMirrorImage(curNode.left)
            findMirrorImage(curNode.right)
            curNode.left, curNode.right = curNode.right,
                                          curNode.left


root=None
while True:
    print("\nPROGRAM TO IMPLEMENT BINARY SEARCH TREE")
    print("======================================")
    print(" 1.Insert Node")
    print(" 2.Preorder Traversal")
    print(" 3.Inorder Traversal")
    print(" 4.Postorder Traversal")
    print(" 5.Delete a Node")
    print(" 6.Search an element")
    print(" 7.Find Largest Node")
    print(" 8.Find smallest Node")
    print(" 9.Count total number of nodes")
    print("10.Count External nodes")
    print("11.Count Internal nodes")
    print("12.Determine height of the Tree")
    print("13.Find Mirror Image of the Tree")
    print("14.Exit")
    print("======================================")
    choice=int(input("Enter your Choice : "))
    if choice==1 :
        num=int(input("Enter the Data: "))
        root=insert_rec(root,num)
    elif choice==2 :
        print("Preorder : ", end = ' ')
        preorder_rec(root)
    elif choice==3 :
        print("Inorder : ", end = ' ')
        inorder_rec(root)
    elif choice==4 :
        print("Postorder : ", end = ' ')
        postorder_rec(root)
    elif choice==5 :
        num=int(input("Enter The Data You Want To Delete : "))
        root=delete_rec(root, num)
    elif choice==6 :
```

```
        num=int(input("Enter The Data You Want To Search : "))
        findNode=search_rec(root, num)
        if findNode is None:
            print("Node not found")
        else:
            print("Node found")
    elif choice==7 :
        if root is None:
            print("Null Tree")
        else:
            max=findLargest_rec(root)
            print("Largest element: ",max.data)
    elif choice==8 :
        if root is None:
            print("Null Tree")
        else:
            min=findSmallest_rec(root)
            print("Smallest element: ",min.data)
    elif choice==9 :
        c=countNode(root)
        print("Total number of nodes: ", c)
    elif choice==10:
        c=countExternal(root)
        print("Total number of External nodes: ", c)
    elif choice==11:
        c=countInternal(root)
        print("Total number of Internal nodes: ", c)
    elif choice==12:
        h=findHeight(root)
        print("Height of the tree: ", h)
    elif choice==13:
        findMirrorImage(root)
    elif choice==14:
        print("\nQuiting.......")
        break
    else:
        print("Invalid choice. Please Enter Correct Choice")
        continue
```

Program 10.3: Write a program to demonstrate level order traversal on a a binary search tree.

```python
class Queue:
    def __init__(self):
        self.items = []
    def isEmpty(self):
        return self.items == []
    def enqueue(self, item):
        self.items.append(item)
    def dequeue(self):
        return self.items.pop(0)
    def peek(self):
        return self.items[0]
    def size(self):
        return len(self.items)

class TreeNode :
    def __init__(self,Newdata=None,lchild=None,rchild=No
                                                    ne):
        self.left  = lchild
        self.data  = Newdata
        self.right = rchild

def insert_rec(curNode,newData):
    if curNode is None:
        return TreeNode(newData)
    elif newData<curNode.data:
        curNode.left=insert_rec(curNode.left, newData)
    else:
        curNode.right=insert_rec(curNode.right, newData)
    return curNode

def levelorder(rootNode):
    q=Queue()
    q.enqueue(rootNode)
    while not q.isEmpty():
        curNode= q.dequeue()
        if curNode.left is not None:
            q.enqueue(curNode.left)
        if curNode.right is not None:
            q.enqueue(curNode.right)
        print(curNode.data, end=" ")

root=None
while True:
```

```
print("\nPROGRAM TO IMPLEMENT LEVEL ORDER TRAVERSAL ON A
                            BINARY SEARCH TREE")
print("====================================================
                        ================")
print(" 1.Insert Node")
print(" 2.Level order Traversal")
print(" 3.Exit")
print("====================================================
                        ================")
choice=int(input("Enter your Choice : "))
if choice==1 :
    num=int(input("Enter the Data: "))
    root=insert_rec(root,num)
elif choice==2 :
    print("Level order : ", end = ' ')
    levelorder(root)
elif choice==3 :
    print("\nQuiting.......")
    break
else:
    print("Invalid choice. Please Enter Correct Choice")
    continue
```

10.10 Threaded Binary Tree

When we traverse a binary tree, whether recursive or non-recursive, a stack is required. Hence, extra memory space is needed. On the other hand, in linked list representation more than half of the nodes contain None reference in their left child or right child reference fields or in both. These spaces basically are wasted by storing None values. One solution is a threaded binary tree, which solves both the problems. Instead of storing None values we may store the references of predecessor nodes and/or successor nodes so that we traverse smoothly throughout the tree. Such references are known as threads and the tree as a binary threaded tree. There are several types of threaded binary trees based on how the tree is traversed. For example, a preorder threaded binary tree, by which we can traverse the tree in preorder fashion without using any stack. Similarly, an inorder threaded binary tree helps us to traverse a binary tree in inorder fashion without using any stack. Again based on the number of threads in a node, a threaded binary tree may be further classified into two types – one-way threaded binary tree and two-way threaded binary tree. One-way threaded binary tree stores either the reference of the predecessor or successor node whereas the two-way threaded binary tree stores the both. If the nodes of a one-way threaded binary tree stores the references of predecessor nodes, then to store the reference of the predecessor, the left child reference part of the node is used and the tree is known as a left threaded binary tree. Similarly, a right threaded binary tree stores the references of successor nodes in the right child reference part of each node. Here are some examples of a threaded binary tree:

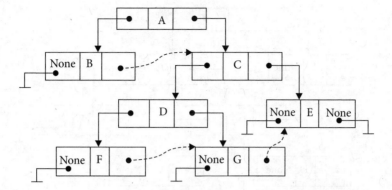

Figure 10.22 Right threaded preorder binary tree

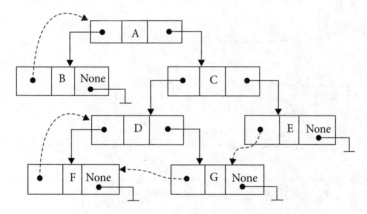

Figure 10.23 Left threaded preorder binary tree

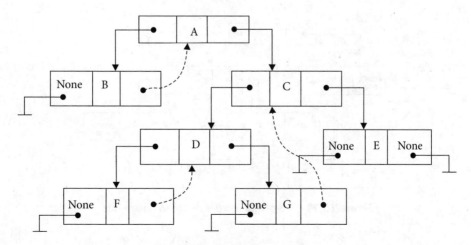

Figure 10.24 Right threaded inorder binary tree

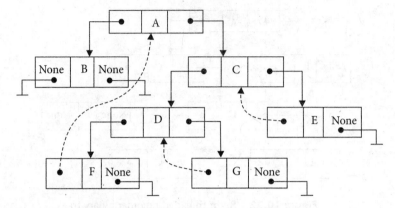

Figure 10.25   Left threaded inorder binary tree

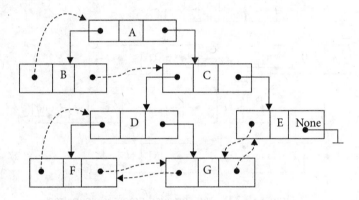

Figure 10.26   Two-way preorder threaded binary tree

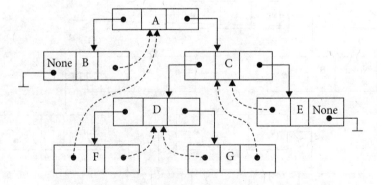

Figure 10.27   Two-way inorder threaded binary tree

10.10.1 Representation of a Threaded Binary Tree

Representation of threaded binary tree in memory is almost like a normal binary tree. The only difference is that we have to keep track of whether the reference is a child reference or a thread. For that we may include an extra attribute, `thread`, to specify whether the reference is a child reference or a thread. If the value of `thread` is True, it indicates it is a thread, otherwise it is a child reference. Consider the following class design to represent a node of a right threaded binary tree:

```
class ThreadedNode :
    def __init__(self,Newdata=None,lchild=None,rchild=None):
        self.left  = lchild
        self.data  = Newdata
        self.right = rchild
        self.thread = False
```

The above class represents a node of a one-way threaded binary tree. For two-way threaded binary tree, two thread attributes are required – one for the left thread and another for the right thread. Among all threaded binary trees the most popular is the right threaded inorder binary tree. Hence, here we are showing all the operations of a threaded binary tree on a right threaded inorder binary tree. Based on the above class design the schematic diagram of a right threaded inorder binary tree is shown in Figure 10.28. Here, T in the thread field denotes True and F denotes False.

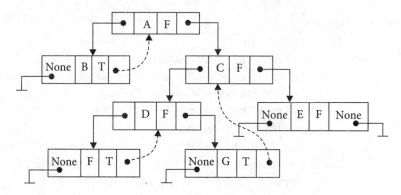

Figure 10.28   Right threaded inorder binary tree

10.10.2 Operations on an Inorder Threaded Binary Tree

Operations on an inorder threaded binary tree are almost similar to a binary tree. It differs on traversing the tree, inserting new nodes, and deleting nodes from a tree. In the following sections we are discussing these operations.

10.10.2.1 Inorder Traversal of an Inorder Threaded Binary Tree

We have already discussed that the main advantage of a threaded binary tree is in traversing as no stack is required. This technique saves both space and time because the extra overhead related to stack operations will now not be required and it makes the data structure more efficient. To implement inorder traversing on a threaded binary tree, we will follow the basic iterative algorithm of inorder traversal with the modification of eliminating stack and introducing thread. The following algorithm shows that:

1. Ser curNode = Root

2. While curNode is not None, do

    a. While left child of curNode is not None, do

        i.   Set left child of curNode as curNode

    b. Print data part of curNode

    c. Set parentNode = curNode

    d. Set right child of curNode as curNode

    e. While both thread part of parentNode and curNode is not None, do

        i.   Print data part of curNode

        ii. Set parentNode = curNode

        iii. Set right child of curNode as curNode

Here is a function to implement inorder traversal of a right threaded binary tree:

```python
def inorder(self):
    curNode=self.Root
    while curNode is not None:
        while curNode.left is not None:
            curNode=curNode.left
        print(curNode.data, end=" ")
        parentNode=curNode
        curNode=curNode.right
        while parentNode.thread and curNode:
            print(curNode.data, end=" ")
            parentNode=curNode
            curNode=curNode.right
```

10.10.2.2 Inserting a New Node in an Inorder Threaded Binary Search Tree

The algorithm to insert a node in a threaded BST is similar to that of a simple BST. For introducing thread we have to keep in mind the following points:

1. While finding the position of the new node, if the data value of the new node is greater than the current, then we will move to the right child only if the thread part of current node contains false.

2. If the new node is inserted as the left child of a leaf node, its right child part will be the thread. Thus the thread part of the new node becomes True and the right child part will contain the reference of the parent node.

3. If the new node is inserted as the right child of a leaf node, then also its right child part will be treated as the thread. Thus the thread part of the new node will be True and for the right child part there may be two cases:

   a. If parentNode contains a thread, then the right child part of the new node contains the content of the right child part of the parent node

   b. Otherwise, the right child part of the new node contains None

The general algorithm to insert a new node in a right threaded BST may be defined as follows:

1. Create a new node.

2. Update its data part with the function argument.

3. Update both the reference parts of the left child and the right child with None.

4. If the Root is None, then

   a. Update the Root with new node

5. Else

   a. Set current node = Root

   b. Set parent node = None

   c. While current node is not None do

      i. Set Parent node = current node

      ii. If the data value of new node is less than data value of current node,

      Set left child of current node as current node

      iii. Otherwise,

         • If thread part of current node is True, then

           o Set None to current node

         • Otherwise,

           o Set right child of current node as current node

   d. If the data value of new node is less than data value of parent node, then

      i. Set the new node as left child of parent node

      ii. Right child part of new node contains the reference of parent node

iii. Thread part of new node becomes True

e. Otherwise,

i. If parentNode contains a thread, then

- Change the thread part of parentNode to False
- Thread part of new node becomes True
- Right child part of new node contains the content of right child part of parent node
- Right child part of parent node contains the reference of new node

ii. Otherwise,

- Thread part of new node becomes False
- Right child part of new node contains None
- Right child part of parent node contains the reference of new node

Using the above algorithm we can write the following code:

```
# Function to insert a new node in a Right threaded Binary
# Search Tree
    def insert(self,newData):
        newNode=ThreadedNode(newData)
        if self.Root is None:
            self.Root=newNode
        else:
            curNode = self.Root
            parentNode = None
            while curNode is not None :
                parentNode=curNode
                if newData<curNode.data:
                    curNode = curNode.left
                else:
                    if curNode.thread is True:
                        curNode=None
                    else:
                        curNode = curNode.right
            if newData<parentNode.data:
                parentNode.left=newNode
                newNode.right=parentNode
                newNode.thread=True
            else:
                if parentNode.thread is True:
```

```
                        parentNode.thread=False
                        newNode.thread=True
                        newNode.right=parentNode.right
                        parentNode.right=newNode
              else:
                        newNode.thread=False
                        newNode.right =None
                        parentNode.right=newNode
```

10.10.2.3 Deletion of a Node from an Inorder Threaded Binary Search Tree

Deletion of nodes from a threaded binary search tree is little bit tricky. Here whether a node has a right child or not has to be decided on the value of the thread, not with the value of the right child. For all cases of deletion it needs to be kept in mind that the corresponding thread should not be lost and the value of the thread is properly maintained. Here is the function to delete a node from a right inorder threaded binary search tree.

```
def findNodeWithParent(self, key):
    parent = None
    curNode= self.Root
    while curNode is not None:
        if key == curNode.data :
            return (parent, curNode)
        elif key < curNode.data :
            parent = curNode
            curNode = curNode.left
        else:
            parent = curNode
            if curNode.thread is True:
                curNode=None
            else:
                curNode = curNode.right
    return (parent, curNode)

def delete(self, key):
    parent, curNode = self.findNodeWithParent(key)
    if curNode is None:
        print("Node not Found")
    elif curNode.left is None and      #No child case
          (curNode.right is None or curNode.thread):
        if parent is not None:
            if parent.right is curNode:
                parent.right = curNode.right
```

```
                    parent.thread= True
            else:
                parent.left = None
        else:
            self.Root = None
        del(curNode)
    elif curNode.left is None or        #One child case
            (curNode.right is None or curNode.thread):
        if curNode.left is None:
            childNode = curNode.right
        else:
            childNode = curNode.left
        if parent is not None:
            if parent.left is curNode:
                parent.left = childNode
                if curNode.thread is True:
                    childNode.right=curNode.right
            else:
                parent.right= childNode
                if childNode.thread is True and
                            curNode.left is childNode:
                    childNode.right=parent.right
        else:
            self.Root = childNode
        del(curNode)
    else:                               #Two children case
        parentLeft = curNode
        largestLeft = curNode.left
        while largestLeft.thread is False:
                # finding largest node of left subtree
            parentLeft = largestLeft
            largestLeft = largestLeft.right
        curNode.data = largestLeft.data
        if parentLeft.right == largestLeft:
            if largestLeft.left is None:
                parentLeft.thread=True
                parentLeft.right = largestLeft.right
            else:
                parentLeft.right = largestLeft.left
                if largestLeft.left.thread:
                    largestLeft.left.right=
                                        largestLeft.right
```

```
        else:
            if largestLeft.left is not None:
                if largestLeft.left.thread:
                    largestLeft.left.right=
                                        largestLeft.right
            parentLeft.left = largestLeft.left
        del(largestLeft)
```

Here is a complete program to show the implementation of a right threaded inorder binary search tree.

Program 10.4: Write a program to demonstrate the various operations on a right threaded inorder binary search tree.

```
#PRGD10_4: Program to demonstrate Inorder Threaded Binary
#Search Tree

class ThreadedNode :          # Declaration of Node of a
                              #Threaded Binary Search Tree
    def __init__(self,Newdata=None,lchild=None,rchild=No
                                                    ne):
        self.left  = lchild
        self.data  = Newdata
        self.right = rchild
        self.thread = False

class TBST :                  # class to represent Threaded BST
    def __init__( self ):
        self.Root = None

    def insert(self,newData):
        newNode=ThreadedNode(newData)
        if self.Root is None:
            self.Root=newNode
        else:
            curNode = self.Root
            parentNode = None
            while curNode is not None :
                parentNode=curNode
                if newData<curNode.data:
                    curNode = curNode.left
                else:
```

```python
                    if curNode.thread is True:
                        curNode=None
                    else:
                        curNode = curNode.right
            if newData<parentNode.data:
                parentNode.left=newNode
                newNode.right=parentNode
                newNode.thread=True
            else:
                if parentNode.thread is True:
                    parentNode.thread=False
                    newNode.thread=True
                    newNode.right=parentNode.right
                    parentNode.right=newNode
                else:
                    newNode.thread=False
                    newNode.right =None
                    parentNode.right=newNode

    def inorder(self):
        curNode=self.Root
        while curNode is not None:
            while curNode.left is not None:
                curNode=curNode.left
            print(curNode.data, end=" ")
            parentNode=curNode
            curNode=curNode.right
            while parentNode.thread and curNode:
                print(curNode.data, end=" ")
                parentNode=curNode
                curNode=curNode.right

    def findNodeWithParent(self, key):
        parent = None
        curNode= self.Root
        while curNode is not None:
            if key == curNode.data :
                return (parent, curNode)
            elif key < curNode.data :
                parent = curNode
                curNode = curNode.left
            else:
```

```
                    parent = curNode
                    if curNode.thread is True:
                        curNode=None
                    else:
                        curNode = curNode.right
            return (parent, curNode)

    def delete(self, key):
        parent, curNode = self.findNodeWithParent(key)
        if curNode is None:
            print("Node not Found")
        elif curNode.left is None and          #No child case
                (curNode.right is None or curNode.thread):
            if parent is not None:
                if parent.right is curNode:
                    parent.right = curNode.right
                    parent.thread= True
                else:
                    parent.left = None
            else:
                self.Root = None
            del(curNode)
        elif curNode.left is None or           #One child case
                (curNode.right is None or curNode.thread):
            if curNode.left is None:
                childNode = curNode.right
            else:
                childNode = curNode.left
            if parent is not None:
                if parent.left is curNode:
                    parent.left = childNode
                    if curNode.thread is True:
                        childNode.right=curNode.right
                else:
                    parent.right= childNode
                    if childNode.thread is True and
                                curNode.left is childNode:
                        childNode.right=parent.right
            else:
                self.Root = childNode
            del(curNode)
        else:                                  #Two children case
```

```python
                parentLeft = curNode
                largestLeft = curNode.left
                while largestLeft.thread is False:
                        # finding largest node of left subtree
                    parentLeft = largestLeft
                    largestLeft = largestLeft.right
                curNode.data = largestLeft.data
                if parentLeft.right == largestLeft:
                    if largestLeft.left is None:
                        parentLeft.thread=True
                        parentLeft.right = largestLeft.right
                    else:
                        parentLeft.right = largestLeft.left
                        if largestLeft.left.thread:
                            largestLeft.left.right=
                                        largestLeft.right
                else:
                    if largestLeft.left is not None:
                        if largestLeft.left.thread:
                            largestLeft.left.right=
                                        largestLeft.right
                    parentLeft.left = largestLeft.left
                del(largestLeft)

tbst=TBST()
while True:
    print("\nPROGRAM TO IMPLEMENT THREADED BINARY SEARCH
                                                TREE")
    print("=============================================
                                                ====")
    print("1.Insert Node")
    print("2.Inorder Traversal")
    print("3.Delete a Node")
    print("4.Exit")
    print("=============================================
                                                ====")
    choice=int(input("Enter your Choice : "))
    if choice==1 :
        num=int(input("Enter the Data: "))
        tbst.insert(num)
    elif choice==2 :
        print("Inorder : ", end = ' ')
        tbst.inorder()
```

```
    elif choice==3 :
        num=int(input("Enter The Data You Want To Delete :
                                                            "))
        tbst.delete(num)
    elif choice==4 :
        print("\nQuiting.......")
        break
    else:
        print("Invalid choice. Please Enter Correct Choice")
        continue
```

10.11 AVL Tree

An AVL tree is a height-balanced binary search tree, which means it is a binary search tree with an extra property of a balance factor that indicates that the height of the two sub-trees of each node differs at the most by one. It is named AVL to honor the inventors of this tree – Adelson-Velsky and Landis. The advantage of the AVL tree is that the worst case time complexity to search an element is $O(\log_2 n)$. This is also true for insertion and deletion operations.

The height balance is achieved by introducing a balance factor in each node. The balance factor is calculated by subtracting the height of the right sub-tree from that of the left sub-tree. The permissible values of the balance factor are 1, 0, and -1. If the height of a left sub-tree is denoted by H_L and the height of a right sub-tree is denoted by H_R, then $|H_L - H_R| <= 1$. If any node possesses any other value as balance factor, the node requires some balancing operations. In the following section we will discuss these balancing operations. Now consider the following AVL tree:

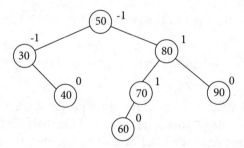

Figure 10.29 An AVL tree with balance factor in each node

In the above tree, consider the root node, 50. The height of its left sub-tree is 2 and that of right sub-tree is 3. Thus, the balance factor is 2-3=-1. For the node 30, the height of the left sub-tree is 0 as it does not have any left child, and the height of right sub-tree is 1 as it contains only a single node. Hence, the balance factor is 0-1=-1. The Balance factor of node 40 is 0 because it is a leaf node. Similarly the balance factor of all other nodes have been calculated. Since the balance factor of all the nodes of the tree is either 0, 1, or -1 and the tree possesses the rules of a binary search tree, the above tree can be treated as an AVL tree.

10.11.1 Operations on an AVL Tree

All operations on binary search tree are similarly applicable on an AVL tree except insertion and deletion operations. Hence, we discuss only these two operations in the following sections.

10.11.1.1 Insertiing a Node in an AVL Tree

To insert a node in an AVL tree, first we have to follow the same operation as we have done in a binary search tree. After inserting the node, the balance factor of all nodes of the tree has to be calculated to check whether any node or nodes possess the value beyond the permissible value. If so, rotation is required to rebalance the tree. Sometimes it may happen that with a single insertion of a node more than one node's balance factor crosses the restricted limit. In those cases, we have to consider the node at the highest level. For example, if the nodes at level 3 and level 4 both have the balance factor more than 1 or less than -1, we have to consider the node at level 4 for rotation. There may be four cases: LL, RR, LR, and RL. We shall discuss all these cases here.

LL: When a new node is inserted in the left sub-tree of the left sub-tree of the node in which balance is disturbed.

RR: When a new node is inserted in the right sub-tree of the right sub-tree of the node in which balance is disturbed.

LR: When a new node is inserted in the right sub-tree of the left sub-tree of the node in which balance is disturbed.

RL: When a new node is inserted in the left sub-tree of the right sub-tree of the node in which balance is disturbed.

The rotation for LL and RR cases are similar in nature but the rotations are in opposite directions. In both cases, a single rotation is required to rebalance the tree and the rotation needs to apply on the node in which balance is disturbed. For the LL case, rotation will be rightwards and for the RR case, rotation will be leftwards.

The rotation for LR and RL cases are a little bit complicated and are similar in nature. In both cases, a single rotation is not sufficient. We have to apply double rotation. The first rotation is at the child node (which has larger height) of the node whose balance factor crosses the limit and after that on the node whose balance factor crosses the limit. The following examples clarify the cases in details:

Case 1: Insert nodes in the following order: 30, 20, 10.

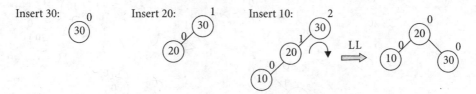

Figure 10.30 LL rotation in an AVL tree

In the above tree, first node 30 is inserted. As it is the first node, it does not have any child and the balance factor is calculated as 0. Next 20 is inserted. Following the rules of BST it is inserted as a left child. The balance factor of the node 20 and 30 are 0 and 1 respectively. Up to this, the balance factors of the nodes are within limit. But after the insertion of node 10, the balance factor of node 30 becomes 2. Since the new node 10 is inserted in the left sub-tree of the left sub-tree of the node 30, i.e. in which balance is disturbed, we have to follow the rotation rule for the LL case and a right rotation has to be given on node 30 and we get the balanced tree as shown in Figure 10.30.

Case 2: Insert nodes in the following order: 10, 20, 30.

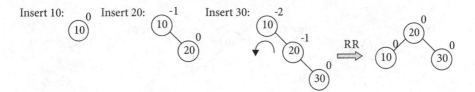

Figure 10.31 RR rotation in an AVL tree

In the above tree, after the insertion of nodes 10 and 20, the balance factors of the nodes are within range. After the insertion of node 30, the balance factor of node 10 becomes -2. Since the new node 30 is inserted in the right sub-tree of the right sub-tree of the node 10, i.e. in which balance is disturbed, we have to follow the rotation rule for the RR case and a left rotation has to be given on node 10 and we get the balanced tree as shown in Figure 10.31.

Case 3: Insert nodes in the following order: 30, 10, 20.

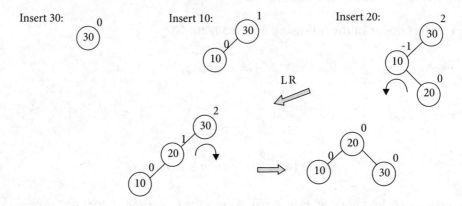

Figure 10.32   LR rotation in an AVL tree

Here also, after the insertion of nodes 30 and 10, the balance factors of the nodes are within range. After the insertion of node 20, the balance factor of node 30 becomes 2. Since the new node 20 is inserted in the right sub-tree of the left sub-tree of the node 30, i.e. in which node balance is disturbed, we have to follow the rotation rule for the LR case. So, first a left rotation has to be given on the child node of node 30, i.e. left rotation on node 10, and after that a right rotation on node 30. Finally, we get the balanced tree as shown in Figure 10.32.

Case 4: Insert nodes in the following order: 10, 30, 20.

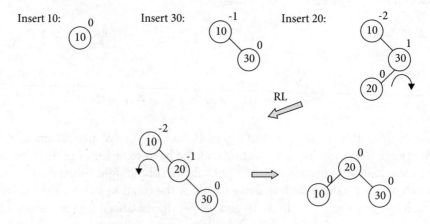

Figure 10.33   RL rotation in an AVL tree

In the above tree, after the insertion of node 20, the balance factor of node 10 becomes -2. Since the new node 20 is inserted in the left sub-tree of the right sub-tree of the node 10, i.e. in which balance is disturbed, we have to follow the rotation rule for the RL case. Thus first a right rotation will be given on the child node of node 10, i.e. on node 30. Next a left rotation is given on node 10 and the tree becomes balanced as shown in Figure 10.33.

Case 5: Insert 20 in the following tree:

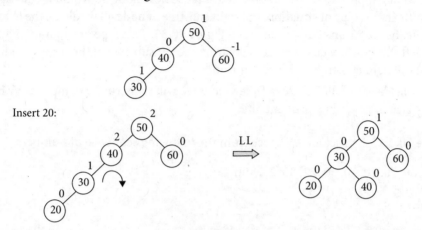

Figure 10.34   Special case when balance factors exceed limit in more than one node

In the above tree, after the insertion of node 20, the balance factor of node 40 as well as of node 50 becomes 2. As 40 is at a higher level than 50, we have to give the rotation on node 40 and the new node 20 is inserted in the left sub-tree of the left sub-tree of node 40; thus we have to follow the rotation rule for the LL case and a right rotation has to be given on node 40 as shown in Figure 10.34.

Case 6: Insert 10 in the following tree:

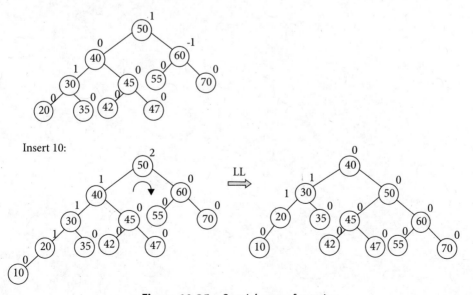

Figure 10.35   Special case of rotation

In the above example, it is very clear that after the insertion of node 10, the balance factor of node 50 becomes 2 and it is a case of LL. So, we have to give a right rotation on node 50. Now to complete the rotation process, node 40 moves to the root along with its left sub-tree. But what happens to its right sub-tree (because now node 50 would be the right child of node 40)? In this type of situation, the right sub-tree of node 40 would be the left sub-tree of node 50 after rotation. This is shown in Figure 10.35. This type of situation may arise in case of a left rotation as well. Then after rotation the left sub-tree of the corresponding node would be the right sub-tree of its ancestor node.

Now consider the following example where we will construct a complete AVL tree by inserting a set of key values sequentially:

Example 10.4: Construct an AVL tree from the following sequence of numbers:

50, 60, 70, 20, 10, 30, 22, 35, 25, and 45.

Solution:

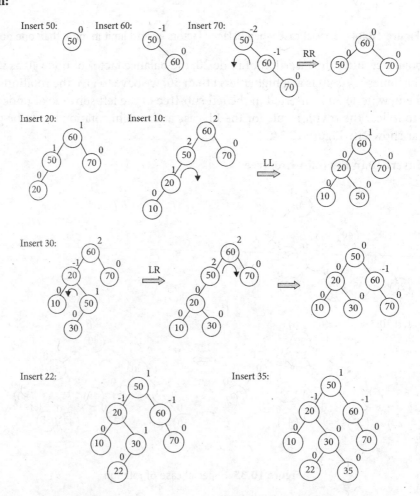

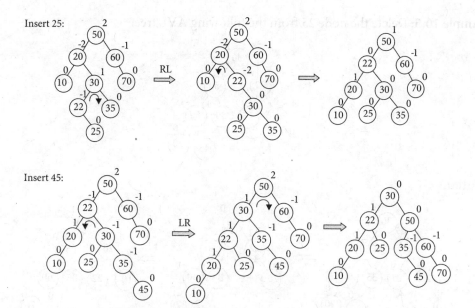

Figure 10.36 Steps to construct an AVL tree

10.11.1.2 Deleting a Node from an AVL Tree

To delete a node from an AVL tree, first we have to follow the basic rules of deleting a node from a binary search tree. Then we will check the balance factors of all nodes. If the tree remains well balanced, then it is okay. Otherwise, we have to provide some rotation operation to rebalance the tree. First we will consider the node where balance is disturbed. If it is found that the balance factor of more than one node exceeds the limit, we will have to consider the node with the highest level. Next we will calculate the height of its children and grandchildren. Based on these, there is also the chance of four possible cases of rotation.

LL: If height of **left** child is greater than its right child and height of **left** grandchild is greater than right grandchild (here grandchildren are the children of left child).

RR: If height of **right** child is greater than its left child and height of **right** grandchild is greater than left grandchild (here grandchildren are the children of right child).

LR: If height of **left** child is greater than its right child and height of **right** grandchild is greater than left grandchild (here grandchildren are the children of left child).

RL: If height of **right** child is greater than its left child and height of **left** grandchild is greater than right grandchild (here grandchildren are the children of right child).

Based on these cases, we have to apply same rotation strategies as was done for insertion. Remember that, unlike insertion, fixing the problem of one node may not completely balance an AVL tree. So, we need to check the balance factors of all nodes once again and, if problem persists, we have to follow the rotation strategies as discussed above.

Example 10.5: Delete the node 25 from the following AVL tree.

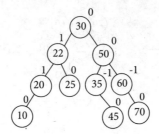

Solution:

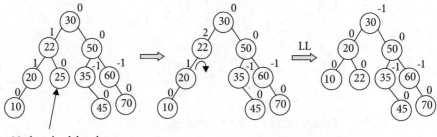

Node to be deleted

Figure 10.37 Deletion of a node from an AVL tree

As 25 is in a leaf node, deletion is simple. The node will be deleted and the right reference of 22 becomes None. But deletion of 25 makes node 22 unbalanced. We need to give a rotation. As it is a case of LL, a right rotation has to be given on 22 and we get the final balanced AVL tree.

10.12 Red–Black Tree

A red–black tree is another self-balancing binary search tree invented by Rudolf Bayer in 1972. The specialty of this tree is that every node of this tree is colored either red or black. That is why it is named as red–black tree. It is similar in kind to an AVL tree but it is not as balanced as an AVL tree. But the advantage of a red–black tree over an AVL tree is it requires less rotation to balance the tree. Thus the search operation is better in an AVL tree whereas insertion and deletion operations are faster in case of a red–black tree. As the tree is roughly balanced, the time complexity of insertion, deletion, and search operations in a red–black tree is also $O(\log_2 n)$.

A red–black tree has the following properties:

- Every node is either red or black.
- The color of the root node is always black.

- All the leaf nodes are black.

- Children of every red node is black, i.e. no two adjacent red nodes is possible.

- All the paths from a particular node to its leaf node contain an equal number of black nodes.

To maintain the color of the node an extra bit is used which contains 0 or 1 to indicate the color red or black. In the red–black tree, all the leaf nodes are considered as external nodes and these nodes do not contain any data. These are basically left and right references and contain None. So, in our diagram we are not showing these. The following are some examples of red–black trees.

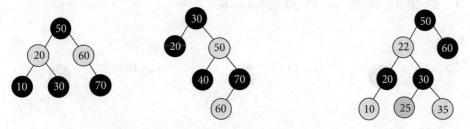

Figure 10.38   Examples of some red–black trees

10.12.1 Inserting a New Node in a Red–Black Tree

As a red–black tree basically is a binary search tree, whenever a new element is added, first it will be inserted in the tree following the basic rules of a binary search tree. Next, to balance the tree, we use two mechanisms:

1. Recolor or repaint

2. Rotation

Recolor means changing the color of the node. We have to keep in mind about color that the color of the root is always black and no two adjacent nodes will be red. The rotations are the same as rotations of an AVL tree. Any one among the four cases, i.e., LL, RR, LR, and RL, may apply.

The general algorithm to insert a new node in a red–black tree can be defined as:

1. Insert the new node following the rules of a BST.

2. If it is inserted as the root, set the color of the node as black.

3. Otherwise, set the color of the node as red.

4. If the parent of the new node is black, then exit.

5. But if it is red, check the uncle node of the new node.

   a. If the color of the uncle node is black or None, then

i.   Do suitable rotation and recolor.

b.   Otherwise, i.e. if it is red, then

i.   Recolor

6.   If the grandparent of the new node is not the root, check it. If it violates the color rule, follow step 5 for grandparent.

Now consider the following example where based on the above algorithm we will construct a complete red–black tree by inserting a set of key values sequentially:

Example 10.6: Construct a red–black tree from the following sequence of numbers:

12, 23, 10, 18, 20, 30, 28, 45, 50, 8, 5, and 60.

Solution:

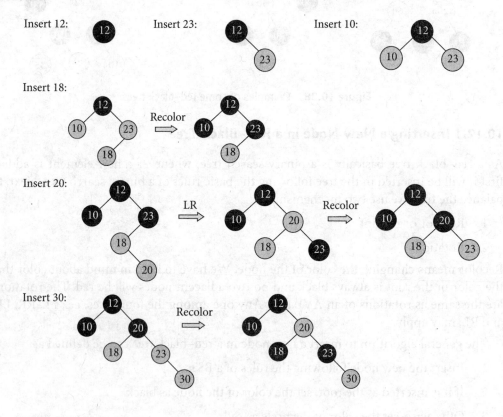

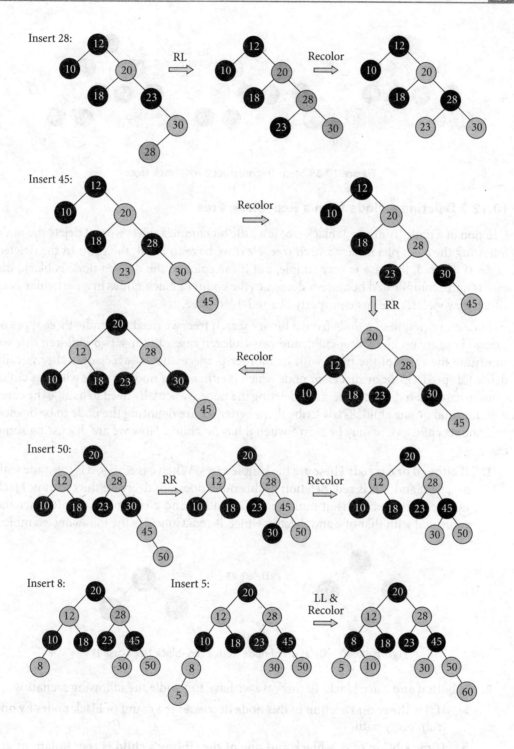

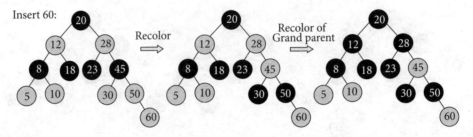

Figure 10.39 Steps to construct a red–black tree

10.12.2 Deleting a Node from a Red–Black Tree

Deletion of a node from a red–black tree is a little bit complex. First we will delete the node following the rules of a binary search tree. Next we have to check the color of the deleted node. If it is red, the case is very simple, but if the color of the deleted node is black, the case is quite complicated because it decreases the count of black nodes in a particular path which may violates the basic property of a red–black tree.

In case of deletion of a node from a binary search tree, we need to handle three types of cases. These are no-child, one-child, and two-children cases. But in a two-children case we substitute the value of the node with its inorder predecessor or successor and physically delete this predecessor or successor node which is either a leaf node or node with one child. Thus in case of a red–black tree, after deleting the node we actually need to handle the cases with no child or one child. To describe them better we are denoting the node to be deleted as d and its child as c (c may be None when d has no child). Now we are discussing some cases.

1. **If either d or c is red:** These are the simple cases. When c is None, d is the node with no child, and if it is red, deletion of this node does not decrease the count of black nodes. If c is not None it must be red as both d and c cannot be red. Replace the value of d with that of c and delete c which is red. Consider the following example:

Figure 10.40 Deletion of node from a red–black tree (case 1)

2. **If both d and c are black:** In this case we have to handle the following scenarios:

   a. **If d is the root:** Deletion of this node decreases the count of black nodes by one from every path.

   b. **If the sibling of d is black and one of the sibling's child is red:** Rotations are needed. Based on the position of the sibling and its child there may be four cases:

i. LL: when both the sibling and its red child are left children of their parents

ii. RR: when both the sibling and its red child are right children of their parents

iii. LR: when the sibling is a left child of its parent and its right child is red

iv. RL: when the sibling is a right child of its parent and its left child is red

In case of LL or RR rotation, the value of the parent node would be shifted to the node to be deleted. The value of the red node and its parent node would be shifted to their parent node and the red node would be actually deleted.

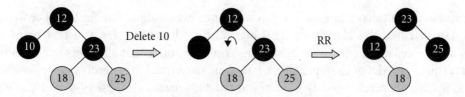

Figure 10.41 Deletion of a node from a red–black tree (case II)

In case of LR or RL, in first rotation, child will be inserted in between its parent and grandparent and its color will be changed to black and its parent now becomes red. Thus after the final rotation, the old sibling node, which now becomes red, is moved up and becomes black again. Consider the following example:

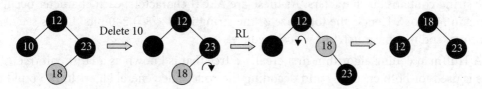

Figure 10.42 Deletion of a node from a red–black tree (case III)

c. **If the sibling of d is black and both the children siblings are black:** Recolor the sibling and repeat the operation for parent if parent is black.

Figure 10.43 Deletion of a node from a red–black tree (case IV)

d. **If the sibling of d is red:** If the sibling is a left child, give a right rotation, otherwise give a left rotation on the parent to move the old sibling up and recolor the old sibling and parent.

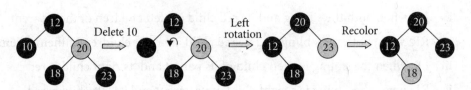

Figure 10.44   Deletion of node from a red–black tree (case V)

10.13 Huffman Coding

A Huffman coding algorithm is a lossless data compression algorithm. In 1952 David Albert Huffman invented this algorithm. This algorithm reduces the size of a text or message using a variable length encoding technique. You may notice that all letters in the alphabet are not equally used. For example, *a, e, i, r*, etc., are used much frequently in words, whereas *x, y, z, w*, etc., are rarely used. In case of punctuation marks also, use of '.' and ',' are used much more than others. The basic philosophy of this algorithm is that the more frequent characters use shorter length code while less frequent characters use relatively larger length code. This makes a great reduction in size of the text.

Suppose we have the following string:

ACCBFAAADCBBEAACFDABCCEDCAAAEC

The string contains 30 characters. As these are ASCII characters, each character occupies 8 bits in memory. Hence, the total size of the string is $30 \times 8 = 240$ bits. Let us see using Huffman coding how much bits we can reduce.

A Huffman coding algorithm first creates a tree that is known as a Huffman tree. This tree is used for both encoding and decoding the code. The general algorithm to build the Huffman tree is as follows:

1. Find the frequency of each character in the string.

2. Arrange these characters in ascending order of their frequency. These forms the leaf nodes of the tree.

3. An intermediate node will be formed by combining the least frequented nodes/characters. The value of the node will be the sum of the frequency of these leaf nodes.

4. Repeat step 3 until total tree is formed. Note that at the time of considering least frequented nodes those nodes already used to form an intermediate node are never used again.

5. After formation of tree assign 0 to each left edge and assign 1 to each right edge.

Let us apply this algorithm on the above string to build the Huffman tree. Our first task is to find the frequency of each character and arrange them in ascending order of their frequency.

F	D	E	B	C	A
2	3	3	4	8	10

These will be considered as leaf nodes of the tree and the least frequented nodes form the intermediate node.

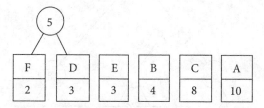

The next least frequented nodes are E and B with values 3 and 4 respectively.

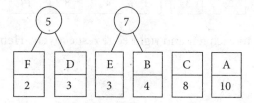

Now intermediate nodes are containing the least values 5 and 7.

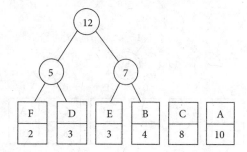

The next least frequented nodes are C and A with values 8 and 10 respectively.

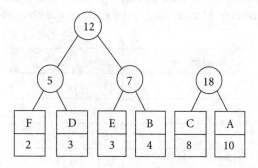

Now the intermediate nodes are containing the least values 12 and 18. Hence, the final tree is:

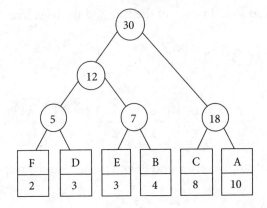

Now we assign 0 and 1 to each left and right edge respectively. Hence we get the Huffman tree.

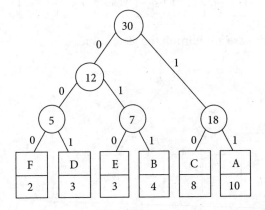

From this tree we are now able to encode the characters. To get the code of each character we traverse from the root to the corresponding character and the corresponding path will be the code for that character. Hence, we get the code of the characters as:

Character	Code
A	11
B	011
C	10
D	001

E	010
F	000

Applying these codes we can encode the above string as:

11101001100011111100110011011010101111100000011101110100100011011111101010.

Now we will find the size of this encoded string.

Character	Code	Size in bits	Frequency	Total Size
A	11	2	10	20
B	011	3	4	12
C	10	2	8	16
D	001	3	3	9
E	010	3	3	9
F	000	3	2	6

Thus, total size of the encoded string = 20+12+16+9+9+6 = 72. But along with the encoded string we also need to store/send the code table. In the code table, there are 6 ASCII characters, for which 6x8 = 48 bits are required, and for the code 2+3+2+3+3+3 = 16 bits are required. Hence, the total size of the code table = 48+16=64 bits. So, to encode the string total 72+64, i.e. 136, bits are required, which is much less than the original string (240 bits).

To decode the string, we have to use the same code table. We read each character from the encoded string and start traversing through the path starting from the root of the Huffman tree. When we reach at the leaf node we will get the decoded character. Again we start from the root and follow the same procedure. In our encoded string, the first 11 represent A, the next 10 represent C, and so on.

10.14 M-way Search Trees

M-way search trees are the generalized version of binary search trees. Here m-way represents multi-way search tree, which means each node of these trees can have a maximum of m number of children and m-1 key values and these key values maintain the search order. We can say that the binary search tree is also an m-way search tree whose value of m = 2. Thus each of its nodes has a maximum of two children – left sub-tree and right sub-tree – and the number of key values is 2-1 = 1. But generally, in case of m-way search trees the value of m is greater than 2. An m-way tree does not mean the tree has exactly m number of children in each node; rather, it indicates that the order of the tree is m, which means that each node may have a maximum of m number of children and the number of key values is one less than the number of children.

The advantage of m-way search trees is that the search, insertion, and deletion operations are much faster in comparison to a binary search tree. Since the data elements are distributed among m paths, the height of the tree is reduced to $\log_m n$, where n is the number of key values in the tree. Thus the time complexity of these operations is reduced to $O(\log_m n)$. The general structure of each node of an m-way search tree is:

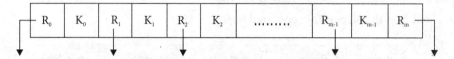

Figure 10.45   Structure of a node of an m-way search tree

where $R_0, R_1, R_2, ..., R_m$ are the references of child nodes and $K_0, K_1, K_2, ..., K_{m-1}$ are the key values. The key values in the node are in ascending order, i.e. $K_0 < K_1 < K_2 < .... < K_{m-1}$, and all the key values in nodes of the sub-tree whose reference is at R_i are less than key value K_i for i = 0, 1, 2, ..., m-1. Similarly, all the key values in nodes of the sub-tree whose reference is at R_m are greater than key value K_{m-1}. Figure 10.46 shows an m-way search tree of order 4.

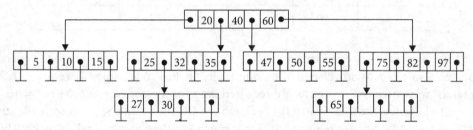

Figure 10.46   Example of a four-way search tree

To search an element, say x, from an m-way search tree we have to start from the root. Within the root, compare x with the key values of the root. If $x < k_i$, then the searching process will be continued in the sub-tree whose reference is at R_i for i = 0 to m-1. But if $x > k_{m-1}$, the searching process will be continued in the sub-tree whose reference is at R_m. This process will be continued until x is matched with some key value or the search ends with an empty sub-tree. Consider the above example and we want to search the key value 30. As 20<30<40 at the root, we have to move through the sub-tree whose reference is in between 20 and 40. Now within the root of this sub-tree, 30 is greater than the first key value, 25, but less than the next key value, 32. So, we have to move through the sub-tree whose reference is in between 25 and 32 and we will find 30 at the k_1 position of this node.

10.15 B Tree

A B tree is a very popular and efficient m-way search tree. Its application is found widely in database management systems. The B tree was developed by Rudolf Bayer and Ed McCreight in 1970.

A B tree of order m is an m-way search tree that has the following properties:

1. All leaves of the tree are at the same level.

2. All internal nodes except the root can have a maximum of **m** children and a minimum of $\left\lceil \dfrac{m}{2} \right\rceil$ children.

3. The root node has a maximum of **m** children but a minimum of 2 children if it is not a leaf node.

4. The number of key values in a node is one less than its child and the key values maintain the search order.

From the first property it is clear that a B tree is a strictly balanced tree and thus the time complexity of insertion, deletion, and search operations are calculated as $O(\log_m n)$. Figure 10.47 shows a B tree of order 3.

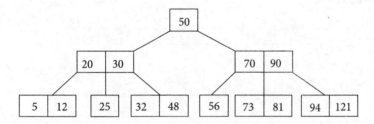

Figure 10.47   Example of a B tree of order 3

10.15.1 Inserting a New Element in a B Tree

To insert an element in a B tree, first we have to follow the basic search operation that is followed in any m-way search tree to find the leaf node where the new element is to be inserted. If the node has sufficient space to accommodate the new element, then the new element will be inserted in that node maintaining the search order. But if the node does not have sufficient space to accommodate the new element, the node splits into three parts. The middle part is moved upward and inserted into the parent node. If this parent node is unable to accommodate the new element, the parent node may be split further and the splitting propagates upwards. This splitting process may propagate up to the root. If the root splits, a new node with a single element is created and the height of the B tree increases by one. The following example illustrates the total insertion process:

Example 10.6: Construct a B tree of order 5 from the following sequence of numbers:

35, 22, 57, 41, 72, 15, 65, 97, 39, 92, 45, 90, 63, 85, 95, 60, 50, 94, 99 and 20.

Solution:

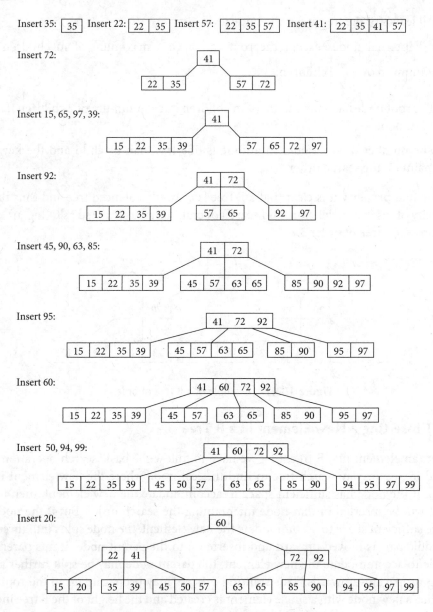

Figure 10.48   Steps to construct a B tree

10.15.2 Deleting Elements from a B Tree

To delete an element from a B tree, first we have to search the element in the tree. After finding the element, check whether the element is in a leaf node or not. If it is in a leaf node and the node contains more than the minimum number of elements, i.e. more than m/2 key values, then simply delete the element. But if the element is in a leaf node and the node does not contain sufficient number of elements, we have to fill the position by borrowing elements from its siblings via the root. The largest element of the left sibling or the smallest element of the right sibling (whichever is available) would be moved into the parent node and the intervening element from the parent node moves to the node where the deletion takes place. But if both the left and right siblings do not have sufficient number of elements, we have to merge the two leaf nodes along with their intervening element in the parent node into a single leaf node. For this reason, if the parent node suffers from less than the minimum number of key values, the process of merging propagates upwards. This may propagate up to the root, causing the height of the tree to decrease by one. If the element is in some internal node, the inorder predecessor or successor of the element has to be fetched from the corresponding leaf node to fill up the position of the deleted element. The following example illustrates the various cases that may arise due to the deletion of elements from a B tree.

Example 10.7: Delete 50, 92, 90 and 35 from the following B tree:

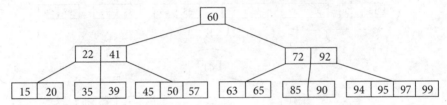

Solution:

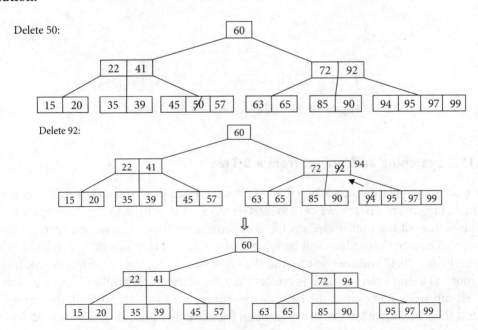

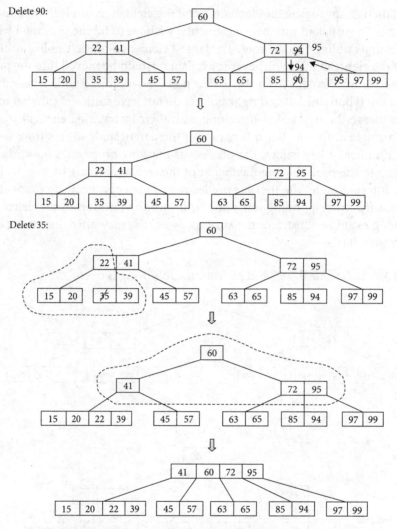

Figure 10.49   Deletion of nodes from a B tree

10.15.3 Searching an Element from a B Tree

The searching operation in a B tree is similar to that in an m-way search tree. To search an element, say x, from a B tree, we have to start from the root. Within the root, compare x with the key values of the root. Based on the comparison we have to move the corresponding sub-tree. The same procedure will be followed for this sub-tree as well. Consider the final tree in Figure 10.48 and we want to find the key value 50. So, we start from the root. Here the root has a single element and is greater than the searching key value. Thus we move to the left sub-tree. The root of the left sub-tree contains 22 and 41. So, both the key values are less than 50. So, we have to move through the extreme right sub-tree of this node. This sub-tree contains a single node with key values 45, 50, and 57. On finding the value 50, the search operation is completed with success.

10.16 B+ Tree

A B+ tree is another m-way search tree. Basically it is a variant of the B tree. In a B tree, only direct access of keys is possible. We do not have any scope of traversing the elements sequentially. A B+ tree provides this opportunity. It supports direct access as well as sequential access among the keys. In a B+ tree, all the key values are stored in the leaves and some key values are replicated in the internal nodes to define the paths to locate individual records. All the leaf nodes are linked together forming a linked list to provide sequential access. Another important difference with a B tree is that while a B tree stores the key values as well as records in their nodes, a B+ tree stores only the key values in their internal nodes and all the records in leaf nodes. These leaf nodes are connected through a linked list to provide the sequential access. Thus internal nodes are known as index nodes and leaf nodes are data nodes. A B+ tree is widely used in DBMS, especially in maintaining indexed and multi-level indexed structures. Since the size of the main memory is always limited, it is used to store large amounts of data with the trick that the key values are stored in the main memory and the records are stored in a secondary storage device and references are maintained with the key values of leaf nodes to point to the records stored in the secondary device. Figure 10.50 shows a B+ tree of order 3.

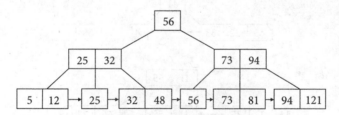

Figure 10.50 Example of a B+ tree of order 3

10.16.1 Inserting a New Element in a B+ Tree

The process of insertion of a new element in a B+ tree is almost similar to that in a B tree. But as we discussed, unlike a B tree, since it stores data values only at the leaf nodes, we need to follow some deviations in implementation. Again the leaf nodes are connected through a linked list. So, care has to be taken for that also. To insert an element, first we will locate the node where the new element will be inserted. Now if the node has sufficient space to accommodate the new element, it will be inserted smoothly (maximum capacity is m-1 key values). Otherwise, the node will be split into two parts. The left part will contain $\left\lceil \dfrac{m}{2} \right\rceil$

– 1 elements ($\left\lceil \dfrac{m}{2} \right\rceil$ is also considered) and the right part will contain the rest. The smallest element in the right part, i.e. the left-most element of the right part, will be pushed up into the parent node maintaining the ascending order of the elements in the parent node. Next, the left part points to the right part and the right part points to the node that was pointed to by the node of insertion before splitting. The addition of an element in the parent node follows exactly the same rules that have been followed in the case of a B tree. The following example illustrates the insertion operation in detail:

Example 10.8: Construct a B tree of order 5 from the following sequence of numbers:

35, 22, 57, 41, 72, 15, 65, 97, 39, 92, 45, 63, 85, 90, 60, 94 and 20.

Solution:

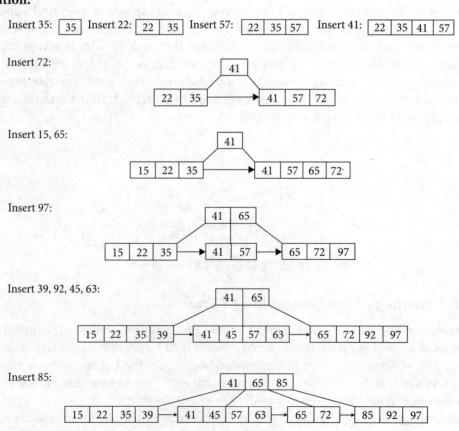

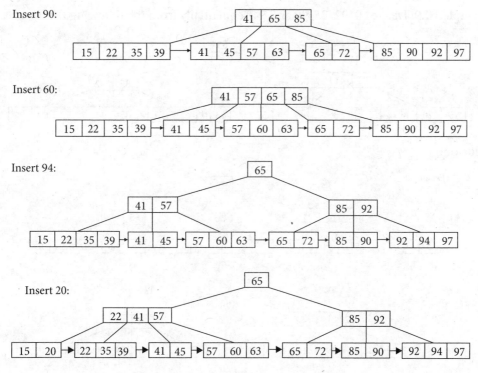

Figure 10.51   Steps to construct a B+ tree

10.16.2 Deleting Elements from a B+ Tree

To delete an element, we have to delete in two steps. First from a leaf node and then from an intermediate node, if it exists. After the deletion of an element from the leaf node if it is found that the node has more than or equal to the requisite minimum number of key values, then it is okay. Next we have to check if there is an entry in the intermediate node for that element. If it is there, the entry should be removed from the node and replaced with the copy of the left-most element of the immediate right child. But after deletion if the number of elements in the leaf node becomes less than the minimum number of key values, the node will be merged with its left or right siblings and the intermediate index key value will be removed from the parent node. This may cause underflow for the parent node. To fulfill the criteria then we have to borrow from the siblings of this parent node via its parent node (i.e. grandparent node) if they have more than the minimum number of keys. But if they do not have so, we need to merge the node with its left or right siblings along with the intervening element in the parent node. This may cause underflow to its parent node. The process of merging propagates upward and in extreme cases it may propagate up to the root, causing the height of the tree to decrease by one. Now we discuss several cases that may arise at the time of deletion. Consider the following examples:

Example 10.9: Delete 60, 92, 85, 90 and 94 sequentially from the following B+ tree.

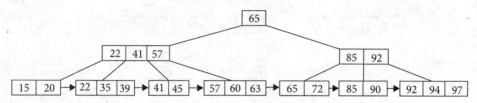

Solution:

Delete 60:

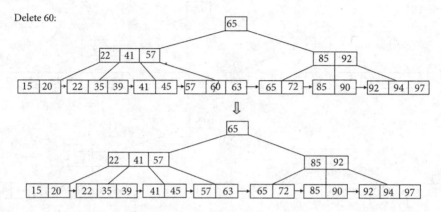

Figure 10.52   Deletion of node from a B+ tree (Case I)

This is the simplest case. The node where deletion occurs has the required minimum number of key values after deleting the element from the node and the element has no entry in intermediate nodes.

Delete 92 :

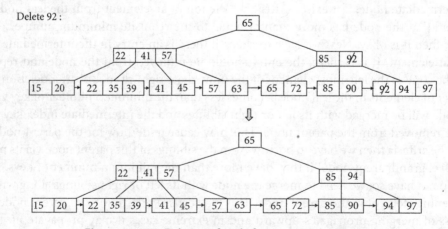

Figure 10.53   Deletion of node from a B+ tree (Case II)

In this case, after deleting the element from the node, it has the required minimum number of key values. So, there is no problem in deletion. But the element has an entry in its parent node. This entry needs to be removed. This vacant position will be replaced by 94, which is now the left-most element in its right child node.

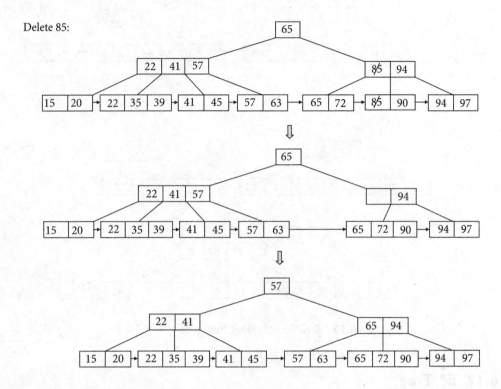

Figure 10.54   Deletion of node from a B+ tree (Case III)

After deleting 85, the node containing 85 becomes underflow. Thus we merge this node with its left sibling and remove the entry of 85 from the parent node. But now the parent node becomes underflow. To balance it again, we borrow an element from its sibling via the root. Thus 65 moves down to this node from the root and 57 moves up from its sibling to the root. The inorder successor node of 57 now becomes the inorder predecessor of 65 and maintains the search order.

Deletion of 90 does not violate any rule; thus simply its entry will be removed from the node. But deletion of 94 makes the corresponding node underflow. So, this node is merged with its left sibling, and also the entry of 94 has been removed from its parent node. But this makes the parent node underflow. So, we need to borrow an element from its sibling. But at this situation the node has a single sibling and it has exactly the minimum number of required elements. Thus borrowing is not possible and we merge the node with its sibling along with the parent.

Delete 90,94:

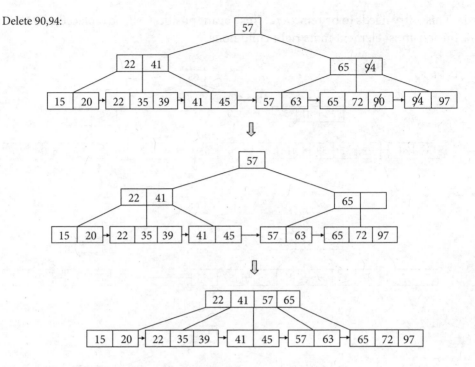

Figure 10.55 Deletion of nodes from a B+ tree (Case IV)

10.17 B* Tree

A B* tree is another variation of a B tree where each node except the root node is at least two-third full rather than half full. The basic idea to construct a B* tree is to reduce the splitting of nodes. In this tree, when a node gets full, instead of splitting the node, keys are shared between adjacent siblings, and when two adjacent siblings become full, both of them are merged and split into three. The insertion and deletion operations are somehow similar to a B tree but quite complex and that is why it has not become that much popular in comparison to a B tree or a B+ tree.

10.18 2–3 Tree

A 2–3 tree is nothing but a B tree of order 3. Each node of a B tree of order 3 can have either two children or three children. That is why sometimes it is called a 2–3 tree. Similarly, a B tree of order 4 is also known as a 2–3–4 tree as each node of this tree can have either 2, 3, or 4 children. The following is an example of a 2–3 tree.

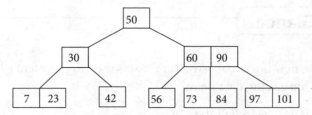

Figure 10.56   Example of a 2–3 tree

10.19 Trie Tree

A Trie tree is a special type of a search tree. The term 'Trie' comes from the word 'retrieval' because it is used for efficient retrieval of a key from a set of key values. Generally these keys are in the form of strings. Instead of storing key values in the nodes, it stores a single character and a set of pointers. If we think about a dictionary, i.e. words are constructed only with letters of the alphabet, the maximum number of pointers may be 26. To access a key the tree is traversed from the root through a specific path that matches with the prefix of a string up to the leaf node. Thus all the children of a particular node have a common prefix of string. That is why it is also known as a prefix tree. Application of a Trie tree is mainly found in string matching operations such as predictive text, auto completing a word, spell checking, etc. The following example shows the creation of a Trie tree:

Example 10.10: Construct a Trie tree for the following:

"A", "TO", "THE", "TED", "TEN", "I", "IN", "AND", "INN", "TEA", "THEN", "THAT".

Solution:

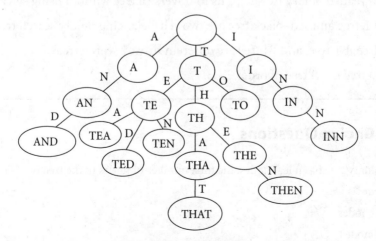

Figure 10.57   TRIE tree

Trees at a Glance

✓ A tree is a non-linear data structure that is used to represent a hierarchical relationship among data items.

✓ A forest is a collection of trees.

✓ A binary tree is a tree of degree 2, i.e. each node of this tree can have a maximum of two children.

✓ If each node of a binary tree has exactly zero (in case of leaf node) or two non-empty children, the binary tree is known as a strictly binary tree or 2-tree.

✓ A complete binary tree is a binary tree whose all levels, except possibly the last level, have the maximum number of nodes and at the last level all the nodes appear as far left as possible.

✓ A binary tree whose all levels have the maximum number of nodes is called a full binary tree.

✓ When every null sub-trees in a binary tree is replaced by some special nodes, it is known as an extended binary tree.

✓ A binary search tree (BST) is an ordered binary tree whose left sub-tree always possesses less value than its root node and right sub-tree always possess larger value than its root node.

✓ Preorder, inorder, and postorder are the three main traversal techniques.

✓ A threaded binary tree helps us to traverse a tree without using stack.

✓ AVL tree and red–black tree are two self-balancing binary search trees.

✓ B tree, B+ tree, and B* tree are different m-way search trees.

✓ 2–3 tree is a B tree of order 3.

Multiple Choice Questions

1. If a full binary tree has n leaf nodes, the total number of nodes in the tree is
   a) n nodes
   b) $\log_2 n$ nodes
   c) 2n-1 nodes
   d) 2n nodes

2. The maximum number of nodes of a binary tree of depth 5 is (considering depth of the root is 1)

   a) 32

   b) 63

   c) 31

   d) 16

3. The maximum number of nodes in a complete binary tree of depth k is

   a) 2^k

   b) 2k

   c) 2k-1

   d) None of these.

4. Which of the following need not be a binary tree?

   a) BST

   b) AVL Tree

   c) Heap

   d) B tree.

5. If a binary tree has n leaf nodes, the number of nodes of degree 2 in the tree is

   a) $\log_2 n$

   b) n

   c) n-1

   d) 2^n

6. If a binary tree has n internal nodes, the number of external nodes in a full binary tree is

   a) n

   b) n+1

   c) 2n

   d) 2n+1

7. Which of the following need not be a balance tree?

   a) BST

   b) AVL Tree

   c) Red–black Tree

   d) B Tree.

8. In an AVL tree, at what condition is balancing to be done?

   a) If the balance factor is greater than -1 or less than 1.

   b) If the balance factor is greater than -2 or less than 2.

   c) If the balance factor is greater than -2 or less than 1.

   d) If the balance factor is greater than 1 or less than -1.

9. If the preorder and postorder traversal of a binary tree generates the same output, the tree can have a maximum of
   a) Three nodes
   b) One node
   c) Two nodes
   d) Any number of nodes

10. The height of a complete binary tree with 32 nodes is
    a) 4
    b) 5
    c) 6
    d) 7

11. The root node is visited after visiting its child in
    a) Preorder Traversal
    b) Inorder Traversal
    c) Postorder Traversal
    d) Level order Traversal

12. To reconstruct a binary tree
    a) Both preorder and postorder traversal paths are required.
    b) Preorder, inorder, and postorder traversal paths are required.
    c) Inorder and any one between preorder and postorder traversal paths are required.
    d) Only preorder and inorder traversal paths are required.

13. Postorder traversal path helps us to identify the
    a) Root node
    b) Left sub-tree
    c) Right sub-tree
    d) Sibling nodes

14. The maximum height of a binary tree with n nodes is
    a) n
    b) 2^n
    c) $\log_2 n$
    d) $2^n - 1$

15. Which of the following is not a search tree?
    e) Binary Tree
    f) B Tree
    g) B+ Tree
    h) B* Tree

16. Which of the following need not be a balance tree?

a)   2–3 Tree

b)   AVL Tree

c)   Red–black Tree

d)   Threaded Binary Tree

17. Which of the following is a search tree

a)   Binary Tree

b)   Threaded Binary Tree

c)   Huffman Tree

d)   B+ Tree

18. All leaves of the tree must be at the same level in

a)   BST

b)   Threaded Binary Tree

c)   Huffman Tree

d)   2–3 Tree

19. It is found that all leaves are linked with a linked list in

a)   B Tree

b)   B+ Tree

c)   Red–black Tree

d)   2–3 Tree

20. In a B Tree of order m, the number of children of any internal node except the root is at least

a) $\dfrac{m}{2} - 1$

b) $\dfrac{m}{2}$

c) $\left\lceil \dfrac{m}{2} \right\rceil$

d) $\left\lfloor \dfrac{m}{2} \right\rfloor$

Review Exercises

1.   What is tree data structure?

2.   What do you mean by a binary tree?

3.   Discuss different types of binary trees.

4. Differentiate between a full binary tree and a complete binary tree.

5. What is a strictly binary tree?

6. Draw the expression tree for the following expressions:

   a) a + b * c – d / e

   b) a – (b – c * d) + (g / h – e) * f

   c) (a * b – c) % (d / e + f)

   d) 2 * (a + b) – 3 * (c – d)

7. What do you mean by a binary search tree?

8. How can the following tree be represented in memory when an array will be used?

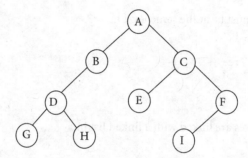

9. How can a binary tree be represented using a linked list? Explain with an example.

10. Explain the different traversal algorithms of a binary tree.

11. Write down the preorder, inorder, and postorder traversal paths for the following binary tree:

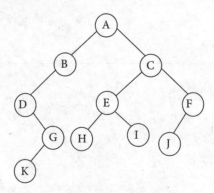

12. Consider the following sequence of binary tree traversals:

   Preorder: A B C E F G H D

   Inorde: A E C G F H B D

   Construct the binary tree.

13. Consider the following sequence of binary tree traversals:

Postorder: C G F I H E B D A

Inorder: C B G F E I H A D

Construct the binary tree.

14. Consider the following sequence of binary tree traversals:

Preorder: P Q R S T

Inorder: Q S T R P

Postorder: T S R Q P

Construct the binary tree.

15. Is it possible to reconstruct a binary tree with the preorder and postorder traversal sequences of a binary tree? Explain.

16. Write down the preorder, inorder, postorder, and level order traversal paths for the following binary tree:

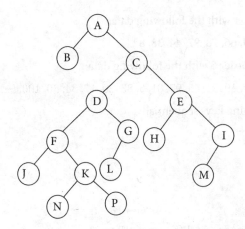

17. Compare and contrast between array representation and linked list representation of a binary tree.

18. Write a non-recursive algorithm to traverse a binary tree with preorder fashion.

19. Write a non-recursive algorithm to traverse a binary tree with postorder fashion.

20. Write a function to implement a non-recursive inorder traversal algorithm of a binary tree.

21. Write a function to search an element from a binary search tree whose leaves are all tied to a sentinel node.

22. Draw a BST with the following sequence of numbers:

57, 32, 45, 69, 65, 87, 5, 40, 43, 12, 80.

Then delete 5, delete 87, and delete 57 in the sequence.

23. Explain threaded binary tree with examples.

24. Define an AVL tree and give examples of AVL and non-AVL trees.

25. Draw an AVL tree with the following list of names by clearly mentioning the different rotations used and the balance factor of each node:

    Bikash, Palash, Ishan, Nimai, Lakshmi, Perth, Jasmin, Arijit, Himesh, Dibyendu.

26. Draw an AVL tree with the following sequence of numbers:

    52, 67, 72, 17, 9, 35, 21, 37, 24, 44.

    Next delete 35 from the above tree maintaining the AVL structure.

27. Draw an AVL tree with the following strings:

    MAR, NOV, MAY, AUG, APR, JAN, DEC, JUL, FEB, JUN, OCT, SEP.

28. What is a red–black tree? Draw a red–black tree from the following sequence of numbers:

    25, 37, 48, 12, 7, 33, 27, 15, 10.

29. What is B tree? Construct a B tree of order 3 with the following data:

    85, 69, 42, 12, 10, 37, 53, 71, 94, 99.

30. Draw a B tree of order 4 with the following data:

    35, 10, 52, 40, 27, 5, 19, 66, 78, 97, 44, 38, 82.

31. Construct a B tree of order 5 with the following data:

    25, 32, 10, 15, 67, 7, 11, 19, 22, 45, 97, 81, 5, 88, 20, 17, 34, 30, 100, 52.

    Then delete the following keys sequentially:

    i.   Delete 97

    ii. Delete 67

    iii. Delete 15

    iv. Delete 81.

32. What is a B+ tree ? How does it differ from a B tree?

33. Construct a B+ tree of order 4 with the following data:

    33, 88, 66, 44, 11, 22, 55, 77, 111, 99, 50, 70, 100.

34. Compare B tree, B+ tree, and B* tree.

35. Draw the Huffman tree for encoding the string 'successiveness'. How many bits are required to encode the string? Write down the encoded string too.

36. What do you mean by 2–3 tree? Explain with example.

37. Construct a Trie tree for the following names:

    Ram, Ramen, Ramesh, Suva, Samir, Subir, Rama, Samu, Raktim, Rakhi, Suvas, Subinoy.

Problems for Programming

1. Write a function to insert a node in a binary tree.

2. Write a function to insert a node in a binary search tree.

3. Write a function to delete a node from a binary search tree.

4. Write a function to find the average of the values of keys of a binary tree.

5. Write a function to count the number of nodes containing odd values in a binary tree.

6. Write a function to find the path from the root to a particular node in a binary search tree.

7. Write a function to calculate the balance factor of a node in a binary tree.

8. Write a function to insert a node in a preorder threaded binary tree.

9. Write a function to traverse preorderly in a preorder threaded binary tree.

10. Write a function to delete a node from a preorder threaded binary tree.

11. Write a function to implement the Huffman encoding.

12. Write a function to implement the Huffman decoding.

Heap

In this chapter we will discuss an important data structure: a heap. Though there are several variations of this data structure, such as binary heap, d-ary heap, B heap, Fibonacci heap, etc., we will discuss here the most popular heap data structure – the binary heap. In the following sections we will mention heap to indicate the binary heap.

11.1 Definition and Concept

Heap is a very important tree-based data structure. It is widely used in computer science. We can define a heap as a binary tree that has two properties. These are: *shape* property and *order* property. By shape property, a heap must be a complete binary tree. By order property, there are two types of heaps. One is *max* heap and the other is *min* heap. By default, a heap means it is a max heap. In max heap, the root should be larger than or equal to its children. There is no order in between the children. This is true also for its sub-trees. In min heap the order is the reverse. Here the root is smaller than or equal to any of its children. Thus the root of a max heap always provides the largest element of a list whereas the root of a min heap always provides the smallest element. As a heap is a complete binary tree, its maximum height is $O(\log_2 n)$ where n is the total number of elements. Thus both the insertion of new node and the deletion of an existing node can be done in $O(\log_2 n)$ time. Figure 11.1 shows a max heap and a min heap.

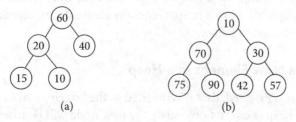

Figure 11.1 (a) Max heap and (b) Min heap

11.2 Representation of a Heap in Memory

Like other data structures, a heap also can be represented in memory using an array (or a list in Python) and a linked list. The main problem in tree representation using arrays is in wastage of memory. But in case of complete binary tree representation, that chance is almost nil. Moreover, we need not waste space for storing references of left and right children. So, using arrays (or lists in Python) we can represent the heap data structure efficiently.

As we discussed in the previous chapter, we can start storing from the zeroth index position or from index position 1 For simplicity we are starting from index position 1. So, root will be stored at index position 1 and the position of the immediate left and right children of the root will be calculated as

Position of left child   = 2 * Position of root

Position of right child = 2 * Position of root + 1

These rules are applicable also for sub-trees. The memory representation of the heaps shown in Figure 11.1 is shown in Figure 11.2.

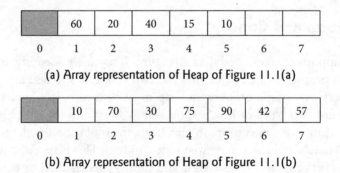

(a) Array representation of Heap of Figure 11.1(a)

(b) Array representation of Heap of Figure 11.1(b)

Figure 11.2   Array representation of Heap

11.3 Operations on a Heap

The main operations related to a heap are insertion of new elements into a heap and deletion of an existing node from a heap. Generally elements are accessed from the root of the heap. These are discussed below.

11.3.1 Inserting a New Element in a Heap

When a new element is inserted, first it is inserted as the last element in the heap if the heap is not empty. If the heap is empty, obviously the new node will be inserted as a root. Thus the shape property has been maintained. Now we need to check whether the order property has been established or not. If it is violated, we need to readjust the structure so that it again becomes a heap. To maintain the order property, first the newly inserted element is compared with its parent. If it is greater than its parent, values are exchanged among these two nodes. This readjustment operation moves upwards until the order property satisfies for all nodes or the root is reached. The following example illustrates the insertion operation in a heap.

Example 11.1: Construct a max heap from the following data:

> 12 15 10 20 18 4 27 16 23

Solution:

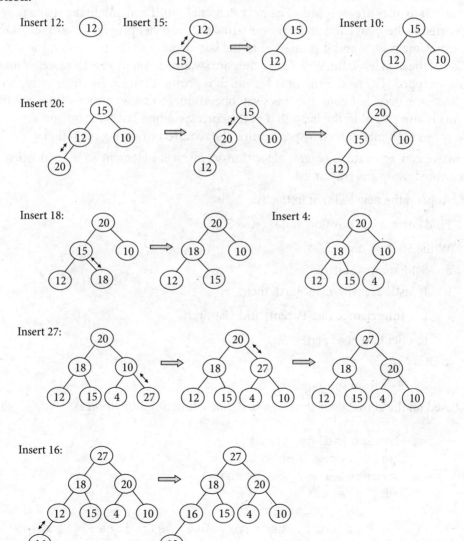

Insert 23:

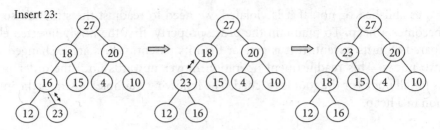

Figure 11.3 Stepwise construction of a heap

Explanation: Here, the first element is 12; thus it is inserted as the root. The next element is 15. To maintain the complete tree property it is inserted as the left child of 12. But 12 is less than 15; so, they are swapped. The next element is 10. To maintain the shape property it is inserted as the right child of the root. As 10 < 15, the order property is also maintained. The next element is 20 and it is inserted as the last element in the tree, i.e. at the leftmost position of the next level. But 20 > 12; so, they are swapped. Again 20 > 15 as well; thus they are also swapped. The next element is 18, which is greater than 15, and thus swapped. But 18 < 20; so, we need not continue this swap operation. In this way, each of the rest of the elements is also stored in the heap first at the corresponding last position and then order property has maintained by performing the required swapping operation.

Now we can generate a general algorithm to insert an element in a heap when it is implemented using an array or list.

1.   Append the new element in the list

2.   Find current last position and set it as Start

3.   While Start >1 do

    a.   Set Parent = Start/2

    b.   If List[Parent] < List[Start], then

        i.   Interchange List[Parent] and List[Start]

        ii.   Set Parent as Start

   c. Otherwise,

        i.   Exit from the loop.

Now based on the above algorithm we can define a function in Python as:

```python
def insert(self, item):
    self.items.append(item)
    start=len(self.items)-1
    while start>1:
        parent=start//2
        if self.items[parent]<self.items[start]:
            self.items[parent],self.items[start] =
```

```
                    self.items[start],self.items[parent]
            start=parent
    else:
            break
```

11.3.2 Deleting an Element from a Heap

In a heap, deletion takes place always from the root. But to maintain the shape property, i.e. to retain it as a complete tree, we always physically delete the last element and obviously before deleting the last element it should be copied to the root. Now we need to check whether in any position the order property is violated or not. For that we start from the root and check whether the root is greater than both of its children. If not, the root is swapped with its largest child. Next this child node is compared against its children, and so on. This process continues up to the leaf. The following example illustrates the deletion operation in heap:

Example 11.2: Delete an element from the following heap.

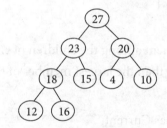

Solution:

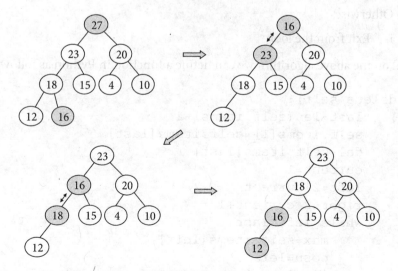

Figure 11.4 Stepwise deletion of a node from a heap

Explanation: Deletion is done always from the root of the heap. So, the root, 27, is deleted here. To delete the root, first we replace the value of the root with the value of the last node. Thus 27 is replaced by 16 and the last node, i.e. the node originally containing the value 16, is now physically deleted. Next we have to check the order property. So, the node 16 is compared with its children. Between the children, 23 is larger and it is also larger than 16. Thus, 16 and 23 are swapped. Next, 16 is compared with 18 and 15. As 18 is greater than 16, they are interchanged. Now 16 has only one child and it is smaller than it. So, we need not do anything more and we get the final tree.

The general algorithm to delete an element from a heap may be defined as:

1. Find current last position and set it as Last

2. Replace the value of the root with the value of Last position

3. Now delete the last element

4. Set Current = 1

5. Set Left = 2 * Current

6. Set Right = 2 * Current + 1

7. While Left < Last, do

    a. Find the largest element among the children of Current

    b. If Current is smaller than the largest member of the children, then

        i. Swap them

        ii. Set largest child as Current

        iii. Based on the new value of Current recalculate Left and Right

    c. Otherwise,

        i. Exit from the loop.

Now based on the above algorithm we can define a function in Python as follows:

```python
def delete(self):
        last=len(self.items)-1
        self.items[1]=self.items[last]
        del self.items[last]
        current=1
        left=2*current
        right=2*current+1
        while left<last:
            max=self.items[left]
            posn=left
            if right<last and self.items[right]>max:
                max=self.items[right]
```

```
                posn=right
            if self.items[current]<self.items[posn]:
                self.items[current],self.items[posn] =
                        self.items[posn],self.items[current]
                current=posn
                left=2*current
                right=2*current+1
            else:
                break
```

Here is a complete program to demonstrate the operations of a heap.

Program 11.1: Write a program to demonstrate the operations of a heap.

```
# Program to demonstrate the operations of a Heap.

class Heap:
    def __init__(self):
        self.items = [0]

    def isEmpty(self):
        return len(self.items) == 1

    def insert(self, item):
        self.items.append(item)
        start=len(self.items)-1
        while start>1:
            parent=start//2
            if self.items[parent]<self.items[start]:
                self.items[parent],self.items[start] =
                        self.items[start],self.items[parent]
                start=parent
            else:
                break

    def delete(self):
        last=len(self.items)-1
        self.items[1]=self.items[last]
        del self.items[last]
        current=1
        left=2*current
        right=2*current+1
        while left<last:
```

```
            max=self.items[left]
            posn=left
            if right<last and self.items[right]>max:
                max=self.items[right]
                posn=right
            if self.items[current]<self.items[posn]:
                self.items[current],self.items[posn] =
                        self.items[posn],self.items[current]
                current=posn
                left=2*current
                right=2*current+1
            else:
                break

    def display(self):
        count=len(self.items)-1
        print()
        print("------"*count+"-")
        for i in range(1,count+1):
            print('|',format(self.items[i],'>3'), end="
                                                       ")

        print("|")
        print("------"*count+"-")

h=Heap()
while(True):
    print("\nPROGRAM TO IMPLEMENT HEAP ")
    print("=========================")
    print("\t1. Insert")
    print("\t2. Delete")
    print("\t3. Display")
    print("\t4. Exit")
    print("=========================")
    choice=int(input("Enter your Choice : "))
    if choice==1 :
        num=int(input("Enter the Data: "))
        h.insert(num)
    elif choice==2 :
        if h.isEmpty() :
            print("Heap Underflow")
        else :
            h.delete();
```

```
                  print("Item deleted successfully")
           elif choice==3 :
               if h.isEmpty() :
                   print("Heap is Empty")
               else :
                   h.display()
           elif choice==4 :
               print("\nQuiting.......")
               break
           else:
               print("Invalid choice. Please Enter Correct
                                                    Choice")
               continue
```

11.4 Applications of Heap

Heap is mostly used in implementation of priority queues. Again, priority queue is further used in implementation of several graph algorithms such as Dijkstra's algorithm to find the shortest path in a graph, Prim's algorithm to find minimal spanning tree, etc. Another important use is found in implementation of *heap sort* algorithm. In the following section we will discuss the implementation of a priority queue using heap. Implementation of heap sort is discussed in Chapter 13.

11.4.1 Implementing a Priority Queue Using Heap

We have already discussed the priority queue in Chapter 9. There we have also discussed a number of ways of implementing this important data structure. But here we are going to discuss the most efficient implementation of a priority queue, which is using a heap. Because insertion and deletion operations in a heap are done in a running time of $O(\log_2 n)$ whereas for an array or a linked list representation, though the deletion operation is done with the running time complexity of $O(1)$, for the insertion operation it is $O(n)$.

We know that in priority queue implementation every element is associated with some priority and the highest priority element leaves the queue first. Thus when we use a heap to implement a priority queue, the enqueue operation is nothing but the insertion operation in a heap where the heap will be formed on the basis of priority of the element. Whether we create a max heap or a min heap depends on the nature of the priority value. If larger value indicates higher priority, then we need to create a max heap. But if smaller value represents the higher priority, we have to create a min heap. For the dequeue operation we simply use the deletion operation of a heap with a single addition, which is that it returns the value of the root node. The peek operation is very simple; it returns the root node without deleting it. The following program shows how a priority queue can be implemented efficiently using a heap. Here the larger value is considered as higher priority and thus max heap has been used.

Program 11.2: Write a program to demonstrate the operations of a priority queue.

```python
# PRGD11_2: Program to implement Priority Queue Using Heap

class Node :
    def __init__ ( self, Newdata, NewPriority ) :
        self.data = Newdata
        self.priority= NewPriority


class Heap:
    def __init__ (self):
        self.items = [0]

    def isEmpty(self):
        return len(self.items) == 1

    def enqueue(self, item):
        self.items.append(item)
        start=len(self.items)-1
        while start>1:
            parent=start//2
            if self.items[parent].priority<self.
                                items[start].priority:
                self.items[parent],self.items[start]=
                    self.items[start],self.items[parent]
                start=parent
            else:
                break

    def dequeue(self):
        temp=self.items[1]
        last=len(self.items)-1
        self.items[1]=self.items[last]
        del self.items[last]
        current=1
        left=2*current
        right=2*current+1
        while left<last:
            max=self.items[left].priority
            posn=left
```

```python
                if right<last and self.items[right].
                                            priority>max:
                    max=self.items[right].priority
                    posn=right
                if self.items[current].priority<self.
                                    items[posn].priority:
                    self.items[current],self.items[posn]=
                        self.items[posn],self.items[current]
                    current=posn
                    left=2*current
                    right=2*current+1
            else:
                break
        return temp

    def peek(self):
        return self.items[1]
    def display(self):
        count=len(self.items)-1
        print()
        print("---------"*count+"-")
        for i in range(1,count+1):
            print('|',format(str(self.items[i].data)+
        "("+str(self.items[i].priority)+")",'>6'), end=" ")
        print("|")
        print("---------"*count+"-")

q=Heap()
while(True):
    print("\nPROGRAM TO IMPLEMENT PRIORITY QUEUE")
    print("==================================")
    print("\t1. Enqueue")
    print("\t2. Dequeue")
    print("\t3. Peek")
    print("\t4. Display")
    print("\t5. Exit")
    print("==================================")
    choice=int(input("Enter your Choice : "))
    if choice==1 :
        num=int(input("Enter the Data: "))
        prio=int(input("Enter Priority value: "))
        newNode=Node(num,prio)
        q.enqueue(newNode)
```

```
elif choice==2 :
    if q.isEmpty() :
        print("Queue Underflow")
    else :
        popNode=q.dequeue()
        print("Item dequeued = ",popNode.data," with
                        Priority ", popNode.priority)
elif choice==3 :
    if q.isEmpty() :
        print("Queue Underflow")
    else :
        popNode=q.peek()
        print("Item at the front of the Queue =
    ",popNode.data," with Priority ",popNode.priority)
elif choice==4 :
    if q.isEmpty() :
        print("Queue is Empty")
    else :
        q.display()
elif choice==5 :
    print("\nQuiting.......")
    break
else:
    print("Invalid choice. Please Enter Correct
                                Choice")

    continue
```

Heap at a Glance

- ✓ A heap is a complete binary tree which must satisfy the order property.

- ✓ By order property there are two types of heap – Max heap and Min heap.

- ✓ In max heap, root should be larger than or equal to its children.

- ✓ In min heap, the root is smaller than or equal to any of its child.

- ✓ The time complexity of insertion and deletion operation on heap is O(log2n), where n is the number of elements in a heap.

- ✓ In memory, heap can be represented using array as well as linked list. In Python, heap is better represented using in-built list data structure.

- ✓ Efficient use of heap is found in representation of priority queue and heap sort.

Multiple Choice Questions

1. If the following array represents a heap, the largest element in the heap is

A	B	C	D	E	F	G

   a) A

   b) G

   c) Cannot say

   d) None of these

2. If the following array represents a min heap, the smallest element in the heap is

A	B	C	D	E	F	G

   a) A

   b) G

   c) Cannot say

   d) None of these

3. If the following array represents a heap, the smallest element in the heap is

A	B	C	D	E	F	G

   a) A

   b) Any one among D, E, F, and G

   c) Cannot say

   d) Either B or C

4. The height of a heap of n elements is

   a) n

   b) n–1

   c) $\log_2 n$

   d) n/2

5. The worst case time complexity to search for an element from a heap of n elements is

   a) O(n)

   b) $O(n^2)$

   c) $O(\log_2 n)$

   d) $O(n \log_2 n)$

6. A heap is a
   a) binary tree
   b) complete tree
   c) Both (a) and (b)
   d) None of these

7. A heap can be used as
   a) stack
   b) a decreasing order array
   c) priority queue
   d) an increasing order array

8. Consider a heap has been implemented using an array. Which of the following arrays perfectly represents a min heap?
   a) 10, 18, 20, 15, 25, 27, 30
   b) 10, 18, 15, 30, 25, 27, 20
   c) 10, 20, 25, 18, 15, 30, 27
   d) 10, 20, 18, 25, 27, 15, 30

9.

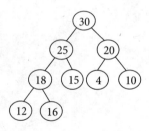

10. If we delete the root node of the above heap, by which value the root will be replaced?
    a) 4
    b) 16
    c) 12
    d) 10

11. Which data structure does this array represent?

| 25 | 20 | | 18 | 12 | 10 | 7 |

   a) Binary tree
   b) Binary search tree
   c) Heap
   d) None of these

Review Exercises

1. Define a heap.

2. Differentiate between max heap and min heap.

3. Write an algorithm to insert elements into an empty heap.

4. Construct a max heap from the following data:

   23 72 35 49 62 87 12 58 93 76

5. Delete three consecutive elements from the heap constructed in question no. 4.

6. Construct a min heap from the following data:

   82 45 70 35 18 49 27 2 23 15

7. Delete the root from the heap constructed in question no. 6.

8. Does the sequence "57, 32, 47, 22, 17, 38, 42, 20, 9" represent a max heap?

9. Does the sequence "5, 12, 27, 22, 17, 38, 42, 28, 39, 19" represent a min heap?

10. How does a heap differ from a binary search tree?

11. What is a priority queue? How can a heap be used to implement a priority queue?

12. Illustrate the insertion operation for a min heap.

13. Illustrate the deletion operation for a min heap.

14. Discuss the utility of the heap data structure.

Problems for Programming

1. Write a function to insert a new node in a min heap.

2. Write a function to delete a node from a min heap.

3. Write a menu driven program to implement a min heap.

4. Write a menu driven program to implement a priority queue.

5. Write a function to find the largest node in a min heap.

6. Write a function to find the smallest node in a max heap.

7. Write a function to check whether a binary tree is a heap or not.

Graphs

In this chapter we will discuss another non-linear data structure: graph. We have already discussed a non-linear data structure, tree, where we found the hierarchical relation among nodes. Every parent node may have zero or more child nodes, i.e. the relationship is one-to-many. In graph, we will find that every node may be connected to any node, i.e. the relationship is many-to-many. Here we will discuss various terms related to a graph and then its representation in memory. We will also discuss the operations on a graph as well as its different applications.

12.1 Definition and Concept

A graph is a very important non-linear data structure in computer science. A graph is a non-linear data structure that basically consists of some vertices and edges. We can define a graph, G, as an ordered set of vertices and edges, i.e. $G = \{v, e\}$, where v represents the set of vertices, which is also called nodes, and e represents the edges, i.e. the connectors between the vertices. Figure 12.1 shows a graph where the vertex set $v = \{v1, v2, v3, v4, v5, v6\}$ and the edge set $e = \{e1, e2, e3, e4, e5, e6, e7, e8, e9\}$, i.e. the graph has 6 vertices and 9 edges.

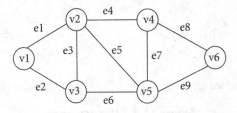

Figure 12.1 A graph

12.2 Terminology

In this section we will discuss the various terms related to graphs.

Directed graph: If the edges of a graph are associated with some directions, the graph is known as a directed graph or digraph. If the direction of an edge is from v_i to v_j, it means we can traverse the nodes from v_i to v_j but not from v_j to v_i. An edge may contain directions in both sides. Then we may traverse from v_i to v_j as well as from v_j to v_i. Figure 12.2 shows a directed graph.

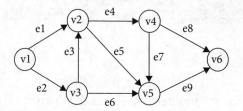

Figure 12.2   Directed graph

Undirected graph: When there is no direction associated with an edge, the graph is known as undirected graph. In case of undirected graph, if there is an edge between the vertex v_i and v_j, the graph can be traversed in both directions, i.e. from v_i to v_j as well as from v_j to v_i. The graph shown in Figure 12.1 is an undirected graph.

Weighted Graph: When the edges of a graph are associated with some value, it is known as a weighted graph. This value may represent the distance between two places or may represent the cost of transportation from one to place to another, etc. A weighted graph may be of two types: directed weighted graph and undirected weighted graph. If the edge contains weight as well as direction, it is known as a directed weighted graph but if the edge contains weight but there is no direction associated with that edge, it is known as an undirected weighted graph. Figure 12.3 shows both directed weighted graph and undirected weighted graph.

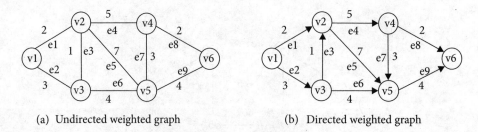

(a) Undirected weighted graph   (b) Directed weighted graph

Figure 12.3   Directed graph

Adjacent vertex: If an edge, e, connects two vertices, v_i and v_j, then v_i and v_j are called adjacent vertices or neighbors. In Figure 12.1, v1 and v2 are two adjacent vertices.

Degree of a vertex: In an undirected graph the number of edges connected to a vertex is known as the degree of that vertex. In Figure 12.3(a) the degree of vertex v1 is 2 and that of v2 is 4. In case of a directed graph, the number of edges originating from a particular vertex is known as the out-degree of that vertex and the number of edges incident to a particular vertex is known as the in-degree of that vertex. Thus, in Figure 12.3(b), the in-degree of vertex v1 is 0 but the out-degree of vertex v1 is 2. The in-degree of vertex v2 is 2 and the out-degree of vertex v2 is 2.

Isolated vertex: An isolated vertex is a vertex whose degree is 0.

Source: The vertex whose in-degree is 0 but out-degree is greater than 0 is known as a source. In Figure 12.3(b) v1 is a source vertex.

Sink: The vertex whose in-degree is greater than 0 but out-degree is 0 is known as a sink. In Figure 12.3(b) v6 is a sink vertex.

Path: A path is a sequence of vertices that can be traversed sequentially from one point of the graph to another point. In Figure 12.3, v1-> v2-> v5-> v6 is a path. v1-> v3-> v5-> v6 is also a path. If the end points of a path are the same, the path is called a **closed path**. If all the vertices in a path are distinct, the path is called **simple**.

Cycle: If a path ends at a vertex from which the path started, the path is called a **cycle**. In Figure 12.3(a), v1-> v2-> v3-> v1 is a cycle or v1-> v2-> v4-> v6-> v5-> v3-> v1 is another cycle. But there is no cycle in Figure 12.3(b).

Connected graph: If there is a path between any two vertices of a graph, then the graph is known as a connected graph. In connected graph there will be no isolated vertex.

Complete graph: A graph is said to be complete if every two vertices in that graph are adjacent. In a complete graph, if there are n number of vertices, there should be n(n-1)/2 edges.

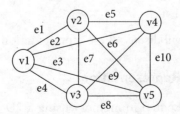

Figure 12.4 Complete graph

Multiple edges: If there are multiple edges between the same two vertices, then it is called multiple edges or parallel edges. Figure 12.5 shows multiple edges, e1, e2, and e3 between the vertices, v1 and v2.

Multigraph: A graph that has multiple edges is known as a multigraph.

Loop: If any edge has the same end points, then it is called a loop or self-loop. In Figure 12.5, e7 is a loop or self-loop.

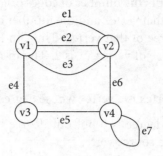

Figure 12.5 Multigraph with self-loop

Cut vertex: If there is any such vertex whose deletion makes the graph disconnected, such a vertex is known as a cut vertex.

12.3 Representation of a Graph

Like other data structures a graph is also represented in memory using an array or a linked list. However, to represent a graph in memory, a 2D array is required. There are two ways by which a graph can be represented. These are:

- Using adjacency matrix
- Using incidence matrix

To represent a graph using a linked list there are also two ways. These are:

- Using adjacency list
- Using adjacency multi-list

In the following sections we will discuss these representation.

12.3.1 Adjacency Matrix Representation

An adjacency matrix is represented in memory using a 2D array whose number of rows and columns are the same and is equal to the number of vertices in the graph. Rows and columns are labeled with the name of the vertices. If the name of the 2D array is arr, then $arr[v_i][v_j] = 1$ represents that there is an edge from the vertex v_i to vertex v_j. In case of an undirected graph, suppose there is an edge between v_i and v_j. It indicates we have an edge from the vertex v_i to vertex v_j as well as from v_j to v_i. Thus both $arr[v_i][v_j] = 1$ and $arr[v_j][v_i] = 1$; and we get a symmetric matrix. In case of a weighted graph, the value of $arr[v_i][v_j]$ is the weight of the corresponding edge. Hence, if the weight of the edge (v_i, v_j) is w, then the expression will be arr[v_i][v_j]=w. In the following figure, adjacency matrices of an undirected graph, a directed graph, an undirected weighted graph, and a directed weighted graph have been shown.

	v1	v2	v3	v4	v5	v6
v1	0	1	1	0	0	0
v2	1	0	1	1	1	0
v3	1	1	0	0	1	0
v4	0	1	0	0	1	1
v5	0	1	1	1	0	1
v6	0	0	0	1	1	0

(a) Adjacency matrix of the undirected graph shown in Figure 12.1

	v1	v2	v3	v4	v5	v6
v1	0	1	1	0	0	0
v2	0	0	0	1	1	0
v3	0	1	0	0	1	0
v4	0	0	0	0	1	1
v5	0	0	0	0	0	1
v6	0	0	0	0	0	0

(b) Adjacency matrix of the directed graph shown in Figure 12.2

	v1	v2	v3	v4	v5	v6
v1	0	2	3	0	0	0
v2	2	0	1	5	7	0
v3	3	1	0	0	4	0
v4	0	5	0	0	3	2
v5	0	7	4	3	0	4
v6	0	0	0	2	4	0

(c) Adjacency matrix of the undirected weighted graph shown in Figure 12.3(a)

	v1	v2	v3	v4	v5	v6
v1	0	2	3	0	0	0
v2	0	0	0	5	7	0
v3	0	1	0	0	4	0
v4	0	0	0	0	3	2
v5	0	0	0	0	0	4
v6	0	0	0	0	0	0

(d) Adjacency matrix of the directed weighted graph shown in Figure 12.3(b)

Figure 12.6   Adjacency matrix representation

The advantage of this representation is that the implementation is very easy and searching an edge is very fast if the adjacent vertices of the edge are known. The disadvantage is that it consumes much space. Specially, if the graph is sparse, the wastage is much more.

12.3.2 Incidence Matrix Representation

An incidence matrix is also represented in memory using a 2D array. But in this representation, rows of the matrix represent the vertices of the graph, and columns of the matrix represent the edges. In this representation if an edge is incident to a vertex, the corresponding cell value is set to 1. Suppose we have a 2D array, say, arr, and an edge e_i is incident to the vertex v_i. Then the value of arr[v_j][e_i] will be 1. In case of a directed graph, if an edge e_i starts from vertex v_i and is incident to vertex v_j, then arr[v_i][e_i] will be 1 and arr[v_j][e_i] will be -1. In Figure 12.7, incidence matrices of an undirected graph, a directed graph, an undirected weighted graph, and a directed weighted graph have been shown.

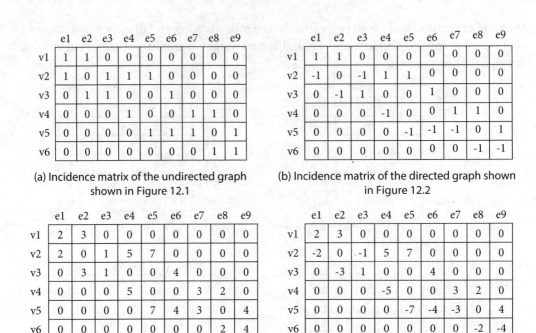

	e1	e2	e3	e4	e5	e6	e7	e8	e9
v1	1	1	0	0	0	0	0	0	0
v2	1	0	1	1	1	0	0	0	0
v3	0	1	1	0	0	1	0	0	0
v4	0	0	0	1	0	0	1	1	0
v5	0	0	0	0	1	1	1	0	1
v6	0	0	0	0	0	0	0	1	1

(a) Incidence matrix of the undirected graph shown in Figure 12.1

	e1	e2	e3	e4	e5	e6	e7	e8	e9
v1	1	1	0	0	0	0	0	0	0
v2	-1	0	-1	1	1	0	0	0	0
v3	0	-1	1	0	0	1	0	0	0
v4	0	0	0	-1	0	0	1	1	0
v5	0	0	0	0	-1	-1	-1	0	1
v6	0	0	0	0	0	0	0	-1	-1

(b) Incidence matrix of the directed graph shown in Figure 12.2

	e1	e2	e3	e4	e5	e6	e7	e8	e9
v1	2	3	0	0	0	0	0	0	0
v2	2	0	1	5	7	0	0	0	0
v3	0	3	1	0	0	4	0	0	0
v4	0	0	0	5	0	0	3	2	0
v5	0	0	0	0	7	4	3	0	4
v6	0	0	0	0	0	0	0	2	4

(c) Incidence matrix of the undirected weighted graph shown in Figure 12.3(a)

	e1	e2	e3	e4	e5	e6	e7	e8	e9
v1	2	3	0	0	0	0	0	0	0
v2	-2	0	-1	5	7	0	0	0	0
v3	0	-3	1	0	0	4	0	0	0
v4	0	0	0	-5	0	0	3	2	0
v5	0	0	0	0	-7	-4	-3	0	4
v6	0	0	0	0	0	0	0	-2	-4

(d) Incidence matrix of the directed weighted graph shown in Figure 12.3(b)

Figure 12.7 Incidence matrix representation

12.3.3 Adjacency List Representation

An adjacency list is an array of linked lists. In this representation, first we need to declare an array of reference in which each cell contains the references of linked lists. The array size should be the same as the total number of vertices in the graph. Each cell in the array represents a vertex and contains the reference of a linked list. Each node of the linked list stores the information about the adjacent vertices of the corresponding vertex. In case of an unweighted graph, only names of the adjacent vertices are stored, but for a weighted graph, corresponding weights are also stored within the linked list. Consider the graph shown in Figure 12.1. As the number of vertices in that graph is 6, to construct the adjacency list first we need to declare an array (or list in case of Python) of size 6. Now the vertex v1 has two adjacent vertices – v2 and v3. Thus a linked list is needed to be created containing v2 and v3 and the reference of the first node of the list will be stored within the cell that will represent v1. Similarly, the cell for v2 contains the reference of a linked list that contains 4 nodes for storing v1, v3, v4, and v5. In this way the entire list will be created. In the Figure 12.8, the adjacency lists of an undirected graph, a directed graph, an undirected weighted graph, and a directed weighted graph have been shown.

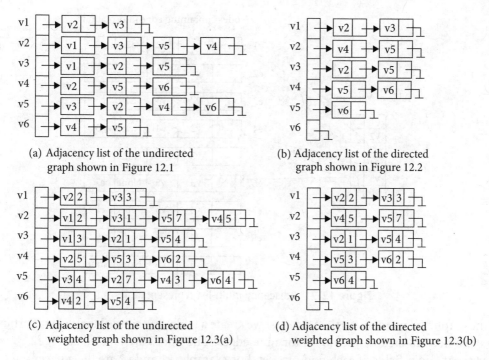

Figure 12.8   Adjacency list representation

The advantage of an adjacency list is that it requires less space in comparison to an adjacency matrix representation.

12.3.4 Adjacency Multi-list Representation

An adjacency multi-list representation is an edge-based representation rather than vertex-based. In this representation, there are two parts. One is a table containing information about the vertices and other is a set of linked lists containing information about the edges. For each vertex, there is an entry in the vertex table and for each entry a reference is stored to point to another node of a linked list which stores the information about the adjacent edge. This node structure contains five fields.

M	v_i	v_j	Link fo v_i	Link fo v_j

Here, the first field M is a single bit representation which denotes whether the edge is visited or not. The next two fields are v_i and v_j, which are the two adjacent vertices of the edge. The last two fields are 'Link for v_i' and 'Link for v_j', which are the references of the nodes that have an edge incident on v_i and v_j, respectively. Now to understand how the multi-list is created, consider the undirected graph of Figure 12.1.

Nodes containing edge information

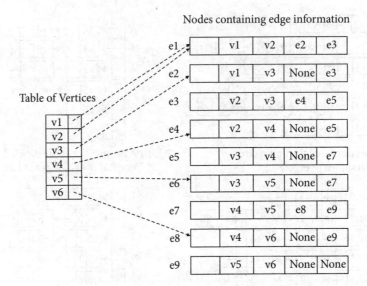

Figure 12.9 Adjacency multi-list representation

In the graph, there are six vertices. So, first we create a table containing labels of six vertices. Next we need to create nine nodes for nine edges. The nodes are labeled as e1, e2, ... e9. Next the v_i and v_j fields of each node are set. For example, v1 and v2 are the adjacent nodes of the edge e1. Thus v_i and v_j fields of e1 are set as v1 and v2, respectively. Similarly for e2, these values are v1 and v3. Now to set the link fields we need to look down. Consider the node for e1 first. To set the link for v1, we look below and find v1 is at e2 and v2 is at e3. Thus in the Link for v1 field e2 is set and in the Link for v2 field e3 is set. In the next node e2, to set the link for v1, we look below but do not find any entry for v1. Thus in the Link for v1 field of e2, None is set. The second vertex of e2, i.e. v3, has an entry in the node e3. Hence, e3 is set in the Link for v3 field. In this way all the values are set. Now we update the reference field in the vertices table. As v1 and v2 first appear in the node e1, both v1 and v2 point to e1. v3 first appeared in e2. So, v3 points to e2. Similarly, we find that v4, v5, and v6 first appear in e4, e6, and e8 nodes, respectively. Thus they point to the corresponding node in the vertices table and we get the above adjacency multi-list.

From the above adjacency multi-list we can easily find the adjacency list for the vertices as shown below.

Vertex	List of edges
v1	e1, e2
v2	e1, e3, e4
v3	e2, e3, e5, e6
v4	e4, e5, e7 e8
v5	e6, e7
v6	e8, e9

12.4 Operations on a Graph

In this section we will discuss how we can insert a vertex in a graph or how a new edge can be added or how a vertex or edge can be deleted, several traversing algorithms, printing a graph, etc.

12.4.1 Insertion Operation

The insertion operation means we can insert a vertex or an edge into a graph. In adjacency matrix representation we have to declare a 2D array. In Python it may be a list of lists. Now, if we want to insert a new vertex we need to insert a new row as well as a new column whereas insertion of a new edge is quite simple. If the graph is undirected and the adjacent vertices of the edge is v_i and v_j, then we have to consider an edge from v_i to v_j and another from v_j to v_i. Thus if the array/list name is arr, we have to set $arr[v_i][v_j] = 1$ as well as $arr[v_j][v_i] = 1$. If the graph is a weighted graph and the weight of the edge is w, then instead of 1, it will be $arr[v_i][v_j] = w$ and $arr[v_j][v_i] = w$. For a directed graph if the source vertex is v_i and end vertex is v_j, then only set $arr[v_i][v_j] = 1$ and for a weighted graph set $arr[v_i][v_j] = w$.

In an adjacency list representation we need to declare an array of references. We may also include an extra field to store the name of the vertices. The size of the array is the same as the number of vertices in the graph. If we insert a new vertex, the array size increases by one. To store adjacent vertices of a particular vertex, we have to create a linked list whose every node contains the vertex name. If the graph is a weighted graph, then the node contains an extra field to store the corresponding weight. Reference of the first node of the linked list is stored at the corresponding reference position of the vertex in the array. Now if a new edge is added in an undirected graph and the adjacent vertex of the edge is v_i and v_j, then a new node containing v_j is inserted in the linked list of the vertex v_i and another new node containing v_i is inserted in the linked list of the vertex v_j. In case of a directed graph only a single new node containing the end vertex name is inserted in the linked list of the source vertex. For a weighted graph, the weight of the edge is also stored within the node.

12.4.2 Deletion Operation

The deletion operation includes deletion of vertices as well as deletion of edges from a graph. In an adjacency matrix representation, the deletion of a vertex causes the deletion of the corresponding entire row as well as the entire column. To delete an edge whose adjacent vertices are v_i and v_j from an undirected graph, we have to set $arr[v_i][v_j] = 0$ as well as $arr[v_j][v_i] = 0$. In case of a directed graph, if the source vertex is v_i and the end vertex is v_j, we have to set only $arr[v_i][v_j] = 0$.

In an adjacency list representation, if we delete a vertex v, first we have to delete all the nodes containing v; then we delete the entry of vertex v from the list. To delete an edge from an directed adjacency list, simply find the source vertex in the list; traverse through the corresponding list and delete the node containing the end vertex. For an undirected graph do the same operation again considering the source vertex as the end vertex and vice versa.

Here are some complete programs showing these insertion and deletion operations for different types of graphs. The first program is an implementation of an undirected graph using an adjacency matrix.

Program 12.1: Write a program to implement a graph using an adjacency matrix.

```python
# PRGD12_1: Program to implement a graph using adjacency
# matrix

class Graph:
    def __init__(self,size=0):
        self.size=size
        self.items = [[0 for i in range(size)] for j in
                                              range(size)]

    def isEmpty(self):
        return self.size == 0

    def insert_vertex(self):            #Function to insert a
                                                    #vertex
        for i in range(self.size):
            self.items[i].append(0)
        self.items.append([0 for i in range(self.
                                              size+1)])
        self.size+=1

    def insert_edge(self, vi, vj):   #Function to insert
                                                #an edge
        self.items[vi][vj]=1
        self.items[vj][vi]=1
    def delete_vertex(self,v):              #Function to
                                         #delete a vertex
        if v>=self.size:
            print("vertex not found..")
            return
        for i in range(self.size):
            del self.items[i][v]
        del self.items[v]
        self.size-=1
        print("Vertex Removed")
```

```
    def delete_edge(self,vi, vj):   #Function to delete
                                    #an edge
        if vi>=self.size or vj>=self.size:
            print("vertex not found..")
            return
        self.items[vi][vj]=0
        self.items[vj][vi]=0
        print("Edge Removed")


    def display(self):
        for i in range(self.size):
            print("v{}|".format(i),end=' ')
            for j in range(self.size):
                print(self.items[i][j],end=' ')
            print("|")


g=Graph()
while(True):
    print("\nPROGRAM TO IMPLEMENT GRAPH USING ADJACENCY
                                    MATRIX")
    print("=============================================")
    print("\t1. Insert a Vertex")
    print("\t2. Insert an edge")
    print("\t3. Remove a vertex")
    print("\t4. Remove an edge")
    print("\t5. Display")
    print("\t6. Exit")
    print("=============================================")
    choice=int(input("Enter your Choice : "))
    if choice==1 :
        g.insert_vertex()
    elif choice==2 :
        vs = int(input("Enter Source Vertex:"))
        ve = int(input("Enter End Vertex:"))
        g.insert_edge(vs,ve)
    elif choice==3 :
        v = int(input("Enter the Vertex:"))
        g.delete_vertex(v)
    elif choice==4 :
        vs = int(input("Enter Source Vertex:"))
        ve = int(input("Enter End Vertex:"))
        g.delete_edge(vs,ve)
```

```
    elif choice==5 :
        if g.isEmpty() :
            print("Graph is Empty")
        else :
            g.display()
    elif choice==6 :
        print("\nQuiting.......")
        break
    else:
        print("Invalid choice. Please Enter Correct
                                        Choice")
        continue
```

The above program is on an undirected graph. For a directed graph the program is almost the same, the only difference being that we need to consider only v_i to v_j, not v_j to v_i. For a weighted graph, instead of 1, we have to set the corresponding weight, w.

The next two programs show the implementation of a graph using an adjacency list. The first one is on an undirected graph and the second one is on a weighted directed graph.

Program 12.2: Write a program to implement an undirected graph using adjacency list.

```
# PRGD12_2: Program to implement an undirected graph using
# adjacency list

class Node:
    def __init__(self,vName):
        self.vName=vName
        self.next=None

class Graph:
    def __init__(self):
        self.size=0
        self.items = []

    def isEmpty(self):
        return self.size == 0

    def insert_vertex(self,v):
        self.items.append([v,None])
        self.size+=1
```

```python
def insert_edge(self, vi, vj):
    for i in range(self.size):
        if self.items[i][0]==vi:
            newNode=Node(vj)
            if self.items[i][1] is None:
                self.items[i][1]=newNode
            else:
                last=self.items[i][1]
                while last.next:
                    last=last.next
                last.next=newNode
        if self.items[i][0]==vj:
            newNode=Node(vi)
            if self.items[i][1] is None:
                self.items[i][1]=newNode
            else:
                last=self.items[i][1]
                while last.next:
                    last=last.next
                last.next=newNode

def search(self,v):
    for i in range(self.size):
        if self.items[i][0]==v:
            return True
    return False

def delete_vertex(self,v):
    for i in range(self.size):
        if self.items[i][0]==v:
            curNode=self.items[i][1]
            while curNode:
                self.delete_edge(curNode.vName,v)
                curNode=curNode.next
            del self.items[i]
            break
    self.size-=1
    print("Vertex Removed")

def delete_edge(self,vi, vj):
    for i in range(self.size):
        if self.items[i][0]==vi:
```

```
                        curNode=self.items[i][1]
                        if curNode.vName==vj:
                            self.items[i][1]=curNode.next
                        else:
                            prev=None
                            while curNode.vName!=vj:
                                prev=curNode
                                curNode=curNode.next
                            prev.next=curNode.next
                        del curNode
                    if self.items[i][0]==vj:
                        curNode=self.items[i][1]
                        if curNode.vName==vi:
                            self.items[i][1]=curNode.next
                        else:
                            prev=None
                            while curNode.vName!=vi:
                                prev=curNode
                                curNode=curNode.next
                            prev.next=curNode.next
                        del curNode

    def display(self):
        for i in range(self.size):
            print(self.items[i][0],":",end=' ')
            curNode=self.items[i][1]
            while curNode:
                print(curNode.vName,end='->')
                curNode=curNode.next
            print("None")

g=Graph()
while(True):
    print("\nPROGRAM TO IMPLEMENT GRAPH USING ADJACENCY LIST")
    print("=============================================")
    print("\t1. Insert a Vertex")
    print("\t2. Insert an Edge")
    print("\t3. Remove a Vertex")
    print("\t4. Remove an Edge")
    print("\t5. Display")
    print("\t6. Exit")
    print("=============================================")
```

```python
choice=int(input("Enter your Choice : "))
if choice==1 :
    v = input("Enter the Vertex:")
    if g.search(v):
        print("Vertex already exists..")
        continue
    g.insert_vertex(v)
elif choice==2 :
    vs = input("Enter Source Vertex:")
    if not g.search(vs):
        print("Source Vertex not found..")
        continue
    ve = input("Enter End Vertex:")
    if not g.search(ve):
        print("End Vertex not found..")
        continue
    g.insert_edge(vs,ve)
elif choice==3 :
    v = input("Enter the Vertex:")
    if not g.search(v):
        print("Vertex not found..")
        continue
    g.delete_vertex(v)
elif choice==4 :
    vs = input("Enter Source Vertex:")
    if not g.search(vs):
        print("Source Vertex not found..")
        continue
    ve = input("Enter End Vertex:")
    if not g.search(ve):
        print("End Vertex not found..")
        continue
    g.delete_edge(vs,ve)
    print("Edge Removed")
elif choice==5 :
    if g.isEmpty() :
        print("Graph is Empty")
    else :
        g.display()
elif choice==6 :
    print("\nQuiting.......")
    break
```

```
        else:
            print("Invalid choice. Please Enter Correct Choice")
            continue
```

Program 12.3: Write a program to implement a weighted directed graph using an adjacency list.

```
# PRGD12_3: Program to implement a directed weighted graph
#using adjacency list

class Node:
    def __init__(self,vName,weight):
        self.vName=vName
        self.weight=weight
        self.next=None

class Graph:
    def __init__(self):
        self.size=0
        self.items = []
    def isEmpty(self):
        return self.size == 0
    def insert_vertex(self,v):
        self.items.append([v,None])
        self.size+=1

    def insert_edge(self, vi, vj, wt):
        for i in range(self.size):
            if self.items[i][0]==vi:
                newNode=Node(vj,wt)
                if self.items[i][1] is None:
                    self.items[i][1]=newNode
                else:
                    last=self.items[i][1]
                    while last.next:
                        last=last.next
                    last.next=newNode

    def search(self,v):
        for i in range(self.size):
            if self.items[i][0]==v:
                return True
```

```
        return False

def delete_vertex(self,v):
    for i in range(self.size):
        curNode=self.items[i][1]
        if curNode is not None:
            if curNode.vName==v:
                self.items[i][1]=curNode.next
            else:
                prev=None
                while curNode:
                    if curNode.vName==v:
                        prev.next=curNode.next
                        del curNode
                        break
                    else:
                        prev=curNode
                        curNode=curNode.next
    for i in range(self.size):
        if self.items[i][0]==v:
            del self.items[i]
            self.size-=1
            break
    print("Vertex Removed")
def delete_edge(self,vi, vj):
    for i in range(self.size):
        if self.items[i][0]==vi:
            curNode=self.items[i][1]
            if curNode.vName==vj:
                self.items[i][1]=curNode.next
            else:
                prev=None
                while curNode.vName!=vj:
                    prev=curNode
                    curNode=curNode.next
                prev.next=curNode.next
            del curNode

def display(self):
    for i in range(self.size):
        print(self.items[i][0],":",end=' ')
        curNode=self.items[i][1]
```

```python
            while curNode:
                print(curNode.vName,"(",curNode.weight,")",end='
                                                    -> ')
                curNode=curNode.next
            print("None")

g=Graph()
while(True):
    print("\nPROGRAM TO IMPLEMENT DIRECTED WEIGHTED GRAPH")
    print("==========================================")
    print("\t1. Insert a Vertex")
    print("\t2. Insert an Edge")
    print("\t3. Remove a Vertex")
    print("\t4. Remove an Edge")
    print("\t5. Display")
    print("\t6. Exit")
    print("==========================================")
    choice=int(input("Enter your Choice : "))
    if choice==1 :
        v = input("Enter the Vertex: ")
        if g.search(v):
            print("Vertex already exists..")
            continue
        g.insert_vertex(v)
    elif choice==2 :
        vs = input("Enter Source Vertex: ")
        if not g.search(vs):
            print("Source Vertex not found..")
            continue
        ve = input("Enter End Vertex: ")
        if not g.search(ve):
            print("End Vertex not found..")
            continue
        wt= int(input("Enter weight: "))
        g.insert_edge(vs,ve,wt)
    elif choice==3 :
        v = input("Enter the Vertex: ")
        if not g.search(v):
            print("Vertex not found..")
            continue
        g.delete_vertex(v)
    elif choice==4 :
```

```
        vs = input("Enter Source Vertex: ")
        if not g.search(vs):
            print("Source Vertex not found..")
            continue
        ve = input("Enter End Vertex: ")
        if not g.search(ve):
            print("End Vertex not found..")
            continue
        g.delete_edge(vs,ve)
        print("Edge Removed")
    elif choice==5 :
        if g.isEmpty() :
            print("Graph is Empty")
        else :
            g.display()
    elif choice==6 :
        print("\nQuiting.......")
        break
    else:
        print("Invalid choice. Please Enter Correct Choice")
        continue
```

12.4.3 Graph Traversal

Traversal of a graph means examining or reading data from each and every vertex and edge of the graph. There are two standard algorithms to traverse a graph. These are:

- BFS (Breadth First Search)
- DFS (Depth First Search)

In the following sections these two algorithms are discussed. Both algorithms are discussed considering the adjacency list representation of the graph.

12.4.3.1 Breadth First Search Algorithm

In Breadth First Search (BFS) algorithm, starting from a source vertex all the adjacent vertices are traversed first. Then the adjacent vertices of these traversed vertices are traversed one by one. This process continues until all the vertices are traversed. This algorithm is quite similar to the level order traversal of a tree. But the difference is that a graph may contain cycles; thus we may traverse a vertex again and again. To solve this problem we may use a flag variable for each vertex to denote whether the vertex is previously traversed or not. We may set 0, 1, and 2 to this flag variable; where 0 denotes the vertex is not traversed at all, 1 denotes the vertex is in the queue, and 2 denotes all the adjacent vertices of the vertex are traversed. Similar to the level order traversal of a tree, here also we need to use the queue data structure. The general algorithm of BFS is given here:

1. Create a queue.
2. Set Flag = 0 to all the vertices of the graph.
3. Enqueue the source vertex and set its Flag =1.
4. While the queue is not empty, do
    a. Dequeue from queue and store into a variable, v.
    b. Enqueue all the adjacent vertices of v whose Flag value is 0.
    c. Set Flag = 1 for these adjacent vertices.
    d. Print v and set Flag = 2 for this vertex.

Now consider the following graph and we want to traverse using the BFS method considering source vertex as v1.

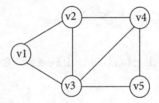

First we create a queue and a dictionary named flag. Within the dictionary we insert all the vertices as key and set 0 to all the elements.

Vertex	v1	v2	v3	v4	v5
Flag Value	0	0	0	0	0

We start the algorithm by enqueueing the source vertex v1 and update the flag value of v1 to 1.

Queue	v1

Vertex	v1	v2	v3	v4	v5
Flag Value	1	0	0	0	0

Next dequeue from queue and we get v1. Now we traverse the adjacent list of v1. v2 and v3 are the adjacent vertices of v1 and flag value of both vertices is 0. Thus we enqueue both vertices and set their corresponding flags as1. The next task is to print this dequeued element and set its flag value = 2 as this vertex is completely processed.

Queue		v2	v3

Vertex	v1	v2	v3	v4	v5
Flag Value	2	1	1	0	0

Print	v1

This last step repeats until the queue becomes empty. Thus in the next iteration, v2 is dequeued. Its adjacent vertices are v1, v3, and v4. But the flag value of v1 is 2, which means it is completely processed; the flag value of v3 is 1, which means it is already in the queue. Thus we enqueue only v4 as its flag value is 0. After inserting we change its flag value as 1. Now we print v2 and set its flag value as 2.

Queue		v3	v4

Vertex	v1	v2	v3	v4	v5
Flag Value	2	2	1	1	0

Print	v1 v2

Similarly, in the next iteration v3 is dequeued. Among its adjacent vertices only v5's flag value is 0; so it is enqueued and its flag value becomes 1. Now v3 is printed and its flag value becomes 2.

Queue		v4	v5

Vertex	v1	v2	v3	v4	v5
Flag Value	2	2	2	1	1

Print	v1 v2 v3

In the next iteration v4 is dequeued. But there is no adjacent vertex of v4 whose flag value is 0. So no new element is enqueued. Next v4 is printed and its flag value becomes 2.

Queue	v5

Vertex	v1	v2	v3	v4	v5
Flag Value	2	2	2	2	1

Print	v1 v2 v3 v4

Finally v5 is dequeued. As there is no adjacent vertex of v5 whose flag value is 0, no new element is enqueued. Next v5 is printed and its flag value becomes 2.

Queue	

Vertex	v1	v2	v3	v4	v5
Flag Value	2	2	2	2	2

Print	v1 v2 v3 v4 v5

Now the queue becomes empty and we get the BFS traversal order of vertices as v1 v2 v3 v4 v5. Remember, this order is not unique for any graph. Suppose, if we are processing the vertex v1, instead of v2 one may insert v3 first and then v2. Then we get a different order. This is true for all other vertices as well.

Here is a function that implements the above BFS algorithm:

```python
# Function to implement Breadth First Search
  def BFS(self,s):
          q=Queue()
          self.flag={}
          for i in range(self.size):
              self.flag[self.items[i][0]]=0
          for i in range(self.size):
              if self.items[i][0]==s:
                  break
          q.enqueue(s)
          self.flag[s]=1
          while not q.isEmpty():
              v=q.dequeue()
              for i in range(self.size):
                  if self.items[i][0]==v:
                      break
              next=self.items[i][1]
              while next is not None:
                  if self.flag[next.vName]==0:
                      q.enqueue(next.vName)
                      self.flag[next.vName]=1
                  next=next.next
              print(v,end=' ')
              self.flag[v]=2
```

To find the time complexity of BFS, if we consider the adjacency matrix representation, it solely depends on the number of vertices and is calculated as $O(v^2)$, where v is the number of vertices. But if we consider an adjacency list representation, it is calculated as $O(|V|+|E|)$, where $|V|$ is the total number of vertices and $|E|$ is the total number of edges in a graph.

12.4.3.2 Depth First Search Algorithm

A Depth First Search (DFS) algorithm is another graph traversal algorithm. In this algorithm, starting from the source vertex, instead of traversing all the adjacent vertices, we need to move deeper and deeper until we reach a dead end. Then by backtracking we return to the most recently visited vertex and form that position again we start to move deeper level through unvisited vertices. This process continues until we reach the goal node or traverse the entire tree. As backtracking is required, the stack data structure is used here. So, starting from a source vertex we push all the adjacent vertices into the stack. Then we pop a vertex from the stack and move to that vertex. The same operation is done for that vertex also. This process continues until the stack becomes empty. Like BFS, here too we need to use a flag variable for each vertex to denote whether the vertex is previously traversed or not. We may set 0, 1, and 2 to these flag variable, where 0 denotes the vertex is not traversed at all, 1 denotes the vertex is in the stack, and 2 denotes all the adjacent vertices of the vertex are traversed. The general algorithm of DFS is given here:

1. Create a stack.
2. Set Flag = 0 to all the vertices of the graph.
3. Push the source vertex and set its Flag =1.
4. While the stack is not empty, do
   a. Pop from stack and store into a variable, v.
   b. Push all the adjacent vertices of v whose Flag value is 0.
   c. Set Flag = 1 for these adjacent vertices.
   d. Print v and set Flag = 2 for this vertex.

Now consider the following graph and we want to traverse using the DFS method considering source vertex as v1.

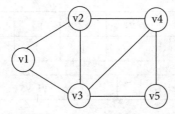

First we create a stack and a dictionary named flag. Within the dictionary we insert all the vertices as key and set 0 to all the elements.

Vertex	v1	v2	v3	v4	v5
Flag Value	0	0	0	0	0

At the very beginning we push the source vertex v1 into the stack and update the flag value of v1 to 1.

Stack	v1

Vertex	v1	v2	v3	v4	v5
Flag Value	1	0	0	0	0

Next pop from stack and we get v1. Now traversing the adjacent list of v1, we find v2 and v3 are the adjacent vertices of v1 and flag value of both vertices is 0. Thus we push both the vertices and set their corresponding flags as 1. The next task is to print this popped element and set its flag value = 2 as this vertex is completely processed.

Stack		v2	v3	

Vertex	v1	v2	v3	v4	v5
Flag Value	2	1	1	0	0

Print	v1

This last step repeats until the stack becomes empty. Thus in the next iteration, v3 is popped. Its adjacent vertices are v1, v2, v4, and v5. But the flag value of v1 is 2, which means it is completely processed, and the flag value of v2 is 1, which means it is already in the stack. Thus we push v4 and v5 as their flag values are 0 and update their flag values to 1. Now we print v3 and set its flag value as 2.

Stack	v2	v4	v5

Vertex	v1	v2	v3	v4	v5
Flag Value	2	1	2	1	1

Print	v1 v3

Similarly, in the next iteration the popped element is v5. Among its adjacent vertices there is no vertex whose flag value is 0; thus no element is pushed. Now v5 is printed and its flag value becomes 2.

Stack		v2	v4

Vertex	v1	v2	v3	v4	v5
Flag Value	2	1	2	1	2

Print	v1 v3 v5

In the next iteration v4 is popped. Here also no adjacent vertex is found whose flag value is 0. So no new element is pushed. Next v4 is printed and its flag value becomes 2.

Stack	v2

Vertex	v1	v2	v3	v4	v5
Flag Value	2	1	2	2	2

Print	v1 v3 v5 v4

Finally v2 is popped. As there is no adjacent vertex of v2 whose flag value is 0, no new element is pushed. Next v2 is printed and its flag value becomes 2.

Stack	

Vertex	v1	v2	v3	v4	v5
Flag Value	2	2	2	2	2

Print	v1 v3 v5 v4 v2

Now the stack becomes empty and we get the DFS traversal order of vertices as v1   v3   v5   v4   v2. Remember, in case of DFS also this order is not unique for any graph. At the time of processing the vertex v1, instead of v2 one may insert v3 first and then v2. Then we get a different order. This is true for all other vertices as well.

Here is a function that implements the above DFS algorithm:

```
# Function to implement Depth First Search
def DFS(self,s):
        st=Stack()
        self.flag={}
        for i in range(self.size):
                self.flag[self.items[i][0]]=0
        for i in range(self.size):
```

```
            if self.items[i][0]==s:
                break
    st.push(s)
    self.flag[s]=1
    while not st.isEmpty():
        v=st.pop()
        for i in range(self.size):
            if self.items[i][0]==v:
                break
        next=self.items[i][1]
        while next is not None:
            if self.flag[next.vName]==0:
                st.push(next.vName)
                self.flag[next.vName]=1
            next=next.next
        print(v,end=' ')
        self.flag[v]=2
```

The time complexity of DFS is also calculated as $O(v^2)$, where v is the number of vertices when we consider the adjacency matrix representation, and in case of an adjacency list representation, it is calculated as $O(|V|+|E|)$, where $|V|$ is the total number of vertices and $|E|$ is the total number of edges in a graph.

12.5 Minimum Spanning Tree

A spanning tree of a graph is a subset of that graph where all the vertices of the graph are connected with the minimum number of edges. As it does not have any cycle, it is called a tree. Another thing is that all the vertices are connected through edges; so, we can find a spanning tree only if the graph is connected. In a connected graph, there may be any number of spanning trees but at least one spanning tree should exist. In a spanning tree, the number of edges is always one less than the number of vertices.

If the graph is a weighted graph, then we may find the minimum spanning tree. A minimum spanning tree of a weighted graph is a subset of the graph where all the vertices of the graph are connected with the minimum number of edges in such a way that the sum of the weight of the edges is minimum. In other words, a minimum spanning tree is the spanning tree whose total weight of the tree is the minimum compared to all other spanning trees of the graph. Consider the following weighted graph.

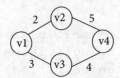

The spanning trees of the above graph are the following:

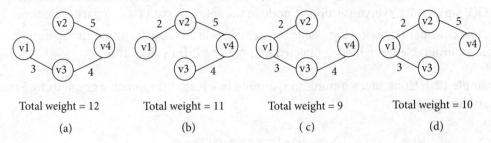

| Total weight = 12 | Total weight = 11 | Total weight = 9 | Total weight = 10 |
| (a) | (b) | (c) | (d) |

Figure 12.10 Spanning trees

All the above four trees are the spanning trees of the above graph but the one in (c) has the smallest total weight. Hence it is the minimum spanning tree of the above graph.

In the following sections we will discuss two popular algorithms to find the minimum spanning tree. These are Prim's algorithm and Kruskal's algorithm.

12.5.1 Prim's Algorithm

Prim's algorithm is one of the most popular algorithms to find the minimum spanning tree of a connected weighted graph. It is a greedy algorithm that may start with any arbitrary vertex. The algorithm starts with an empty spanning tree and in each step one edge is added to this spanning tree. After choosing the starting vertex our task is to find the edge with the smallest weight among the edges that are connected to that starting vertex. This edge and the corresponding vertex are then added to the spanning tree. In the next step we will find the edge with the smallest weight among the edges that are connected to the vertices that are already in the spanning tree and obviously not already included in the minimum spanning tree. If the inclusion of this new smaller edge does not form a cycle within the spanning tree, we will include the edge and its corresponding vertex. This process continues until all the vertices of the original graph have been added to the spanning tree. Prim's algorithm can be represented as:

1. Select a vertex as starting vertex.

2. Take an empty graph, T, as the minimum spanning tree.

3. Add the starting vertex to T.

4. Repeat until T does not contain all the vertices of the given graph, do

   a. Consider the vertices that are already in T.

   b. Consider the edges that are connected to these vertices but not included in T.

   c. Choose the edge with the smallest weight among them.

   d. If inclusion of this edge does not form a cycle within the spanning tree, then

      i. Include the edge and its corresponding vertex in T.

The running time of Prim's algorithm can be calculated as O(V logV + E logV), where E is the number of edges and V is the number of vertices. This calculation can be made simpler as O(E logV) since every insertion of node in the solution path takes logarithmic time.

Now consider the following example where we will construct a minimum spanning tree from an undirected weighted connected graph using Prim's algorithm:

Example 12.1: Construct a minimum spanning tree from the following graph using Prim's algorithm:

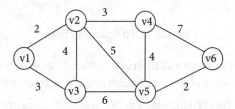

Solution:

Step 1: Suppose we are choosing the vertex v1 as the starting vertex.

Step 2: Taking an empty graph and adding v1 to it.

Step 3: Now we have to consider the edges that are connected to v1 and among them (v1,v2) is with the smallest weight. This edge and the corresponding vertex v2 would be added.

Step 4: Now we would consider all the edges that are connected to v1 or v2 except the edge (v1,v2). There are two vertices (v2,v4) and (v1,v3); both have weight 3 and are smaller than others. We may consider any one among them. Here, we are considering (v2,v4).

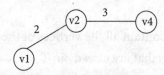

Step 5: Next we need to consider all the edges that are connected to v1, v2, or v4 except the edges (v1,v2) and (v2,v4). Now (v1,v3) is the smallest one. So, we add it.

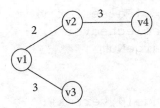

Step 6: In the next step, we consider the edges connected to v1, v2, v3, or v4 excluding the edges (v1,v2), (v2,v4), and (v1,v3). Now there are two vertices (v2,v3) and (v4,v5); both have weight 4 and are smaller than others. If we consider (v2,v3), it will form a cycle. Hence, we cannot consider it. We will add (v4,v5).

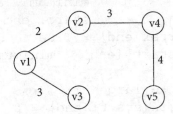

Step 7: Among the edges that are connected to v1, v2, v3, v4, or v5, but not already included in the spanning tree, (v5, v6) is the smallest and we include it.

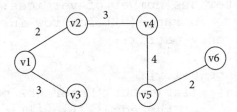

Step 8: As all the vertices of the original graph are now included in the spanning tree, this is our final spanning tree of the given graph.

Here is a complete program to implement Prim's algorithm:

Program 12.4: Write a program to implement Prim's Algorithm to find the minimum spanning tree.

```
# PRGD12_4: Program to implement Prim's Algorithm
def Prims(adjMatrix):
    vertex=len(adjMatrix)
    mstMatrix = [[0 for col in range(vertex)] for row in
                                        range(vertex)]

    largeNum = float('inf')
    # list of vertices which are already selected
```

```
        selectedvertex = [False for v in range(vertex)]
        while(False in selectedvertex):
            minimum = largeNum
            start = 0
            end = 0
            for i in range(0,vertex):
                if selectedvertex[i]:
                    for j in range(0+i,vertex):
                        if (not selectedvertex[j] and
                                        adjMatrix[i][j]>0):
                            if adjMatrix[i][j] < minimum:
                                minimum = adjMatrix[i][j]
                                start, end = i, j
            selectedvertex[end] = True
            mstMatrix[start][end] = minimum
                                        # Set the edge in MST
            if minimum == largeNum:
                mstMatrix[start][end] = 0
            mstMatrix[end][start] = mstMatrix[start][end]
        return mstMatrix

v=int(input('Enter the number of vertices: '))
adj = [[0 for col in range(v)] for row in range(v)]
# Input to adjacency matrix:
for i in range(0,v):
    for j in range(0+i,v):
        adj[i][j] = int(input('Enter the path weight of
                        the edge: ({}, {}):  '.format(i,j)))
        adj[j][i] = adj[i][j]
mst=Prims(adj)
for i in range(v):
    print(mst[i])
```

12.5.2 Kruskal's Algorithm

Kruskal's algorithm is another popular algorithm to find the minimum spanning tree of a connected weighted graph. It is also a greedy algorithm and starts with a null graph containing only all the vertices of the given graph. There will be no edge in that graph. All the edges of the given graph are then kept in a sorted list in ascending order. Next one by one the edges are taken from the list and added to the spanning tree such that no cycle is formed. This process completes when (n-1) edges are added in the new graph and forms the spanning tree. Kruskal's algorithm can be represented as:

1.   Take a null graph, T.

2.   Add all the vertices of the given graph to T.

3.   Create a list of edges in ascending order of weight.

4.   Repeat until T does not contain (n-1) edges where n is the number of vertices, do

   a.   Select the edge with lowest weight from the list.

   b.   Add the edge to T if it does not form a cycle.

   c.   Remove the edge from the list.

The running time of Kruskal's algorithm can be calculated as O(E logV) or O(E logE), where E is the number of edges and V is the number of vertices.

Now consider the following example where we will construct a minimum spanning tree from an undirected weighted connected graph using Kruskal's algorithm:

Example 12.2: Construct a minimum spanning tree from the following graph using Kruskal's algorithm:

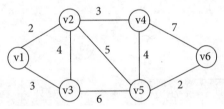

Solution:

Step 1: Taking an empty graph and adding all the vertices to it.

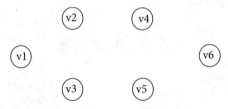

Step 2: Next we create a list containing all the edges of the given graph and sort them in ascending order of weight.

(v1,v2)	(v5,v6)	(v1,v3)	(v2,v4)	(v2,v3)	(v4,v5)	(v2,v5)	(v3,v5)	(v4,v6)
2	2	3	3	4	4	5	6	7

Step 3: Now we have to add the edge that has the least weight. There are two edges that have the least weight. These are (v1,v2) and (v5,v6). Both have weight 2. We can choose any one of them. Here we are choosing (v1,v2). It will be added in the graph and removed from the list.

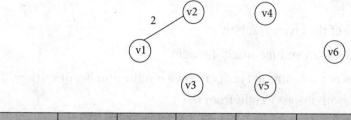

(v5,v6)	(v1,v3)	(v2,v4)	(v2,v3)	(v4,v5)	(v2,v5)	(v3,v5)	(v4,v6)
2	3	3	4	4	5	6	7

Step 4: Now the edge (v5,v6) has the least weight in the list. Hence it will be added in the graph and remove from the list.

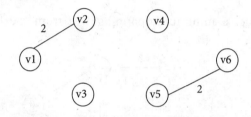

(v1,v3)	(v2,v4)	(v2,v3)	(v4,v5)	(v2,v5)	(v3,v5)	(v4,v6)
3	3	4	4	5	6	7

Step 5: The next edge with lowest weight in the list is (v1,v3). Hence it will be added in the graph and removed from the list.

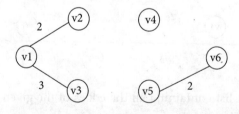

(v2,v4)	(v2,v3)	(v4,v5)	(v2,v5)	(v3,v5)	(v4,v6)
3	4	4	5	6	7

Step 6: Now the edge (v2,v4) has the least weight in the list. Hence it will be added in the graph and removed from the list.

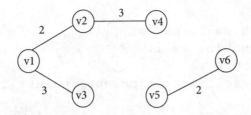

(v2,v3)	(v4,v5)	(v2,v5)	(v3,v5)	(v4,v6)
4	4	5	6	7

Step 7: Again there are two edges that have the least weight in the list. These are (v2,v3) and (v4,v5). But inclusion of the edge (v2,v3) forms a cycle. Thus we have to discard it. So, in next step, (v4,v5) will be added in the graph and removed from the list.

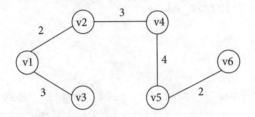

(v2,v5)	(v3,v5)	(v4,v6)
5	6	7

Step 7: Now the number of edges in the graph becomes 5, which is 1 less than the total number of vertices. Hence our algorithm terminates here and we get the required minimum spanning tree.

Here is a complete program to implement Kruskal's algorithm:

Program 12.5: Write a program to implement Kruskal's algorithm to find the minimum spanning tree:

```
# PRGD12_5: Program to implement Kruskal's Algorithm
class Graph:
    def __init__(self, vertex):
        self.vertex = vertex
        self.edges = []

    def add_edge(self, vi, vj, wt):
        self.edges.append([vi, vj, wt])
```

```python
def search(self, parent, i):
    if parent[i] == i:
        return i
    return self.search(parent, parent[i])


def doUnion(self, parents, rank, a, b):
    root_a = self.search(parents, a)
    root_b = self.search(parents, b)
    if rank[root_a] < rank[root_b]:
        parents[root_a] = root_b
    elif rank[root_a] > rank[root_b]:
        parents[root_b] = root_a
    else:
        parents[root_b] = root_a
        rank[root_a] += 1


def Kruskals(self):
    mst = []
    i, e = 0, 0
    self.edges = sorted(self.edges, key=lambda
                                    element: element[2])
    parents = []
    rank = []
    for node in range(self.vertex):
        parents.append(node)
        rank.append(0)
    while e < self.vertex - 1:
        vi, vj, wt = self.edges[i]
        i = i + 1
        a = self.search(parents, vi)
        b = self.search(parents, vj)
        if a != b:
            e = e + 1
            mst.append([vi, vj, wt])
            self.doUnion(parents, rank, a, b)
    minCost=0
    for vi, vj, wt in mst:
        print("{} --> {} = {}".format(vi,vj,wt))
        minCost+=wt
    print("Cost of MST=",minCost)
```

```
v=int(input('Enter the number of vertices: '))
gr = Graph(v)
ch="y"
while(ch.upper()=="Y"):
    i=int(input('Enter Source Vertex: '))
    j=int(input('Enter Destination Vertex: '))
    wt = int(input('Enter the path weight of the edge:
                            ({}, {}): '.format(i,j)))
    gr.add_edge(i,j,wt)
    ch=input('Continue?(y/n)')
gr.Kruskals()
```

12.6 Shortest Path Algorithm

The shortest path between two vertices in a graph indicates the path between these two vertices having the lowest weight; there is no other path between these vertices with a lower weight than this path. Finding the shortest path is a very interesting and useful study under graphs. The shortest path can be found between two vertices or between one source vertex and any other vertex or between any vertex and any other vertex in a graph.

12.6.1 Within a Given Source and Destination

Dijkstra's algorithm is used for the single source shortest path problem. More precisely it is used to find the shortest path between one vertex and every other vertex for any weighted graph – directed or undirected. This algorithm is very useful in networking for routing protocols as well as to find the shortest path between one city and any other cities or to find the path to set a waterline system, etc. The disadvantage of this algorithm is that it may not work properly for negative weights. Dijkstra's algorithm can be represented as:

1. Take a square matrix of size equals to the number of vertices+1.

2. Leave the first column empty.

3. Fill the other column of the first row with the name of the vertices.

4. Next rows will contain the corresponding shortest distance from the source vertex.

5. Initially set all columns except the first column of next row, i.e. the second row, with infinity except the column under source vertex, which will store 0.

6. Find the smallest value in the row and fill the first column with the vertex name of the smallest distance.

7. Consider the vertex with the smallest value as u and visit all its adjacent vertices (v). In the next row, calculate the distance of each vertex as:

   a. If distance(u)+weight(u,v) < distance(v), then

Set distance(v) = distance(u)+weight(u,v)

    b.   Otherwise, set distance(v) with its old value.

8.   Repeat steps 6 and 7 until all the vertex is traversed.

Above algorithm creates a table which shows the shortest distance of all other vertices from the source vertex. To find the shortest path between source vertex and given vertex,

1.   First we have to find the vertex from the first row.

2.   Find the last written value at the corresponding column. This represents the shortest distance.

3.   Now move upward until the value ∞ is reached.

4.   On that row find the marked smallest value and the corresponding vertex name.

5.   Note this vertex as the previous vertex of the destination vertex in the path.

6.   From this point again move upward and follow the same procedure (i.e. steps 3 to 5) to get its previous node. This process continues until we reach the source vertex.

As we are creating a square matrix of size v (where v is the number of vertices in the graph), the time complexity of Dijkstra's algorithm is $O(v^2)$.

Now consider the following example to find the shortest path using Dijkstra's algorithm:

Example 12.3: Find the shortest path from vertex v1 to all other vertices in the following graph using Dijkstra's algorithm:

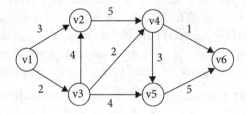

Solution:

	v1	v2	v3	v4	v5	v6
v1	0	∞	∞	∞	∞	∞
v3		3	2	∞	∞	∞
v2		3		4	6	∞
v4				4	6	∞
v6					6	5
v5					6	

From the above table it is clear that the shortest distance from v1 to v2 is 3, from v1 to v3 is 2, from v1 to v4 is 4, from v1 to v5 is 6, and from v1 to v6 is 5. Now if we want to find the shortest path between v1 and v6, first we have to find v6 in the first row. Next moving downward we find that the last entry is 5. So, the shortest distance between v1 and v6 is 5. From this point we are moving upward and the first ∞ is found in its previous row. The smallest value in that row is 4 and the corresponding vertex is v4. Thus we get the previous vertex of v6.

    v4 -> v6

From this point we again move upward and find ∞ in the row whose first column contains v3. Thus we get

    v3 -> v4 -> v6

Again moving upward, we find ∞ in its previous row and its first column contains the source vertex v1. Thus the final shortest path between v1 to v6 is:

    v1 -> v3 -> v4 -> v6

Similarly, we may get the shortest path between v1 to v5 is   v1 -> v3 -> v5

    The shortest path between v1 to v4 is   v1 -> v3 -> v4 and so on.

    In the above example, we consider a directed graph. If the graph is an undirected graph, we need to consider each edge (u,v) as a combination of two directed edges of the same weight – one from u to v and the other from v to u.

    Here is a complete program to implement Dijkstra's algorithm to find the shortest paths from any source vertex to all other vertices in the graph:

Program 12.6: Write a program to implement Dijkstra's algorithm to find the shortest paths from source vertex to other vertices.

```
# PRGD12_6: Program to implement Dijkstra's Algorithm
class Node:
      def __init__(self,vName,weight):
            self.vName=vName
            self.weight=weight
            self.next=None

class Graph:
      def __init__(self):
            self.vertex=0
            self.items = []
```

```python
    def isEmpty(self):
        return self.vertex == 0

    def insert_vertex(self,v):
        self.items.append([v,None])
        self.vertex+=1

    def insert_edge(self, vi, vj, wt):
        for i in range(self.vertex):
            if self.items[i][0]==vi:
                newNode=Node(vj,wt)
                if self.items[i][1] is None:
                    self.items[i][1]=newNode
                else:
                    last=self.items[i][1]
                    while last.next:
                        last=last.next
                    last.next=newNode

    def search(self,v):
        for i in range(self.vertex):
            if self.items[i][0]==v:
                return True
        return False

    def Dijkstra(self,source):
        selectedvertices=[]
        largeNum = float('inf')
        temp= [[largeNum for col in range(self.vertex+1)]
                        for row in range(self.vertex+1)]
        for i in range(self.vertex):
            temp[0][i+1]= self.items[i][0]
        i=0
        while(self.items[i][0]!=source):
            i=i+1
        temp[1][i+1]=0
        row=1
        while(row<=self.vertex):
            minm=temp[row][1]
            j=1
            for i in range(1,self.vertex+1):
                if temp[row][i]<minm:
```

```
                    minm=temp[row][i]
                    j=i
        minVertex=temp[0][j]
        temp[row][0]=minVertex
        selectedvertices.append(minVertex)
        curNode=self.items[j-1][1]
        if row==self.vertex:
            break
        for i in range(1,self.vertex):
            if temp[0][i] not in selectedvertices:
                temp[row+1][i]=temp[row][i]
        while curNode:
            vName=curNode.vName
            k=1
            while(temp[0][k]!=vName):
                k=k+1
            cumWt=temp[row][j]+curNode.weight

            if cumWt<temp[row][k]:
                temp[row+1][k]= cumWt
            curNode=curNode.next
        row=row+1
    for i in range(1,self.vertex+1):
        print(temp[i])
# Now table has been prepared. Next we find the
# shortest path from source vartex to other vertices
    print('Shortest path from source to other
                                vertices:-')
    for row in range(2,self.vertex+1):
        path=[]
        r=row
        flag=True
        while(r>0):
            minm=largeNum
            for i in range(1,self.vertex+1):
                if temp[r][i]<minm:
                    minm=temp[r][i]
                    j=i
            path.append(temp[r][0])
            if flag:
                minDist=minm
                flag=False
```

```
                        curVal=temp[r][j]
                        while(temp[r][j]==curVal):
                            r=r-1
                    l=len(path)-1
                    while(l>=0):
                        print(path[l]+'->',end='')
                        l=l-1
                    print('\b\b : ',minDist)

    v=int(input('Enter the number of vertices: '))
    gr = Graph()
    for i in range(v):
        vert=input('Enter the name of the vertex {}:
                                                '.format(i+1))
        gr.insert_vertex(vert)
    ch="y"
    print('Enter the details of the edges:-')
    while(ch.upper()=="Y"):
        vs=input('Enter Source End Vertex: ')
        ve=input('Enter Destination End Vertex: ')
        wt = int(input('Enter the path weight of the edge:
                            ({}, {}):  '.format(vs,ve)))
        gr.insert_edge(vs,ve,wt)
        ch=input('Continue?(y/n)')
    sr=input('Enter Source Vertex: ')
    gr.Dijkstra(sr)
```

12.6.2 Among All Pairs of Vertices

In the previous section we have learnt that using Dijkstra's algorithm we can find the shortest path from a single source vertex to any other vertex in the graph. Now to find the shortest path among all pairs of vertices we may apply the same algorithm for each vertex. As the time complexity to find the single source shortest path using Dijkstra's algorithm in a graph of n vertices is $O(n^2)$, for all pairs of vertices it will be $O(n^2)$ x n, i.e. $O(n^3)$. Another drawback of this algorithm is that it does not work properly for negative weight. The Floyd–Warshall algorithm solves this problem. The single execution of this algorithm finds the shortest path among all pairs of vertices in a directed weighted graph where the edges may have positive or negative weights. Though the time complexity of this algorithm is also $O(n^3)$, it shows better performance in comparison to Dijkstra's algorithm applied for each vertex.

The Floyd–Warshall algorithm uses the dynamic programming approach where a problem is decomposed into several sub-problems of similar type, and the solution of each sub-program is constructed from previously found ones. This algorithm shows only the shortest distance but does not construct the paths. We can reconstruct the path with a simple modification of this algorithm.

The main motive of the Floyd–Warshall algorithm is to find the shortest path between two vertices considering all possible paths one by one. According to this algorithm, first we have to consider the adjacency matrix of the given graph. Using this matrix, first we will find the shortest path between all pairs of vertices via the first vertex and then via the second vertex, and so on. To explain the algorithm we are considering the following graph:

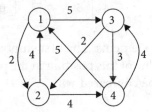

The adjacency matrix of the above graph is

	1	2	3	4
1	0	2	5	0
2	4	0	0	4
3	0	2	0	3
4	5	0	4	0

From this adjacency matrix we prepare the initial matrix, A^0. In this matrix, if there is a direct path between two vertices, v_i and v_j, the distance between v_i and v_j (i.e. the weight of the edge (v_i, v_j)) will be the value of $A^0[v_i, v_j]$. but if there is no direct path, it will be considered as ∞. Hence, the initial matrix A^0 will be

$$A^0 =$$

	1	2	3	4
1	0	2	5	∞
2	4	0	∞	4
3	∞	2	0	3
4	5	∞	4	0

Let us first choose an intermediate vertex as vertex 1. Here we will find whether any shorter path exists through vertex 1. For this we will keep all the paths belonging to vertex 1 as unchanged. So, we need not calculate. We will copy all the elements of row 1 and column 1 from A^0 matrix. If there is no self-loop, the diagonal elements will contain 0 (zero). So, we get the following matrix:

		1	2	3	4
$A^1 =$	1	0	2	5	∞
	2	4	0		
	3	∞		0	
	4	5			0

Now we calculate the remaining elements. The first empty position is $A^1[2,3]$. To find this value we have to compare the value of this position in the previous matrix with the path via vertex1, if any, i.e. $A^0[2,3]$ will be compared with $A^0[2,1] + A^0[1,3]$ and the smaller value will be accepted.

$A^0[2,3]$		$A^0[2,1] + A^0[1,3]$
∞	>	4+5=9

Thus the value of $A^1[2,3]$ will be 9 and we put it there.

		1	2	3	4
$A^1 =$	1	0	2	5	∞
	2	4	0	9	
	3	∞		0	
	4	5			0

Similarly we calculate rest portions as

$A^0[2,4]$		$A^0[2,1] + A^0[1,4]$	$A^1[2,4]$
4	<	4+∞=∞	4
$A^0[3,2]$		$A^0[3,1] + A^0[1,2]$	$A^1[3,2]$
2	<	∞+2=∞	2
$A^0[3,4]$		$A^0[3,1] + A^0[1,4]$	$A^1[3,4]$
3	<	∞+∞=∞	3

$A^0[4,2]$		$A^0[4,1] + A^0[1,2]$	$A^1[4,2]$
∞	>	5+2=7	7
$A^0[4,3]$		$A^0[4,1]+ A^0[1,3]$	$A^1[4,3]$
4	<	5+5=10	4

And the matrix becomes

$$A^1 = \begin{array}{c|cccc} & 1 & 2 & 3 & 4 \\ \hline 1 & 0 & 2 & 5 & \infty \\ 2 & 4 & 0 & 9 & 4 \\ 3 & \infty & 2 & 0 & 3 \\ 4 & 5 & 7 & 4 & 0 \end{array}$$

Now the same operation will be done on vertex 2. Thus this time we will copy the elements of the second row and second column of A^1 matrix and all the diagonal elements remain 0 as there is no self-loop. Hence, the A^2 matrix looks like as follows:

$$A^2 = \begin{array}{c|cccc} & 1 & 2 & 3 & 4 \\ \hline 1 & 0 & 2 & & \\ 2 & 4 & 0 & 9 & 4 \\ 3 & & 2 & 0 & \\ 4 & & 7 & & 0 \end{array}$$

The rest of the elements will also be calculated in the same way:

$A^1[1,3]$		$A^1[1,2] + A^1[2,3]$	$A^2[1,3]$
5	<	2+9=11	5
$A^1[1,4]$		$A^1[1,2] + A^1[2,4]$	$A^2[1,4]$
∞	>	2+4=6	6
$A^1[3,1]$		$A^1[3,2] + A^1[2,1]$	$A^2[3,1]$
∞	>	2+4=6	6
$A^1[3,4]$		$A^1[3,2] + A^1[2,4]$	$A^2[3,4]$
3	<	2+4=6	3
$A^1[4,1]$		$A^1[4,2] + A^1[2,1]$	$A^2[4,1]$

5	<	7+4=11	5
$A^1[4,3]$		$A^1[4,2]+ A^1[2,3]$	$A^2[4,3]$
4	<	7+9=16	4

Thus the final A^2 matrix will be:

$$A^2 = \begin{array}{c|cccc} & 1 & 2 & 3 & 4 \\ \hline 1 & 0 & 2 & 5 & 6 \\ 2 & 4 & 0 & 9 & 4 \\ 3 & 6 & 2 & 0 & 3 \\ 4 & 5 & 7 & 4 & 0 \end{array}$$

Now we consider the vertex 3 as intermediate vertex and will create the A^3 matrix. For that first we copy the elements of row 3 and column 3 and the diagonals of A^2 matrix.

$$A^3 = \begin{array}{c|cccc} & 1 & 2 & 3 & 4 \\ \hline 1 & 0 & & 5 & \\ 2 & & 0 & 9 & \\ 3 & 6 & 2 & 0 & 3 \\ 4 & & & 4 & 0 \end{array}$$

Calculations for the rest of the elements are as follows:

$A^2[1,2]$		$A^2[1,3] + A^2[3,2]$	$A^3[1,2]$
2	<	5+2=7	2
$A^2[1,4]$		$A^2[1,3] + A^2[3,4]$	$A^3[1,4]$
6	<	5+3=8	6
$A^2[2,1]$		$A^2[2,3] + A^2[3,1]$	$A^3[2,1]$
4	<	9+6=15	4
$A^2[2,4]$		$A^2[2,3] + A^2[3,4]$	$A^3[2,4]$
4	<	9+3=12	4
$A^2[4,1]$		$A^2[4,3] + A^2[3,1]$	$A^3[4,1]$
5	<	4+6=10	5
$A^2[4,2]$		$A^2[4,3]+ A^2[3,2]$	$A^3[4,2]$
7	>	4+2=6	6

Thus the final A^3 matrix will be:

$$A^3 = \begin{array}{c|c|c|c|c|} & 1 & 2 & 3 & 4 \\ \hline 1 & 0 & 2 & 5 & 6 \\ \hline 2 & 4 & 0 & 9 & 4 \\ \hline 3 & 6 & 2 & 0 & 3 \\ \hline 4 & 5 & 6 & 4 & 0 \\ \hline \end{array}$$

Finally we consider the vertex 4 as intermediate vertex and will create the A^4 matrix. For that again we copy the elements of row 4 and column 4 and the diagonals of A^3 matrix.

$$A^4 = \begin{array}{c|c|c|c|c|} & 1 & 2 & 3 & 4 \\ \hline 1 & 0 & & & 6 \\ \hline 2 & & 0 & & 4 \\ \hline 3 & & & 0 & 3 \\ \hline 4 & 5 & 6 & 4 & 0 \\ \hline \end{array}$$

Calculations for the rest elements are as follows:

$A^3[1,2]$		$A^3[1,4] + A^3[4,2]$	$A^4[1,2]$
2	<	6+6=12	2
$A^3[1,3]$		$A^3[1,4] + A^3[4,3]$	$A^4[1,3]$
5	<	6+4=10	5
$A^3[2,1]$		$A^3[2,4] + A^3[4,1]$	$A^4[2,1]$
4	<	4+5=9	4
$A^3[2,3]$		$A^3[2,4] + A^3[4,3]$	$A^4[2,3]$
9	>	4+4=8	8
$A^3[3,1]$		$A^3[3,4] + A^3[4,1]$	$A^4[3,1]$
6	<	3+5=8	6
$A^3[3,2]$		$A^3[3,4]+ A^3[4,2]$	$A^4[3,2]$
2	<	3+6=9	2

Hence the final A^4 matrix will be:

$$
A^4 =
\begin{array}{c|cccc}
 & 1 & 2 & 3 & 4 \\
\hline
1 & 0 & 2 & 5 & 6 \\
2 & 4 & 0 & 8 & 4 \\
3 & 6 & 2 & 0 & 3 \\
4 & 5 & 6 & 4 & 0 \\
\end{array}
$$

Now we can formulate the calculation as:

$$A^k[i,j] = \min\{\, A^{k-1}[i,j]\,,\, A^{k-1}[i,k] + A^{k-1}[k,j]\,\}$$

To write the code we may use this formula to find the elements of the successive arrays.

If we want to find the complexity of this algorithm, it is clear that if there are n vertices in a graph the adjacency matrix will be n × n. Thus to prepare a single matrix the running time complexity is $O(n^2)$. Now here we need to prepare n number of this type of matrix. Hence, the time complexity of the Floyd–Warshall algorithm is $O(n^3)$.

```python
# PRGD12_7: Program to implement Floyd-Warshall Algorithm
def FloydWarshall(adjMatrix):
    vertex=len(adjMatrix)
    spMatrix = [[INF for col in range(vertex)] for row in
                                        range(vertex)]
    for i in range(vertex):
        for j in range(vertex):
            if i==j:
                spMatrix[i][j]=0
            else:
                spMatrix[i][j]=adjMatrix[i][j]
    for k in range(vertex):
        for i in range(vertex):
            for j in range(vertex):
                spMatrix[i][j]=min(spMatrix[i][j],
                        spMatrix[i][k]+spMatrix[k][j])
    return spMatrix

v=int(input('Enter the number of vertices: '))
INF = float('inf')
adj = [[INF for col in range(v)] for row in range(v)]
ch="y"
print('Enter the details of the edges:-')
while(ch.upper()== "Y"):
    vs=int(input('Enter Source End Vertex: '))
```

```
ve=int(input('Enter Destination End Vertex: '))
wt = int(input('Enter the path weight of the edge:
                        ({}, {}):  '.format(vs,ve)))
adj[vs][ve]=wt
ch=input('Continue?(y/n)')

spm=FloydWarshall(adj)
print('Shortest Distance Matrix:-')
for i in range(v):
    print(spm[i])
```

12.7 Applications of Graph

In computer science, graph has various applications. Some of them are as follows:

- Graph is used to represent various cities and their connecting roads.
- Graph is used to show the flow of controls.
- Graph is used to show the network of communications.
- Graph is used to find the shortest path among various locations.
- Graph is used to find the shortest path to implement pipe lining.
- Graph is used to represent the state transition diagram.

Graph at a Glance

✓ A graph is a non-linear data structure that basically consists of some vertices and edges.

✓ If the edges of a graph are associated with some directions, the graph is known as a directed graph or digraph.

✓ When the edge of a graph is associated with some value, it is known as a weighted graph.

✓ In an undirected graph the number of edges connected to a vertex is known as the degree of that vertex.

✓ The vertex whose in-degree is 0 but out-degree is greater than 0 is known as source and the vertex whose in-degree is greater than 0 but out-degree is 0 is known as sink.

✓ A path is a sequence of vertices that can be traversed sequentially from one point of the graph to another point.

✓ If a path ends at a vertex from which the path started, the path is called cycle.

✓ If there is a path between any two vertices of a graph, then the graph is known as a connected graph.

✓ A graph is said to be complete if every two vertices in that graph are adjacent.

✓ If there are multiple edges between same two vertices, then it is called multiple edges or parallel edges, and the graph which has multiple edges is known as a multigraph.

✓ If any edge has the same end points, then it is called a loop or self-loop.

✓ If there is any such vertex whose deletion makes the graph disconnected, then such a vertex is known as a cut vertex.

✓ In memory, there are two ways to represent a graph using arrays. These are: using adjacency matrix and using incidence matrix.

✓ To represent a graph using linked lists there are also two ways. These are: using adjacency list and using adjacency multi-list.

✓ Breadth First Search (BFS) and Depth First Search (DFS) are two most common graph traversal algorithms.

✓ BFS algorithm uses queue and DFS algorithm uses stack as auxiliary data structure.

✓ Prim's algorithm and Kruskal's algorithm are two most common algorithms to find the minimum spanning tree.

✓ Dijkstra's algorithm is used for the single source shortest path problem whereas the Floyd–Warshall algorithm is used to find the shortest path between all pairs of vertices.

Multiple Choice Questions

1. If a connected acyclic graph has v vertices and e edges, which of the following statements is true?

   a) $e = v + 1$

   b) $v = e + 1$

   c) $v = e$

   d) $v = e - 1$

2. Which of the following is true?

    a) A graph may have many vertices but no edges.

    b) A graph may have many edges but no vertices.

    c) A graph may have no vertices and no edges.

    d) All of the above.

3. Which of the following ways can be used to represent a graph in memory?

    a) Incidence matrix only

    b) Adjacency list and adjacency matrix only

    c) Adjacency list, adjacency matrix as well as incidence matrix

    d) None of these

4. Which algorithm is used to find the shortest path among all pairs of vertices?

    a) Dijkstra's algorithm

    b) Floyd–Warshall algorithm

    c) Prim's algorithm

    d) Kruskal's algorithm

5. Which algorithm is used to find the shortest path from a particular vertex to all other vertices?

    a) Dijkstra's algorithm

    b) Floyd–Warshall algorithm

    c) Prim's algorithm

    d) Kruskal's algorithm

6. Prim's algorithm follows

    a) Greedy method

    b) Dynamic programming

    c) Divide and conquer strategy

    d) Backtracking

7. Which auxiliary data structure is used to implement BFS?

    a) Linked list

    b) Stack

    c) Queue

    d) Tree

8. Which auxiliary data structure is used to implement DFS?

    a) Linked list

    b) Stack

    c) Queue

    d) Tree

9. The vertex whose in-degree is greater than 0 but out-degree is 0 is known as
    a) Isolated vertex
    b) Source vertex
    c) Sink vertex
    d) None of these

10. The vertex whose in-degree is 0 but out-degree is greater than 0 is known as
    a) Isolated vertex
    b) Source vertex
    c) Sink vertex
    d) None of these

11. The vertex whose both in-degree and out-degree is 0 is known as
    a) Isolated vertex
    b) Source vertex
    c) Sink vertex
    d) None of these

12. Floyd–Warshall algorithm follows
    a) Greedy method
    b) Dynamic Programming
    c) Divide and conquer strategy
    d) Backtracking

13. Kruskal's algorithm follows
    a) Greedy method
    b) Dynamic Programming
    c) Divide and conquer strategy
    d) Backtracking

14. If all the vertices of a graph are connected to each other, it is known as
    a) Connected graph
    b) Complete graph
    c) Forest
    d) None of these

15. The number of edges in a complete graph of n vertices is
    a) $n(n - 1)/2$
    b) $2n - 1$
    c) $2^n - 1$
    d) None of these

Review Exercises

1. Define a graph.

2. What do you mean by a directed graph and an undirected graph?

3. What is a weighted graph?

4. Find the adjacency matrix, incidence matrix, adjacency list, and adjacency multi-list of the following graph:

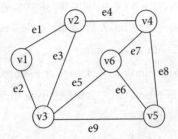

5. Find the adjacency matrix, incidence matrix, adjacency list, and adjacency multi-list of the following directed graph:

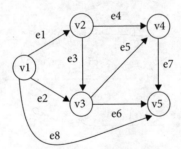

6. Find the adjacency matrix, incidence matrix, and adjacency list of the following weighted graph:

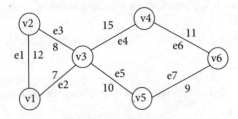

7. Find the adjacency matrix, incidence matrix, and adjacency list of the following weighted directed graph:

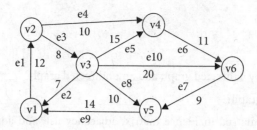

8. Consider the graph given in question no. 6. Find the degree of each vertex.

9. Consider the graph given in question no. 7. Find the in-degree and out-degree of each vertex.

10. What is a cut vertex? Explain with an example.

11. Consider the graph given in question no. 5. Is there any source and sink? Explain.

12. Consider the graph given in question no. 7. Is there any source and sink? Explain.

13. Differentiate between BFS and DFS.

14. Consider the graph given in question no. 7. Find out the DFS and BFS paths in this graph.

15. What do you mean by a spanning tree? What is a minimum spanning tree?

16. Find out the minimum spanning tree from the following graph using Prim's algorithm.

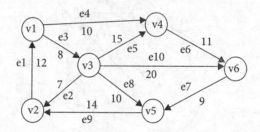

17. Find out the minimum spanning tree from the graph given in question no. 16 using Kruskal's algorithm.

18. Consider the graph given in question no 16. Find the shortest path

    a.   from v1 to v6

    b.   from v5 to v6

    c.   from v5 to v4

19. Consider the graph given in question no. 16. Find the shortest distance among all pair of vertices.

Problems for Programming

1. Write a function to check whether a graph contains any loops or not. If a loop exists, remove it.

2. Write a function to implement BFS.

3. Write a function to implement DFS.

4. Write a function to check whether a graph is a complete graph or not.

5. Write a function to construct a minimum spanning tree from a given graph.

6. Write a function to check whether a path exists between two vertices. If it exists, print the path.

7. Write a function to find the shortest path between two given vertices.

Searching and Sorting

In this chapter we will discuss two important operations in programming languages. These are searching and sorting. There are several algorithms for both searching and sorting. Every algorithm has some merits and demerits. In this chapter we will discuss some important searching algorithms as well as sorting algorithms. We will discuss the working principles of these algorithms in detail and how they can be implemented in Python, we will derive their time complexity, and finally we will compare them with each other.

13.1 Introduction to Searching

Searching is a process by which we can check whether an element is present within a set of elements or not. If it is present, we can say that the search operation is 'Successful' and this process also find the position of the element in the list. But if the element is not present, the search operation is considered as 'Failure' and the process terminates with an appropriate failure message. In traditional programming languages searching operations are generally implemented using arrays. In Python we can implement searching algorithms using arrays as well as in-built list data structures. There are several searching algorithms to search for an element from an array/list. Here we will discuss the three most common searching algorithms.

- Linear Search
- Binary Search
- Interpolation Search

Among the above three searching algorithms, to implement linear search the array/list need not be sorted necessarily. But the initial requirement for the other two algorithms is that the array/list must be sorted.

13.1.1 Linear Search

The algorithm which checks each element of a list starting from the first position is known as Linear Search. As this algorithm checks each element in a list sequentially it is also known as Sequential Search. When the elements in a list are unsorted, i.e. not in proper order, this searching technique is used. Suppose we have the following list of elements:

arr	25	12	57	40	63	32
	0	1	2	3	4	5

And the key element is 40, i.e. we want to search whether 40 is present in the list or not and if it is present, then we also need to know its position in the list. In case of linear search, we start checking from the beginning of the list, i.e. from the index position 0. So, we first compare whether arr[0]==40. As the comparison fails, we check for the next index position. Now arr[1] contains 12. So, the comparison arr[1]==40 becomes false. Next we need to compare with the value of next index position, i.e. arr[2], and the comparison arr[2]==40 becomes false again. Again we compare the key element with the next index position, i.e. whether arr[3]==40 Now the condition becomes true and the search operation terminates here returning the index position 3.

But what happens if the element is not present in the list at all? Let us see. Suppose the key element is 50. The search operation starts from index position 0. The element in the zeroth position is 25 here. So the first comparison would be failed and we need to move to the next index position. Again the comparison arr[1]==50 becomes false and we move to the next index position. In this way we compare the value of each index position sequentially and all the comparisons become false. When the last comparison, i.e. arr[5]==50, becomes false, we can say that the search fails and the key element, 50, is not present in the list.

The general algorithm of linear search may be defined as follows.

Linear_Search(List, Key_Value)

Here *List* is either an array or a Python list and *Key_Value* is the element to be searched.

```
1. Set Index = 0
2. While Index < Size of the List do,
   a. If List[Index] == Key_Value, then
      i. Return Index
   b. Index = Index + 1
3. Return -1
```

Here the algorithm is written as a function that returns the corresponding index position when the element is found in the list; otherwise, it returns -1 to indicate the failure of the search operation.

Here is the implementation of linear search technique:

Program 13.1: Program to implement linear search

```
#PRGD13_1: Program to implement Linear Search
def linear_search(list, key):
    size=len(list)
    index=0
    while index<size:
        if list[index]==key:
            return index
        index=index+1
    return -1

n=int(input('Enter number of elements: '))
lst=[]
for i in range(n):
    num = int(input('Enter element {}: '.format(i+1)))
    lst.append(num)
key=int(input('Enter the element to be searched: '))
position = linear_search(lst, key)
if position == -1:
    print('Element not Found')
else:
    print('{} found at position {}'.format(key, position))
```

Analysis of linear search: If there are n number of elements in the list, we need to compare n number of times in the worst case. Thus the worst case time complexity of linear search is O(n). This is the situation when the key element is at the last position, or the key element is not present at all in the list. However, the best case is when the key element is at the very first position in the list. In that case, the element would be found with the first comparison. Thus the best case time complexity of linear search is O(1).

13.1.2 Binary Search

Whatever we have discussed in the previous section that is used mostly with the unsorted element. If the elements are in proper order, most of the time we never follow sequential searching. Suppose we need to open a particular page in a book; we never check each and every page starting from page 1. What we do is that we move to an arbitrary page and check whether we have crossed the required page or we need to move further. Based on that decision we consider the book separated into two portions and we repeat the same action in the appropriate portion of the book until we reach the required page. For example, if we want to move to page number 359 of a book of, say, 500 pages, first we move to an arbitrary page which is at nearly the middle of the book. Suppose the page number of this page is 273. As the required page number is greater than this, it should be on the right half of the book and we need not check in between 1 and 273. So we repeat the same operation on the portion that consists of page numbers 274 to 500. Hence we again move to an arbitrary page that is nearly at the middle of this portion and, say, it is page number 403. So we need to check again in between 274 and 402. This process continues until we reach the required page. This is also true for finding any word from a dictionary or finding any name from a voter list, etc.

Binary search works based on this principle. It is now clear that to implement this working principle the list should be sorted. Thus to implement binary search the prerequisite condition is that the array/list must be sorted. According to binary search algorithm, the search key value is compared with the middle element of the sorted array/list. If it matches, the array/list index is returned. Otherwise, if the search key is less than the middle element, then the algorithm repeats its action on the sub-array/list to the left of the middle element or if the search key is greater, then the algorithm repeats its action on the sub-array/list to the right of the middle element. This process continues until the match is found or the remaining array to be searched becomes empty. If it is empty, it indicates that the searched element is not found. This algorithm runs much faster than linear search.

Consider the following example. We have the following list of elements and the search key element is 32.

Arr	12	25	32	40	57	63	76
	0	1	2	3	4	5	6

As we need to find the middle position of the array/list, we start the operation considering **low** as the staring index and **high** as the last index of the array/list. Thus here

Low = 0 and High = 6

So, Mid = (Low+High)/2 = (0+6)/2 = 3

And arr[Mid] = arr[3]=40

As the key element, 32, is less than arr[Mid], we need to search within the left half of the array/list. So, the lower bound of the array/list remains the same and the new upper bound would be

High = Mid-1=3-1=2

Now, Mid = (Low+High)/2 = (0+2)/2 = 1

And arr[Mid]= arr[1] = 25

As the key element, 32, is greater than arr[Mid], we need to search within the right half of the sub-array/list. So, the upper bound of the sub-array/list remains the same and the new lower bound would be

Low = Mid + 1 = 1+1 = 2

Now, Mid = (Low+High)/2 = (2+2)/2 = 2

And arr[Mid]= arr[2] = 32 which is equal to the key element.

This indicates that the search element is found at position 2, i.e. the final position of Mid.

Now, we are considering another example where the key element is not present in the array/list. Suppose, the key element is 35. Proceeding in the same way, we get

Low = 0 and High = 6

So, Mid = (Low+High)/2 = (0+6)/2 = 3

And arr[Mid] = arr[3]=40

As the key element, 35, is less than arr[Mid], we need to search within the left half of the array/list. Thus,

High = Mid-1=3-1=2

Now, Mid = (Low+High)/2 = (0+2)/2 = 1

And arr[Mid]= arr[1] = 25

As the key element, 35, is greater than arr[Mid], we need to search within the right half of the sub-array/list. Hence,

Low = Mid + 1 = 1+1 = 2

Now, Mid = (Low+High)/2 = (2+2)/2 = 2

And arr[Mid]= arr[2] = 32

As the key element, 35, is greater than arr[Mid], we need to search within the right half of the sub-array/list. Hence,

Low = Mid + 1 = 2+1 = 3

Now, see the situation. The value of the upper bound, i.e. High, is 2 and the value of lower bound, i.e. Low, is 3, which cannot be possible. This indicates we do not have any sub-array/list to search more, which means that the search operation fails here, and we can say that the key element, 35, is not present in the list.

The general algorithm of binary search may be defined as follows:

Binary_Search(*List, Key_Value*)

Here *List* is either a sorted array or Python list and *Key_Value* is the element to be searched.

```
1.  Set Low = 0
2.  Set High = Length of List - 1
3.  While Low <= High do,
    a. Mid = (Low+High)/2
    b. If Key_Value == List[Mid], then
        i. Return Mid
```

```
c. Else if Key_Value < List[Mid], then
    i. High = Mid - 1
d. Else,
    i. Low = Mid + 1
4. Return -1
```

Here the algorithm is written as a function that returns the corresponding index position when the element is found in the list; otherwise, it returns -1 to indicate the failure of the search operation.

Here is the implementation of binary search operation:

Program 13.2: Program to implement binary search

```
#PRGD13_2: Program to implement Binary Search
def binary_search(list, key):
    low = 0
    high = len(list)-1
    while low<=high:
        mid=(low+high)//2
        if key==list[mid]:
            return mid
        elif key<list[mid]:
            high=mid-1
        else:
            low=mid+1
    return -1

n=int(input('Enter number of elements: '))
lst=[]
for i in range(n):
    num = int(input('Enter element {}: '.format(i+1)))
    lst.append(num)
key=int(input('Enter the element to be searched: '))
position = binary_search(lst, key)
if position == -1:
    print('Element not Found')
else:
    print('{} found at position {}'.format(key, position))
```

Analysis of Binary search: Like linear search, the calculation of the complexity of binary search too depends on the number of comparisons. But this calculation is not as simple as linear search because with each comparison the effective size of the array/list reduces to half.

Therefore if the total number of required comparisons among n elements is T_n, we can say

$$T_n = 1 + T_{\frac{n}{2}} \qquad => 1 + T_{\frac{n}{2^1}}$$

$$= 1 + \left(1 + T_{\frac{n}{4}}\right) \quad => 2 + T_{\frac{n}{2^2}}$$

$$= 2 + \left(1 + T_{\frac{n}{8}}\right) \quad => 3 + T_{\frac{n}{2^3}}$$

....

$\therefore$ After y-th search, $T_n = y + T_{\frac{n}{2^y}}$ .... (1)

Suppose the y-th search is the last search. Hence in the worst case the number of elements in the sub-array/list would be 1.

Thus, we can say $\frac{n}{2^y} = 1$

Or, $n = 2^y$

Or, $\log_2 n = \log_2 2^y$ [Taking log on both sides]

$= y \log_2 2$

$= y$ [$\therefore \log_2 2 = 1$]

$\therefore y = \log_2 n$ ....(2)

Putting the value of y in Equation (1), we get

$$T_n = \log_2 n + T_{\frac{n}{2^y}}$$

$$= \log_2 n + T_1 \quad \left[\because \frac{n}{2^y} = 1\right]$$

$$= \log_2 n + 1 \quad [\because T_1 = 1]$$

Hence, the worst case time complexity of binary search is $O(\log_2 n)$.

However, the best case is when the key element would be at the middle position. In that case, the element would be found with the first comparison. Thus the best case time complexity of binary search is also O(1).

13.1.3 Interpolation Search

The working principle of interpolation search is just like binary search but we can consider it as an improved version of binary search. In binary search we always find the exact middle position. But in real life, when we search a page from a book instead of finding the middle position we use some intuition. If the page number is towards the end of the book, we try to find a page nearer to the end. Similarly if the page is nearer to the beginning of the book, we try to find the page nearer to the desired page, i.e. nearer to the beginning of the book. This concept is used in interpolation search.

Interpolation search works on a sorted list of elements and it performs better when the elements are uniformly distributed in the array/list. Though it follows the basic logic of binary search, instead of finding middle position, to find the intermediate position it uses the following formula:

```
Position=low+((keyValue-Arr[low])*(high-low)/(Arr[high]-
                                              Arr[low]))
```

where **Arr** is an array/list, **keyValue** is the element to be searched, **low** is the starting index of the array/list or the sub-array/list and **high** is the last index of array/list or sub-array/list.

After calculating the intermediate position, the algorithm checks whether the keyValue is equal, smaller, or larger than the element of the calculated intermediate position. If it is equal, the search operation terminates by returning the value of the position, otherwise the position divides the array into two sub-arrays/lists; if the keyValue is smaller, the same operation repeats with the lower half of the array/list; and if the keyValue is larger, the same operation repeats with the upper half of the array/list.

Consider the following example. Suppose we have the following list of elements and the search key element is 32.

arr	12	25	32	40	57	63	76
	0	1	2	3	4	5	6

We start the operation considering **low** as the staring index and **high** as the last index of the array/list. Thus here

Low = 0 and High = 6

Now, Position = Low+((keyValue–arr[low])*(high–low)/(arr[high]– arr[low]))

= 0+((32-12)*(6-0)/(76-12)) = 20*6/64=1.875

Considering integer division, value of Position = 1

And arr[Position] = arr[1]=25

As the key element, 32, is larger than arr[Position], we need to search within the right half of the array/list. So, the upper bound of the array/list remains the same and the new lower bound would be

Low = Position+1=1+1=2

Now, Position = 2+7*6/44 = 2+0.95 = 2.95

Considering integer division, value of Position = 2

And arr[Position] = arr[2]=32 which is equals to the key element.

This indicates that the search operation is successful and the search element is found at position 2.

The general algorithm of interpolation search may be defined as follows:

`Interpolation_Search(List, Key_Value)`

Here *List* is either a sorted array or Python list and *Key_Value* is the element to be searched.

```
1.  Set Low = 0
2.  Set High = Length of List - 1
3.  While Low <= High do,
    a.  Position = Low+((keyValue-arr[low])*(high-low)/
            (arr[high]- arr[low]))
    b.  If Key_Value == List[Position], then
            i. Return Position
    c.  Else if Key_Value < List[Position], then
            i. High = Position - 1
    d.  Else,
            i. Low = Position + 1
4. Return -1
```

Here the algorithm is written as a function that returns the corresponding index position when the element is found in the list; otherwise it returns -1 to indicate the failure of the search operation.

Here is the implementation of interpolation search operation:

Program 13.3: Program to implement interpolation search

```
#PRGD13_3: Program to implement Interpolation Search
def interpolation_search(list, key):
    low = 0
    high = len(list)-1
    while low<=high:
```

```
            if low == high:
                if list[low]==key:
                    return low
                else:
                    return -1
            position=low+((key-list[low])*(high-low)//
                                (list[high]-list[low]))
            if key==list[position]:
                return position
            elif key<list[position]:
                high=position-1
            else:
                low=position+1
        return -1

n=int(input('Enter number of elements: '))
lst=[]
for i in range(n):
    num = int(input('Enter element {}: '.format(i+1)))
    lst.append(num)
key=int(input('Enter the element to be searched: '))
position = interpolation_search(lst, key)
if position == -1:
    print('Element not Found')
else:
    print('{} found at position {}'.format(key, position))
```

Analysis of Interpolation search: Interpolation search gives the best performance when the elements are evenly distributed. In that situation the time complexity of interpolation search is measured as $O(\log_2(\log_2 n))$. But if the elements are distributed exponentially, it shows the worst case performance and the worst case performance is $O(n)$. However, the elements may be found with the first comparison and it is denoted as $O(1)$.

13.2 Introduction to Sorting

Sorting is a process by which we can arrange the elements in a specific order. The order may be increasing or decreasing. By default it is increasing. Basically sorting is of two types: *internal sort* and *external sort*. When the amount of data is less, which easily fits into the main memory (i.e. RAM), internal sorting is used. Whereas for huge amounts of data which do not fit completely into the main memory, external sorting is required. In this chapter, we will discuss some internal sorting techniques. There are several internal sorting algorithms to sort an array/list. Here we discuss a few of them.

13.2.1 Bubble Sort

It is very simple and the most common sorting technique for beginners. In this sorting technique, the adjacent elements are compared. If the previous element is larger than the successor, elements are interchanged. This continues from the first two elements to the last two elements. At the end of the comparison of last two elements, the first pass is completed. At the end of the first pass, we will find that the largest element has moved to the last position. This process continues. As in each pass a single element will move to its required position, n-1 passes will be required to sort the array. The following example illustrates the working principle of bubble sort:

| arr | 85 | 33 | 57 | 12 | 40 | 2 |

| arr | 85 | 33 | 57 | 12 | 40 | 2 |

First arr[0] will be compared with arr[1], i.e. 85 with 33. As the first element is larger than the next one, the elements will be interchanged and we will get to the next state.

| arr | 33 | 85 | 57 | 12 | 40 | 2 |

Next arr[1] will be compared with arr[2], i.e. 85 with 57. Again 85 is larger than 57. So, the elements will be interchanged. This process continues.

| arr | 33 | 57 | 85 | 12 | 40 | 2 |

| arr | 33 | 57 | 12 | 85 | 40 | 2 |

| arr | 33 | 57 | 12 | 40 | 85 | 2 |

| arr | 33 | 57 | 12 | 40 | 2 | 85 |

This is the end of the first pass and we get the largest element at the last position. Now the second pass will start.

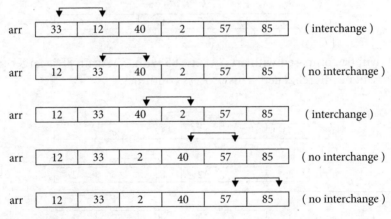

This is the end of the second pass and the second largest element, i.e. 57, is now in its proper position. In this way in each pass a single element will get its proper position. Resembling the formation of bubbles, in this sorting technique the array is sorted gradually from the bottom. That is why it is known as bubble sort. As the sorting process involves exchange of two elements, it is also known as exchange sort. Other passes are described below:

Third pass:

| arr | 33 | 12 | 40 | 2 | 57 | 85 | (interchange) |

| arr | 12 | 33 | 40 | 2 | 57 | 85 | (no interchange) |

| arr | 12 | 33 | 40 | 2 | 57 | 85 | (interchange) |

| arr | 12 | 33 | 2 | 40 | 57 | 85 | (no interchange) |

| arr | 12 | 33 | 2 | 40 | 57 | 85 | (no interchange) |

Fourth pass:

| Arr | 12 | 33 | 2 | 40 | 57 | 85 | (no interchange) |

| Arr | 12 | 33 | 2 | 40 | 57 | 85 | (interchange) |

| Arr | 12 | 2 | 33 | 40 | 57 | 85 | (no interchange) |

| Arr | 12 | 2 | 33 | 40 | 57 | 85 | (no interchange) |

| Arr | 12 | 2 | 33 | 40 | 57 | 85 | (no interchange) |

Fifth pass:

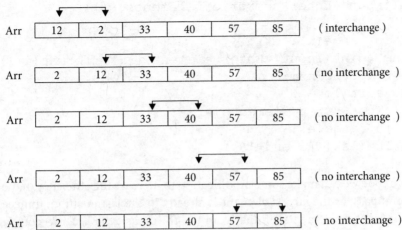

Now the array becomes sorted.

The general algorithm of a bubble sort algorithm is as follows:

Bubble_Sort(*List*)

Here *List* is either an array or Python list.

```
1. size = len(list)
2. For i=0 to size-2 do
       a. For j=0 to size-2 do
              i.  if list[j]>list[j+1], then
                      1. set temp=list[j]
                      2. set list[j]=list[j+1]
                      3. set list[j+1]=temp
3. exit
```

On the basis of this algorithm now we can write the corresponding program.

Program 13.4: Program to sort a list using bubble sort algorithm

```
#PRGD13_4: Program to implement Bubble Sort
def bubble_sort(list):
    size = len(list)
    for i in range(size-1):
        for j in range(size-1):
            if list[j]>list[j+1]:
                temp=list[j]
                list[j]=list[j+1]
                list[j+1]=temp
```

```
n=int(input('Enter number of elements: '))
lst=[]
for i in range(n):
    num = int(input('Enter element {}: '.format(i+1)))
    lst.append(num)
bubble_sort(lst)
print('The Sorted Elements are : ')
for i in range(n):
    print(lst[i], end=' ')
```

In the above code we can make some modification to increase the efficiency of the program. In the second pass, as the largest element is already in the last position, unnecessarily we compare the last two elements. Similarly, in the third pass, the last two comparisons are unnecessary. We can modify our code in such a way that in the first pass n-1 comparisons are made, in the second pass n-2 comparisons are made, in the third pass n-3 comparisons are made, and so on. In this way, in the last pass, i.e. the (n-1)th pass, only one comparison will be required. Thus the process speeds up as it proceeds through successive passes. To implement this concept we can rewrite the function as:

```
def bubble_sort(list):
    size = len(list)
    for i in range(size-1):
        for j in range(size-i-1):
            if list[j]>list[j+1]:
                temp=list[j]
                list[j]=list[j+1]
                list[j+1]=temp
```

Another drawback of this algorithm is that if the elements are already sorted or the array becomes sorted in any intermediate stage, still we have to proceed for n-1 passes. But if we carefully notice, if the elements have become sorted, then no further interchange is made. In other words, if no interchange takes place in a pass, we can say that the elements are sorted and it can be easily implemented by using an extra variable, say, flag. Considering this modification, the modified version of the basic technique of bubble sort is given below:

Program 13.5: Modified version of bubble sort algorithm

```
#PRGD13_5: Program to implement Modified Bubble Sort
def modified_bubble_sort(list):
    size = len(list)
    for i in range(size-1):
```

```
        flag=True
        for j in range(size-i-1):
            if list[j]>list[j+1]:
                temp=list[j]
                list[j]=list[j+1]
                list[j+1]=temp
                flag=False
        if flag:
            break

n=int(input('Enter number of elements: '))
lst=[]
for i in range(n):
    num = int(input('Enter element {}: '.format(i+1)))
    lst.append(num)
modified_bubble_sort(lst)
print('The Sorted Elements are : ')
for i in range(n):
    print(lst[i], end=' ')
```

Analysis of Bubble Sort: In bubble sort, if there are n number of elements, in the first pass the number of comparisons is n-1. In the second pass it is n-2, and so on. As there would be n-1 passes to sort an array/list, in the (n-1)th pass the number of comparisons is n-(n-1) = 1. In the (n-2)th pass, the number of comparisons is n-(n-2) = 2.

Thus, the total number of comparisons T_n = (n-1) + (n-2) + …….. + 3 + 2 +1

$$= n(n-1)/2$$

$$=\frac{1}{2}n^2 -\frac{1}{2}n$$

Hence, the time complexity of bubble sort is $O(n^2)$. In basic bubble sort algorithm, whatever may be the initial position of the elements, the time complexity is always $O(n^2)$. But in modified bubble sort, if the elements are already in sorted order, the algorithm terminates with the first pass. In the first pass, the number of comparisons is n-1. Hence, in the best case, the modified bubble sort shows the time complexity as $O(n)$. But in the worst case, time complexity of modified bubble sort is $O(n^2)$.

13.2.2 Selection Sort

In this sorting technique, first the smallest element is selected and then this element is interchanged with the element of the first position. Now the first element is in its proper position and the rest of the elements are unsorted. So, consider the rest of the elements. The second element is now logically the first element for the remaining set. Again we select the smallest element from this remaining set and interchange with the currently logical first position. This process continues by selecting the smallest element from the rest and placing it into its proper position by interchanging with the logical first element. As in each iteration, the corresponding smallest is selected and placed into its proper position, this algorithm is known as selection sort. Since in each pass a single element will move to its required position, n-1 passes will be required to sort the array/list. The following example illustrates the working principle of selection sort:

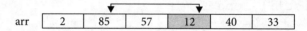

| arr | 33 | 85 | 57 | 12 | 40 | 2 |

| arr | 33 | 85 | 57 | 12 | 40 | 2 |

Here, the smallest element is 2. So, it will be interchanged with the first element, i.e. 33, and we get the next state.

| arr | 2 | 85 | 57 | 12 | 40 | 33 |

Now 2 is placed in its proper position. So, we consider only the rest of the elements. Among the rest of the elements 12 is the smallest. It will be interchanged with the second position, which is currently the logical first position.

| arr | 2 | 12 | 57 | 85 | 40 | 33 |

This process continues.

| arr | 2 | 12 | 33 | 85 | 40 | 57 |

| arr | 2 | 12 | 33 | 40 | 85 | 57 |

| arr | 2 | 12 | 33 | 40 | 57 | 85 |

Based on the above working principle, we may define the general algorithm of selection sort as follows:

```
Selection_Sort(List)
```

Here *List* is a Python list.

```
1.    size = length of list
2.    for i=0 to size-2 do
      a. min=list[i]
      b. posn=i
      c. for j in range(i+1,size):
             i.  if list[j]<min:
                     1. min=list[j]
                     2. posn=j
      d. if i!=posn:
             i.   temp=list[i]
            ii.   list[i]=list[posn]
           iii.   list[posn]=temp
3.    exit
```

On the basis of this algorithm now we write a program to sort an array using selection sort.

Program 13.6: Program to sort elements using selection sort algorithm

```python
#PRGD13_6: Program to implement Selection Sort
def selection_sort(list):
    size = len(list)
    for i in range(size-1):
        min=list[i]
        posn=i
        for j in range(i+1,size):
            if list[j]<min:
                min=list[j]
                posn=j
        if i!=posn:
            temp=list[i]
            list[i]=list[posn]
            list[posn]=temp

n=int(input('Enter number of elements: '))
lst=[]
for i in range(n):
    num = int(input('Enter element {}: '.format(i+1)))
    lst.append(num)
selection_sort(lst)
print('The Sorted Elements are : ')
for i in range(n):
    print(lst[i], end=' ')
```

Analysis of Selection Sort: In selection sort, in each pass we need to find the smallest element. To find the smallest element, if there are n number of elements, the number of required comparisons in the first pass is n-1. In the second pass it is n-2, and so on. As there would be n-1 passes to sort an array/list, in the (n-1)th pass, the number of comparisons is n-(n-1) = 1. In the (n-2)th pass, the number of comparisons is n-(n-2) = 2.

Thus, the total number of comparisons $T_n = (n-1) + (n-2) + \ldots\ldots + 3 + 2 + 1$

$$= n(n-1)/2$$

$$= \frac{1}{2}n^2 - \frac{1}{2}n$$

Hence, the time complexity of selection sort is $O(n^2)$. As there is no scope to understand whether the array is already sorted or not, we need to complete all the (n-1) passes. Thus selection sort always shows $O(n^2)$ time complexity. However, with slight modification we may decrease the running time a bit.

13.2.3 Insertion Sort

The basic theory of this sorting technique is that each element is inserted into its proper position in a previously sorted array/list. The process starts from the second element of the array/list. Before this element there is a single element only and it can be considered as a sorted array/list which has only one element. Now insert the second element in this array/list so that we get a sorted array/list of two elements. Next consider the third element. Before this element, we have a sorted array/list of two elements. Insert the third element into its proper position in this sorted array/list and we will get the first three elements sorted. This process continues up to the last element for the array/list to become fully sorted. As the sorting technique grows by inserting each element into its proper position, this sorting technique is known as Insertion sort. The following example illustrates the working principle of insertion sort:

Consider the initial list as:

arr	85	33	57	12	40	2

According to this technique the sorting procedure starts from the second position of the list. So, we have to consider the second element, i.e. arr[1], which is 33, and the situation is:

arr | 85 → | (33)

To become sorted 85 will be shifted to its next position, i.e. into arr[1], and 33 will be inserted to arr[0] position. So, the new state will be:

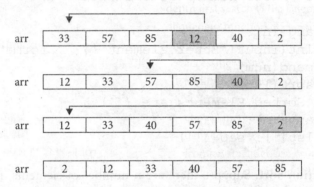

| arr | 33 | 85 | 57 | 12 | 40 | 2 |

In the next iteration we have to consider the third element, i.e. arr[2]. Now the situation is:

As 57 is smaller than 85 but larger than 33, 57 should be inserted in between these two. So, 85 will be shifted to arr[2] position and 57 will be inserted in arr[1] and we will get:

| arr | 33 | 57 | 85 | 12 | 40 | 2 |

This process continues and we get the following states:

| arr | 33 | 57 | 85 | 12 | 40 | 2 |

| arr | 12 | 33 | 57 | 85 | 40 | 2 |

| arr | 12 | 33 | 40 | 57 | 85 | 2 |

| arr | 2 | 12 | 33 | 40 | 57 | 85 |

Based on the above working principle we may define the general algorithm of insertion sort as follows:

Insertion_Sort(*List*)

Here *List* is a Python list.

```
1.    size = length of list
2.    for i=1 to size-1 do
      a. temp=list[i]
      b. j=i-1
      c. while temp<list[j] and j>=0 do
             i.  list[j+1]=list[j]
             ii. j=j-1
      d. list[j+1]=temp
3. exit
```

The following code shows the implementation of the above algorithm.

Program 13.7: Program to sort elements using insertion sort algorithm

```
#PRGD13_7: Program to implement Insertion Sort
def insertion_sort(list):
    size = len(list)
    for i in range(1,size):
        temp=list[i]
        j= i-1
        while temp<list[j] and j>=0:
            list[j+1]=list[j]
            j=j-1
        list[j+1]=temp

n=int(input('Enter number of elements: '))
lst=[]
for i in range(n):
    num = int(input('Enter element {}: '.format(i+1)))
    lst.append(num)
insertion_sort(lst)
print('The Sorted Elements are : ')
for i in range(n):
    print(lst[i], sep=' ')
```

Analysis of Insertion Sort: Suppose there are n number of elements in an array/list. In insertion sort, in the first pass, the first two elements get sorted. In the second pass the first three elements get sorted. So, the total number of required passes is (n-1). In the first pass, the maximum number of comparisons is 1. In the second pass it is 2, and so on. So, in the (n-1)th pass, the number of comparisons is (n-1). In (n-2)th pass, the number of comparisons is (n-2).

Thus, the total number of comparisons $T_n = 1 + 2 + 3 + \ldots\ldots + (n-2) + (n-1)$

$$= n(n-1)/2$$

$$= \frac{1}{2}n^2 - \frac{1}{2}n$$

Hence, the time complexity of insertion sort is $O(n^2)$. But if the array is already sorted, in each pass the maximum number of comparisons would be 1. Hence,

Total number of comparisons $T_n = 1 + 1 + 1 + \ldots\ldots\ldots$ upto (n-1) terms

$$= n-1$$

Thus, insertion sort shows the best performance when the elements are already sorted and the best case performance of insertion sort is O(n).

13.2.4 Quick Sort

Quick sort is a very efficient algorithm that follows the 'divide and conquer' strategy. The first task in this algorithm is to select the pivot element. It may be the first element, the last element, the middlemost element, or any other element. As this choice does not provide any extra advantages, we are choosing the first element as the pivot element. Next, the algorithm proceeds with the motivation that this pivot element partitions the array/list into two sub-arrays/lists such that all the elements smaller than the pivot element is on the left side of the pivot element and all the larger elements are on the right side. The same operation would be then applied to both sub-arrays/lists until the size of the sub arrays/lists becomes one or zero. Consider the following example:

33	85	40	12	57	2	25

As we select the first element, i.e. the leftmost, as pivot, scanning starts from the right side. We also need to set two variables – left and right. They will contain the starting index and the end index of the array/list. Thus, initially, left = 0 and right = 6 here.

Starting from the right, we find that arr[right]<pivot; so, we need to interchange these elements.

After interchange we have to change the direction of scanning. Now we scan from left.

Now, arr[left]<pivot; thus the value of the left variable will be increased by 1 to point to the next element.

This time arr[left]>pivot. So, these values need to interchange.

With this interchange we again change the direction of scanning.

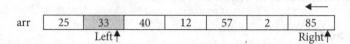

Now, arr[right]>pivot; thus the value of the right variable will be decreased by 1 to point to the next element. This time arr[right]<pivot. So, we interchange these values.

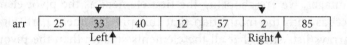

Again we scan from the left.

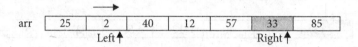

Now, arr[left]<pivot; hence the value of the left variable will be increased to point to the next element.

This time arr[left]>pivot. So, these values would be interchanged.

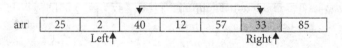

Now we scan from the right.

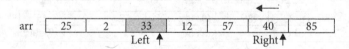

Again, arr[right]>pivot and the value of the right variable will be decreased by 1 to point to the next element.

arr | 25 | 2 | 33 | 12 | 57 | 40 | 85 |

Left ⬆ Right ⬆

Again, arr[right]>pivot and once again the value of right variable will be decreased by 1. Now, arr[right]<pivot. So, we will interchange these values.

arr | 25 | 2 | 33 | 12 | 57 | 40 | 85 |

Left ⬆ Right ⬆

Now we scan from the left.

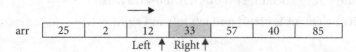

Now, arr[left]<pivot; hence the value of the left variable will be increased.

arr | 25 | 2 | 12 | 33 | 57 | 40 | 85 |
Right↑
Left↑

Now the left and the right become equal, which indicates the end of this procedure and the pivot element finds its proper position and divides the array/list into two sub-arrays/lists where all the smaller elements are on the left side and the larger elements on the right side.

The same procedure now will be applied on both the sub-arrays/lists.

arr | 25 | 2 | 12 |
Left↑   Right↑

On the left sub-array/list, again we choose the first element as pivot element and scanning starts from the right side. Now, left = 0 and right = 2. As arr[right]<pivot, we will interchange these values.

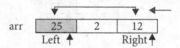

Now we scan from the left. Since arr[left]<pivot, the value of the left variable will be increased.

arr | 12 | 2 | 25 |
Left↑ Right↑

Again, arr[left]<pivot; thus the value of the left variable will be incremented and we get:

arr | 12 | 2 | 25 |
Right↑
Left↑

Now the left and the right become equal, which indicates the end of this procedure and this pivot element, i.e. 25, finds its proper position. But this time, there will be no element on right sub-array/list and all the rest of the elements will be in the left sub-array/list. So, we need to apply the same procedure on this left sub-array/list.

Now, the pivot element is arr[0] and left = 0 and right = 1.

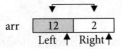

```
arr   | 12 |  2 |
      Left ↑ Right↑
```

Scanning from the right we find that arr[right]<pivot and we interchange these values.

```
arr   | 12 |  2 |
      Left ↑ Right↑
```

And we get:

```
arr   |  2 | 12 |
      Left ↑ Right↑
```

Now arr[left]<pivot; thus the value of the left variable will be increased and we get:

```
Arr   |  2 | 12 |
            Right↑
            Left ↑
```

Now the left and the right become equal; thus this procedure is terminated here. As the size of the newly formed left sub-array/list is 1 and of the right sub-array/list is 0, we need not proceed further. Now we have to consider the first right sub-array/list.

Now the pivot element is arr[4], which is the leftmost or the first element of the right sub-array/list and left = 4 and right = 6.

```
arr   | 57 | 40 | 85 |
      Left ↑    Right↑
```

Starting scanning from the right side, we find arr[right]>pivot. So, the value of the right variable is decreased by 1.

```
arr   | 57 | 40 | 85 |
      Left ↑ Right↑
```

Now, arr[right]<pivot. So, we will interchange these values.

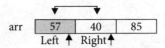

And we get:

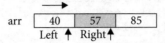

Now we scan from the left and find that arr[left]<pivot; thus the value of the left variable will be increased and we get:

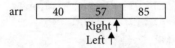

As the left and the right become equals, this procedure will terminate here and we get two sub-arrays/lists each of which contains a single element. So, we need not proceed further and we get the final sorted array/list as follows:

arr	2	12	25	33	40	57	85

Based on this working principle, we may now write the algorithm of quick sort. As we find that the partitioning procedure is called recursively, we divide the algorithm into two modules where one module does the process of partitioning and the other module is the driver module that calls the partitioning module recursively.

Here is the general algorithm of quick sort:

Quick_Sort(*Arr, left, right*)

Here *Arr* is an array or python list, *left* is the starting index, and *right* is the end index of the array/list or sub-array/list.

```
1.  If left<right, then
    a.  Set loc=PartitionList(arr,left,right)
    b.  call Quick_Sort(arr,left,loc-1)
    c.  call Quick_Sort(arr,loc+1,right)
2.  end
```

PartitionList(*Arr, left, right*)

Here *Arr* is an array or Python list, *left* is the starting index, and *right* is the end index of the array/list or sub-array/list.

```
1. Set loc=left
2. while True, do
      a. while arr[loc]<=arr[right] and loc!=right, do
            i. Set right=right-1
      b. if loc==right, then
            i. break
      c. elif arr[loc]>arr[right], then
            i. swap arr[loc] and arr[right]
           ii. set loc=right

      d. while arr[loc]>=arr[left] and loc!=left, do
            i. set left=left +1
      e. if loc==left, then
            i. break
      f. elif arr[loc]<arr[left], then
            i. swap arr[loc] and arr[left]
           ii. set loc=left
3. return loc
```

The following code shows the implementation of quick sort algorithm:

Program 13.8: Program to sort elements using quick sort algorithm

```python
#PRGD13_8: Program to implement Quick Sort
def partitionlist(arr, left, right):
    loc=left
    while True:
        while arr[loc]<=arr[right] and loc!=right:
            right-=1
        if loc==right:
            break
        elif arr[loc]>arr[right]:
            arr[loc],arr[right]=arr[right],arr[loc]
            loc=right

        while arr[loc]>=arr[left] and loc!=left:
            left+=1
        if loc==left:
            break
        elif arr[loc]<arr[left]:
            arr[loc],arr[left]=arr[left],arr[loc]
            loc=left
    return loc

def quickSort(arr,left,right):
    if left<right:
```

```
            loc=partitionlist(arr,left,right)
            quickSort(arr,left,loc-1)
            quickSort(arr,loc+1,right)

    arr=[]
    n=int(input("Enter number of elements: "))
    for i in range(n):
        arr.append(int(input("Enter number {}: ".format(i+1))))
    print(arr)
    quickSort(arr,0,n-1)
    print(arr)
```

Analysis of Quick Sort: The time complexity of the partitioning procedure, i.e. finding the proper position of the pivot element by dividing the array/list into two sub-arrays/lists, is O(n) because the pivot element is compared with each and every element in the array. After splitting each sub-array/list, again the same partitioning procedure is performed. But this splitting depends on the initial order of the elements. Hence, the performance of quick sort also depends on the initial order of the elements. In the best case, the array/list is divided into two equal halves. So, there will be $\log_2 n$ number of splits. Hence,

Total number of comparison, $T_n = n \times \log_2 n$.

And we can say that in the best case, the time complexity of quick sort is O(n $\log_2 n$).

But in the worst case, i.e. when the elements are already in sorted order, pivot elements would divide the array/list into two sub-arrays/lists, one of which contains zero element and the other contains n-1 elements. Then,

$$T_n = (n-1) + (n-2) + (n-3) + \ldots\ldots\ldots + 3 + 2 + 1$$

$$= n(n-1)/2$$

$$= \frac{1}{2}n^2 - \frac{1}{2}n$$

Hence, the worst case time complexity of quick sort is O(n²).

13.2.5 Merge Sort

Merge sort is another very efficient algorithm to sort a list of elements. It also follows the 'divide and conquer' strategy. The basic policy of this algorithm is to merge two sorted arrays. As we may consider every single element as a sorted array of one element, first we divide the array into a set of arrays of single elements and then merge them one by one to get the final sorted array. To divide the array, first we divide it into two halves. Then each half will be divided again into two halves. These halves will be then again divided.

These processes will go on until the size of each half becomes one. The following example illustrates the total algorithm. Consider the following unsorted array/list.

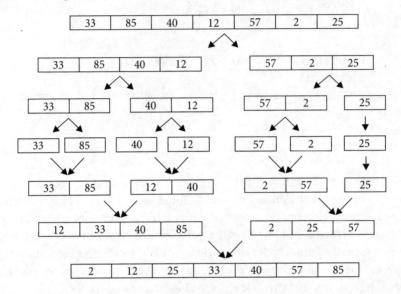

First we divide the array/list into two halves. As the array/list contains 7 elements, the first half contains 4 elements and the other half contains 3 elements. The first half is then again divided into two halves where each half contains 2 elements. Next these halves are further divided. From this first half we get two single elements – one is 33 and the other is 85. Now merging operation is applied on these two elements and we get a sorted array/list of 33 and 85. Similarly, the second half is divided into two single elements and these are 40 and 12. Applying merging operation we get another sorted array/list containing 12 and 40. Now these two sorted arrays/lists are further merged and we get a sorted array/list containing 12, 33, 40, and 85. Now the three-element array/list is further divided into two halves where the first half contains two elements and the second half contains a single element. So the first half will be further divided and we get two single elements, 57 and 2. These two elements will be merged now to produce a single sorted array/list containing 2 and 57. This merged array/list will be further merged with 25 and we get a single sorted array/list containing 2, 25, and 57. Finally this array/list will be merged with the array containing 12, 33, 40, and 85 and we get the final sorted array/list.

Based on this working principle, now we may define the merge sort algorithm. This algorithm is also divided into two modules. One, the driver module, which divides the array/list recursively, and the other module merges two sorted arrays/lists that will be called recursively to get back the undivided array/list that was divided previously at that level but is now in sorted form.

The general algorithm of merge sort may be defined as follows:

```
Merge_Sort(Arr, left, right)
```

Here *Arr* is an array or Python list, *left* is the starting index, and *right* is the end index of the array/list or sub-array/list.

```
1. If left<right, then
       a. Set mid=(left+right)/2
       b. Call Merge_Sort(arr,left,mid)
       c. Call Merge_Sort(arr,mid+1,right)
       d. MergeList(arr,left,mid,mid+1,right)
2. end
```

MergeList(*Arr, lst, lend, rst, rend*)

Here *Arr* is an array or Python list, *lst* and *lend* are the starting index and end index of left array/list or sub-array/list, and *rst* and *rend* are the starting index and end index of the right array/list or sub-array/list.

```
1. Create an empty list named temp
2. Set i=lst
3. Set j=rst
4. while i<=lend and j<=rend, do
       a. if arr[i] < arr[j], then
             i.  append arr[i] into temp
             ii. set i=i+1
       b. else:
             i.  append arr[j] into temp
             ii. set j=j+1
5. while i<=lend, do
       a. append arr[i] into temp
       b. set i=i+1
6. while j<=rend, do
       a. append arr[j] into temp
       b. set j=j+1
7. Set j=0
8. for i=lst to rend, do
       a. set arr[i]=temp[j]
       b. set j=j+1
9. End
```

The following code shows the implementation of merge sort algorithm.

Program 13.9: Program to sort elements using merge sort algorithm

```
#PRGD13_9: Program to implement Merge Sort
def mergeList(arr, lst, lend, rst, rend):
    temp=[]
    i=lst
```

```
        j=rst
        while i<=lend and j<=rend:
            if arr[i] < arr[j]:
                temp.append(arr[i])
                i+=1
            else:
                temp.append(arr[j])
                j+=1
        while i<=lend:
            temp.append(arr[i])
            i+=1
        while j<=rend:
            temp.append(arr[j])
            j+=1
        j=0
        for i in range(lst, rend+1):
            arr[i]=temp[j]
            j+=1

def mergeSort(arr,left,right):
    if left<right:
        mid=(left+right)//2
        mergeSort(arr,left,mid)
        mergeSort(arr,mid+1,right)
        mergeList(arr,left,mid,mid+1,right)

arr=[]
n=int(input("Enter number of elements: "))
for i in range(n):
    arr.append(int(input("Enter number {}: ".format(i+1))))
print(arr)
mergeSort(arr,0,n-1)
print(arr)
```

Analysis of Merge Sort: The time complexity of the mergeList procedure, i.e. merging two sorted arrays/lists, is $O(n)$ since to merge the lists we need to traverse both the lists just once. This operation is done after the array/list is divided into two halves and finally, by applying the mergeList operation, the divided halves are merged and sorted. As at each level the array/list is divided into two halves, there are total $\log_2 n$ divisions. Hence,

Total number of comparison $T_n = n \times \log_2 n$.

As this operation does not depend on the initial order of the elements, there is no such best or worst case found. Thus the time complexity of merge sort is always $O(n \log_2 n)$. However, the disadvantage of this algorithm is that it uses extra spaces. We need to declare a temporary array/list whose size is the same as the original array/list.

13.2.6 Heap Sort

We have already discussed the heap data structure in the previous chapter. Now we shall see one of its applications. As we know the root of a max heap contains the largest element and the root of a min heap contains the smallest element, we can use this property to sort an array. When we sort the elements in ascending order, max heap is used, and if we want to sort in descending order, min heap is used. In this section we shall discuss the heap sort algorithm to sort an array/list in ascending order. Thus max heap will be used in our algorithm. The working principle of heap sort is like selection sort. In selection sort the smallest element is selected and it is placed in its proper position, and in heap sort the largest element is selected and placed in its proper position. But the difference is that to find the smallest element we need $O(n)$ comparisons whereas in heap sort $O(\log_2 n)$ comparisons are sufficient because by shape property a heap is a complete binary tree.

In heap sort, first a max heap is built from the initial array/list. Then repeated deletion of the root sorts the array/list. More precisely, as the root contains the largest element, it will be interchanged with the element of the last position and, excluding this last element, we again apply these two operations, i.e. rebuild the heap and delete the root. The following example illustrates this. Consider the following array/list:

33	85	40	12	57	2	25

First we need to build a heap from these elements and we get:

85	57	40	12	33	2	25

As now it is a heap and more precisely max heap, the largest element is at the root and it is at the first position. So, we need to swap it with the last element.

25	57	40	12	33	2	85

The largest element is now in its proper position. Thus, we ignore this element and logically decrease the array/list size by 1.

25	57	40	12	33	2	85

From these remaining elements we again rebuild the heap and we get:

| 57 | 33 | 40 | 12 | 25 | 2 | 85 |

The first element now will be interchanged with the current last position, i.e. with the sixth element.

| 2 | 33 | 40 | 12 | 25 | 57 | 85 |

Now we decrease the array/list size by 1.

| 2 | 33 | 40 | 12 | 25 | 57 | 85 |

From these remaining elements we again rebuild the heap and we get:

| 40 | 33 | 2 | 12 | 25 | 57 | 85 |

The first element now will be interchanged with the current last position, i.e. with the fifth element, and the array/list size will be decreased by 1.

| 25 | 33 | 2 | 12 | 40 | 57 | 85 |

From these remaining elements we need to rebuild the heap again.

| 33 | 25 | 2 | 12 | 40 | 57 | 85 |

Now we swap the first element and the logical last element, i.e. the fourth element, and decrease the array/list size by 1.

| 12 | 25 | 2 | 33 | 40 | 57 | 85 |

Again we rebuild the heap from these remaining elements.

| 25 | 12 | 2 | 33 | 40 | 57 | 85 |

Now we swap the first element and logical last element, i.e. the third element, and decrease the array/list size by 1.

| 2 | 12 | 25 | 33 | 40 | 57 | 85 |

From these two elements we again rebuild the heap.

| 12 | 2 | 25 | 33 | 40 | 57 | 85 |

Now we swap the first element and the second element and decrease the array/list size by 1.

2	12	25	33	40	57	85

As now the array/list size becomes 1, our operation terminates here and we get the sorted array/list.

Based on this working principle we may define the basic steps as follows:

1. Create the heap from initial elements.

2. Interchange the root element with the logical last element.

3. Decrease the array/list size by 1.

4. Rebuild the heap from the remaining elements.

5. Repeat steps 2, 3, and 4 until the array/list size becomes 1.

Considering the basic steps we may now define the general algorithm of heap sort. For ease of implementation, we are dividing the algorithm into two modules. The second module is a recursive module which will build the heap and the first module is the driver module which controls the basic steps of the algorithm.

Heap_Sort(Arr)

Here *Arr* is an array or Python list.

```
1. Set n=length of arr - 1
2. Set i=n/2
3. while i>0, do
       a. call heapify(arr,n,i)
       b. set i=i-1
4. set i=n
5. while i>0, do
       a. swap arr[1] and arr[i]
       b. call heapify(arr,i,1)
       c. set i=i-1
6. End
```

Heapify(Arr, n, i)

Here *Arr* is an array or Python list, *i* is the index position of the element from where the heapify operation starts, and *i* is the index position of the last element of the heap.

```
1. Set largest=i
2. Set left=2*i
3. Set right=2*i+1
4. if left<n and arr[left]>arr[largest], then
       a. largest=left
```

```
5. if right<n and arr[right]>arr[largest], then
      a. largest=right
6. if largest!=i, then
      a. swap arr[i] and arr[largest]
      b. call heapify(arr,n,largest)
7. End
```

The following code shows the implementation of heap sort algorithm:

Program 13.10: Program to sort elements using the heap sort algorithm

```python
#PRGD13_10: Program to implement Heap Sort
def heapify(arr, n, i):
    largest=i
    left=2*i
    right=2*i+1
    if left<n and arr[left]>arr[largest]:
        largest=left
    if right<n and arr[right]>arr[largest]:
        largest=right
    if largest!=i:
        arr[i],arr[largest]=arr[largest],arr[i]
        heapify(arr,n,largest)


def heapSort(arr):
    n=len(arr)-1
    i=n//2
    while i>0:                    #Max heap creation
        heapify(arr,n,i)
        i-=1

    i=n
    while i>0:                    # Heap sort
        arr[1],arr[i]=arr[i],arr[1]
        heapify(arr,i,1)
        i-=1

arr=[0]
n=int(input("Enter number of elements: "))
for i in range(1,n+1):
    arr.append(int(input("Enter number {}: ".format(i))))
print(arr)
heapSort(arr)
print(arr)
```

Analysis of Heap Sort: In the heap sort algorithm, first we create an initial heap from n elements, which requires $O(\log_2 n)$ operations. Next, a loop is executed n-1 times in which first a swapping takes place that requires constant times and then the *heapify* function is called. In the *heapify* function, the root element is moved down up to a certain level. As the maximum height of a complete binary tree may be $O(\log_2 n)$, the maximum number of comparisons in the *heapify* function wll be $O(\log_2 n)$. As this function executes (n-1) times, the worst case time complexity of heap sort is $(n-1) \times O(\log_2 n)$, i.e. $O(n \log_2 n)$.

13.2.7 Radix Sort

Radix sort is a very efficient sorting algorithm that sorts the elements digit by digit if the elements are numbers and letter by letter if the elements are strings. When the elements are numbers, the sorting process starts from the least significant digit to the most significant digit, whereas in case of string, first it sorts the strings based on the first letter, then the second letter, then the third letter, and so on. This algorithm is also known as bucket sort since it requires some buckets. The number of buckets required depends on the base or radix of the number system. That is why it is called radix sort. Thus to sort some decimal numbers we need 10 buckets, to sort octal numbers we need 8 buckets, and to sort some name we need 26 buckets as there are 26 letters in the alphabet. For decimal numbers buckets are numbered as 0 to 9. To illustrate the working principle consider the following example. Suppose we have the following list of elements:

57	234	89	5	367	74	109	35	48	37

In the first pass, the numbers would be sorted based on the digits of the unit place. Hence, we consider the unit place digit of each number and put them at the corresponding buckets. For example, we put 57 in bucket number 7, 234 in bucket number 4, and so on.

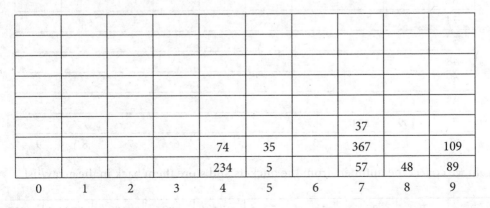

0	1	2	3	4	5	6	7	8	9
							37		
				74	35		367		109
				234	5		57	48	89

Now we collect the numbers from the buckets sequentially and store them back in the array/list.

234	74	5	35	57	367	37	48	89	109

We may notice that after this first pass, numbers are already sorted on the last digit. In the next pass, we would repeat the same operation but on the decimal place digit. Thus we get:

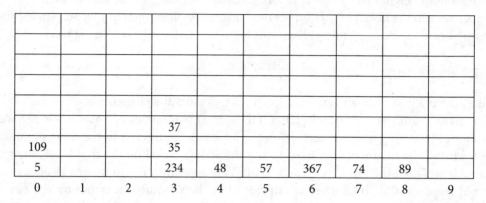

			37						
109			35						
5			234	48	57	367	74	89	
0	1	2	3	4	5	6	7	8	9

Again we collect the numbers from the buckets sequentially and store them back in the array/list.

5	109	234	35	37	48	57	367	74	89

After this second pass, numbers are sorted based on last two digits. In the third pass, we need to repeat the same operation but on the hundredth place digit and we get:

89									
74									
57									
48									
37									
35									
5	109	234	367						
0	1	2	3	4	5	6	7	8	9

Again we collect the numbers from the buckets and store them back in the array/list.

5	35	37	48	57	74	89	109	234	367

And we get the final sorted list.

From the above working principle, it is clear that the number of passes depends on the number of digits of the largest number. Now we may define the general algorithm of the radix sort as:

Radix_Sort(Arr)

Here *Arr* is an array or Python list.

```
1. Set n = length of Arr
2. Find the largest element from the list.
3. Count number of digits of the largest element and set it
   as digitCount.
4. For I = 1 to digitCount, do
      a. Initialize buckets
      b. For j=0 to n-1, do
            i.   Set Digit = i-th positioned digit of Arr[i]
            ii.  Put Arr[i] in the Digit-th Bucket
            iii. Increment count of the Digit-th Bucket
      c. Collect elements from bucket and store back into the
         list
5. End
```

Based on the above algorithm we may now write a program to implement radix sort.

Program 13.11: Program to sort elements using radix sort algorithm

```python
#PRGD13_11: Program to implement Radix Sort
def radixSort(arr):
    n=len(arr)
    Max=arr[0]
    for i in range(n):   # Finding Largest element
        if arr[i]>Max:
            Max=arr[i]

    digitCount=0
    while Max>0:              # counting number of digits of
                                      #largest element
        digitCount+=1
        Max//=10
    divisor=1
    for p in range(digitCount):
        bucket=[[0 for i in range(n)] for j in range(10)]
        bucketCount=[0]*10  # Initialize the bucket count
        for i in range(n):
            rem=(arr[i]//divisor)%10
```

```
            bucket[rem][bucketCount[rem]]=arr[i]
            bucketCount[rem]+=1
        k=0
        for i in range(10):       # Collect elements from
                                                    #bucket
            for j in range(bucketCount[i]):
                arr[k]=bucket[i][j]
                k+=1
        divisor*=10

arr=[]
n=int(input("Enter number of elements: "))
for i in range(n):
    arr.append(int(input("Enter number {}: ".format(i+1))))
print(arr)
radixSort(arr)
print(arr)
```

Analysis of Radix Sort: If the number of digits of the largest element in the list is d, the number of passes to sort the elements is also d. In each pass we need to access all the elements of the list. If there are n number of elements in the list, the total number of executions would be O(dn). If the value of d is not very high, the running time complexity of radix sort is O(n), which indicates its efficiency. But the main drawback of this algorithm is that it takes much more space in comparison to other sorting algorithms. To sort decimal numbers, apart from the list of numbers it requires 10 buckets each of size n. To sort strings containing only letters, number of buckets required is 26, each of size n. If the strings contain other characters such as punctuation marks or digits, the number of buckets will increase.

13.2.8 Shell Sort

Shell sort algorithm was invented by Donald Shell in 1959. The basic principle of this algorithm is designed observing the fact that more the elements are towards the sorted order, the better the insertion sort performs. Thus shell sort may be considered as an improved version of insertion sort. In this algorithm several passes are used and in each pass equally distanced elements are sorted. Instead of applying the basic insertion sort algorithm for the whole set of elements, elements with a certain interval are used for this purpose and they get sorted. In each pass this interval is reduced by half. So, at the earlier passes when the elements are fully unsorted, the list size is very small. So it takes less time. On the other hand, at the later passes when more elements are involved, elements are almost sorted. Hence, better performance of insertion sort is achieved. This policy reduces the overall execution time.

The following example illustrates the working principle of shell sort. Consider the following set of elements:

92	57	61	12	77	48	25	6	34	39	50
0	1	2	3	4	5	6	7	8	9	10

We start the algorithm with gap size as half of the number of elements. Here, n = 11. So, gap = 11/2 = 5 (considering integer division since array/list index should be integer). At this first pass, first we will apply insertion sort on the zeroth , fifth, and tenth elements of the list.

92	57	61	12	77	48	25	6	34	39	50
0	1	2	3	4	5	6	7	8	9	10

And we get:

48	57	61	12	77	50	25	6	34	39	92
0	1	2	3	4	5	6	7	8	9	10

Next insertion sort will be applied on the first and sixth elements.

48	57	61	12	77	50	25	6	34	39	92
0	1	2	3	4	5	6	7	8	9	10

And we get:

48	25	61	12	77	50	57	6	34	39	92
0	1	2	3	4	5	6	7	8	9	10

Following the sequence, the next insertion sort will be applied on the second and seventh elements, the third and eighth elements, and the fourth and ninth elements.

48	25	61	12	77	50	57	6	34	39	92
0	1	2	3	4	5	6	7	8	9	10

Hence, after the first pass, we get:

48	25	6	12	39	50	57	61	34	77	92
0	1	2	3	4	5	6	7	8	9	10

In the next pass, the gap size will be half. Thus gap = 5/2 = 2 (considering integer division). Now in the second pass, first insertion sort will be applied on the zeroth, second, fourth, sixth, eighth, and tenth elements.

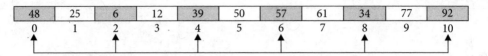

And we get:

6	25	34	12	39	50	48	61	57	77	92
0	1	2	3	4	5	6	7	8	9	10

The next insertion sort will be applied on the first, third, fifth, seventh, and ninth elements.

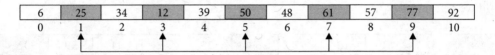

Thus, after the second pass, we get:

6	12	34	25	39	50	48	61	57	77	92
0	1	2	3	4	5	6	7	8	9	10

Now, in the third pass, gap = 2/2 = 1. So, insertion sort will be applied on the total set.

6	12	34	25	39	50	48	61	57	77	92
0	1	2	3	4	5	6	7	8	9	10

And we get the final sorted list.

6	12	25	34	39	48	50	57	61	77	92
0	1	2	3	4	5	6	7	8	9	10

Based on this working principle, we may now define the algorithm of shell sort.

```
Shell_Sort(Arr)
```

Here *Arr* is an array or Python list.

```
1. Set n = length of Arr
2. Set gap = n/2
3. While gap>= 1, do
      a. For i=gap to n-1, do
           i.   Set temp = Arr[i]
           ii.  Set j = i
           iii. While j>=gap and Arr[j-gap]>temp, do
                    1. Set Arr[j] = Arr[j-gap]
                    2. Set j = j - gap
           iv.  Set Arr[j] = temp
      b. Set gap = gap/2
```

Here is the implementation of shell sort.

Program 13.12: Program to sort elements using shell sort algorithm

```
#PRGD13_12: Program to implement Shell Sort
def shellSort(arr):
    n=len(arr)
    gap=n//2
    while gap>=1:
        for i in range(gap,n):
            temp=arr[i]
            j=i
            while j>=gap and arr[j-gap]>temp:
                arr[j]=arr[j-gap]
                j-=gap
            arr[j]=temp
        gap//=2

arr=[]
n=int(input("Enter number of elements: "))
for i in range(n):
    arr.append(int(input("Enter number {}: ".format(i+1))))
print(arr)
shellSort(arr)
print(arr)
```

Analysis of Shell Sort: It is very difficult to calculate the exact time complexity of shell sort. In shell sort we are applying insertion sort using gaps such as n/2, n/4, n/8, ... 4, 2, 1. Thus in the best case the time complexity of shell sort would be nearer to $O(n)$. As the earlier passes set the elements towards the sorted order, in the worst case the time complexity would be less than $O(n^2)$.

13.3 Comparison of Different Sorting Algorithms

We have already discussed the time complexity of different sorting algorithms. The following table shows the comparative study of different sorting techniques in Big Oh notation.

Algorithm	Best case	Worst Case
Bubble Sort	$O(n^2)$	$O(n^2)$
Selection Sort	$O(n^2)$	$O(n^2)$
Insertion Sort	$O(n)$	$O(n^2)$
Quick Sort	$O(n \log_2 n)$	$O(n^2)$
Merge Sort	$O(n \log_2 n)$	$O(n \log_2 n)$
Heap Sort	$O(n \log_2 n)$	$O(n \log_2 n)$
Radix Sort	$O(n)$	$O(d\,n)$
Shell Sort	$O(n)$	$O(n^2)$

13.4 Concept of Internal and External Sorting

So far in the sorting algorithms we discussed, all the elements are stored in the main memory. i.e. within RAM, and then the sorting procedure takes place in the main memory considering all the elements at a time. This type of sorting is known as *internal sorting*. But when we need to deal with huge data, then such amounts of data cannot be placed in the main memory at a time. We need to store data in a secondary storage device, and part by part data are loaded into memory and then sorted. This type of sorting is known as *external sorting*. An example of external sorting is external merge sort.

Searching and Sorting at a Glance

✓ Searching is a process by which we can check whether an element is present within a set of elements or not.

✓ The algorithm that checks each and every element of a list one by one sequentially starting from the first position is known as linear search.

✓ The time complexity of linear search is $O(n)$.

✓ Binary search works on sorted elements only. It is much faster than linear search and the time complexity of binary search is $O(\log_2 n)$.

✓ Interpolation search is more realistic and faster than binary search.

✓ The time complexity of interpolation search is measured as $O(\log_2(\log_2 n))$.

✓ When the amount of data is less such that it easily fits into the main memory (i.e. RAM), internal sorting is used.

✓ For huge amounts of data, which do not fit completely in the main memory, external sorting is required.

✓ In basic bubble sort algorithm, whatever may be the initial position of the elements, the time complexity is always $O(n^2)$.

✓ In best case, modified bubble sort shows the time complexity as $O(n)$.

✓ In selection sort technique, in each pass the smallest element is selected and then this element is interchanged with the element of the relative first position. The time complexity of selection sort is always $O(n^2)$.

✓ The basic theory of insertion sort technique is that each element is inserted into its proper position in a previously sorted array/list.

✓ The worst case time complexity of insertion sort is $O(n^2)$ whereas the best case time complexity of insertion sort is $O(n)$.

✓ Quick sort and merge sort both are sorting algorithms that follow the 'divide and conquer' strategy.

✓ Quick sort algorithm proceeds with the motivation that the pivot element partitions the array/list into two sub-arrays/lists such that all the elements smaller than the pivot element are on the left side of the pivot element and all the larger elements are on the right side. The same operation will then be applied to both the sub-arrays/lists until the size of the sub arrays/lists become one or zero.

✓ In the best case the time complexity of quick sort is $O(n \log_2 n)$ but in the worst case it is $O(n^2)$.

✓ Merge sort first divides the list into several lists such that each list contains a single element and then merge these lists one by one maintaining the concept of 'merge two sorted lists into a single sorted list'. The time complexity of merge sort is always $O(n \log_2 n)$ but extra spaces are required.

✓ In heap sort, first a max heap is built from the initial array/list. Then repeated deletion of the root sorts the array/list. The time complexity of heap sort is $O(n \log_2 n)$.

✓ Radix sort or bucket sort uses the base or radix number of buckets. Its time complexity is O(n) but uses huge space in comparison to others.

✓ In shell sort several passes are used and in each pass equally distanced elements are sorted. Its time complexity is between O(n) and O(n²).

Multiple Choice Questions

1. Quick sort uses
   a) Divide and conquer strategy
   b) Backtracking approach
   c) Heuristic search
   d) Greedy approach

2. Merge sort uses
   a) Divide and conquer strategy
   b) Backtracking approach
   c) Heuristic search
   d) Greedy approach

3. How many swaps are required to sort the given array using bubble sort: 12, 15, 11, 13, 14
   a) 5
   b) 15
   c) 4
   d) 14

4. The time complexity of linear search is
   a) $O(n^2)$
   b) $O(n)$
   c) $O(n \log n)$
   d) $O(\log n)$

5. The time complexity of binary search is
   a) $O(n^2)$
   b) $O(n)$
   c) $O(n \log n)$
   d) $O(\log n)$

6. The time complexity of interpolation search is
   a) O(log n)
   b) O(n)
   c) O(n log n)
   d) None of these

7. The best case time complexity of insertion sort is
   a) $O(n^2)$
   b) O(n)
   c) O(n log n)
   d) O(log n)

8. The worst case time complexity of quick sort is
   a) $O(n^2)$
   b) O(n)
   c) O(n log n)
   d) O(log n)

9. The time complexity of merge sort is
   a) $O(n^2)$
   b) O(n)
   c) O(n log n)
   d) O(log n)

10. The time complexity of heap sort is
    a) $O(n^2)$
    b) O(n)
    c) O(n log n)
    d) O(log n)

11. In general which of the following sorting algorithms requires the least number of assignment operations?
    a) Selection sort
    b) Insertion sort
    c) Quick sort
    d) Merge sort

12. When the input array is sorted or nearly sorted, which algorithm shows the best performance?
    a) Selection sort
    b) Insertion sort
    c) Quick sort
    d) Merge sort

13. Suppose we have two sorted lists: one of size *m* and the other of size *n*. What will be the running time complexity of merging these two lists?

    a)   O(*m*)

    b)   O(*n*)

    c)   O(*m+n*)

    d)   O(*log m* + *log n*)

14. Which of the following sorting algorithms least bother about the ordering of the elements in the input list?

    a)   Selection sort

    b)   Insertion sort

    c)   Quick sort

    d)   all of these

Review Exercises

1.   What is searching?

2.   What are the different searching techniques?

3.   Compare and contrast between different searching techniques?

4.   How does binary search give benefit over linear search?

5.   What is the difference between binary search and interpolation search?

6.   Write an algorithm for binary search.

7.   Consider the following list of elements:

     23 34 45 49 53 67 72 78 83 88

     Show the steps to search for (a) 83 and (b) 33 using binary search method.

8.   Show the steps to sort the following elements using bubble sort algorithm:

     25 10 18 72 40 11 32 9

9.   Show the steps to sort the following elements using selection sort algorithm:

     25 10 18 72 40 11 32 9

10. Show the steps to sort the following elements using insertion sort algorithm:

     25 10 18 72 40 11 32 9

11. Show the steps to sort the following elements using quick sort algorithm:

     25 10 18 72 40 11 32 9

12. Show the steps to sort the following elements using merge sort algorithm:

     25 10 18 72 40 11 32 9

13. Show the steps to sort the following elements using heap sort algorithm:

    25 10 18 72 40 11 32 9

14. Show the steps to sort the following elements using radix sort algorithm:

    40 525 18 172 11 310 32 9 68 81

15. Show the steps to sort the following elements using shell sort algorithm:

    25 37 48 10 56 89 18 5 72 40 31 11 45 32 9

16. Consider the following initial elements of a list. Certain sorting algorithm has been applied on these elements.

    53 29 78 46 12 121 34 68

    After two passes, the arrangement of the elements in the list is as follows:

    12 29 78 46 53 121 34 68

    Identify and explain which sorting algorithm has been applied.

17. Consider the following initial elements of a list. Certain sorting algorithm has been applied on these elements.

    53 29 78 46 12 121 34 68

    After two passes, the arrangement of the elements in the list is as follows:

    29 53 78 46 53 121 34 68

    Identify and explain which sorting algorithm has been applied.

18. Consider the following initial elements of a list. Certain sorting algorithm has been applied on these elements.

    53 29 78 46 12 121 34 68

    After two passes, the arrangement of the elements in the list is as follows:

    29 46 12 53 34 68 78 121

    Identify and explain which sorting algorithm has been applied.

19. Consider the following initial elements of a list. Certain sorting algorithm has been applied on these elements.

    53 29 78 46 12 121 34 68

    After two passes, the arrangement of the elements in the list is as follows:

    68 34 53 29 12 46 78 121

    Identify and explain which sorting algorithm has been applied.

20. Compare insertion sort, heap sort, and quick sort according to the best case, worst case, and average case behaviors.

Programming Exercises

1. Write a function to implement a searching algorithm whose worst case time complexity is $O(\log_2 n)$.

2. Write a menu-driven program to implement the following searching algorithms:
   a) Linear search
   b) Binary search
   c) Interpolation search

3. Write a menu-driven program to sort an inputted list of elements using:
   a) Bubble sort
   b) Selection sort
   c) Insertion sort
   d) Quick sort
   e) Merge sort
   f) Heap sort
   g) Radix sort
   h) Shell sort

4. Write a function to sort a list of elements using an algorithm whose best case time complexity is $O(n \log_2 n)$ but worst case time complexity is $O(n^2)$.

5. Write a function to sort a list of elements using an algorithm whose best case time complexity $O(n)$ but worst case time complexity is $O(n^2)$.

6. Write a function to sort a list of strings using insertion sort.

7. Write a function to sort a list of octal numbers using radix sort.

Hashing

In the previous chapter we have discussed three different searching techniques. Linear search works on both ordered and unordered data but time complexity is O(n). Binary search works on only ordered data but time complexity is $O(\log_2 n)$ which is much faster than linear search. Interpolation search generally works faster than binary search and its time complexity is $O(\log_2(\log_2 n))$ when elements are evenly distributed. But there is another application where, irrespective of the size of the array/list, a search operation can be performed with time complexity O(1), i.e. in constant time. This is possible due to *hashing*. In this chapter we will discuss this.

14.1 Definitions and Concept

Hashing is a procedure by which we can store or retrieve data in constant time, i.e. with time complexity O(1). To achieve O(1) time complexity we may follow a simple process. Suppose we have to store the data of students whose roll numbers range from 1 to 60. For this purpose we may take an array/list and store the data of each student at the corresponding index position which matches with the roll number. In this situation, to access a student, if we know his/her roll number, we can directly access his/her data. For example, if we want to read the data of the student whose roll number is 27, we may directly access the 27th index position of the array/list. But the problem is that in real life key values are not always as simple. You may find that in a certain university someone's roll number may be 21152122027. This does not imply that it is a sequential number, nor that this number of students are admitted in a year in that university. It may be a nomenclature of a key value where the first two digits may denote the year of registration, the next three digits are the college code, the next two digits may indicate stream, and so on. This is true for not only roll numbers but also any other key value. Thus it is clear that the number of digits does not indicate the total number of elements. In the above example hardly 10,000 or 20,000 students may take admission in that university in a year. So, it would not be a wise decision to store the data of a student if we declare an array/list of size which is equal to the last student's roll number. Rather what we can do is declare an array/list of size equal to the total number of elements and map the roll numbers of the students to the index position such that each and every record is accommodated properly and we can also access them directly. This is hashing.

To implement hashing we need to use a data structure named **hash table** where each key value is mapped to a particular array/list index position by using some procedure which is known as **hash function**. If we have key values such as $k_1, k_2, k_3, \ldots.. k_n$, in direct addressing system the record with key value k_1 would be stored at k_1 index position, the record with key value k_2 at k_2 index position, and so on. But in case of hashing we need to use a hash function, say h(k), which uses the key value k and returns an index position where the particular record would be stored. Hence, the record with key value k_1 would not be stored at k_1 index position. It may be stored at the i_1th position if $h(k_1)$ returns i_1. Figures 14.1 and 14.2 show these concepts.

In Figure 14.1, we are assuming the value of k_1 is 1 and it is stored at position 1, value of k_2 is 2 and it is stored at position 2, and so on. But in Figure 14.2, the hash function h(k) has been used. We are assuming $h(k_1)$ returns 7 and thus it is stored at position 7. Similarly, if $h(k_3)$, $h(k_4)$, and $h(k_6)$ return 1, 5, and 2 respectively, they would be stored at the corresponding position as shown in the figure.

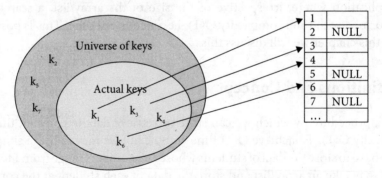

Figure 14.1 Direct relationship between keys and index positions

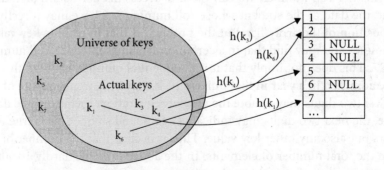

Figure 14.2 Relationship between keys and hash table index positions

14.2 Hash Functions

A hash function is a procedure that calculates a unique index position using the key value. Sometimes it may happen that for two or more key values a hash function may return identical index value. This is known as collision. Though it is a problem, it is not possible to avoid collision completely. Thus main aim of a hash function is to produce unique hash values as far as possible within a defined range for a set of key values by evenly distributing the values for that range. There are several standard hash functions. We will now discuss them in this section. But it is not that we have to use any from only among those. We may define our own hash functions. After defining a hash function we need to pass the probable set of key values in that function and then we have to study the returned hash values. If it is found that all the values are unique or almost unique, we accept the hash function. Now we discuss some popular hash functions.

14.2.1 Division Method

It is the simplest hash function. When key values are integers and consecutive and there is no gap in the sequence in the possible set of values, this method is very effective. If k is the key value and the size of the hash table is n, the remainder value of k/n is the hash value of k which is considered as the index of the hash table. Hence, we may define the hash function, $h(k)$, as:

$$h(k) = k \bmod n$$

Here, *mod* is the modulus operator which returns the remainder value of k/n.

This mathematical formula is suitable for programming languages such as C, C+, Java, Python, etc., where the array/list index starts from 0. But for a programming language where the index position starts from 1, we may rewrite the hash function as:

$$h(k) = k \bmod n + 1$$

If the possible key values are not consecutive, we need to be careful in choosing the value of n. Studies have shown that any prime number nearer to the size of the hash table is a good choice whereas any number closest to the exact power of 2 is the worst choice.

Example 14.1: Consider a hash table of size 100. Map the keys 329 and 4152 to appropriate locations using the division method.

Solution: Here, size of the hash table is 100. Thus, n = 100.

Hence, h(329) = 329 mod 100 = 29

And h(4152) = 4152 mod 100 = 52

∴ The keys 329 and 4152 will be mapped to positions 29 and 52 respectively.

14.2.2 Multiplication Method

This method operates in two steps. In the first step, a constant value, c, is chosen such that $0 < c < 1$. Then the key value, k, is multiplied by c and the fractional part of this product is considered. In the next step, this fractional value is further multiplied by the size of the hash table, n. Finally, the floor value of the result is considered as the hash value. Hence, we may define the hash function, $h(k)$, as:

$$h(k) = \left\lfloor n\left(k\,c\,mod\,1\right)\right\rfloor,$$

where $(k\,c\,mod\,1)$ represents the fractional part of $k\,c$.

The advantage of this method is that it works with almost any value of c. However, Knuth has suggested in his study the best value of c is

$$c = (\sqrt{5} - 1)/2 = 0.61803398874 \ldots$$

Example 14.2: Consider a hash table of size 100. Calculate the hash values for the keys 329 and 4152 using the multiplication method.

Solution: Here, size of the hash table is 100. Thus, n = 100. We are considering c = 0.6180339887.

$$\text{Hence, } h(329) = \left\lfloor n\left(k\,c\,mod\,1\right)\right\rfloor$$

$$= \left\lfloor 100\left(329 * 0.6180339887\,mod\,1\right)\right\rfloor$$

$$= \left\lfloor 100\left(203.3331822823\,mod\,1\right)\right\rfloor$$

$$= \left\lfloor 100\left(0.3331822823\right)\right\rfloor$$

$$= \left\lfloor 33.31822823\right\rfloor$$

$$= 33$$

$$h(4152)) = \left\lfloor n\left(k\,c\,mod\,1\right)\right\rfloor$$

$$= \left\lfloor 100\left(4152 * 0.6180339887\,mod\,1\right)\right\rfloor$$

$$= \left\lfloor 100\left(2566.0771210824\,mod\,1\right)\right\rfloor$$

$$= \lfloor 100(0.0771210824) \rfloor$$

$$= \lfloor 7.71210824 \rfloor$$

$$= 7$$

∴ The hash values of the keys 329 and 4152 are 33 and 7 respectively.

14.2.3 Mid-square Method

The mid-square method is a very effective hash function. In this method the key value is squared first. Then the middlemost d digits are taken as the hash value. Hence, we may define the hash function, $h(k)$, as:

$h(k)$ = middlemost d digits of k^2.

It is to be remembered that always the same d digits must be taken. The value of d depends on the size of the hash table. If we have a hash table of size 100, the index positions in the table are from 0 to 99. So, the value of d would be taken as 2.

Example 14.3: Consider a hash table of size 100. Map the keys 329 and 4152 to appropriate locations using the mid-square method.

Solution: Here, size of the hash table is 100. Thus, d = 2, i.e. the middlemost 2 digits need to be selected.

Hence, h(329) = Middlemost 2 digits of 329^2

= Middlemost 2 digits of 108241

= 82

h(4152) = Middlemost 2 digits of 4152^2

= Middlemost 2 digits of 1723080

= 30

∴ The keys 329 and 4152 will be mapped to positions 82 and 30 respectively.

Note that in both case, the third and fourth digits from the right are considered.

14.2.4 Folding Method

Another important hash function is the folding method. Generally this method is used when the keys are relatively large. In this method, the key is divided into parts and then combined or folded together to achieve the desired index in the hash table. To implement it, first the key value is logically divided into a number of parts where each part contains the same number of digits except the last part, which may contain fewer digits. Next, all the parts are added together and the result is considered as the hash value. If the summation contains some carry, that value must be ignored. In this method also, the number of digits in each part depends on the size of the hash table. If we have a hash table of size 100, the index positions in the table are from 0 to 99. So, the number of digits of each part and the summation of these parts after ignoring the last digit, which is considered the hash value, would be 2.

Example 14.4: Consider a hash table of size 10000. Map the keys 21152122027 and 191880101023 to appropriate locations using the folding method.

Solution: Here, size of the hash table is 10000. Thus, number of digits of each part would be 4.

Hence,   key = 21152122027

Parts = 2115, 2122, 027

Sum of the parts = 2115+2122+027=4294

h(21152122027) = 4294

And key = 191880101023

Parts = 1918,8010,1023

Sum of the parts = 1918+8010+1023=10951

h(191880101023) = 0951(Ignoring 1, the carry)

∴ The keys 21152122027 and 191880101023 will be mapped to positions 4294 and 951 respectively.

14.2.5 Length Dependent Method

In this method the key value or some portion of the key and the length of the key are somehow combined to generate the index position in the hash table or an intermediate key. There are several processes of combining keys and the length of the keys. One common example is to multiply the first two digits of the key with the length of the key and then divide the result with the last digit to find the hash value. We may consider this value or may use it as an intermediate key on which another hash function may be applied to get the desired hash value.

Example 14.5: Consider a hash table of size 100. Map the keys 329 and 4152 to appropriate locations using the length dependent method.

Solution: Here, key $\quad$ = 329

$\quad$ First two digits $\quad$ = 32

$\quad$ Last digit $\quad$ = 9

$\quad$ Length of key $\quad$ = 3

$\quad \therefore h(329) \quad$ = $(32 \times 3)/9 = 96/9 = 10.66 \approx 10$(truncating fractional part)

$\quad$ key $\quad$ = 4152

$\quad$ First two digits $\quad$ = 41

$\quad$ Last digit $\quad$ = 2

$\quad$ Length of key $\quad$ = 4

$\quad \therefore h(4152) \quad$ = $(41 \times 4)/2 = 164/2 = 82$

$\therefore$ The keys 329 and 4152 will be mapped to positions 10 and 82 respectively.

14.2.6 Digit Analysis Method

In this method extracting and manipulating the digits or bits of a key produces the hash value for that key. There is no fixed rule for this approach. It provides a general idea. In this method first we need to select a certain number of digits from the key based on the size of the hash table. We may select these digits from any position. For example, we may select the third, fourth, and fifth digits or we may select the second, fifth, and seventh digits. Now these digits have to be extracted to form a new number. Next, all or some of the digits of this new number will be manipulated. To manipulate we may perform a circular shift of the digits clockwise or anticlockwise, or the digits may be reversed, or some pair of digits may be swapped, or something else. This manipulation produces the address of the hash table. In our example we are selecting odd positioned digits from the left and then performing a circular shift to the left. Consider the following example:

Example 14.6: Consider a hash table of size 1000. Map the keys 123456 and 32759 to appropriate locations using the digit analysis method.

Solution: Here, size of the hash table is 1000. Thus, the number of digits of the hash value would be 3.

> Now, key = 123456

After extracting odd positioned digits from the key, we get 135.

> Finally, a circular shift to the left produces the hash value.

> Thus, h(123456) = 351

> When key = 32759

After extracting odd positioned digits from the key, we get 379.

> Thus, h(32759) = 793.

∴ The keys 123456 and 32759 will be mapped to positions 351 and 793 respectively.

14.3 Collision Resolution Technique

We have already discussed that when a hash function produces same hash value for more than one key, collision occurs. Though the basic target of any hash function is to produce a unique address within a given range, yet it is hardly achieved. Collisions may occur. Chances of collision depend on various factors. One major factor is the load factor. The ratio of the number of keys in a hash table and the size of the hash table is known as the load factor. Larger the value of the load factor, larger is the chance of collision. However, if collision occurs, we have to resolve the problem. There are several collision resolution techniques. The most two common techniques are:

- Open addressing
- Chaining.

In the following sections we will discuss these in detail.

14.3.1 Open Addressing

In open addressing all the key elements are stored within the hash table. When a collision occurs, a new position is calculated in some free slots within the hash table. Thus the hash table contains either the key elements or some sentinel value to indicate that the slot is empty. When we apply a hash function for a particular key, it returns an index position of the hash table. If this index position contains a sentinel value, it represents that the slot is empty and we store the key element at that position. But if the index position is already occupied by some key element, we will find some free slots in the hash table moving forward in some systematic manner. The process of examining slots in the hash table is known as probing. Linear probing, quadratic probing, and double hashing are common open addressing schemes for collision resolution.

14.3.1.1 Linear Probing

In linear probing, when collision occurs the key element is stored in the next available slot. Hence, linear probing can be represented with the hash function as:

```
h(k,i) = [h'(k) + i] mod n        for i=0,1,2,.... n-1,
```

where h'(k) is the basic hash function, n is the size of the hash table and i is the probe number. For a given key k, first probe is at h'(k) memory location. If it is free, the element would be stored at this position. Otherwise, next probe generates the slot number h'(k) + 1. Similarly, subsequent probes generate slot numbers h'(k) + 2, h'(k) + 3, ... up to h'(k) + (n-1) and then wrap around to slots 0, 1, 2, ... up to h'(k) - 1 until a free slot is found. The following example illustrates this:

Example 14.7: Consider a hash table of size 10 and the basic hash function $h'(k) = k \bmod n$ is used. Insert the following keys into the hash table using linear probing.

34, 71, 56, 14, 69, 45, and 9.

Solution: Initially, the hash table can be shown as:

—	—	—	—	—	—	—	—	—	—
0	1	2	3	4	5	6	7	8	9

First key, k =34.

h(34,0) = [(34 mod 10) + 0] mod 10 = [4+0] mod 10 = 4 mod 10 = 4.

Since slot 4 is free, 34 will be inserted at this position.

—	—	—	—	34	—	—	—	—	—
0	1	2	3	4	5	6	7	8	9

Next key, k =71.

h(71,0) = [(71 mod 10) + 0] mod 10 = [1+0] mod 10 = 1 mod 10 = 1.

Since slot 1 is free, 71 will be inserted at position 1.

—	71	—	—	34	—	—	—	—	—
0	1	2	3	4	5	6	7	8	9

Next key, k =56.

$h(56,0) = [(56 \bmod 10) + 0] \bmod 10 = [6+0] \bmod 10 = 6 \bmod 10 = 6.$

Since slot 6 is free, 56 will be inserted at slot 6.

—	71	—	—	34	—	56	—	—	—
0	1	2	3	4	5	6	7	8	9

Next key, k =14.

$h(14,0) = [(14 \bmod 10) + 0] \bmod 10 = [4+0] \bmod 10 = 4 \bmod 10 = 4.$

Since slot 4 is occupied, the next probe position is calculated as:

$h(14,1) = [(14 \bmod 10) + 1] \bmod 10 = [4+1] \bmod 10 = 5 \bmod 10 = 5.$

Since slot 5 is free, 14 will be inserted at slot 5.

—	71	—	—	34	14	56	—	—	—
0	1	2	3	4	5	6	7	8	9

Next key, k =69.

$h(69,0) = [(69 \bmod 10) + 0] \bmod 10 = [9+0] \bmod 10 = 9 \bmod 10 = 9.$

Since slot 9 is free, 69 will be inserted at slot 9.

—	71	—	—	34	14	56	—	—	69
0	1	2	3	4	5	6	7	8	9

Next key, k =45.

$h(45,0) = [(45 \bmod 10) + 0] \bmod 10 = [5+0] \bmod 10 = 5 \bmod 10 = 5.$

Since slot 5 is occupied, the next probe position is calculated as:

$h(45,1) = [(45 \bmod 10) + 1] \bmod 10 = [5+1] \bmod 10 = 6 \bmod 10 = 6.$

Since slot 6 is occupied, the next probe position is calculated as:

$h(45,2) = [(45 \bmod 10) + 2] \bmod 10 = [5+2] \bmod 10 = 7 \bmod 10 = 7.$

Since slot 7 is free, 45 will be inserted at slot 7.

—	71	—	—	34	14	56	45	—	69
0	1	2	3	4	5	6	7	8	9

Next key, k =9.

$h(9,0) = [(9 \bmod 10) + 0] \bmod 10 = [9+0] \bmod 10 = 9 \bmod 10 = 9.$

Since slot 9 is occupied, the next probe position is calculated as:

h(9,1) = [(9 mod 10) + 1] mod 10 = [9+1] mod 10 = 10 mod 10 = 0.

Since slot 0 is free, 9 will be inserted at slot 0.

9	71	—	—	34	14	56	45	—	69
0	1	2	3	4	5	6	7	8	9

The main disadvantage of linear probing is that it suffers from primary clustering. Here clusters means blocks of occupied slots, and primary clustering means there are many such clusters which are separated by a few free slots. When a new item is inserted, if its calculated position is within any cluster, it is inserted at the end of the cluster, which increases the cluster length. With the insertion of new items, if the free slots in between two clusters are filled up, the two clusters will be merged, causing a great increase in cluster length. As a result, to find a free slot, more probes will be required, which degrades the performance. To overcome this problem, quadratic probing and double hashing may be used.

14.3.1.2 Quadratic Probing

In quadratic probing, when collision occurs, to find the free slot quadratic search is used instead of linear search. Quadratic probing uses the following hash function:

```
h(k,i) = [h'(k) + c₁i + c₂i²] mod n for i=0,1,2, .... n-1,
```

where **h'(k)** is the basic hash function, **n** is the size of the hash table, **i** is the probe number, and c_1 and c_2 are two constants and $c_1 \neq 0$ and $c_2 \neq 0$. For a given key **k**, first probe is at **h'(k)** memory location. If it is free, the element would be stored at this position. Otherwise, next probes are generated in a quadratic manner on probe number **i**. The performance of quadratic probing is better than linear probing, and for better performance the values of c_1, c_2, and **n** are constrained. The following example illustrates the working principle of quadratic probing:

Example 14.8: Consider a hash table of size 10 and the basic hash function $h'(k) = k\ mod\ n$ is used. Further consider that c1=1 and c2=2. Insert the following keys into the hash table using quadratic probing:

34, 71, 56, 14, 69, 45, and 9.

Solution: Initially, the hash table can be shown as:

—	—	—	—	—	—	—	—	—	—
0	1	2	3	4	5	6	7	8	9

First key, k =34.

$h(34,0) = [(34 \bmod 10) + 1 \times 0 + 2 \times 0^2] \bmod 10 = [4+0+0] \bmod 10 = 4 \bmod 10 = 4.$

Since slot 4 is free, 34 will be inserted at this position.

—	—	—	—	34	—	—	—	—	—
0	1	2	3	4	5	6	7	8	9

Next key, k =71.

$h(71,0) = [(71 \bmod 10) + 1 \times 0 + 2 \times 0^2] \bmod 10 = [1+0+0] \bmod 10 = 1 \bmod 10 = 1.$

Since slot 1 is free, 71 will be inserted at position 1.

—	71	—	—	34	—	—	—	—	—
0	1	2	3	4	5	6	7	8	9

Next key, k =56.

$h(56,0) = [(56 \bmod 10) + 1 \times 0 + 2 \times 0^2] \bmod 10 = [6+0+0] \bmod 10 = 6 \bmod 10 = 6.$

Since slot 6 is free, 56 will be inserted at slot 6.

—	71	—	—	34	—	56	—	—	—
0	1	2	3	4	5	6	7	8	9

Next key, k =14.

$h(14,0) = [(14 \bmod 10) + 1 \times 0 + 2 \times 0^2] \bmod 10 = [4+0+0] \bmod 10 = 4 \bmod 10 = 4.$

Since slot 4 is occupied, the next probe position is calculated as:

$h(14,1) = [(14 \bmod 10) + 1 \times 1 + 2 \times 1^2] \bmod 10 = [4+1+2] \bmod 10 = 7 \bmod 10 = 7.$

Since slot 7 is free, 14 will be inserted at slot 7.

—	71	—	—	34	—	56	14	—	—
0	1	2	3	4	5	6	7	8	9

Next key, k =69.

$h(69,0) = [(69 \bmod 10) + 1 \times 0 + 2 \times 0^2] \bmod 10 = [9+0+0] \bmod 10 = 9 \bmod 10 = 9.$

Since slot 9 is free, 69 will be inserted at slot 9.

—	71	—	—	34	—	56	14	—	69
0	1	2	3	4	5	6	7	8	9

Next key, k =45.

h(45,0) = [(45 mod 10) + 1 x 0 + 2 x 0^2] mod 10 = [5+0+0] mod 10 = 5 mod 10 = 5.

Since slot 5 is free, 45 will be inserted at slot 5.

—	71	—	—	34	45	56	14	—	69
0	1	2	3	4	5	6	7	8	9

Next key, k =9.

h(9,0) = [(9 mod 10) + 1 x 0 + 2 x 0^2] mod 10 = [9+0+0] mod 10 = 9 mod 10 = 9.

Since slot 9 is occupied, the next probe position is calculated as:

h(9,1) = [(9 mod 10) + 1 x 1 + 2 x 1^2] mod 10 = [9+1+2] mod 10 = 12 mod 10 = 2.

Since slot 2 is free, 9 will be inserted at slot 2.

—	71	9	—	34	45	56	14	—	69
0	1	2	3	4	5	6	7	8	9

Though quadratic probing solves the problem of primary clustering, it suffers in secondary clustering. When collision occurs for multiple keys, the same probe sequence will be followed for these keys. Another problem is that a sequence of successive probes may explore only certain portions of the hash table. It may happen that though there are some empty slots, we are not able to find any.

14.3.1.3 Double Hashing

In double hashing, as the name suggests, instead of a single hash function, two hash functions are used. The first hash function is used to probe a location in the hash table and the second hash function is used to find the interval that is to be added with the address determined by the first hash function. Since the interval may vary for each probe as the value generated by the second hash function, it is one of the best collision resolution techniques available for open addressing. The hash function for double hashing may be defined as:

```
h(k,i) = [h₁(k) + i h₂(k)] mod n        for i=0,1,2,.... n-1,
```

where h_1(k) and h_2(k) are two hash function, n is the size of the hash table, and i is the probe number. The hash functions are defined as h_1(k) = k mod n and h_2(k) = k mod n'. The value of n' is slightly less than n. We may consider n' = n-1 or n-2. For a given key k, first we probe at h_1(k) memory location as first time i=0. If it is free, the element will be stored at this position. Otherwise, next probes are generated with the offset value generated by h_2(k). Since the offset values are generated by a hash function, double hashing is free from primary and secondary clustering and its performance is very close to the ideal case of uniform hashing. The following example illustrates the working principle of double hashing.

Example 14.9: Consider a hash table of size 10 and the hash functions $h_1(k) = k \bmod 10$ and $h_2(k) = k \bmod 8$ are used. Insert the following keys into the hash table using double hashing:

34, 71, 56, 14, 69, 45, and 9.

Solution: Initially, the hash table can be shown as:

—	—	—	—	—	—	—	—	—	—
0	1	2	3	4	5	6	7	8	9

First key, k =34.

  h(34,0) = [(34 mod 10) + 0 x (34 mod 8)] mod 10 = [4+0] mod 10 = 4 mod 10 = 4.

Since slot 4 is free, 34 will be inserted at this position.

—	—	—	—	34	—	—	—	—	—
0	1	2	3	4	5	6	7	8	9

Next key, k =71.

  h(71,0) = [(71 mod 10) + 0 x (71 mod 8)] mod 10 = [1+0] mod 10 = 1 mod 10 = 1.

Since slot 1 is free, 71 will be inserted at position 1.

—	71	—	—	34	—	—	—	—	—
0	1	2	3	4	5	6	7	8	9

Next key, k =56.

  h(56,0) = [(56 mod 10) + 0 x (56 mod 8)] mod 10 = [6+0] mod 10 = 6 mod 10 = 6.

Since slot 6 is free, 56 will be inserted at slot 6.

—	71	—	—	34	—	56	—	—	—
0	1	2	3	4	5	6	7	8	9

Next key, k =14.

  h(14,0) = [(14 mod 10) + 0 x (14 mod 8)] mod 10 = [4+0] mod 10 = 4 mod 10 = 4.

Since slot 4 is occupied, the next probe position is calculated as:

  h(14,1) = [(14 mod 10) + 1x (14 mod 8)] mod 10 = [4+6] mod 10 = 10 mod 10 = 0.

Since slot 0 is free, 14 will be inserted at slot 0.

14	71	—	—	34	—	56	—	—	—
0	1	2	3	4	5	6	7	8	9

Next key, k =69.

h(69,0) = [(69 mod 10) + 0 x (69 mod 8)] mod 10 = [9+0] mod 10 = 9 mod 10 = 9.

Since slot 9 is free, 69 will be inserted at slot 9.

14	71	—	—	34	—	56	—	—	69
0	1	2	3	4	5	6	7	8	9

Next key, k =45.

h(45,0) = [(45 mod 10) + 0 x (45 mod 8)] mod 10 = [5+0] mod 10 = 5 mod 10 = 5.

Since slot 5 is free, 45 will be inserted at slot 5.

14	71	—	—	34	45	56	—	—	69
0	1	2	3	4	5	6	7	8	9

Next key, k =9.

h(9,0) = [(9 mod 10) + 0 x (9 mod 8)] mod 10 = [9+0] mod 10 = 9 mod 10 = 9.

Since slot 9 is occupied, the next probe position is calculated as:

h(9,1) = [(9 mod 10) + 1 x (9 mod 8)] mod 10 = [9+1] mod 10 = 10 mod 10 = 0.

Since slot 0 is also occupied, the next probe position is calculated as:

h(9,2) = [(9 mod 10) + 2 x (9 mod 8)] mod 10 = [9+2] mod 10 = 11 mod 10 = 1.

Since slot 1 is also occupied, the next probe position is calculated as:

h(9,3) = [(9 mod 10) + 3 x (9 mod 8)] mod 10 = [9+3] mod 10 = 12 mod 10 = 2.

Since slot 2 is free, 9 will be inserted at slot 2.

14	71	9	—	34	45	56	—	—	69
0	1	2	3	4	5	6	7	8	9

You can note that for the last value 9 we have to probe 4 times. Though double hashing is a very efficient technique, yet in this example we have found some degraded performance. This is due to the value of **n**. If we consider the value of **n** as some prime number, we will always get efficient performance. Thus in the above example instead of 10 if we consider **n**=11, we will get much better performance.

14.3.2 Chaining

In chaining, when a collision occurs, the elements are not stored in some free slots. Instead, the hash table maintains separate linked lists for each slot to store the elements/records. All the elements for which the hash function returns the same slot in a hash table are put in a single linked list. Initially all the slots in a hash table contain None or NULL value. When an element is hashed to a particular slot, a linked list is created containing the element, and the slot contains the address or reference of the first node (now it contains only one) of the list. Next, if any element is hashed to same slot, the element is inserted as a new node in the linked list of that slot. How the elements are mapped in the hash table and are stored in a linked list is shown in Figure 14.3.

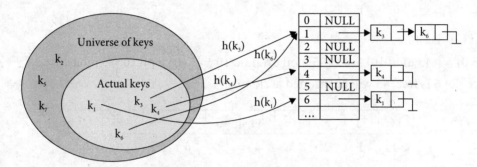

Figure 14.3   Mechanism of collision resolution by chaining method

The advantage of chaining is that it is free from primary and secondary clustering. Another advantage is that when the hash table is almost filled up, i.e. load factor is close to 1, the performance of the chaining method does not degrade. Even if the number of key elements is higher than the number of slots, i.e. the load factor is greater than 1, it still remains effective. The only disadvantage is that in this method extra space is required. First, on collision, elements/records are stored in a linked list, not in the hash table. So, extra memory is required. Second, due to the linked list, extra space is required for each node.

Example 14.10: Consider a hash table of size 10 and the basic hash function $h'(k) = k \bmod n$ is used. Insert the following keys into the hash table using the chaining method:

34, 71, 56, 14, 69, 45, and 9.

Solution: Initially, the hash table can be shown as:

First key, k =34.
h(34) = 34 mod 10 = 4.
Since slot 4 is containing NULL, a linked list will be created for the slot 4 and its only node will contain 34.

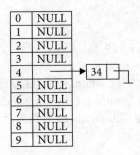

Next key, k =71.
h(71) = 71 mod 10 = 1.
Since slot 1 is containing NULL, a linked list will be created for the slot 1 and its only node will contain 71.

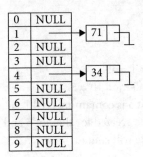

Next key, k =56.
h(56) = 56 mod 10 = 6.
Since slot 6 is containing NULL, a linked list will be created for the slot 6 and its only node will contain 56.

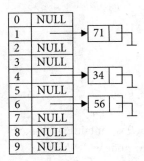

Next key, k =14.
h(14) = 14 mod 10 = 4.
Since slot 4 is containing a linked list, a new node with 14 will be inserted at the end of this list.

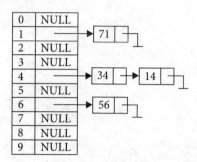

Next key, k =69.
h(69) = 69 mod 10 = 9.
Since slot 9 is containing NULL, a linked list will be created for the slot 9 and its only node will contain 69.

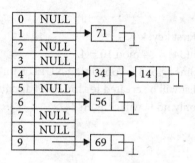

Next key, k =45.
h(45) = 45 mod 10 = 5.
Since slot 5 is containing NULL, a linked list will be created for the slot 5 and its only node will contain 45.

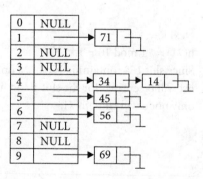

Next key, k =9.
h(9) = 9 mod 10 = 9.
Since slot 9 is containing a linked list, a new node with 9 will be inserted at the end of this list.

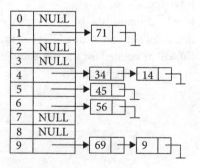

14.4 Rehashing

Sometimes it may happen that with exhaustive use the hash table may be nearly full. At this stage, performance is very much degraded with open addressing. In case of quadratic probing, a free slot may not be found for inserting a new record. In this situation a new hash table of size double the current one is created and existing elements/records are remapped in the new table. This is called rehashing.

14.5 Applications of Hashing

As the insertion, deletion, and search operations in hashing take constant order of time on an average, hashing is used as a data structure in various areas for quick retrieval of data. Some common examples are given here:

- In some database management software where indexing is used, hashing is used for database indexing. In an index file system, to retrieve a record first the key information is searched in the appropriate index file and from that location the actual record is found in the database file through a pointer. Hashing is used to store these key values in the index file.

- Sometimes hashing is used in a compiler to accelerate retrieval of keywords for fast compilation.

- A famous string search algorithm, Rabin–Karp algorithm, uses hashing to find patterns in a string.

- In a disk file system, hashing is used to map the file name and its path.

- Cryptographic hash functions are used for message digest and password verification.

Hashing at a Glance

✓ Hashing is a procedure by which we can store or retrieve data in constant time, i.e. with time complexity O(1).

✓ A hash table is a data structure where each key value is mapped to a particular array/list index position by using a procedure known as the hash function.

✓ Some popular hash functions are division method, multiplication method, folding method, mid-square method, etc.

✓ When a hash function produces same hash value for more than one key, it is known as collision.

✓ The most two common collision resolution techniques are open addressing and chaining.

✓ In open addressing all the key elements are stored within the hash table.

✓ Linear probing, quadratic probing, and double hashing are common open addressing schemes for collision resolution.

✓ In linear probing, when the collision occurs the key element is stored in the next available slot using the hash function

```
h(k,i) = [h'(k) + i] mod n for i= 0,1,2,.... n-1
```

✓ Quadratic probing use the hash function

```
h(k,i) = [ h'(k) + c₁i + c₂i² ] mod n for i =
0,1,2,.... n-1
```

✓ Linear probing faces the problem of primary clustering whereas quadratic probing suffers in secondary clustering.

✓ In double hashing two hash functions are used in which the first hash function is used to probe a location in the hash table and the second hash function is used to find the interval that is to be added with the address determined by the first hash function.

✓ Double hashing is free from primary and secondary clustering.

✓ In chaining the hash table maintains a separate linked list for each slot to store the elements.

✓ When an old hash table is nearly full, a new hash table of size double the current one is created and existing elements/records are remapped in the new table. This is called rehashing.

Multiple Choice Questions

1. Which of the following is a hash function?
   a) Open addressing
   b) Quadratic probing
   c) Folding
   d) Chaining

2. The ratio of the number of items in a hash table to the table size is called
   a) Load factor
   b) Item factor

c) Balance factor

d) All of these

3. Which of the following is not a hash function?

a) Mid-square method

b) Multiplication method

c) Folding

d) Chaining

4. Which of the following is not a collision resolution technique under the open addressing scheme?

a) Linear addressing

b) Quadratic probing

c) Double Hashing

d) Rehashing

5. Which of the following is a collision resolution technique?

a) Mid-square method

b) Multiplication method

c) Folding

d) Chaining

6. When multiple elements are mapped for a same location in the hash table, it is called

a) Repetition

b) Replication

c) Collision

d) Duplication

7. If n is the size of a hash table, which one of the following may be a hash function for implementing linear probing?

```
a)  h(k) = h'(k) mod n
b)  h(k) = h'(k) mod 10
c)  h(k, i) = ( h'(k) + f(i) ) mod n
d)  h(k, i) = ( h'(k) + f(i²) ) mod n
```

8. Suppose the size of a hash table is 7 whose starting index is 0 and initially empty. If the mid-square method is used as a hash function, what will be the contents of the hash table when the sequence 147, 99, 231, 81 is inserted into the table using linear probing? ['_' denotes an empty location in the hash table.]

a) 147, 231, 81, 99,_, _, _

b) 99, _, _, 231, _, _, 147, 81

c) 99, 81, _, 231, _, _, 147

d) 81, 99, _, _, 231, _, 147

9. Suppose the hash function $h(k) = k\ mod\ 10$ is used. Which of the following statements is true for the following inputs?

   2322, 1634, 1571, 8679, 2989, 7171, 6173, 3199

   i.   8679, 2989, 3199 hash to the same location

   ii. 1571, 7171 hash to the same location

   iii. All elements hash to the same location

   iv. Each element hashes to a different location

   a) i only

   b) ii only

   c) i and ii only

   d) iii or iv

10. Consider the size of a hash table as 10 whose starting index is 0 and initially empty. If the division method is used as a hash function, what will be the contents of the hash table when the sequence 55, 367, 29, 83, 10,121 is inserted into the table? ['_' denotes an empty location in the hash table.]

    a) 55, 367, 29, 83, 10, 121, _, _, _, _.

    b) 10, 121, _, 83, _, 55, _, 367, _, 29.

    c) 121, _, 83, _, 55, _, 367, _, 29, 10.

    d) 10, 29, _, _, 55, 83, _,121, _, 367.

11. Consider the size of a hash table as 10 whose starting index is 0 and initially empty. If the division method is used as a basic hash function and linear probing is used for collision resolution, what will be the contents of the hash table when the sequence 55, 67, 105, 26, 19, 35, 119 is inserted into the table? ['_' denotes an empty location in the hash table.]

    a) 55, 67, 105, 26, 19, 35, 119, _, _, _.

    b) 35,119, _, _, _, 55, 26, 67, 105, 19.

    c) 35,119, _, _, _, 55, 105, 67, 26, 19.

    d) None of these.

12. Consider the size of a hash table as 10 whose starting index is 0 and initially empty. If the division method is used as a basic hash function and quadratic probing is used for collision resolution, what will be the contents of the hash table when the sequence 55, 67, 105, 26, 19, 35, 119 is inserted into the table? ['_' denotes an empty location in the hash table.]

    a) 26, _, _, 119, 35, 55, 105, 67, _, 19.

    b) 35,119, _, _, _, 55, 26, 67, 105, 19.

    c) 35,119, _, _, _, 55, 105, 67, 26, 19.

    d) None of these.

13. Consider a hash table of size 10 whose starting index is 0. Map the key 568 to an appropriate location using the folding method.

   a) 9

   b) 8

   c) 1

   d) 0

14. Consider a hash table of size 100 whose starting index is 0. Map the key 56 to an appropriate location using the folding method.

   a) 6

   b) 56

   c) 1

   d) 11

Review Exercises

1. What is hashing? What is its utility?

2. What do you mean by a hash table?

3. What is a hash function? Give examples of some standard hash functions.

4. Explain with example the different hash functions.

5. What is collision? How it is resolved in hashing?

6. What is open addressing?

7. What are the different open addressing collision resolution techniques? Explain with examples.

8. What is chaining? How does it work? Explain.

9. What is rehashing?

10. What is the importance of double hashing?

11. Consider a hash table of size 1000. Map the keys 29 and 5162 to appropriate locations using the division method.

12. Consider a hash table of size 1000. Map the key 23401 to an appropriate location using the mid-square method.

13. Consider a hash table of size 100. Map the keys 153249 and 513 to appropriate locations using the folding method.

14. Consider a hash table of size 1000. Map the keys 57 and 4392 to appropriate locations using the multiplication method.

15. Consider a hash table of size 10 and the basic hash function $h'(k) = k \bmod n$ is used. Insert the following keys into the hash table using linear probing:

   68, 23, 57, 83, 77, 98, 47, 50, and 9.

16. Consider a hash table of size 10 and the basic hash function $h'(k) = k \bmod n$ is used. Further consider that c1=0 and c2=1. Insert the following keys into the hash table using quadratic probing:

    45, 56, 78, 36, 27, 15, 89, and 66.

17. Consider a hash table of size 11 and the hash functions $h_1(k) = k \bmod 11$ and $h_2(k) = k \bmod 7$ are used. Insert the following keys into the hash table using double hashing:

    29, 56, 73, 43, 89, 51, and 16.

18. Consider a hash table of size 10 and the basic hash function $h'(k) = k \bmod n$ is used. Insert the following keys into the hash table using the chaining method:

    37, 46, 92, 87, 29, 66, 69, 96, and 7.

Appendix

Answers of Multiple Choice Questions

Chapter 1: Data Structure Preliminaries

1. b	2. d	3. c	4. d	5. d	6. a
7. b	8. d	9. b	10. d	11. c	12. b
13. a	14. d	15. d	16. d		

Chapter 2: Introduction to Algorithm

1. c	2. b	3. a	4. b	5. c	6. a
7. b	8. a	9. b	10. c	11. c	12. d
13. b	14. d	15. d			

Chapter 3: Array

1. a	2. a	3. d	4. a	5. b	6. d
7. b	8. d	9. c	10. d	11. a	12. c
13. c	14. c				

Chapter 4: Python Data Structures

1. c	2. d	3. a	4. b	5. a	6. b
7. c	8. d	9. a	10. c	11. d	12. b
13. a	14. b	15. b	16. a	17. d	18. b

Chapter 5: Strings

1. a	2. c	3. b	4. d	5. b	6. d
7. d	8. b	9. d	10. d	11. d	12. c
13. b	14. a	15. c			

Chapter 6: Recursion

1. b	2. a	3. b	4. d	5. a	6. d
7. b	8. d	9. c	10. d	11. c	

Chapter 7: Linked List

1. d	2. d	3. b	4. a	5. d	6. b
7. c	8. d	9. d	10. c	11. b	12. c
13. b	14. c	15. d	16. d	17. b	18. b

Chapter 8: Stack

1. c	2. d	3. a	4. b	5. d	6. c
7. b	8. d	9. d	10. c	11. b	12. d
13. b	14. b	15. a	16. c	17. c	18. a
19. a	20. c	21. b	22. a	23. d	24. a
25. d	26. b	27. a	28. a		

Chapter 9: Queue

1. c	2. c	3. a	4. c	5. a	6. c
7. d	8. d	9. a	10. c	11. a	12. c

Chapter 10: Trees

1. c	2. c	3. d	4. d	5. c	6. b
7. a	8. d	9. b	10. c	11. c	12. c
13. a	14. a	15. a	16. d	17. d	18. d
19. b	20. c				

Chapter 11: Heap

1. a	2. a	3. b	4. c	5. c	6. c
7. c	8. b	9. b	10. d		

Chapter 12: Graph

1. b	2. a	3. c	4. b	5. a	6. a
7. c	8. b	9. c	10. b	11. a	12. b
13. a	14. b	15. a			

Chapter 13: Searching and Sorting

1. a	2. a	3. c	4. b	5. d	6. d
7. b	8. a	9. c	10. c	11. a	12. b
13. c	14. a				

Chapter 14: Hashing

1. c	2. a	3. d	4. d	5. d	6. c
7. c	8. b	9. c	10. b	11. c	12. a
13. a	14. b				

Index